BI 3428154 1

DFJIm

Deploying IP and MPLS QOS for Multiservice Networks

The Morgan Kaufmann Series in Networking
Series Editor, David Clark, M.I.T.

*For further information on these books and for a list of
forthcoming titles, please visit our Web site at
http://www.mkp.com.*

Deploying IP and MPLS QOS for Multiservice Networks
Theory and Practice

John Evans
Cisco Systems, London, UK

Clarence Filsfils
Cisco Systems, Brussels, Belgium

AMSTERDAM • BOSTON • HEIDELBERG • LONDON
NEW YORK • OXFORD • PARIS • SAN DIEGO • SAN
FRANCISCO • SINGAPORE • SYDNEY • TOKYO

Morgan Kaufmann Publishers is an imprint of Elsevier

ELSEVIER

MORGAN KAUFMANN PUBLISHERS

T.I.C.
MILLENNIUM
POINT
LEARNING CENTRE

Acquisitions Editor	Rick Adams
Publishing Services Manager	George Morrison
Production Editor	Renata Corbani
Associate Acquisitions Editor	Rachel Roumeliotis
Cover Design	Alisa Marie Andreola
Composition	Charon Tec Ltd (A Macmillan Company)
Technical Illustration	Charon Tec Ltd (A Macmillan Company)
Copyeditor	Debbie Puleston
Proofreader	Joe Haworth
Indexer	Indexing Specialists
Interior Printer	Sheridan
Cover Printer	Sheridan

Morgan Kaufmann Publishers is an imprint of Elsevier.
500 Sansome Street, Suite 400, San Francisco, CA 94111

This book is printed on acid-free paper.

Library of Congress Cataloging-in-Publication Data
Application submitted

ISBN 13: 978-0-12-370549-5
ISBN 10: 0-12-370549-5

Typeset by Charon Tec Ltd (A Macmillan Company), Chennai, India
www.charontec.com

For information on all Morgan Kaufmann publications, visit our web site at www.mkp.com or www.books.elsevier.com

Printed in the United States of America
07 08 09 10   5 4 3 2 1

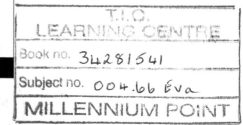

Contents

3

Deploying Diffserv   209

5 SLA and Network Monitoring 335

6 Core Capacity Planning and Traffic Engineering   375

Preface

Traditionally, Internet Protocol or IP networks have only offered a "best effort" delivery service for IP traffic; in these best-effort networks all traffic is treated equally. The service requirements – or more specifically service level agreement (SLA) requirements – of, voice, video, and mission critical data applications, for example, are not the same. Consequently, "best effort" IP networks have not been able to provide optimal support for multiservice applications with different SLA requirements.

Broadly speaking "quality of service" or QOS (either pronounced "Q-O-S" or "kwos") is the term used to describe the science of engineering a network to make it work well for applications by treating traffic from applications differently depending upon their SLA requirements. In the 5–10 years preceding this publication there have been significant developments in IP QOS to the point where the mechanisms, architectures, and deployment experience are now available to enable optimized support for multiservice applications on an integrated IP network. IP is becoming the convergence technology for multimedia services and consequently QOS is one of the hottest topics in IP networking, and yet currently it is still one of the least well understood from a practical perspective. Ten years ago, the design and implementation of large IP networks using routing protocols like OSPF and BGP was seen as a very specialist subject, restricted to the gurus of the networking community. Today, however, with the proliferation of the Internet and large IP networks, much of the mysticism associated with these technologies has gone, and an understanding of them has moved into the mainstream. IP QOS today is seen as a specialist subject, much as OSPF and BGP were ten years ago.

In this book we hope to help to bring IP QOS more into the mainstream, through bridging the theory of QOS with the practice of deployment, from SLA definition to detailed design and configuration. We describe the key application SLA requirements, QOS functions, and architectures to help readers understand the concepts of IP QOS; case studies and examples are used to show how these concepts are applied in practice. In the process, we address some of the most common QOS questions:

- What's the difference between QOS, COS, and TOS? (Chapter 2, Section 2.1.1)

- Why use IP QOS rather than using layer 2 QOS capabilities? (Chapter 2, Section 2.1.4)

- What's the difference between a queue and a buffer? (Chapter 2, Section 2.2.4.2)

- What's the difference between a shaper and a policer? (Chapter 2, Section 2.2.4.3)

- Which QOS architecture should be used? (Chapter 2, Section 2.3)

- How do you assure an end-to-end SLA for Voice over IP (VoIP) traffic? (Chapter 3, Section 3.2.2.1.1)

- How many Diffserv classes should be used? (Chapter 3, Section 3.2.2.6)

- What packet marking scheme should be used? (Chapter 3, Section 3.2.2.7)

- Why isn't ECN widely deployed? (Chapter 2, Section 2.3.4.4)

- How do you convert between TOS, IP precedence, and DSCP? (Chapter 2, Appendix 2.A)

- How do you tune RED and WRED? (Chapter 3, Section 3.4)

- What options are there for admission control? (Chapter 4)

- How do you manage an IP QOS deployment? (Chapters 5 and 6)

In addition, we debunk some common IP QOS myths including:

- Jitter is more important than delay for VoIP. (Chapter 1, Section 1.3.1.2)

- The maximum VoIP load that can be supported on a link is 33%. (Chapter 3, Section 3.2.2.8)

- If a design does not use the recommended Diffserv marking scheme it is not Diffserv compliant. (Chapter 3, Section 3.2.2.7)

- IPv6 provides better QOS than IPv4. (Chapter 2, Section 2.3.5)

- MPLS provides better QOS than IPv4 or IPv6. (Chapter 2, Section 2.3.6)

Audience

We have tried to make this book accessible to a wide audience and to address beginner, intermediate, and advanced IP QOS topics. We hope it will be of value to anyone trying to design, support, or just understand IP QOS from a practical perspective. This includes, but is not limited to, network designers, engineers, administrators, and operators, both in service provider and enterprise environments, together with students looking to gain a more applied understanding of QOS. This book also serves as a general technical reference guide to IP QOS.

Previous knowledge or understanding of QOS is not a prerequisite to reading this book; however, we have assumed that readers have a basic level of knowledge of data networking in general, and of the basic concepts of IP, IP routing, and MPLS, in particular. There are already many good books on these subjects.

Approach

The approach that we have taken in this book is one where we describe both theory and practice, linking them, wherever possible, through the use of case studies and examples.

From a theoretical perspective, we start by describing application SLA requirements, and then explain the range of QOS functions and features that can be used to support such SLAs, within the context of an overriding QOS architecture. Where we address theory and standards, we have aimed not to blindly reproduce information that is freely available in published standards, but rather we reference available standards and augment them with explanation, description, and context which are not available from these sources. The information here will make it easier to understand the technical detail provided in standards documents, such as Internet Engineering Task Force (IETF) drafts and Requests for Comments (RFCs), and the literature provided by network equipment vendors.

Where we use case studies, they are generally based upon real-life networking scenarios, and show how theoretical SLA requirements are translated into practical network designs, which are defined in terms of example configurations. To describe the example configurations we use a Diffserv meta-language. The meta-language provides abstraction from vendor specific configurations, thereby allowing it to be understood by readers that are not familiar with particular vendor QOS implementations and configuration. The meta-language can be easily translated into most vendors' specific configurations. The case studies presented are examples, and as such do not represent the only way of doing things; rather, they aim to describe possible methodologies and to bring out the key considerations.

In focussing on IP QOS, this book centers on the network layer, or layer 3, of the Open Systems Interconnection (OSI) 7 layer reference model. Hence, where we refer to network nodes or devices, in general we are referring to IP routers and where we refer to lower layers, we mean with respect to layer 3. As no two networks are exactly the same, throughout this book we use a generalized network model to explain the application of QOS features and functions. This model is in line with the way in which many networks are designed, consisting of a hierarchy of core, distribution, and access routers; core routers (CRs) provide connectivity between distribution routers (DRs), which in turn aggregate connections to routers at remote sites, each of which have local access routers (ARs). When deploying QOS, there is often a difference between the functionality applied at the edge of the network compared to that applied in the core; in the context of the generalized network model, the edge of the network is represented by the connectivity between the ARs and DRs, while the core of the network provides the interconnectivity between DRs and CRs.

Throughout this book, where we use the terms service provider and customer, we use them generically. These terms are not intended to infer applicability only to network service provider environments, such as virtual private network (VPN) service providers; the networking department of an enterprise organization is also service provider to their enterprise. The terms are instead intended to distinguish between the provider of the service and the user of the service.

Content and Organization

The organization of the chapters is as follows:

- *Chapter 1: QOS Requirements and Service Level Agreements.* Service level agreements (SLAs) provide the context for IP quality of service. Application and service SLA requirements are the inputs and also the qualification criteria for measuring success in a QOS design. Chapter 1 considers the SLAs metrics that are important for IP service performance, reviewing the current industry status with respect to the standardization and support of these metrics, and then describes application SLA requirements and the impacts that these metrics can have on application performance.

- *Chapter 2: Introduction to QOS Mechanics and Architectures.* Chapter 2 provides an introduction and overview to the subject of QOS. In practical terms, QOS involves using a range of functions and features (e.g. classification, scheduling, policing, shaping), within the context of an overriding architecture (e.g. Integrated Service, Differentiated Services) in order to ensure that a network service delivers the SLA characteristics required by applications. This chapter describes and discusses the key QOS functions, features and architectures.

- *Chapter 3: Deploying Diffserv.* Diffserv is by far the most widely deployed IP QOS architecture; it is widely deployed in both private enterprise networks and in service provider networks providing VPN services to enterprises. Hence, in Chapter 3, we build on the foundations set by Chapters 1 and 2, to show how the Differentiated Services architecture (Diffserv) can be practically deployed at the network edge and in the network core in order to satisfy defined application SLA requirements. This is achieved through the use of end-to-end Diffserv design case studies, which are based upon experience gained from real-world deployments. These case studies show how SLA requirements are translated into practical network designs, which are defined in terms of example configurations using the Diffserv meta-language.

- *Chapter 4: Capacity Admission Control.* Capacity admission control is the process that is used to determine whether a new flow can be granted its requested QOS without affecting those flows already granted admission. There are a number of approaches to capacity admission control, and some technologies for admission control are still evolving. Hence, Chapter 4 describes the requirement for admission control and presents a taxonomy and review of the mechanisms available for capacity admission control in IP networks.

- *Chapter 5: SLA and Network Monitoring.* After a network design has been deployed, the ability to ensure that a network service continues to deliver the required SLAs is dependent upon SLA and network monitoring. Chapter 5 discusses the technologies and techniques available for monitoring IP QOS enabled networks, considering both passive and active network monitoring.

- *Chapter 6: Core Capacity Planning and Traffic Engineering.* Capacity planning is the process of ensuring that sufficient bandwidth is provisioned to assure that the committed SLA targets can be met. IP traffic engineering is the process of manipulating traffic on an IP network to make better use of the network capacity, by making use of capacity that would otherwise be unused, for example. Hence, capacity planning and traffic engineering are related, where traffic engineering is a tool that can be used to ensure that the available network capacity is appropriately provisioned. This chapter describes a holistic methodology for capacity planning of the core network, and describes the theory behind traffic engineering in general, and analyses some of the options and deployment considerations for the possible approaches for traffic engineering in IP networks.

Acknowledgments

The task of writing this book has been made easier due to the considerable help received in the process. Acknowledging that help, and thanking the contributors, to whom we are indebted, is truthfully one of the most significant pleasures of the task!

The book has benefitted enormously from the input of both Emmanuel Tychon and Thomas Telkamp, experts in their respective fields. Emmanuel's contribution formed the basis of the active monitoring section in Chapter 5. Thomas's work formed the basis of the capacity planning section in Chapter 6.

Rong Pan provided valuable input and expertise on the subject of RED tuning, which is used in Chapter 3.

This first edition has been improved enormously from the practical and constructive feedback that Ross Munns and the anonymous reviewers provided on the entire manuscript, which has helped in ensuring that our composition is as objective as possible. Fred Serr provided valuable comments on Chapter 5, and Simon Spraggs provided valuable comments on Chapter 1.

This book is a reflection of what we have learned over the years; much of this learning would not have been possible without the help of many colleagues during our time working for Cisco. Our employer Cisco kindly allowed us the latitude to work on this book, as well as providing us with day jobs.

Rick Adams, Rachel Roumeliotis, Brian Randall, and Renata Corbani at Elsevier had the job of actually getting this book to publication, which included the unenviable task of trying to get us to meet deadlines.

Finally, for forgiving my evenings and weekends at work, for her support and for providing enumerable roast potatoes to sustain this endeavor, I would like to thank my lovely wife Nessy.

John Evans

About the Authors

John Evans is a Distinguished Consulting Engineer with Cisco Systems, where he has been instrumental in the engineering and deployment of quality of service and policy control. His current areas of focus include policy/resource control, admission control, QOS, and traffic management with associated work in the DSL Forum, the Multiservice Forum, and ETSI/TISPAN. Prior to joining Cisco in 1998, John worked for BT where he was responsible for the design and development of large-scale networks for the financial community. Prior to BT, he worked on the design and deployment of battlefield communications networks for the military. He received a BEng (Hons) degree in Electronic Engineering from the University of Manchester Institute of Science and Technology (UMIST, now part of the University of Manchester), UK in 1991 and an MSc degree in Communications Engineering from UMIST in 1996. He is a Chartered Engineer (CEng) and Cisco Certified Internetwork Expert (CCIE).

Clarence Filsfils is a Cisco Distinguished System Engineer and a recognized expert in Routing and Quality of Service. He has been playing a key role in engineering, marketing, and deploying the quality of service and fast routing convergence technology at Cisco Systems. Clarence is a regular speaker at conferences. He has published several journal articles and holds over 30 patents on QOS and routing mechanisms.

1

QOS Requirements and Service Level Agreements

1.1 Introduction

When sending a parcel, the sender can generally select from a range of contractual commitments from the postal courier service provider; that the parcel will arrive within two working days of being sent, for example. The commitments may include other parameters or metrics such as the number of attempts at redelivery if the first attempt is unsuccessful, and any compensation that will be owed by the courier if the parcel is late or even lost. The more competitive the market for the particular service, the more comprehensive and the tighter the commitments or service level agreements (SLAs) that are offered.

In the same way, within the networking industry the increased competition between Internet Protocol (IP) [RFC791] service providers (SPs) together with the heightened importance of IP applications to business operations has led to an increased demand and consequent supply of IP services with better defined and tighter SLAs for IP performance. These SLAs represent a contract for the delivery of the service; in this case, it is an IP transport service. The SLA requirements of a service need to be derived from the SLA requirements of the applications they are intended to support; customers utilizing the service rely on this contract to ensure that they can deliver the applications critical to their business. Hence, SLA definitions are key and it is essential they are representative of the characteristics of the IP transport service they define.

For an IP service, the service that IP traffic receives is measured using quality metrics; the most important metrics for defining IP service performance are:

- delay
- delay variation or delay-jitter
- packet loss
- throughput
- service availability
- per flow sequence preservation.

"Quality of service" or QOS (either pronounced "Q-O-S" or "kwos") implies providing a contractual commitment (SLA) for these quality metrics. This contract may be explicitly defined; it is common for an IP transport service to have such an explicit SLA, for example. Alternatively, SLAs may be implied; for example, if you upgrade from a 2 Mbps DSL Internet connection to an 8 Mbps connection then you might expect that the service that you receive improves; however, this need not necessarily be the case. In this example "2 Mbps" and "8 Mbps" define the maximum rates for the service and as DSL services are commonly delivered using contended access networks, the actual usable throughput that users experience may be less than this maximum rate. Hence, the way in which the network has been engineered to deliver the service will determine the throughput that users receive, and it is possible that even though the user's maximum rates are different, their attained usable throughput may be the same. Clearly, there is no incentive for end-users to upgrade from a 2 Mbps service to an 8 Mbps service if they do not perceive a difference between them. Hence, in reality there is an implied SLA difference between the two services even if it is not explicitly specified – that the 8 Mbps service will offer a higher attainable throughput than the 2 Mbps service.

Application and service SLA requirements are the inputs and also the qualification criteria for measuring success in a network QOS design; a network which provides a 500 ms one-way delay would clearly not be able to support a voice over IP (VoIP) service requiring a worst-case one-way delay of 200 ms. Similarly, a network that provides a one-way delay of 50 ms may be over-engineered to support this service, and over-engineering may incur unnecessary cost. In price-sensitive markets, whether customers will be prepared to pay for the facility that QOS provides may depend in part on whether they can detect the effects of QOS; SLAs can provide a means to qualify the difference between services.

Although it is common for SPs, who provide virtual private network (VPN) services to enterprise organizations, to offer an explicit SLA to their enterprise customers, it is less common within enterprise organizations to define explicitly the SLAs that they engineer their networks to support. Nonetheless, enterprise networks support business-critical applications that have bounded SLA requirements; without an understanding of these requirements, it is not possible to engineer a network to ensure that they can be adequately supported without the risk of over- or under-engineering. An understanding of application SLA requirements is therefore as important in enterprise networks as in network SP environments.

In considering SLAs and SLA metrics, because they define a service contract, as with any contract the detail of the contract definition matters. In terms of SLAs for IP service performance, it is important to understand how the SLAs are numerically defined; SLAs may be defined in absolute terms, e.g. a worst-case one-way delay of 100 ms, or may be defined statistically, e.g. a loss rate of 0.01%. In the case of the statistical definition, defining a network loss rate of 0.01% is not sufficient information on its own to be able to determine if an application or service could be supported on that network. How the loss rate is measured and calculated needs to be defined in order to understand what impact the 0.01% loss rate will have on the end applications; 1 lost packet in every one hundred packets may not have a significant impact on a VoIP call, but 10 consecutive packets dropped out of 1000 will cause a glitch in the call that is audible to the end-user.

In order to remove some of the potential ambiguity around SLA definitions, the IP Performance Metrics [IPPM] Working Group (WG) within the Internet Engineering Task Force (IETF) was tasked with defining a set of standard metrics and procedures for accurately measuring and documenting them, which can be applied to the quality, performance, and reliability of IP services. The intent of the IPPM WG was to design metrics such that they can be measured by network operators, end-users, or independent testing groups. Their aim was to define metrics that do not represent a subjective value judgment (i.e. do not define "good" or "bad"), but rather provide unbiased quantitative measures of performance. [RFC2330] defines the "Framework for IP Performance Metrics" within the IETF. It is noted, however, that the SLAs provided by network service providers to customers do not generally use the IPPM definitions; see Section 1.4 for a discussion on "marketing" versus "engineering" SLAs.

In the proceeding sections in this chapter, we consider the SLA's metrics that are important for IP service performance in more detail, review the current industry status with respect to the standardization, and support of these metrics and then describe application SLA requirements and the impacts that these metrics can have on application performance.

1.2 SLA Metrics

1.2.1 Network Delay

SLAs for network delay are generally defined in terms of one-way delay for non-adaptive (inelastic) time-critical applications such as VoIP and video, and in terms of round-trip delay or round-trip time (RTT) for adaptive (elastic) applications, such as those which use the Transmission Control Protocol (TCP) [RFC793].

One-way delay characterizes the time difference between the reception of an IP packet at a defined network ingress point and its transmission at a defined network egress point. A metric for measuring one-way delay has been defined by [RFC2679] in the IETF.

RTT characterizes the time difference between the transmission of an IP packet at a point, toward a destination, and the subsequent receipt of the corresponding reply packet from that destination, excluding end-system processing delays. A metric for measuring RTT has been defined by [RFC2681] in the IETF.

Whether considering one-way delay or round-trip delay, the delays induced in a network are made up of the four following components.

1.2.1.1   Propagation Delay

Propagation delay is the time taken for a single bit to travel from the output port on a router across a link to another router. This is constrained by the speed of light in the transmission medium and hence depends both upon the distance of the link and upon the physical media used. The total propagation delay on a path consisting of a number of links is the sum of the propagation delays of the constituent links. Propagation delay is around 4 ms per 1000 km through coaxial cable and around 5 ms per 1000 km for optical fiber (allowing for repeaters).

In practice, network links never follow the geographical shortest path between the points they connect, hence the link distance, and associated propagation delay, can be estimated as follows:

- Determine the "as the crow flies" geographical distance D between the two end points.

- Obviously, the link distance must be longer than the distance as the crow flies. The route length R can be estimated from D, for example, using the calculation from International Telecommunications Union (ITU) recommendation [G.826], which is summarized in the following table.

D	R
$D < 1000 \text{ km}$	$R = 1.5 * D$
$1000 \text{ km} \leqslant D \leqslant 1200 \text{ km}$	$R = 1500 \text{ km}$
$D > 1200 \text{ km}$	$R = 1.25 * D$

The only way of controlling the propagation delay of a link is to control the physical link routing, which could be controlled at layer 2 or layer 3 of the Open Systems Interconnection (OSI) 7 layer Reference Model. If propagation delays for a link are too large, it may be that the link routing in an underlying layer 2 network is longer than it needs to be, and may be reduced by rerouting the link. Alternatively, a change to the network topology, by the addition of a more direct link for example, may reduce the propagation delay on a path.

1.2.1.2 Switching Delay

The switching or processing delay incurred at a router is the time difference between receiving a packet on an incoming router interface and the enqueuing of the packet in the scheduler of its outbound interface. Switching delays on high-performance routers can generally be considered negligible: for backbone routers, where switching is typically implemented in hardware, switching delays are typically in the order of 10–20 μs per packet; even for software-based router implementations, typical switching delays should only be 2–3 ms.

Little can be done to control switching delays without changing router software or hardware; however, as switching delays are generally a minor proportion of the end-to-end delay, this will not normally be justified.

1.2.1.3 Scheduling Delay

Scheduling (or queuing) delay is defined as the time difference between the enqueuing of a packet on the outbound interface scheduler, and the start of clocking the packet onto the outbound link. This is a function of the scheduling algorithm used and of the scheduler queue utilization, which is in turn a function of the queue capacity and the offered traffic load and profile.

Scheduling delays are controlled by managing the traffic load and by applying appropriate queuing and scheduling mechanisms (see Chapter 2, Section 2.2.4.1).

1.2.1.4 Serialization Delay

Serialization delay is the time taken to clock a packet onto a link and is dependent upon the link speed and the packet size. Serialization

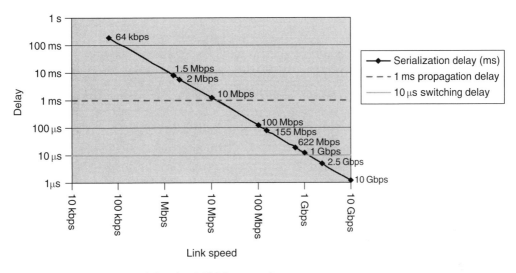

Figure 1.1   Serialization delay for 1500 byte packet

delay is proportional to packet size and inversely proportional to link speed:

$$\text{serialization\_delay} = \frac{\text{packet\_size}}{\text{link\_speed}}$$

Serialization delay can generally be considered negligible at link speeds above 155 Mbps (e.g. STM-1/OC3) such as backbone links, but can be significant on low-speed links. The serialization delay for a 1500-byte packet at link speeds from 64 kbps to 10 Gbps is shown in Figure 1.1, together with a line plotting indicative switching delay and a line showing a propagation delay of 1 ms (e.g. a link distance of ~130 km).

Serialization delay clearly is more significant component of delay for lower-speed links. Serialization delay is a physical constraint and hence there is no way of controlling serialization delay other than changing the link speed.

1.2.2 Delay-jitter

Delay-jitter characterizes the variation of network delay. Jitter is generally considered to be the variation of the one-way delay for two consecutive packets, as defined by [RFC3393] in the IETF. In practice, however, jitter can also be measured as the variation of delay with respect to some reference metric, such as average delay or minimum delay. It is fundamental that jitter relates to one-way delay; the notion of round-trip time jitter does not make sense.

Jitter is caused by the variation in the components of network delay previously described in Section 1.2.1:

- *Propagation delay*. Propagation delay can vary as network topology changes, when a link fails, for example, or when the topology of a lower layer network (e.g. SDH/SONET) changes, causing a sudden peak of jitter.

- *Switching delay*. Switching delay can vary as some packets might require more processing than others might. This effect may be perceptible in software-based router implementations but is becoming less of a consideration as routers implement packet switching in hardware resulting in more consistent switching delay characteristics.

- *Scheduling delay*. Variation in scheduling delay is caused as schedulers' queues oscillate between empty and full.

- *Serialization delay*. Serialization delay is a constant and as such should not contribute to jitter directly. If during a network failure, however, traffic is rerouted over a link with a different speed, then the serialization delay will change as a result of the failure and the change in serialization delay may contribute to jitter.

Some applications, such as those which use TCP, are generally not susceptible to jitter. Applications that are susceptible to jitter use dejitter buffers in order to remove delay variation by turning variable network delays into constant delays at the destination end-systems. Considerations on de-jitter buffers and their tuning are discussed in more detail in Section 1.3.1.2.

1.2.3   Packet Loss

Packet loss characterizes the packet drops that occur between a defined network ingress point and a defined network egress point. A packet sent from a network ingress point is considered lost if it does not arrive at a specified network egress point within a defined time period.

A metric for measuring the one-way packet loss rate (PLR) has been defined by [RFC2680] in the IETF.

One-way loss is measured rather than round-trip loss because the paths between a source and destination may be asymmetrical; that is, the path routing or path characteristics from a source to a destination may be different from the path routing or characteristics from the destination back to the source. Round-trip loss can be estimated by measuring the loss on each path independently.

In addition to the measured loss rate, in some applications the loss pattern or loss distribution is a key parameter that can impact the performance observed by the end-users; the same loss rate can result in significantly different perceptions of performance given two different loss distributions. Consequently, [RFC3357] introduces some additional metrics, which describe loss patterns:

- "loss period" defines the frequency and length of loss (loss burst) once it starts

- "loss distance" defines the spacing between the loss periods.

Packet loss can be caused by a number of factors:

- *Congestion.* When congestion occurs, queues build up and packets are dropped. Loss due to congestion is controlled by managing the traffic load and by applying appropriate queuing and scheduling mechanisms (see Chapter 2, Section 2.2.4).

- *Lower layer errors.* Physical layer bit errors, which may be due to noise or attenuation in the transmission channel, may cause packets to be dropped. Most link layer technologies and IP transport protocols, such as the User Datagram Protocol (UDP) [RFC768], have a cyclic redundancy check (CRC) or parity checksum to detect bit errors; when bit errors occur and the checksum is incorrect, the impacted frames will be dropped. Hence, for packets traversing networks with such capabilities, bit errors will normally result in packet loss, i.e. each packet will either arrive correct or not at all, although there are a few noted exceptions to this (see Section 1.3.2.1.3). In practice, actual bit error rates (BER, also referred to as the bit error ratio) vary widely depending upon the underlying layer 1 or layer 2 technologies used, which is different for different parts of the network:

○ Fiber-based optical links may support bit error rates as low as to $1 * 10^{-13}$

○ Synchronous Digital Hierarchy (SDH) or Synchronous Optical Network (SONET) services typically offer BER of $1 * 10^{-12}$

○ Typical E1/T1 leased line services support BER of $1 * 10^{-9}$

○ The Institute of Electrical and Electronics Engineers (IEEE) standard for local and metropolitan area networks [802-2001] specifies a maximum BER of $1 * 10^{-8}$

○ Typical Asynchronous Digital Subscriber Line (ADSL) services support BER of $1 * 10^{-7}$

○ Satellite services typically support BER of $1 * 10^{-6}$

For link layer technologies that are generally prone to high error rates, it is usual to support some link layer reliability mechanisms, such as Forward Error Correction (FEC), in order to recover from some bit error cases. If, however, the underlying layer 1 or layer 2 technologies cannot provide the BERs necessary to support the packet loss rates (PLRs) required by IP applications, then error correction or concealment techniques need to be used either by higher layer protocols or by the application, or alternate layer 1 or layer 2 technologies are needed.

• *Network element failures*. Network element failures may cause packets to be dropped until connectively is restored around the failed network element. The resulting loss period depends upon the underlying network technologies that are used.

With a "plain" IP (i.e. non-MPLS) deployment, after a network element failure, even if there is an alternative path around the failure, there will be a loss of connectivity which causes packet loss until the interior gateway routing protocol (IGP) converges. In well-designed networks, the IGP convergence time completes in a few hundred milliseconds [FRANCOIS]. If there is not an alternative path available then the loss of connectivity will persist until the failure is repaired. While such outages could be accounted for by the defined loss rate for the service, they are most commonly accounted for in the defined availability for the service (see Section 1.2.6).

Where an alternate path exists, the loss of connectivity following network element failures can be significantly reduced through the use of technologies such as MPLS Traffic Engineering (TE) Fast Reroute (FRR) [RFC4090] or IP Fast Reroute (IPFRR), which are local protection techniques that enable connectivity to be rapidly restored around link and node failures, typically within 50 ms. Equivalent techniques may be employed at layer 2, such as Automatic Protection Switching (APS) for SONET and Multiplex Section Protection (MSP) for SDH.

- *Loss in application end-systems*. Loss in application end-systems can happen due to overflows and underflows in the receiving buffer. An overflow is where the buffer is already full and another packet arrives, which cannot therefore be enqueued in the buffer; overflows can potentially impact all types of applications. An underflow typically only impacts real-time applications, such as VoIP and video, and is where the buffer is empty when the codec needs to play out a sample, and is effectively realized as a "lost" packet.

  Loss due to buffer underflows and overflows can be prevented through careful design both of the network and the application end-systems.

Depending upon the transport protocol or application, there are potentially a number of techniques that can be employed to protect against packet loss including error correction, error concealment, redundant transmission and retransmission.

1.2.4 Bandwidth and Throughput

IP services are commonly sold with a defined "bandwidth," where the bandwidth often reflects the layer 2 access link capacity provisioned for the service; however, when used in the context of networking the term "bandwidth" – which was originally used to describe a range of electromagnetic frequencies – can potentially have a number of different meanings with respect to the capacity of a link, network or service to transport traffic and data. Hence, to avoid confusion we define some more specific terms:

- *Link capacity*. The capacity of a link is a measure of how many bits per second that link can transport; link capacity needs to be considered both at layer 2 and at layer 3.
  - The capacity of a link is normally constant at layer 2 and is a function of the capacity of the physical media (i.e. the layer 1 capacity) and particular layer 2 encoding used. Some media, however, such as ADSL 2/2+ are rate-adaptive, and hence the layer 1 capacity can vary with noise and interference.
  - Link capacity at layer 3 (i.e. the IP link capacity) is a function of the link capacity at layer 2, the layer 2 encapsulation used and the layer 3 packet sizes. The IP link capacity can be derived for IP packets of a specified size, from the available layer 2 link capacity in bits per second, where only those bits of the IP packet are counted. The effect of layer 2 overheads on SLA definitions is discussed in more detail in Section 1.2.4.1.
  Link capacity is also referred to as link bandwidth or link speed.

- *Class capacity*. Where QOS mechanisms are used, an aggregate traffic stream may be classified into a number of constituent classes, and different QOS assurances may be provided to different classes within the aggregate. Where a class has a defined minimum bandwidth assurance, this is referred to as the class capacity, and may also be known as the class bandwidth.

- *Path capacity*. Path capacity is the minimum link capacity on a path between a defined network ingress point and a defined network egress point, consisting of a number of links interconnected by a number of nodes or routers. [CHIMENTO] also provides definitions for link and path capacity. Path capacity may also be referred to as the path bandwidth.

- *Bulk Transport Capacity*. The Bulk Transport Capacity (BTC) is a measure of the attainable user data throughput between a source and a destination; [RFC3148] specifies a framework for Defining Empirical Bulk Transfer Capacity Metrics. BTC is effectively a measure of the long-term average data throughput rate (e.g. in bits per second) a single congestion-aware transport layer connection could achieve over the path from source to destination. "Congestion aware" in this context refers to a transport layer technology that adapts its rate of sending, depending upon what is actually received, in order to try to maximize throughout; a TCP session is an example of such a congestion-aware transport layer connection. BTC is clearly limited by the path capacity, but is also impacted by a number of other factors such as packet loss and RTT (see Section 1.3.3.1), hence it is important to note that the BTC may be significantly lower than the link capacity specified in the SLA. BTC is a representation of the "goodput" available to a user, where the goodput represents the usable portion of the attainable throughput between a source and destination.

  BTC is not applicable to non congestion-aware, i.e. non-adaptive or inelastic, services; for such services, their attainable through-put may not be a meaningful metric, but nonetheless may be derived from the path capacity and the loss rate commitments for the service.

Hence, it is clear that the throughput attained for a service may not be the same as the defined "bandwidth." The following sections consider additional factors that further complicate the relationship between "bandwidth" and attained throughput.

1.2.4.1   Layer 2 Overheads

When considering the capacity of a service the available IP capacity depends upon the layer 2 media, the layer 2 encapsulation used and

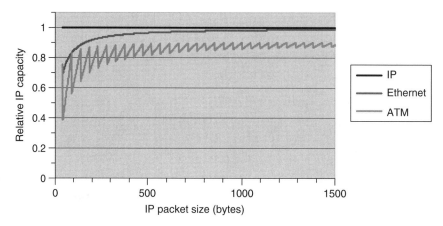

Figure 1.2 Relative IP capacity for different layer 2 media

upon the layer 3 packet sizes. Different layer 2 encapsulations add different sized headers and trailers to each packet; the headers and trailers are an overhead from the perspective of IP services, in that they use available layer 2 capacity, which is therefore not available at layer 3. As the layer 2 headers and trailers are added to each IP packet, the amount of layer 2 overhead incurred, and hence the IP capacity available, is dependent upon the IP packet size. Figure 1.2 shows the relative IP capacity for Ethernet and ATM connections, and how this relative capacity varies with IP packet sizes.

As can be seen from Figure 1.2, the available IP capacity can vary significantly depending upon the overall layer 2 overhead. For Ethernet, the layer 2 overhead in bytes per IP packet is constant, irrespective of the packet size; hence the layer 2 overhead reduces relative to the available IP capacity as the IP packet size increases. This is not the case for ATM, where an IP packet is segmented into cells and the per cell overhead or "cell tax" depends upon the number of cells, which in turn depends on the packet size. Hence, although the trend in the layer 2 overhead is to reduce relative to the available IP capacity as the IP packet size increases, a one-byte increase in packet size can result in an additional ATM cell, which results in an increase in the relative overhead; hence the saw tooth IP capacity characteristic for ATM in Figure 1.2.

Some services use traffic shapers applied to the access links in order to reduce the available capacity of the link; however, shapers, policers and schedulers can also exhibit very different behaviors, depending on whether they account for bandwidths in terms of layer 3 packet sizes or whether they also include all layer 2 overheads, or even account for something in between the two.

We discuss scheduling in detail in Chapter 2, Section 2.2.4.1; however, prior to that, consider for example, a simple two-queue (where a queue is ostensibly a class) scheduler with per-queue minimum bandwidth assurances defined at layer 3 of $X = Y = 50\%$. With IP packet sizes of 100 bytes for queue X and 1000 bytes for queue Y, and assuming a layer 2 overhead of 26 bytes per packet (as is the case with Ethernet v2), the measured bandwidth ratio X:Y at layer 3 is (10 * 100):(1 * 1000) = 50:50, whereas the ratio measured at layer 2 = (10 * 126):(1 * 1026) = ~55:45. Conversely, assuming the same packet sizes and overhead but with per-queue minimum bandwidth assurances of $X = Y = 50\%$ defined at layer 2, the resulting bandwidth ratio at layer 3 = (100 * 1026):(1000 * 126) = ~45:55.

In some cases, there are constraints imposed by the underlying layer 1 and layer 2 technologies, which naturally define the overheads that are taken into account in a particular SLA definition. In other cases there may be no definitive answer as to whether layer 2 overheads should be taken into account:

- Accounting for all layer 2 overheads in actual router implementations can be difficult when, for example, layer 2 fragmentation mechanisms (see Chapter 2, Section 2.2.5) insert additional bytes after a packet has been enqueued.

- Some service SLAs are defined excluding layer 2 overheads; while others to take layer 2 overheads into account; there is no de facto industry approach.

- The IETF's Integrated Services (Intserv) and Differentiated Services (Diffserv) architectures (see Chapter 2, Sections 2.3.3 and 2.3.4) do not discuss or define the accounting of layer 2 overheads.

- There is variation in the overheads accounted for by different vendors' scheduling, shaping, and queuing implementations; in some vendors' implementations the overhead accounting that is taken into account by a QOS policy can be configured.

Whichever approach is adopted, the SLA specification must clearly define which overheads are taken into account and to which layer the bandwidth assurances apply. This has a consequent impact on the overheads that QOS functions such as scheduling, shaping, or policing need to take into account.

1.2.4.2   VPN Hose and Pipe Models

Consider a network connecting four sites (#1, #2, #3 and #4); this could be a layer 2 virtual private network (VPN) offered by a service provider using a technology such as leased lines, Frame-relay or ATM, for example. Whichever underlying technology is used the sites could be interconnected in a hub and spoke arrangement with spoke sites connected back to a hub site using leased lines or virtual circuits (VCs), or they could be interconnected with a full mesh of leased lines or VCs; both options are shown in Figure 1.3.[1]

In both cases shown in Figure 1.3, each leased line or VC may have a defined SLA commitment; this type of point-to-point bandwidth commitment was first termed a "pipe" by [DUFFIELD]; these point-to-point commitments provide isolation between the performance of

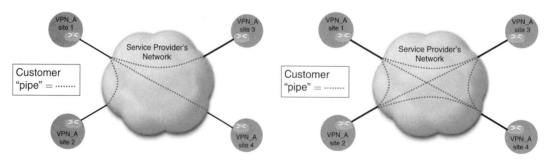

Figure 1.3   Hub and spoke (left) and full mesh (right) VPNs using the "pipe model"

each "pipe." The use of the "pipe model" is obvious for point-to-point services such as leased lines, Frame relay, ATM or layer 2 "pseudo wires" as defined by the Pseudo Wire Emulation Edge-to-Edge Working Group [PWE3] within the IETF. When layer 3 services are built on top of such point-to-point pipes, however, as the number of sites within a VPN increases, provisioning such point-to-point commitments can become cumbersome. For example, a full mesh between n sites requires $n(n-1)/2$ connections, e.g. 100 sites would require $100 * 99/2 = 4950$ such pipes. In addition, such point-to-point commitments can be inefficient with respect to the use of provisioned capacity. For example, site #1 may have 1 Mbps VCs provisioned to each of sites #2, #3, and #4 (i.e. 3 Mbps in total), yet if the VC to site #2 is not busy, this unused capacity to/from site #2 cannot be re-used for traffic between site #1 and sites #3 or #4, i.e. up to 1 Mbps of capacity to/from site #1 would go idle.

VPNs built using IP or MPLS technology, e.g. BGP MPLS VPNs as per [RFC4364], can implicitly provide "any-to-any" connectivity between the sites within the VPN; however, this gives rise to the question of how to define SLAs between sites within VPNs that provide multipoint-to-multipoint connectivity, when you do not have a corresponding pipe (or its SLA assurances) between those sites? [DUFFIELD] addressed this by defining the "hose model" for multipoint-to-multipoint VPN services. With the hose model, rather than defining SLAs on a point-to-point basis between pairs of sites, the SLAs are defined in terms of a "hose" from each site to and from the VPN provider network. From a capacity perspective, the "hose" for each site is defined in terms of the ingress committed rate (ICR) to the provider and the egress committed rate (ECR) from the provider, as shown in Figure 1.4.

Traffic between two sites that is within the ICR contract at the source site, and within the ECR contract at the destination site is assured end-to-end. ICR/ECR could be defined with a single class per site, or in the context of a Diffserv enabled service, could be offered on a per class per site basis.

Hose model SLAs can provide the benefits of statistical multiplexing, where pipe model SLAs cannot. For example, if site #1 has an

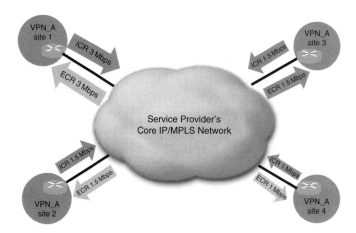

Figure 1.4 Any-to-any VPNs using the "hose model"

ICR and ECR of 3 Mbps, it could use that capacity to communicate with any of sites #2, #3, and #4, i.e. if there were no traffic to site #2, the unused capacity to/from site #2 could potentially be re-used for traffic between site #1 and sites #3 or #4. A consequence of this is that hose model SLAs also need to make provision for mediation between the ICR and ECR between different sites. For example, the ICR for site #1 may be 3 Mbps; however, the attainable capacity to site #4 will be limited by the ECR of site #4, which is 1 Mbps. In addition, hose model SLAs need to take into account cases where the loss of attainable throughput is due to customer-based traffic aggregation. For example, if sites #2, #3 and #4 all attempt to send traffic at their full ICRs (which totals 4 Mbps) to site #1, their aggregate attainable capacity will be limited by the ECR of site #1, which is only 3 Mbps.

1.2.5 Per Flow Sequence Preservation

IP does not guarantee that packets are delivered in the order in which they were sent. As defined in the IETF by [RFC4737], if the packets in a flow were numbered sequentially in the order in which they were sent, a packet that arrived with a sequence number smaller than that of their predecessor would be defined as out-of-order, or re-ordered. For example, if packets in a sequentially number stream were received in the order 1, 2, 3, 4, 7, 5, 6, 8, 9, 10 then packets numbered 5 and 6 would have been re-ordered. The simplest metric by which to measure the magnitude of re-ordering is as a re-ordering ratio, which is the ratio of re-ordered packets that arrived, relative to the total number of packets received. A number of other metrics for quantifying the magnitude of re-ordering are defined in [RFC4737].

Due to the adverse impact that packet re-ordering can have on the performance of some applications, it is accepted best practice in IP network design to prevent packet re-ordering within a flow, although it is not yet a universal component of IP service SLA commitments. There are two key design best practices in order to prevent packet re-ordering within a flow:

- It is important that any IP load balancing across multiple paths within the network is performed on a per flow level rather than on a per packet level such that all packets within a flow follow the same path. This load balancing is performed by Equal Cost Multipath (ECMP) algorithms, where there are multiple IGP paths with the same cost. ECMP algorithms commonly perform a hash function to determine which of the paths a packet will take; where the hash function uses the 5-tuple of IP protocol, source IP address, destination IP address, source UDP/TCP port, and destination UDP/TCP as inputs, and results in packets within a single flow consistently hashing to the same path.

- QOS designs and scheduling algorithms must ensure that packets from the same flow are always serviced in the same order and from the same queue; this is a fundamental principle of both the Integrated Services and Differentiated Services QOS architectures, which are described in Chapter 2.

Re-ordering of packets within a flow is bad practice and designs or implementations, which result in such re-ordering, should be considered broken!

1.2.6 Availability

Availability for IP services is generally defined in one of two ways: either as network availability or as service availability.

1.2.6.1 Network Availability

Network availability (sometimes referred to as connectivity) is defined as the fraction of time that network connectivity is available between a specified network ingress point and a specified network egress point. Availability can be unidirectional or bidirectional; bidirectional connectivity is what matters to the vast majority of IP applications, i.e. that a source can send a packet to a destination that elicits a response which is received by the source. A metric for measuring connectivity has been defined by [RFC2678] in the IETF.

Network availability needs to take into account unavailability due to planned outages, caused by scheduled network maintenance for example, as well as outages due to network failures. The unavailability that results from network failures depends upon the underlying network technologies that are used, as discussed in Section 1.2.3.

The availability of the network can be estimated by calculating the availability of each individual network element and then combining the availabilities in series or in parallel as appropriate using the following formulae.

Component availability

The availability (*A*) of an individual component is the proportion of the time for which the device is working:

$$A = \frac{\text{time\_working}}{\text{total\_time}} = \frac{MTBF}{MTBF + MTTR}$$

Where:
$MTBF$ = mean time between failures
$MTTR$ = mean time to restore

Component unavailability

The unavailability (U) of an individual component is the proportion of the time for which the device is not working:

$$U = \frac{time\_not\_working}{total\_time} = \frac{MTTR}{MTBF + MTTR} = 1 - A$$

Availability of components in series

The availability of components ($a,b,c, \ldots$) in series (A_s) is given by:

$$A_s = [A(a) \times A(b) \times A(c) \times \cdots]$$

Availability of components in parallel

The availability of components ($a,b,c, \ldots$) in parallel (A_p) is given by:

$$A_p = [1 - (U(a) \times U(b) \times U(c) \times \cdots)]$$

For most applications, however, simply having connectivity is not enough. For VoIP for example, it is of little practical use if there is connectivity between two VoIP end-systems but the VoIP packets arrive so delayed that speech between the two calling parties becomes unintelligible, hence service availability is often a more meaningful metric.

1.2.6.2 Service Availability

Service availability is defined as the fraction of time the service is available between a specified ingress point and a specified egress point within the bounds of the other defined SLA metrics for the service, e.g. delay, jitter, and loss. Service availability can be defined in one of two ways: either it can be defined independently of network availability, in which case the service availability cannot exceed the network availability, or it can be defined as being applicable only when the network is considered available. Service availability may encompass application performance as well as network perform-ance. For instance, the service availability may comprise hostname resolution (DNS server) and transaction time, thereby depending on network delay and web server performance.

There may be overlap between the definition of network or service availability and the definition of other SLA parameters. For example, consider two traffic classes, A and B, where Class A supports a tighter delay SLA, which is specified with a 90th percentile (P90) delay for Class A packets of 10 ms – meaning that 99 packets out of 100 were delivered within this delay bound – and a P99 delay of 15 ms, while Class B has a P75 delay of 10 ms with a P99 delay of 30 ms. These SLAs could be expressed by a smaller delay bound for A than B but with the same availability, e.g. Class A has a delay of 15 ms with 99% availability, while Class B has a delay of 30 ms with 99% availability. Alternatively, this SLA could be expressed by the same delay bound but with a higher availability for A than for B, e.g. Class A has a delay of 10 ms with 90% availability, while Class B has a delay of 10 ms with 75% availability.

1.2.7   Quality of Experience

In addition to the metrics already described in this section, which define the characteristics of the network, there are additional metrics, which aim to quantify the performance experienced by the applications using the network. These metrics define the perception of application performance, experienced from the perspective of the end-users, which is also known as the user "quality of experience" (QOE).

For IP-based voice and video applications the QOE is a compound metric dependent upon the quality of the encoder used, the quality of the service delivered by the IP network, and the quality of the decoder used. As such, QOE targets do not directly define the delay, jitter, loss etc., characteristics that a network should provide, but rather for a specified application, using a defined encoder/decoder, the network characteristics may be implied given a particular QOE target.

QOE metrics can be measured subjectively or objectively. Subjective measures rely upon end-user feedback of their perception of the quality of the service. Objective measures use measurements of characteristics of the received stream, and possibly also of the transmitted stream, in order to infer the subjective quality that would be experienced by the end-user.

There are QOE metrics defined for voice, video and on-line gaming applications:

1.2.7.1 Voice

- *Subjective measures*. The Mean Opinion Score (MOS) is a well-established scheme, which provides a numeric measure of the quality of a voice call at the destination. MOS is a formally tested subjective measure, which is defined by the ITU [P.800] and is determined using a number of human listeners participating in a set of standard tests, subjectively scoring the quality of test sentences read aloud over the communications medium being tested using the scale: excellent (5), good (4), fair (3), poor (2) and bad (1). The MOS for the medium under test is calculated by taking the arithmetic mean of all the individual scores. A typical Public Switched Telephony (PSTN) voice service has MOS of 4.3, while mobile telephone services typically have a MOS of between 2.9 and 4.1.

- *Objective measures*. There are several recommendations provided by the ITU, which provide methods for objective voice quality monitoring, and that can also be used to estimate the MOS. These schemes rely on characteristics of the received stream only.
  - ITU P.862 [P.862] defines the Perceptual Evaluation of Speech Quality (PESQ, pronounced "pesk"), and is a full reference (where full information about both the transmitted and received audio signals are available when the audio quality is determined) objective method for predicting the subjective MOS quality of telephony services.
  - ITU G.107 [G.107] defines the so-called "E model" which uses a number of transmission level parameters to rate the quality of a transmission system, in order to assess the effects on telephony services. The primary output from the E model is the "Rating Factor," R, which can be transformed to give estimates of the MOS (an objective MOS score) for calls which use that transmission service.

1.2.7.2 Video

- *Subjective measures*. The main concepts behind the subjective measurement of video quality are the same as for MOS for voice. The most established video subjective testing scheme in the broadcasting world is the Double Stimulus Continuous Quality Scale (DSCQS) method defined in ITU specification [BT.500]. An alternative methodology that The European Broadcasting Union (EBU) [EBU] has defined is called the SAMVIQ Subjective Assessment Methodology for Video Quality [SAMVIQ].

- *Objective measures*. The most established objective measure of video quality is defined in ITU-T standard J.144 [J.144]. This provides guidelines on perceptual video quality measurement for use in digital cable television applications when the full reference video signal is available, i.e. both the transmitted and received video signals are available for comparison when the video quality is determined. It is still a subject of study as to whether reduced reference (where only partial information about transmitted video signal and full information about the received video signal is available when the video quality is determined) or no reference (where only the received video signal is available when the video quality is determined) can be used to accurately infer subjective video quality, i.e. to correctly suggest that the video quality is bad when, and only when, the end viewer also thinks it is bad.

1.2.7.3 On-line Gaming

[DICK] define a MOS metric to classify the player's perceived game quality.

1.3 Application SLA Requirements

Different applications have different SLA requirements; the impact that different network services with different SLAs have on an application is dependent upon the specific application:

- Excessive packet loss or delay may make it difficult to support real-time applications although the precise threshold of "excessive" depends on the particular application.

- The larger the value of packet loss or network delay, the more difficult it is for transport-layer protocols to sustain high bandwidths.

To appreciate these impacts, there is a minimum level of understanding required of how the applications, and the protocols they use, behave as networks SLA characteristics change. It is only through such an understanding that it is possible to engineer the network, using QOS if necessary, to ensure that the specific SLA requirements that applications require can be adequately supported, without over-engineering. Hence, this section aims to provide that minimum level of understanding, together with providing references to further detail on the application and protocol behaviors.

Additionally, by having an understanding of how applications and the protocols behave as networks SLA characteristics change, it is possible to understand where deploying QOS mechanisms may not be sufficient to be able to meet the application SLA requirements and application or network re-engineering may be required instead.

Conversely, to understand the impact that an application has on the network and on other applications, it is important to understand the application's traffic profile. To be meaningful a traffic profile needs to define at least the average rate and the burst characteristic of the application, over a defined time interval; this could be viewed as a virtual simple token bucket (as described in Chapter 2, Section 2.2.3). It can, however, easily be shown that different traffic profiles can share the same average rate and burst characteristics, hence more complex traffic profile descriptors are possible. Some applications will have a constant bit rate (CBR), which means that the burst characteristic of the traffic would relatively be the same over any time interval. Other applications may be described as variable bit rate (VBR), where the burst characteristic is relatively larger over smaller time intervals.

While there are clearly too many applications to describe them all, we consider the most common applications or application types, which impose the tightest SLA requirements on the network. In practice, most applications that have explicit SLA requirements will fall into one of the following categories, or will have SLA requirements, which are similar to one of those categories described:

- voice over IP
- video streaming
- video conferencing
- throughput-focussed TCP applications
- interactive data applications
- on-line gaming.

1.3.1 Voice over IP

Voice over IP (VoIP) is most commonly transported as a digitally encoded stream using the Real-time Protocol (RTP) [RFC3550] over UDP; RTP is the transport layer protocol, which deals with the delivery of the VoIP bearer stream from sender to receiver. Signaling protocols such as the Session Initiation Protocol (SIP) [RFC3261] may be used to set up the RTP bearer streams and to determine the media formats (i.e. codecs) that will be used. The key factors that determine the impact that variations in networks SLA characteristics such as delay and loss have on VoIP are the codec that is used to encode the signal and the specific details of the end-system implementation. For example, some codecs may be less tolerant to loss than others, while a poor end-system implementation may be less tolerant to jitter.

VoIP codecs convert analog voice signals into a digital bit stream at the sender and convert them back to an analog audio signal at the receiver. The most widely used codecs are those defined by the ITU G.71x and G72x standards. The simplest waveform-based codecs, such as that defined by ITU standard G.711, use pulse code modulation (PCM) where the analog signal is sampled at regular intervals; the samples are quantized into a set of discrete values to produce the encoded digital signal. More advanced codecs, such as that defined by ITU standard G.726, use Adaptive Differential PCM (ADPCM). ADPCM predicts the next sample from previous samples and then quantizes only the difference between the actual sample value and the prediction; consequently, ADPCM produces a lower bit rate signal than PCM at equivalent quality.

Frame-based codecs, such as ITU G.729 and ITU G.723, use more complicated techniques such as Algebraic Code Excited Linear Prediction (ACELP). ACELP breaks a sampled input signal into blocks of samples; these blocks or frames, which are typically 20 ms, are processed as whole units. In processing a frame, the encoder uses a technique called analysis-by-synthesis to determine which input parameters, when passed through a synthesizing filter, would result in reconstructed speech closest to the original speech signal. The encoder then uses a codebook to reference the inputs to the filter; the reference is sent to the decoder, which shares the same codebook, and which applies the respective inputs to the same synthesis filter to reconstruct the speech. There are a number of algorithms that have derived from ACELP, including Low-Delay Code Excited Linear Prediction (LD-CELP) and Conjugate Structure ACELP (CS-ACELP).

The codecs available for VoIP vary in complexity, in the bandwidth they need, and in the delivered call quality perceived by the end-user. Algorithms that are more complex may provide better perceived call quality, but may incur longer processing delays; Figure 1.5

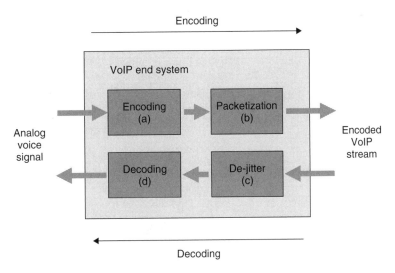

Figure 1.5 VoIP end-systems components of delay

shows the functional components in VoIP end-systems, which contribute to delay.

Some codecs use compression in order to reduce the bandwidth required for a VoIP call, which inevitably results in the loss of detail of the original signal, hence in general the better the call quality required, the more bandwidth that will be required per call. The table in Figure 1.6 compares characteristics of some of the more common VoIP codecs.

ITU-T Codec	Codec type	Maximum codec delay (ms) (a1 d)	Bitrate (bps)	Packetization interval (ms) (b)	pps	Payload size (bytes)	IP pkt size (bytes)[i]	IP bps
G.711	PCM	0.375	64 000	10	100	80	120	96 000
G.711	PCM	0.375	64 000	20	50	160	200	80 000
G.711	PCM	0.375	64 000	30	33.33	240	280	74 659
G.723.1	ACELP	97.5	5 300	30	33.33	20	60	15 998
G.723.1	ACELP	97.5	5 300	15	16.67	40	80	10 669
G.726.16	ADPCM	0.375	16 000	10	100	20	60	48 000
G.726.16	ADPCM	0.375	16 000	20	50	40	80	32 000
G.726.16	ADPCM	0.375	16 000	30	33.33	60	100	26 664
G.726.24	ADPCM	0.375	24 000	10	100	30	70	56 000
G.726.24	ADPCM	0.375	24 000	10	50	60	100	40 000
G.726.24	ADPCM	0.375	24 000	10	33.33	90	130	34 663
G.726.32	ADPCM	0.375	32 000	10	100	40	80	64 000
G.726.32	ADPCM	0.375	32 000	20	50	80	120	48 000
G.726.32	ADPCM	0.375	32 000	30	33.33	120	160	42 662
G.726.40	ADPCM	0.375	40 000	10	100	50	90	72 000
G.726.40	ADPCM	0.375	40 000	20	50	100	140	56 000
G.726.40	ADPCM	0.375	40 000	30	33.33	150	190	50 662
G.728	LD-CELP	1.875	16 000	10	100	20	60	48 000
G.728	LD-CELP	1.875	16 000	20	50	40	80	32 000
G.728	LD-CELP	1.875	16 000	30	33.33	60	100	26 664
G.729A	CS-ACELP	35	8 000	10	100	10	50	40 000
G.729A	CS-ACELP	35	8 000	20	50	20	60	24 000
G.729A	CS-ACELP	35	8 000	30	33.33	30	70	18 665

Figure 1.6   VoIP codec characteristics[2]

The impact that different SLA metric parameters have on VoIP applications is considered in the following sections.

1.3.1.1   VoIP: Impact of Delay

For VoIP the important delay metric is the one-way end-to-end (i.e. from mouth-to-ear) delay, in each direction. The main impact that end-to-end delay has on VoIP is to the interactivity of conversational speech. If the delay is too high, participants find it difficult to discern the difference between natural pauses in speech and the delays introduced by the system. If they mistake system delays for pauses in conversation and take these delays as their cue to begin to speak, by the time their words arrive at the other end, the other speaker may have already started to speak with the result that the normal protocol of conversation breaks down. Excessive end-to-end delay can also impair the effectiveness of mechanisms used for echo-cancellation.

The goal commonly used in designing networks to support voice over IP (VoIP) is the target specified by ITU-T recommendation G.114 [G.114], which uses the E-model (see Section 1.2.7.1) to estimate the effects of delay on mouth-to-ear speech transmission quality. Recommendation G.114 suggests that ~150 ms of end-to-end one-way delay is sufficient to ensure that users will be very satisfied for most applications of telephony. Higher delays may also be acceptable, but with a consequent reduction in user satisfaction, with delays exceeding 400 ms generally considered unacceptable, as shown in the table in Figure 1.7.

Network delay is only one component of the ear-to-mouth delay that impacts a VoIP call. Hence, having determined what the maximum acceptable ear-to-mouth delay is for a particular VoIP service, a network QOS design should take this budget and apportion it to the

Ear-to-mouth delay (D)	R factor	Objective MOS
D < 150 ms	80–89	5
150 ms < D < 250 ms	70–79	4
250 ms < D < 325 ms	60–69	3
325 ms < D < 425 ms	50–59	2
D > 425 ms	90–100	1

Figure 1.7   ITU G.114 Determination of the effects of absolute delay by the E-model

various components of network delay (propagation delay through the backbone, scheduling delay due to congestion, and the access link serialization delay) and end-system delay (due to VoIP codec and de-jitter buffer). The example timeline in Figure 1.8 shows the components of delay, which impact the ear-to-mouth delay of a VoIP service, using typical values for each component.

The codec delays are dependent upon the type of codec used. The table in Figure 1.6 lists the maximum theoretical one-way delay introduced by codec-related processing for a number of different codecs; in practice VoIP end-systems may incur an additional 5–20 ms of delay, depending upon the specific implementation. One-way network delays of 35–100 ms are typically targeted for high quality ("toll quality") VoIP services, in order to ensure that an ear-to-mouth delay of 150 ms can be achieved; an example VoIP delay budget is given in Chapter 3, Section 3.2.2.1.1 QOS mechanisms are typically employed to ensure these targets can be met. Higher delays may be tolerated for lower quality services.

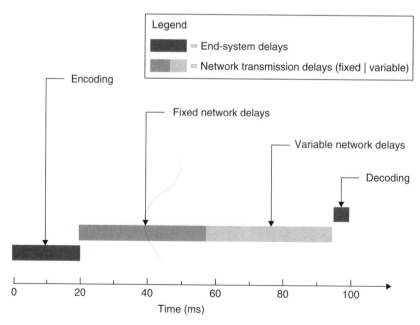

Figure 1.8 VoIP: components of ear-to-mouth delay

1.3.1.2 VoIP: Impact of Delay-jitter

It is a common misconception that jitter has a greater impact on the quality of VoIP calls than network delay. An understanding of how VoIP end-systems deal with delay and jitter is needed to understand why this is incorrect.

Applications which are susceptible to jitter, such as VoIP, use de-jitter buffers (also known as jitter buffers and play-out buffers) to compensate for jitter in packet arrival and for out-of-order packets. This is required because the decoding of the received signal is a synchronous process, and hence data must be fed into the decoder at a constant rate. De-jitter buffers remove delay variation by turning variable network delays into constant delays at the destination end-systems. If the de-jitter buffer play-out delay is set either arbitrarily large or arbitrarily small, then it may impose unnecessary constraints on the characteristics of the network or may affect the quality of the VoIP service. A play-out delay set too large adds unnecessarily to the end-to-end delay, as shown in Figure 1.9, meaning that less of the ear-to-mouth delay budget is available to be apportioned to the network and hence that the network needs to support a tighter delay target than practically necessary.

If the de-jitter buffer play-out delay is too small to accommodate the network jitter then buffer underflows can occur; an underflow is

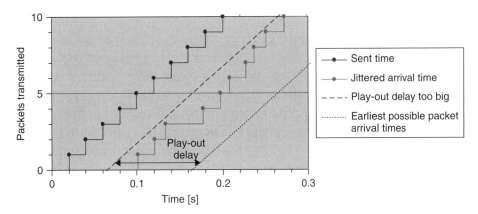

Figure 1.9 VoIP play-out delay unnecessarily large

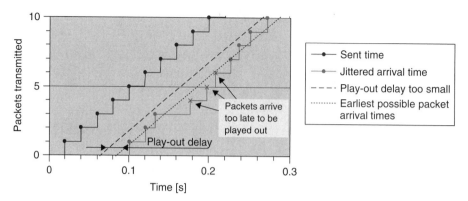

Figure 1.10   VoIP play-out delay too small

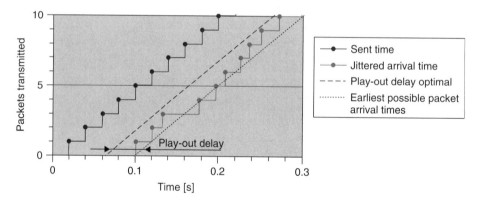

Figure 1.11   Optimal VoIP play-out delay

where the buffer is empty when the codec needs to play out a sample, and is effectively realized as a "lost" packet as shown in Figure 1.10.

Most VoIP end-systems use adaptive de-jitter buffers, which aim to overcome these issues by dynamically tuning the play-out delay to the lowest acceptable value, as shown in Figure 1.11.

Well-designed adaptive de-jitter buffer algorithms should not impose any unnecessary constraints on the network design if they display the following characteristics:

• increasing the play-out delay to the current measured jitter value following an underflow, and using packet loss concealment (see

Section 1.3.1.3) to interpolate for the "lost" packet and for the play-out delay size increase

- if the play-out delay can decrease then it should do so slowly when the measured jitter is less that the current buffer play-out delay.

Where such adaptive de-jitter buffers are used, they dynamically adjust to the maximum value of network jitter. In this case, the jitter buffer does not add delay in addition to the worst-case end-to-end network delay.

1.3.1.3 VoIP: Impact of Loss

Packet Loss Concealment (PLC) is a technique used to mask the effects of lost or discarded VoIP packets; an understanding of PLC is needed to understand the impact that packet loss has on the resultant quality of a VoIP call. The method of packet loss concealment used depends upon the type of codec used.

A simple method of packet loss concealment, used by waveform codecs like G.711 (PLC for G.711 is defined in G.711 Appendix I), is to replay the previously received sample; the concept underlying this approach is that, except for rapidly changing sections, the speech signal is locally stationary. This technique can be effective at concealing the loss of up to approximately 20 ms of samples. The packetization interval determines the size of samples contained within a single packet; assuming a 20 ms packetization interval, the loss of two or more consecutive packets will result in a noticeable degradation of voice quality.[3] From a network design perspective, it is important to note that a design decision to use a 30 ms packetization interval, for a given probability of packet loss, could result in worse perceived call quality than a 20 ms packetization interval, as with a 30 ms interval PLC may not be able to effectively conceal the loss of a single packet. Hence, there is a network design trade-off to be considered; larger packetization intervals may reduce the bandwidth of a VoIP call (there is less IP overhead due to more samples being carried in a single packet) but may also result in lower call quality for a given loss rate.

Low bit rate frame-based codecs, such as G.729 and G.723, use more sophisticated PLC techniques, which can conceal up to 30–40 ms of loss with "tolerable" quality, when the available history used for the interpolation is still relevant. Concealment becomes problematic with short phonemes – *the smallest phonetic unit in a language* – where 30 ms of samples can be over half of a phoneme and previous and subsequent samples may not provide enough information about the lost sample to allow it to be effectively concealed. With frame-based codecs, the packetization interval will determine the number of frames carried in a single packet. Similarly as for waveform-based codecs, if the packetization interval were greater than the loss that the PLC algorithm can interpolate for, then PLC would not be able to conceal the loss of a single packet effectively.

Hence, to summarize the impact that packet loss has on VoIP, with an appropriately selected packetization interval (20–30 ms depending upon the type of codec used) a loss period of one packet may be concealed but a loss period of two or more consecutive packets may result in a noticeable degradation of voice quality. The loss distance targeted for a particular service is a choice for the service provider.

In supporting VoIP services, it is essential to understand what impact these targets have on the network design in practice; consider the impact of the possible causes of packet loss previously defined in Section 1.2.3:

- *Congestion.* When congestion that impacts VoIP traffic occurs, queues build up and VoIP packets are dropped. If congestion occurs, it is not practically possible to engineer the network to ensure that consecutive packets from a single VoIP call are not dropped, nor to ensure that if they are dropped that it is with a controlled distribution. For this reason, networks supporting VoIP are designed to be congestionless from the perspective of the VoIP traffic; that is the available capacity for VoIP traffic is able to cope with the peak of the offered VoIP traffic load. QOS mechanisms, admission control techniques and appropriate capacity planning techniques are deployed to ensure that no packets are lost due to congestion.

- *Lower layer errors*. As described in Section 1.2.3, physical layer bit errors may cause packets to be dropped due to link layer or transport-layer checksums. Hence, bit errors will generally result in packet loss, meaning each packet will either arrive correctly or not at all. QOS mechanisms cannot have any impact on loss due to lower level errors; hence, where the underlying network transport infrastructure cannot meet the loss distance targets required for the VoIP service, PLC techniques will be required.

  Consider for example a typical BER offered for a leased line service of $1 * 10^{-9}$ and assume a random error distribution, that each error causes a lost packet, and that a G.711–20 ms codec is used which produces 200-byte packets at 50 pps; the resultant PLR would be $1 * 10^{-9} * 200 * 8 = 1.6 * 10^{-6}$. Without PLC this would result in an effective loss distance of $1/(1.6 * 10^{-6} * 50\text{pps} * 60)$ seconds = $\sim$208 minutes, which is better than typical service targets, which are in the order of 1 audible artifact every 30 minutes. PLC would further increase the attained loss distance.

  As an alternative example, consider a typical BER offered for an ADSL service of $1 * 10^{-7}$; this would equate to a PLR of $1 * 10^{-7} * 200 * 8 = \sim 1.6 * 10^{-4}$ which, without PLC, would result in a loss distance of $\sim$2 minutes, which is an order of magnitude less than typical service targets. With PLC interpolating for the loss of a single packet, the probability of an audible impairment (due to two consecutive packets lost) would be $(1.6 * 10^{-4})^2 = \sim 2.6 * 10^{-8}$, i.e. an effective loss distance of $1/(2.6 * 10^{-8} * 50\text{pps} * 60$ seconds $* 60$ minutes $* 24$ hours) = $\sim$9 days! Hence, even for ADSL services, the impact on VoIP services of bit errors is unlikely to be significant.

- *Network element failures*. Network element failures may cause packets to be dropped until connectivity is restored around the failed network element. The resulting loss period depends upon the underlying network technologies that are used, as discussed in Section 1.2.3.

  In a "plain" IP (i.e. non-MPLS) deployment, even in a well-designed network where the IGP convergence time is 100s of milliseconds, the packet loss following a network element failure is too significant to be concealed and an audible glitch will result.

Where MPLS TE FRR or equivalent techniques are deployed, reducing the loss of connectivity following network element failures to within 50 ms, PLC may be able to interpolate for the resultant packet loss, but this is not guaranteed.

- *Loss in the application end-systems.* Loss due to buffer underflows and overflows can be prevented through careful design both of the network and the application end-systems, as discussed in Section 1.3.1.2.

Therefore, in practice, networks supporting VoIP should typically be designed for very close to zero percent VoIP packet loss. QOS mechanisms, admission control techniques and appropriate capacity planning techniques are deployed to ensure that no packets are lost due to congestion with the only actual packet loss being due to layer 1 bit errors or network element failures. Where packet loss occurs, the impact of the loss should be reduced to acceptable levels using PLC techniques.

1.3.1.4   VoIP: Impact of Throughput

VoIP codecs generally produce a constant bit rate stream, with bandwidths as shown in Figure 1.6; that is, unless silence suppression is used. Silence suppression, which is also known as voice activation detection (VAD), prevents the transmission of packets carrying "silent" samples. Silence suppression becomes active when it detects periods of silence from the microphone that exceed defined thresholds; when silence suppression is active it prevents the encoder output from being sent to the far end. When silence suppression is active for a leg of a VoIP call, the bandwidth used for that leg of the call is almost zero. As most conversational speech contains approximately 50% silence, this can significantly reduce the average bandwidth used for a call; however, the peak bandwidth used for the call remains unchanged.

As discussed in Section 1.3.1.3, networks supporting VoIP should typically be designed for very close to zero percent VoIP packet loss, and hence are designed to be congestionless from the perspective of the VoIP traffic. This means that the available capacity for VoIP traffic must be able to cope with the peak of the offered VoIP traffic load. Further, in order to ensure that the service availability is maintained, this peak load must be able to be supported without loss while maintaining the required delay and jitter bounds for the VoIP traffic. The bandwidth provisioning required to achieve this is discussed in more detail in Chapter 3, Section 3.2.2.8 and Chapter 6, Section 6.1.3.

Even if VoIP capacity is provisioned to support the peak load, the VoIP service may be statistically oversubscribed. For example, assuming that a link could support a maximum of 30 concurrent VoIP calls while ensuring that the delay, jitter and loss targets are still met, as only a portion of the total number of end-users will have an active call at any particular time, many more than 30 end-users may be supported, resulting in bandwidth efficiencies from statistical multiplexing. If more than 30 users were supported and at peak times, the VoIP load may exceed the available VoIP capacity, then the service to all calls in progress may be degraded. If the probability of this occurring is high enough, then an admission control system may be needed to limit the number of VoIP calls that can be concurrently set up such that the available capacity is never exceeded in practice; admission control is discussed in more detail in Chapter 4.

It is further noted that lower bit rate codecs typically incur greater codec delays, hence when opting for lower bit rate codecs to save bandwidth it should be understood that there may be a consequent increase in terms of ear-to-mouth delay.

1.3.1.5 VoIP: Impact of Packet Re-ordering

VoIP traffic is not commonly impacted by packet re-ordering, as the magnitude of re-ordering would need to be very significant to affect a VoIP flow whose inter-packet gap is a multiple of 20 ms, for example. It is, however, noted that in addition to the impact that it has on application throughput, per-packet load balancing, which is a common cause of packet re-ordering, can also increase the jitter that is experienced within a flow due to the different delays of alternate paths; this effect can impact VoIP services.

1.3.2 Video

1.3.2.1 Video Streaming

With video streaming applications, a client requests to receive a video that is stored on a server; the server streams the video to the client, which starts to play out the video before all of the video stream data has been received. Video streaming is used both for "broadcasting" video channels, which is often delivered as IP multicast, and for video on demand (VOD), which is delivered as IP unicast.

IP-based streaming video is most commonly transported as a data stream encoded using standards defined by the Motion Picture Expert Group (MPEG) and transported using RTP over UDP. MPEG defines the encoding used for the actual video stream, while [RFC2250, RFC 2343, and RFC3640] define how real-time audio and video data are formatted for RTP transport. RTP is the transport layer protocol, which deals with the delivery of that stream from sender to receiver. Protocols such as the Real-time Streaming Protocol (RTSP) [RFC2326] may be used to set up the RTP streams. While other encodings and transport protocols may be used, as this case is the most widespread we consider it in more detail and note that the principles discussed are generally applicable to other encoding schemes and transport layer protocols also.

The MPEG committee [MPEG] is a working group of the International Organization for Standardization/International Electrotechnical Commission (ISO/IEC) working on the development of standards for digital audio and video. MPEG have been responsible for producing a number of standards that can be used for IP-based services including MPEG-2 [MPEG-2] (the video part of which is the same as ITU-T standard H.262), which is used for broadcast quality video encoding including digital television services, and the newer MPEG-4 Advanced Video Coding (AVC) [MPEG-4] (which is also known as MPEG-4 Part 10, and which is technically identical to ITU-T standard H.264) standard which was designed for Internet audio and video encoding. MPEG-2 encoding is most widely used today for television applications; however, newer encoding schemes such as MPEG-4 and the Society of Motion Picture Television Engineers (SMPTE) VC-1

[VC-1] (which was previously known as VC-9 and is the standardized version of Windows Media™ 9) are likely to become more widespread as they offer a potential bit rate reduction by two times over MPEG-2, for comparable quality.

An MPEG encoder converts and compresses a video signal into a series of pictures or frames; as there is generally only a small amount of change between one frame and the next it is possible to compress the video signal significantly by transmitting only the differences. There are three different types of MPEG frames that are used:

- *"I"-frames*. Intra or "I"-frames carry a complete video frame and are coded without reference to other frames. An I-frame may use spatial compression; spatial compression makes use of the fact that pixels within a single frame are related to their neighbors. Therefore, by removing spatial redundancy, the size of the encoded frame can be reduced and prediction can be used in the decoder to reconstruct the frame. A received I-frame provides the reference point for decoding a received MPEG stream.

- *"P"-frames*. Predictive coded or "P"-frames are coded using motion compensation (temporal compression) by predicting the frame to be coded from a previous "reference" I-frame or P-frame. P-frames can provide increased compression compared to I-frames with a P-frame typically 10–30% the size of an associated I-frame.

- *"B"-frames*. Bidirectional or "B"-frames use the previous and next I- or B-frames as their reference points for motion compensation. B-frames provide further compression, still with a B-frame typically 5–15% the size of an associated I-frame.

Frames are arranged into a Group of Pictures or GOP; for example, the European PAL (Phase-Alternating Line) MPEG-2 video format uses a GOP size of 15, while the North American NTSC (National Television Systems Committee) format uses a GOP size of 18. As the frame rate for PAL is 25 frames per second (fps) and for NTSC is 29.97 fps, each GOP will typically encode (15/25) = ~(18/30) = ~0.6 seconds of video. There are many possible GOP structures and the makeup of I, P and B frames within the GOP is determined by the format of the source video signal, any bandwidth constraints on the encoded video stream (which determines the required compression ratio), and possibly constraints on the encoding/decoding delay. Each GOP has one I-frame, and typically 2-to-14 P-frames and 2-to-10 B-frames. A regular GOP structure can be described by the number of frames in the GOP (the GOP size) and the spacing of P-frames within the GOP. A typical GOP structure with GOP size of 15 frames and P-frame spacing of 3 (denoted as a 15/3 GOP structure) is shown below:

$$B_1 \; B_2 \; I_3 \; B_4 \; B_5 \; P_6 \; B_7 \; B_8 \; P_9 \; B_{10} \; B_{11} \; P_{12} \; B_{13} \; B_{14} \; P_{15}$$

The GOP structure shown above is in the order of display; to allow for backward prediction, the encoder re-orders the frames from display order so that B-frames are transmitted after the previous and next frames it references. The resulting order of frames sent to the decoder is:

$$I_3 \; B_1 \; B_2 \; P_6 \; B_4 \; B_5 \; P_9 \; B_7 \; B_8 \; P_{12} \; B_{10} \; B_{11} \; P_{15} \; B_{13} \; B_{14}$$

This re-ordering introduces a delay both on encoding and on decoding dependent on the number of consecutive B-frames.

Unlike with VoIP where codec implementations are very specifically defined, with streaming video there is significant scope for variation in the specific way that an MPEG stream may be encoded, even for a single type of encoding. The specific GOP structure used to encode a video stream can have a major impact on the effect that network loss, latency and throughput have on the video reproduction at the receiver.

1.3.2.1.1 Video Streaming: Impact of Delay

For video streaming, the important delay metric is the one-way end-to-end delay from streaming server to client. The main constraint that end-to-end network delay and jitter have on streaming video is on end-user "interactivity," or the "finger-to-eye" delay. To understand this better we need to consider some of the different types of video streaming applications separately:

1.3.2.1.1.1   Broadcast Video Services Broadcast television services delivered over IP (also known as IPTV) commonly use IP multicast. For IPTV services, the impact that end-to-end delay has is on the time it takes for the end-user to change from one TV channel to another, which is referred to as the "channel change time" or "channel zapping time." Typically, channel change times of 1–2 seconds are targeted (see Section 1.3.3.2 for requirements for interactive applications) although visual feedback is typically provided to the user indicating that the command is being processed within a few hundred milliseconds.

Assuming a broadcast video service being delivered using IP multicast to a receiver – which could be a set-top box (STB) for example – where each channel is a separate multicast group, the overall channel change time is made up of a number of components:

1. *Remote control and STB processing.* The remote control sends the channel change signal to the STB; typically, this takes a few milliseconds. The STB receives the channel change signal, processes the command and issues IGMP group leave and join requests to the network. This delay will be dependent upon the particular STB implementation, but would typically take a few tens of milliseconds; for this example, we assume a worst case of 50 ms.

2. *Network transmission delay.* This is the network transmission delay for the IGMP messages from the STB to the first multicast aware device, which needs to process the IGMP messages; this includes delays due to serialization, switching, propagation and queuing. As the STB and closest multicast aware device are usually physically located relatively near to each other, and QOS mechanism are employed to control queuing delays and ensure IGMP messages are not dropped, this network transmission delay is typically sub-100 ms.

3. *Multicast processing.* When the first multicast aware device receives the IGMP group leave, assuming fast leave processing, it stops

sending the multicast stream from the previous channel on the respective port. When the IGMP group join is received, assuming the multicast stream for the requested channel traffic already exists at the router, the traffic is copied to the egress port. If this assumption is not correct, additional latency may be incurred due to multicast signaling, while the multicast stream is populated to the first multicast aware device.

Multicast processing is dependent upon the particular implementation in the multicast device, but typically takes a few tens of milliseconds in a good implementation; for this example, we assume a worst case of 100 ms.

4. *Network transmission delay*. This is the network transmission delay for the multicast traffic stream to reach the STB; this includes delays due to serialization, switching, propagation and queuing. As the STB and closest multicast aware device are usually physically located relatively near to each other, and QOS mechanism are employed to control queuing delays and ensure that multicast video traffic is not dropped, this delay is typically sub-100 ms.

5. *STB Buffering/processing*. The STB needs to buffer the received video stream, and perform a number of functions before the video can be played out; depending upon the specific STB implementation, some of these functions may be performed in parallel:
   - *De-jitter buffer*. As for VoIP, de-jitter buffers are used in IP-based digital video systems in order to turn variable network delays into constant delays at the receiver. If the de-jitter buffer play-out delay is set either arbitrarily large or arbitrarily small, then it may impose unnecessary constraints on the characteristics of the network or may impact the quality of the video service. The delay incurred by the de-jitter buffer in addition to the worst-case end-to-end network delay depends upon the maximum network jitter and the STB play-out buffer sizing. Considerations on jitter for IP-based video applications are discussed in more detail in Section 1.3.2.1.2. We assume a worst-case play-out delay of 100 ms.

- *FEC or real-time retransmission delay*. If the video system supports FEC or real-time retransmission to protect against network packet loss, then this will incur a delay. This delay will typically be 100–200 ms; see Section 1.3.2.1.3.
- *Decryption delay*. For encrypted streams, the per-channel decryption keys are delivered to each STB periodically as conditional access table information in the transport stream packets; these keys must be received before the channel can be decoded. The frequency of the key distribution therefore has an impact on the channel change time; this delay is typically 200 ms.
- *MPEG decoder buffer*. With MPEG, the amount of data required to represent an image depends upon the image complexity and therefore the output rate of the decoder buffer is not constant. Hence, a buffer is required to ensure that the decoder does not underflow. This buffer is typically 500–1000 ms.
- *IBB frame delay*. The decoder needs to wait until it has received an IBB frame sequence before it can start decoding. For a 15/3 GOP structure, typical for MPEG-2, at 25 fps the worst-case delay for an IBB frame sequence would be $(15 + 2)/25 = {\sim}680$ ms. Longer GOP structures may improve the compression achievable but will also increase the worst-case delay for an IBB-frame sequence, and hence have an impact on the channel change time.

For this example, we assume a total delay incurred at the STB of 1000 ms.

The timeline in Figure 1.12 illustrates the components of channel change time delay described above.

1.3.2.1.1.2 Video-on-demand Services

Video-on-demand (VOD) and network personal video recorder (PVR) services are commonly delivered as unicast. For VOD services the end-to-end delay impacts the finger-to-eye delay, i.e. the response time it takes for user requests to be translated into actions visible to the end-user; for example, how long it takes after pressing play for a VOD to start. Typically,

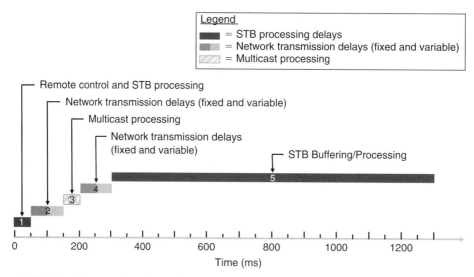

Figure 1.12 Broadcast video channel change time delay components

response times of approximately 1 second are targeted (see Section 1.3.3.2 for requirements for interactive applications), although visual feedback is typically provided to the user indicating that the command is being processed within a few hundred milliseconds.

Assuming a video-on-demand service being delivered over IP unicast to a receiver, which could be a set-top box (STB) for example, the overall response time is made up of a number of components:

1. *Remote control and STB processing.* The remote control sends the control signal to the STB; typically, this takes a few milliseconds. The STB receives the signal, processes the command, and issues the appropriate control request to the video middleware, which is responsible for managing the presentation and delivery of VOD streams. This delay will be dependent upon the particular STB and middleware implementations but would typically take a few tens of milliseconds; we assume a worst case of 50 ms in this example.

2. *Network transmission delay.* This is the network transmission delay for the control messages from the STB to the video middleware; this includes delays due to serialization, switching, propagation and queuing. QOS mechanisms are employed to regulate queuing delays and ensure control messages are not dropped, and hence this network transmission delay is typically sub-100 ms.

3. *Middleware processing.* This is the delay for the video middleware application to process the received request and instruct the VOD server to start streaming the requested VOD. The middleware processing delay is dependent upon the particular middleware implementation, but typically takes a few hundred milliseconds.

4. *Network transmission delay.* This is the network transmission delay for the unicast VOD stream to reach the STB; this includes delays due to serialization, switching, propagation and queuing. QOS mechanisms are employed to regulate queuing delays and ensure control messages are not dropped, and hence this network transmission delay is typically sub-100 ms.

5. *STB buffering/processing.* The STB needs to buffer the received video stream, and perform a number of functions before the video can be played out; depending upon the specific STB implementation, some of these functions may be performed in parallel:
   - de-jitter buffer
   - FEC or real-time retransmission delay
   - decryption delay
   - MPEG decoder buffer.

   The above functions are the same as described for the broadcast video example described in Section 1.3.2.1.1.1. It is noted, however, that for VOD services, unlike broadcast video applications where the STB may need to wait for an I-frame before a stream can start to be decoded, an IBB frame sequence is the first frame that is sent in a VOD stream. Hence the STB buffering and processing delay can be significantly less in the case of VOD, than the channel change time in the broadcast video case. For this example, we assume a total delay incurred at the STB of 500 ms.

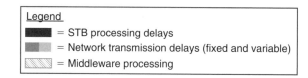

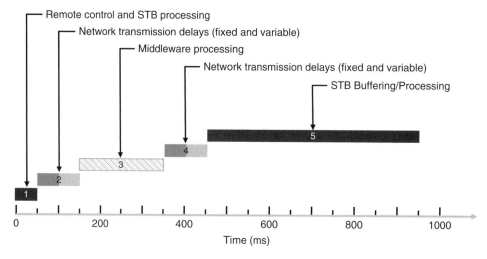

Figure 1.13   VOD response time delay components

The timeline in Figure 1.13 illustrates the components of the VOD response time described above.

Hence, for video streaming applications, one-way network delays of 100 ms are typically targeted in order to try to achieve overall channel change times or VOD response times of 1–2 seconds. QOS mechanisms are typically employed to ensure these targets can be met.

1.3.2.1.2   Video Streaming: Impact of Delay-jitter

Digital video decoders used in streaming video receivers need to receive a synchronous stream, typically with jitter tolerances of only ±500 ns, in order to decode without visible impairments. Such jitter tolerances are not achievable natively in IP networks, hence as for VoIP, broadcast video services use de-jitter buffers (also known as play-out buffers) in receivers to remove delay variation caused by the network and turn variable network delays into constant delays such that the tolerances required by the decoder can be met.

To guarantee that no packet drops are caused by network jitter, QOS mechanism are employed to control queuing delays and hence bound jitter; an STB play-out buffer should be sized at least equal to the resulting maximum possible value of network jitter. As for VoIP, if the video play-out buffer was appropriately sized to the maximum value of network jitter, jitter would not add delay on play-out in additional to the worst-case end-to-end network delay. For streaming video applications, however, unlike for VoIP, the size of jitter buffers is often statically defined. Hence, if the play-out buffer is too small to accommodate the maximum network jitter then buffer underflows can occur; an underflow is where the buffer is empty when the decoder needs to process a frame, and is effectively realized as a lost packet, which may cause a video impairment. A play-out buffer set too large adds unnecessarily to the end-to-end delay, which may increase the channel change time or decrease VOD responsiveness.

Hence, a holistic engineering approach is needed in order to optimize channel change time or VOD responsiveness, employing QOS mechanisms to control queuing delays and hence bound the maximum network jitter, while ensuring that the STB play-out buffer is not set to significantly greater than this value. An STB play-out buffer that is more than 100 ms greater than the maximum network jitter can be considered excessive.

1.3.2.1.3 Video Streaming: Impact of Loss

Each MPEG frame is transported as a number of MPEG transport steam (MPEG-TS) packets, which are typically 188 bytes long. Each IP packet typically carries between 1 and 7 MPEG-TS packets, and an MPEG encoded frame will span multiple IP packets, hence, without employing techniques for loss concealment, the loss of a single IP packet will result in the loss of a complete MPEG frame. Without employing loss concealment techniques, the loss of a frame will generally result in a visible impairment, although the nature of the impairment will depend upon the type of frame lost and on the GOP structure used. The loss of an I-frame can result in a visual impairment until the next I-frame is successfully received; the loss of a P-frame may impact several frames, while the loss of a B-frame may impact that frame only.

Therefore, there is a trade-off to be considered when deciding on which GOP structure to use to support a streaming video service; larger GOP size will give greater compression, which results in more or higher quality video content being transmitted for a given rate than a smaller GOP size; however, the visual impact of packet loss may be more significant for larger GOP, and there may be an impact on the interactivity, e.g. finger-to-eye delay.

The loss distance targeted for a particular video service is a choice for the service provider; however, targets of no more than one visible impairment per hour are typical, such as defined by the Digital Video Broadcasting Project (DVB) in draft [ETSI Ts 102 034], which specifies network requirements for the "Transport of DVB Services over IP." This bound on the rate of visible impairments directly translates into a bound on packet loss. Assuming a 3.7 Mbps MPEG stream with 1356-byte packets (based upon an MPEG transport stream carrying 7×188 bytes of video in each packet, plus 40 bytes for RTP, UDP and IP headers), gives a stream rate of ~350 pps. For this stream, a loss period of one hour would result in a required PLR of no more than $1/(350 \text{ pps} * 60 \text{ seconds} * 60 \text{ minutes}) = \sim1 * 10^{-6}$. We consider what effect targets such as this have on the network design in practice by considering the impact on the possible causes of packet loss previously defined in Section 1.2.3:

- *Congestion.* For the same reasons as discussed in Section 3.1.3 for VoIP, networks supporting streaming video are designed to be congestionless from the perspective of the streaming video traffic; that is, the available capacity for streaming video traffic is able to cope with the peak of the offered video traffic load. QOS mechanisms, admission control and appropriate capacity planning techniques are deployed to ensure that no packets are lost due to congestion.

- *Lower layer errors.* As described in Section 1.2.3, physical layer bit errors may cause packets to be dropped due to link layer or transport-layer checksums. Where this is the case, bit errors will generally result in packet loss, meaning each packet will either arrive correctly or not at all. Consider for example a typical BER offered for a SONET/SDH service of $1 * 10^{-12}$, and assume a random error distribution, and that each error causes a lost packet; for the video stream described above, this would result in a PLR of $1 * 10^{-12} * 1356 * 8 = {\sim}1 * 10^{-8}$; this would result in a loss distance of over 79 hours, which is several orders of magnitude greater than the target. As an alternative example, consider a typical BER offered for an ADSL service of $1 * 10^{-7}$; this would equate to a PLR of $1 * 10^{-7} * 1356 * 8 = {\sim}1 * 10^{-3}$, which would result in a loss distance of less than 3 seconds, and which is several orders of magnitude less than the target.

QOS mechanisms cannot have any impact on loss due to lower level errors, hence where the underlying network transport infrastructure cannot meet the loss distance targets required for the video service, loss concealment techniques may be required. There are two main techniques for loss concealment for streaming video:

○ *Forward error correction (FEC)*. FEC relies on redundancy being built into the transmitted content stream in order to be able to reconstruct lost packets without the need for retransmission. The Professional-MPEG Forum's [PRO-MPEG] published code of practice (COP) number 3 recommends a scheme based on the approach defined in RFC 2733 [RFC2733] which specifies a FEC mechanism for protecting a RTP stream against lost RTP packets. In the Pro-MPEG Forum scheme, XOR operations are performed on a block of packets arranged in a matrix of D rows by L columns to generate redundant parity packets. At the receiver, the FEC information is used to recover from losses within a FEC block.

The structure of the matrix that forms the FEC block impacts the loss burst size the FEC can protect against, the bandwidth overhead associated with the FEC stream and the delay caused by the FEC processing operation. Hence, it is important that the FEC parameters be configured to match the requirements of a particular service, taking into account the characteristics of the underlying network.

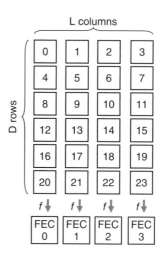

Figure 1.14 Professional-MPEG Forum's COP 3 1D FEC

The Pro-MPEG Forum scheme allows for both one-dimensional (1D) FEC, as shown in Figure 1.14, and two-dimensional (2D) FEC, as shown in Figure 1.15. The FEC information is carried in a separate stream (for 1D FEC) or streams (for 2D FEC) to the video bearer.

One-dimensional FEC is able to recover from 1 error within the FEC block and has an overhead of $L/(L * D)$. The two-dimensional scheme is able to recover from a burst of L errors within a FEC block and has an overhead of $(L + D)/(L * D)$. The additional delay incurred by either scheme is the time to transmit $L * D$ packets. Larger D reduces the overhead at the cost of increasing the additional delay.

For example, assuming a 3.7 Mbps MPEG-2 stream consisting of ~350 pps each with a 1356-byte payload:

– Using a one-dimensional FEC with L = 4 and D = 6 provides the ability to recover from 1 error in 24 packets, while incurring $4/(4 * 6) = $ ~17% overhead and $24/330 = $ ~72 ms of additional delay due to the FEC processing operation.[4]

Assuming a PLR of $1 * 10^{-3}$ (the previously calculated typical PLR for ADSL), with a random packet loss distribution, the

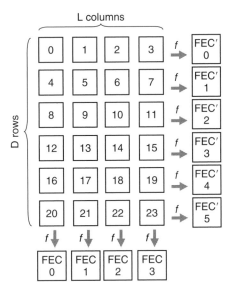

Figure 1.15 Professional-MPEG Forum's COP 3 2D FEC

probability of an unrecoverable loss (i.e. 2 lost packets) within a 24 packet block is $(1 * 10^{-3} * 24) * (1 * 10^{-3} * 23) = \sim 6 * 10^{-4}$; this results in a loss distance of ~ 5 seconds, which is still several orders of magnitude worse than the target.

- By comparison, using a two-dimensional FEC with L = 4 and D = 6 provides the ability to recover from a burst of 4 errors in 24 packets, while incurring $(4 + 6)/(4 * 6) = \sim 42\%$ overhead and $24/330 = \sim 72$ ms of additional delay due to the FEC processing operation.

  Assuming a PLR of $1 * 10^{-3}$, the probability of an unrecoverable loss (i.e. 5 lost packets) within a 24 packet block is $(1 * 10^{-3} * 24) * (1 * 10^{-} * 23) * (1 * 10^{-3} * 22) * (1 * 10^{-3} * 21) * (1 * 10^{-3} * 20) = \sim 5 * 10^{-9}$; this results in a loss distance of greater than ~ 155 hours, which is several orders of magnitude better than the target.

○ *Real-time retransmission.* Media streams that use RTP are to some extent resilient, in that receivers may use the mechanisms defined for the RTP control protocol (also known as RTCP) to report packet reception statistics and thus allow a sender to adapt its transmission behavior. Additional techniques are being defined within the IETF which extend the basic capabilities of RTCP to allow for faster feedback of packet loss from receivers to senders [RFC4584], such that lost packets may be retransmitted [RFC4588]. Within a defined time window, receivers can detect sequence number gaps in the received stream indicating lost packets and report these using RTCP negative acknowledgments (NACKs) to the sender, which retransmits the lost packets.

Real-time retransmission is a reactive scheme, which resends only those packets that are lost, hence it incurs minimal bandwidth overhead. A disadvantage of this approach, however, is that it adds delay equal to the RTT between the receiver and the retransmission source, to the potential worst-case delay that a packet may otherwise experience. Hence, real-time retransmission is only viable in cases where the RTT between the receiver and the retransmission source can be kept small, in order to avoid increasing the channel change time or decreasing VOD responsiveness.

It is noted, however, that some video end-systems disable the UDP checksum, or use "UDP-lite" [RFC3828], such that packets with data bit errors will be received including the error bits, on the premise that it can be better to receive a packet with a bit error, than to receive no packet at all [SINGH]. Currently, however, there is insufficient data on the performance of such implementations to quantify what impact this has on the received video service in practice.

- *Network element failures*. Network element failures may cause packets to be dropped until connectivity is restored around the failed network element; as discussed in Section 1.2.3 the resulting loss period depends upon the underlying network technologies that are used.

  In a "plain" IP (i.e. non-MPLS) deployment, even in a well-designed network where the IGP convergence time is subsecond, the packet loss following a network element failure is too significant to be concealed using any of the techniques described above. For example, assuming a 500 ms loss of connectivity and an impacted 3.7 Mbps MPEG-2 video stream at 350 pps, ~175 packets would be lost due to the outage. Even where MPLS TE FRR or equivalent techniques are deployed, reducing the loss of connectivity following network element failures to within 50 ms, the packet loss may be too significant to be viably concealed using any of the techniques previously described. For example, assuming a 50 ms loss of connectivity and an impacted 3.7 Mbps MPEG-2 video stream at 350 pps, ~18 packets would be lost due to the outage.

Where the impact of network outages is such that the loss distance targets required for the video service cannot be met, techniques using stream redundancy may provide a possible solution; available techniques are either based upon spatial or temporal redundancy:

○ *Spatial redundancy*. Techniques using spatial (physical) redundancy send two streams between the sender and receiver over diverse network paths; diverse path routing can be assured using techniques such as MPLS traffic engineering. In normal working case network conditions, the receiver will effectively receive two copies of each packet, from which one will be selected. If a network failure impacts one of the transmitted streams, the receiver will continue to receive the other and the play-out of the video stream at the receiver will be uninterrupted.

   Schemes using physically redundancy incur a 100% bandwidth overhead per stream, and also must incur a delay on the received stream at least equal to the greatest difference in transmission delays between the two paths, which is likely to be negligible in practice.

○ *Temporal redundancy*. Techniques using temporal redundancy break the stream to be transmitted into blocks: each block is then sent twice, separated in time. The block repetition pattern is such that within a time window greater than the block separation period the receiver should effectively receive two copies of each packet, from which one will be selected. If a network failure occurs, which causes a resulting loss of connectivity of less than the block separation period, at least one packet should be received and the play-out of the video stream at the receiver will be uninterrupted.

Schemes using temporal redundancy incur a 100% bandwidth overhead per stream. Further, to be effective, temporal redundancy must incur a delay on the received stream at least equal to the block separation period, which in turn must be at least as great as the period of loss of connectivity the technique is aiming to protect against. The additional delay, however, need not impact finger-to-eye delay if temporal redundancy is used only in the core network, i.e. does not extend to the end-user.

• *Loss in the application end-systems.* Loss due to buffer underflows and overflows can be prevented through careful design both of the network and the application end-systems, as discussed in Section 1.3.1.2.

Therefore, in practice, networks supporting video streaming services should typically be designed for very close to zero percent video packet loss. QOS mechanisms, admission control techniques and appropriate capacity planning techniques are deployed to ensure that no packets are lost due to congestion, with the only actual packet loss being due to layer 1 bit errors or network element failures. Where packet loss occurs, the impact of the loss should be reduced to acceptable levels using concealment techniques. Different concealment techniques may be employed in different parts of the network. For example, in the core of the network where bandwidth is relatively plentiful and diverse paths exist, spatial redundancy may be used to transport video across the core of a network from a source to distribution points; this would provide protection against both lower layer errors and against network element failures. Other techniques such as FEC could then be used from the video redistribution points to the video receivers, in order to provide protection against lower layer errors in the access network.

1.3.2.1.4   Video Streaming: Impact of Throughput

The bandwidth requirements for a video stream depend upon the video format, the encoder and the specific GOP structure. There are four main video formats used for IP-based video services:

• *Standard definition (SD).* Standard definition format is the conventional format commonly used today for broadcast quality digital video encoding including television services such as cable and satellite. The nomenclature used to refer to digital TV image definitions defines the number of vertical lines and whether the image is interlaced (i) or uses progressive scanning (p); two of the main SD formats are 480i and 576i:

- ○ 480i: 480 vertical lines (interlaced) × 720 horizontal pixels at 29.97 fps (NTSC-based, North America)
- ○ 576i: 576 lines by 720 pixels at 25 fps (PAL-based, Europe)

- *High definition (HD).* High definition has at least twice the resolution (in terms of total number of pixels) as SD and is used for premium broadcast quality digital video encoding including television services. Two of the main HD formats are:
  - ○ 720p: 720 × 1280 at 50 Hz and 60 Hz frame rates (progressive scan)
  - ○ 1080i: 1080 × 1920 at 25 Hz and 30 Hz frame rates (interlaced)

- *Common interchange format (CIF).* CIF is a low definition (LD) format targeted for broadband Internet video delivery applications, such as video conferencing. CIF has one quarter of the full resolution of an SDTV picture (i.e. frame height and width are both halved), which in turn is referred to as 4CIF. Two common 4CIF formats are:
  - ○ 240i: 240 × 352 (NTSC-based)
  - ○ 288i: 288 × 352 (PAL-based)

- *Quarter CIF (QCIF).* QCIF is targeted for mobile handset video applications and has one quarter of the resolution of CIF. Two common QCIF formats are:
  - ○ NTSC-based: 120 × 176
  - ○ PAL-based: 144 × 176.

MPEG allows for streaming video to be encoded either as variable bit rate streams, where the quality of the resultant video is constant, or as constant bit rate streams where the quality of the resultant video is variable. The table in Figure 1.16 gives indicative average bit rates for LD, SD and HD video stream rates using MPEG-2 and MPEG-4 AVC.

McCann observed [MCCANN] that due to the evolution of video encoding implementations, from 1995 to 2002 there was an average

Format	MPEG-2	MPEG-4 AVC
LD QCIF	100–200 kbps	50–100 kbps
LD CIF	0–5–1 Mbps	0.25–0.5 Mbps
SD 4CIF	~3–4 mbps	~2–3 Mbps
HD	~15–20 Mbps	~10–15 Mbps

Figure 1.16 Typical broadcast quality video stream IP rates

of 15% improvement in MPEG-2 encoding efficiency and consequent reduction in stream bandwidth per year. The MPEG-2 bit rates shown in Figure 1.16 are nearing the end of this improvement cycle, whereas there is still scope for reduction in MPEG-4 bit rates.

It is further noted that larger GOP structures, which result in reduced bit rates for equivalent quality streams, have an impact both when considering the effect that packet loss has on the stream and on the channel change time for broadcast video services. Hence, when opting for larger GOP structures to reduce bandwidth, it should be understood that there might be a consequent trade-off in terms of visual quality and channel change time.

From a network design perspective, as discussed in Section 1.3.2.1.3, networks supporting streaming video should typically be designed for very close to zero percent video packet loss, and hence are designed to be congestionless from the perspective of the video traffic. This means that the available capacity for video traffic must be able to cope with the peak of the offered video traffic load. Further, in order to ensure that the service availability is maintained this peak load must be able to be supported without loss while maintaining the required delay and jitter bounds for the video traffic. The capacity planning required to achieve this is discussed in more detail in Chapter 5, Section 6.1.

As for VoIP, as discussed in Section 1.3.1.4, this does not mean that the available capacity for streaming video cannot be oversubscribed. Where oversubscription is used, admission control may be needed to limit the concurrent number of video streams that can be set up; admission control is discussed in more detail in Chapter 4.

1.3.2.1.5 Video Streaming: Impact of Packet Re-ordering

Many real-time video end-systems do not support the re-ordering of received frames, hence packet re-ordering effectively results in higher packet loss and should be avoided.

1.3.2.2 Video Conferencing

Video conferencing sessions are typically set up using the signaling protocols specified in ITU recommendation H.323 [H.323] or SIP. Whichever method is used to establish the connections, from an SLA perspective, the fundamental requirements and principles remain the same. Once the H.323 or SIP end points (also known as terminals) have agreed that they are willing to communicate with each other and have determined the media formats (codecs) that they will use, they then set up the logical channels through which the bearer (media streams such as VoIP and video) traffic itself will be transmitted. Typically, separate logical channels are used for audio and for video, and the setup of these logical channels consists of determining which particular UDP ports the RTP transported media streams will use.

The audio streams will typically use codecs such as those defined by the ITU G.71x/G72x standards. The SLA requirements with respect to delay, jitter, loss, throughput and in-sequence delivery are therefore the same as those already described for VoIP in Section 1.3.1.

The video formats and encoding used for video conferencing applications are less constrained than for broadcast quality video services. Codecs such as MPEG-2/H.262 or MPEG-4 AVC/H.264 are typically used; where bandwidth is constrained, lower definition (e.g. CIF or QCIF) and lower frame rates (e.g. 10 fps), potentially reduce the bandwidths required significantly compared to broadcast video services.

Although the bandwidth requirements for the video streams used for video conferencing may be less than for broadcast video, the delay and jitter requirements will depend upon the quality of the video conferencing service offered. With lower quality services, it may be acceptable for the video stream to have a less stringent delay commitment than the voice stream, in which case participants may experience a time lag between a remote user's audible words, and their associated lip movements. For higher quality services, where lip synchronization is required, one of the media streams may need to be delayed at the receiver, however, subjective studies have shown that the two streams do not have to be exactly matched. [STEINMETZ] shows that the synchronization errors that can be tolerated by human perception vary in different application scenarios; for video conferencing applications, a skew of less than 80 ms is below the limit of human perception. Therefore, even for higher quality services, it may be acceptable for the video stream to be delayed by up to 80 ms with respect to the audio stream, i.e. the end-to-end delay budget for the video stream can be up to 8 ms greater than for the audio stream. Hence, extrapolating from the G.114 targets for voice services, end-to-end (i.e. camera to eye) delay targets of ~250 ms are targeted for the video stream of video conferencing applications.

As for discrete voice and video services, in practice networks supporting video conferencing services should typically be designed for very close to zero percent packet loss for both the VoIP and video streams. QOS mechanisms and appropriate capacity planning techniques may be employed to ensure that no packets are lost due to congestion, with the only actual packet loss being due to layer 1 bit errors or network element failures. Where packet loss occurs, the impact of the loss on voice streams should be reduced to acceptable levels using concealment techniques. The loss rates tolerated for video conferencing are likely higher than those acceptable to broadcast video services, such that the complexity of the video loss concealment techniques may not be required.

1.3.3   Data Applications

QOE requirements for data application, which in turn drive network level SLAs, are less well defined than for voice or video applications. While there are multiple types of data applications that exist, from a QOS perspective they can be broadly divided into interactive data applications and applications that are targeted at data transfer with no requirements on interactivity. An example of an application that is targeted at data transfer, but has no requirements on interactivity, is a data backup application between data centers, where a defined averaged throughput is required in order to ensure that the backup completes within a determined time period.

Throughput focussed applications in general use TCP as their transport layer protocol, due to the reliability and flow control capabilities that it provides. The impact that different SLA metric parameters have on TCP session throughput is considered in Section 1.3.3.1. While there may be some throughput focussed applications that use UDP rather than TCP, such as the Trivial File Transfer Protocol (TFTP) [RFC783] for example, as UDP does not have any implicit reliability or flow control mechanisms these need to be built into the application implementation. Hence, a detailed knowledge of the specific application implementation is required in order to understand what impact different SLA metric parameters have on such UDP applications, which would need to be analyzed on a case-by-case basis.

Interactive data applications require that a transaction be completed within a certain period of time, to ensure that the attention of the end-user is maintained or so that they do not consider that a fault has occurred, for example. The impact that different SLA metric parameters have on interactive data applications is considered in Section 1.3.3.2.

1.3.3.1 Throughput Focussed TCP Applications

In order to understand the impact that metrics such as network delay and loss have on TCP [RFC793], we first need to understand the basic principles of TCP operation. TCP aims to provide a reliable and efficient transport layer protocol on top of IP. Four key mechanisms underlay TCP:

- bidirectional session establishment

- positive acknowledgment with retransmission

- sliding acknowledgment window for flow control between the sender and receiver

- congestion control, for dealing with loss which occurs between the sender and receiver.

The following sections provide an overview of these mechanisms.

1.3.3.1.1   Bidirectional Session Establishment

TCP is a connection oriented transport protocol, which establishes a session between two TCP end-systems before any data can be transferred. TCP session establishment relies on a "three-way handshake." Consider two TCP end-systems, A and B, where A is the initiator of a TCP session to B;

1. A first sends a TCP segment to B with the synchronize bit (SYN) set; this indicates that it is the first segment of the three-way handshake. A segment is the TCP data unit transported in an IP packet.

2. To progress the establishment of the TCP session, B responds by sending a segment back to A with both the SYN and acknowledgment (ACK) bits set.

3. The final segment in the handshake is another ACK, which is sent by A to B to confirm that the session has been successfully established.

During session establishment, a number of parameters are negotiated including the maximum segment size (*MSS*) and the window size, which will be discussed in the following sections, and also whether Explicit Congestion Notification will be used (see Chapter 2, Section 2.3.4.4).

1.3.3.1.2   Positive Acknowledgment with Retransmission

TCP uses a technique known as "positive acknowledgment with retransmission" in order to ensure reliable and efficient data transfer between the TCP end-systems, even if the underlying network may be unreliable. In the context of TCP, positive acknowledgment with retransmission requires that the receiver sends an acknowledgment (ACK) back to the sender on receipt of a TCP segment. In the simplest possible model, the sender keeps a record of each segment it sends and waits for an ACK for the preceding segment, before sending the next. The sender also starts a retransmission timer when it sends a segment; if no ACK is received before the timer times-out the sender retransmits the segment, presuming that the one previously sent was lost.

TCP is a full duplex transport protocol, which means that a single TCP session can support data transfer in both directions. Hence, ACKs from one TCP end-system to another can be piggybacked with segments being sent in the opposite direction.

1.3.3.1.3 Sliding Acknowledgment Window

TCP extends the basic positive acknowledgment with retransmission model by adding the concept of a sliding acknowledgment window, which allows the sender to transmit multiple packets to the receiver before waiting for an ACK. The sliding window acknowledgment scheme is used by TCP for flow control, i.e. adjusting the rate of transmission by the sender so that it does not exceed the receiver's capacity to accept data.

Each TCP end-system advertises the maximum window size (*awnd*) they are prepared to accept to their session-peer within the TCP header. A window aperture or size of X packets means that the sender can have up to X unacknowledged segments outstanding; if the sender has received an ACK for segment Y, then the sender can transmit up to segment Y + X before receiving the ACK for segment Y + 1. There can be a number of packets in transit between sender and receiver with the concept of a sliding window, hence in order to track lost and duplicate segments TCP assigns a sequence number to each segment. If one (or more) of the packets in transit are dropped or resequenced it will appear to the receiver as an out-of-order segment; this causes the receiver to immediately generate an ACK (called a duplicate ACK) for the last segment successfully received in sequence.

1.3.3.1.4 Congestion Control

TCP also implements congestion control, to avoid network "congestion collapse" [JACOBSON] by controlling TCP sessions to adapt to the network and conditions in order to try to maximize throughput for each session. This also maintains fairness between sessions.

To achieve this, the TCP window size is not statically defined but rather a number of control congestion techniques [RFC2581] are used

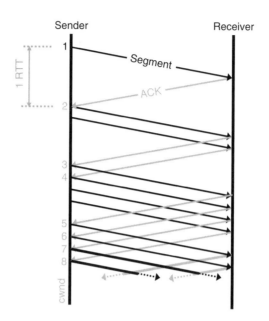

Figure 1.17 TCP slow start

to adjust the window size dynamically. The main techniques used are *slow start, congestion avoidance, fast retransmit* and *fast recovery*:

- *Slow start.* The slow start algorithm aims to control the rate at which a sender transmits segments into a network at the start of a session, in order to reduce the probability that the session will send too many segments and contribute to congestion at a network element on the session's path. To achieve this, slow start applies a constraint to the window size, called the congestion window (*cwnd*). When a new session is established, *cwnd* is set to one segment; for each ACK that is received, *cwnd* is increased by one segment. A sender can send up to whichever is the minimum of *awnd* and *cwnd* (i.e. MIN[*awnd*, *cwnd*]), before another ACK is received. For example, if a sender in slow start with *cwnd* set to one sends one segment; when it receives the first ACK it increases *cwnd* to two and sends two more segments; when each of those two segments are acknowledged, *cwnd* is increased to four as shown in Figure 1.17.

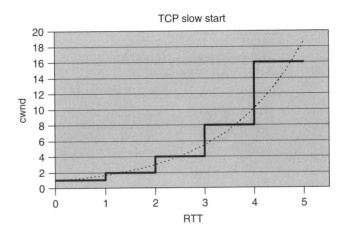

Figure 1.18 TCP slow start

Therefore, slow start provides exponential growth of *cwnd* with RTT as shown in Figure 1.18. You might then question why slow start is so called? The reason is because it is slow relative to the original implementations of TCP, which had no concept of *cwnd* and sent using the maximum negotiated window size at the start of the session.

- *Congestion avoidance.* At some point, the capacity of an intermediate network element between sender and receiver may be exceeded, i.e. congestion occurs and packets may be dropped as a consequence. TCP (without support for ECN as discussed in Chapter 2, Section 2.3.4.4) effectively treats the network as a "black box," in that it does not rely on any explicit network behaviors when performing flow control, in order to determine the status of available network bandwidth and whether congestion has occurred, TCP relies on TCP timeouts or the reception of duplicate ACKs to determine implicitly when packets are dropped. When packet drops within a session are determined, TCP reacts by invoking the following algorithm, which uses an additional variable called the slow start threshold (*ssthresh*):
  1. *ssthresh* is set to whichever is the greater of 2 segments or one-half of the window size before the congestion occurred (i.e. MAX[2, MIN[*awnd, cwnd*]]). The *cwnd* is then halved for every subsequent

loss, hence if loss continues the rate of transmission effectively decreases exponentially.

In addition, if the congestion is indicated by a timeout, *cwnd* is set to one segment.

2. When the next ACK is received:
   - If *cwnd* is less than or equal to *ssthresh*, slow start is invoked as described above until the window size equals *ssthresh*, i.e. half of the window size when the congestion occurred.
   - When *cwnd* is greater than *ssthresh*, invoke the following congestion avoidance algorithm.

     The congestion avoidance algorithm defines that each time an ACK is received *cwnd* is incremented by *segment_size/cwnd*. For example, if a sender in slow start with *cwnd* set to one sends one segment, when it receives the first ACK it increases *cwnd* to two and sends two more segments; when the next two segments are acknowledged, *cwnd* is increased to three as shown in Figure 1.19.

     The increase in *cwnd* is limited to at most one segment during each RTT irrespective of how many ACKS are received in

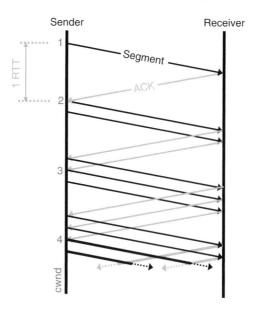

Figure 1.19 TCP congestion avoidance

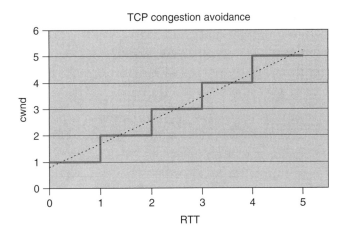

Figure 1.20 TCP congestion avoidance

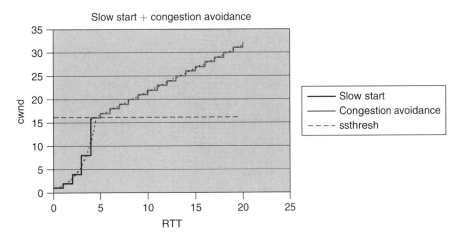

Figure 1.21 Slow start and congestion avoidance example

that interval, whereas slow start increases *cwnd* by the number of ACKs received within a RTT. Therefore, congestion avoidance provides linear growth of *cwnd*, compared to exponential growth with slow start.

Consider the example shown in Figure 1.21; at time $t = 0$, an established TCP session experiences a timeout when *cwnd* = 32 segments;

ssthresh is set to 16 segments and *cwnd* is reduced to 1 segment. *cwnd* then increases with slow start until it equals *ssthresh*, then congestion avoidance is invoked. As can be seen from Figure 1.21, *cwnd* increases exponentially with RTT until it equals *ssthresh*; above *ssthresh cwnd* increases linearly with RTT.

- *Fast retransmit.* Fast retransmit is a performance enhancement to the previously described mechanisms, which determines the sender's behavior when duplicate ACKs are received. When a sender receives a duplicate ACK, it does not know whether the ACK was caused by a lost segment or a re-ordering of segments, hence it waits for a small number of duplicate ACKs to be received before reacting. If two or less duplicate ACKs are received in a row it is assumed that segment re-ordering has occurred. If three or more duplicate ACKs are received, it is taken as an indication that a segment has been lost, and fast retransmit defines that in this case the sender should retransmit the missing segment, without waiting for the retransmission timer to expire.

- *Fast recovery.* Fast recovery is a further performance enhancement, which allows higher throughput under moderate congestion. Fast recovery defines that after fast retransmit resends the missing segment, congestion avoidance should be performed rather than slow start.

Support for the various congestion control techniques in TCP stacks has evolved over time and there is a generally used naming scheme, which derives from the BSD (Berkeley UNIX) TCP stack implementation, and which provides a taxonomy for TCP stack evolution:

- 4.2BSD (1983) was the first widely available release of TCP/IP.

- *Tahoe*: the 4.3BSD Tahoe release (1988) incorporates slow start, congestion avoidance and fast retransmission.

- *Reno*: the 4.3BSD Reno release (1990) added support for fast recovery.

- *Vegas*: the Vegas TCP stack (1994) added support for the additional enhancements described in [BRAKMO], which aim to improve TCP throughput over previous stacks.

- *NewReno*: the NewReno TCP stack (1999) adds support for the enhancements to the fast recovery algorithm described in [RFC3782].

More recently, [RFC 3390] specified an increase in the permitted upper bound for TCP's initial window size from one or two segment(s) to between two and four segments. This change reduces the number of RTTs required to complete some transactions; many email and web page transactions are less than 4 kbytes, hence the larger initial window would reduce the data transfer time to a single RTT.

There are additional subtleties to the implementations of TCP – see [STEVENS, RFC2581] – however, the details provided above are sufficient to understand the impacts that network characteristics such as delay and loss have on TCP, and which are discussed in more detail in the following sections.

1.3.3.1.5 TCP: Impact of Delay

For TCP, the important delay metric is the RTT between TCP end-systems. The maximum number of unacknowledged segments that a TCP sender can have outstanding is limited by the window size. Therefore, for a particular RTT between sender and receiver, the maximum possible TCP session throughput will be determined by *window_size * MSS/RTT*, where *MSS* is the maximum segment size. This is the amount of data that has been sent, but not yet acknowledged and is commonly referred to as the TCP "flight size" [RFC2581] or the "pipesize." Hence, the TCP session throughput is inversely proportional to the RTT.

[MATHIS] shows that maximum theoretical attainable TCP throughput for a single session varies as a function of RTT and packet loss using the following relationship, where p is the probability of packet loss:

$$TCP\_throughput = \frac{MSS}{RTT \times \sqrt{p}}$$

The graph in Figure 1.22 uses this relationship to plot how the theoretical maximum attainable TCP throughput for a single TCP session varies as a function of RTT for a TCP maximum segment size (MSS) of 1460 bytes.

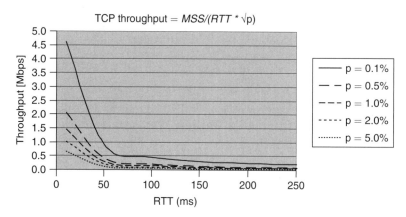

Figure 1.22 TCP throughput as a function of RTT

It is noted that the attained TCP throughput will in practice depend upon a number of additional factors, which vary network-by-network, including:

- the life span of the TCP sessions; long-lived sessions will have more opportunity to open up their maximum window sizes than short-lived sessions

- if congestion occurs:
  - the specific behavior of the participating end-systems in the presence of congestion; for TCP-based applications, this is dependent upon the TCP stacks used
  - the dropping behavior of any routers along the path in the presence of congestion, e.g. tail drop or RED (see Chapter 2, Section 2.2.4.2).

Additionally, it can be seen from Figure 1.22 that even if the attained throughput is close to the theoretical maximum, that at low RTTs and low probabilities of packet loss, the session throughput is limited to a few megabits per second. For some high bandwidth applications these limits can be overly constraining; one such application is Grid computing [BAKER], where geographically distributed computing

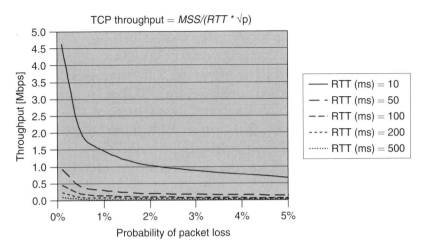

Figure 1.23   TCP throughput as a function of packet loss

resources are networked to act as a single unified computer. Consequently, there have been a number of efforts, although none of which are yet widely deployed, to enhance TCP in order to achieve much greater throughput with a single session; two such efforts are "Fast TCP" [CHENG] and "HighSpeed TCP" [RFC3649].

1.3.3.1.6   TCP: Impact of Delay-jitter

Jitter has no explicit impact on TCP; jitter only has an impact on TCP in that it is a component of delay, which can impact throughput as discussed in Section 1.3.3.1.5.

1.3.3.1.7   TCP: Impact of Loss

As discussed in Section 1.3.3.1.3, TCP implicitly has mechanisms to ensure that packets dropped are resent; however, [MATHIS] shows theoretically that maximum TCP throughput decreases as an inverse of the square root of the probability of packet loss. The graph in Figure 1.23 uses this relationship to plot how the theoretical maximum attainable TCP throughput for a single TCP session varies as a function of packet loss for a TCP maximum segment size (MSS) of 1460 bytes.

As previously noted in Section 1.3.3.1.5 there are a number of factors which will impact the attained TCP throughput in practice.

1.3.3.1.8   TCP: Impact of Throughput

The previous sections have described how the achieved throughput for a TCP session is dependent upon the probability of packet loss and the achieved RTT, as well as a number of practical factors. In addition achieved throughput for a TCP session will obviously be gated by the available capacity on the path between the source and destination. Hence, it is important to note that the actual achieved TCP throughput for a single TCP session may be significantly less than the contracted access bandwidth provided for a service.

1.3.3.1.9   TCP: Impact of Packet Re-ordering

Most deployed TCP implementations will support fast retransmit behavior and hence will interpret the receipt of three consecutive duplicate ACKS as an indication of packet loss and will retransmit the next packet and slow down their rate of sending by invoking the congestion avoidance algorithm. Therefore, re-ordering packets within a TCP stream can have a significant impact on TCP throughput. [LAOR] shows that for TCP traffic with a 0.04% rate of packet re-ordering, achieved application throughput can be reduced to 74% compared to the throughput achieved with no packet re-ordering.

Hence, packet re-ordering should be avoided due to the potential impact on TCP throughput.

1.3.3.2   Interactive Data Applications

Interactive applications depend on providing responses to an end-user in real-time. As the specific implementations of interactive data applications can vary, the impact that network characteristics such as delay have on them can also vary. Hence, it is not possible to provide definitive guidance, but rather we consider the main factors that impact the SLA requirements in support of interactive data applications.

The response time targets for such interactive applications are dependent upon human factors; [DOHERTY] show the economic value of rapid response times to interactive applications. Robert B. Miller's definitive paper from 1968 (when all computers were mainframes) on "Response Time in Man-Computer Conversational Transactions" described three response time thresholds for human attention, which are still generally accepted targets today:

- A response time of less than ~0.1 second is the target where applications need to give the user the feeling that the system is reacting instantaneously. This delay bound target is supported by more recent research in a variety of fields aimed at determining the delay above which performance for interactive applications becomes impaired [G.114, BAILEY, MACKENZIE].

- A response time of less than ~1.0 second is the target where the applications need to keep the user's flow of thought uninterrupted, although the user will notice the delay.

- A response time of less than 10 seconds is the target where the applications need to keep the user's attention focussed on the dialogue; for longer delays, users will want to perform other tasks while waiting for the computer to finish.

  This target was also supported by Peter Bickford's 1997 paper [BICKFORD], which reported research in which half the users abandoned web pages after a wait of 8.5 seconds; the "8-second rule" subsequently become a universal rule of web site design.

These targets relate to the time to complete a user transaction – that is, the time between a user action, and the user receiving the response to their action. For client/server applications which require a network transaction, network delay is but one aspect of the total transactional delay to which these targets refer, which may be comprised of the following components:

- *Client-side processing delays.* The user's system may perform some pre-processing before starting the network transaction, and may perform additional processing on receiving the response from the server.

- *Server-side processing delays.* The server will need to perform some processing before the response can be sent to the user. Some applications may involve a number of distributed server transactions as part of the processing initiated by user request.

- *Network delays.* Network delays will be incurred in sending the request from the client to the server and in sending the response from server to client. Further, some "chatty" applications may require several network transactions between the client and server for a single user transaction. For such applications, relatively small increments in network latency can have a noticeable effect on end-user response times, or conversely, very small network delays may be required in order to achieve the application response time targets.

Hence, for an application targeting a 1-second response time, even if the network RTT may be well below a second, the user response time may still exceed the one-second target. Hence, a good understanding of the specific application behavior is required to understand what impact different network delays have on the application and to be able to translate application response time targets into the corresponding network RTT targets.

Assume, as per the timeline shown in Figure 1.24 for example, that a business-critical interactive application with a 1 second response

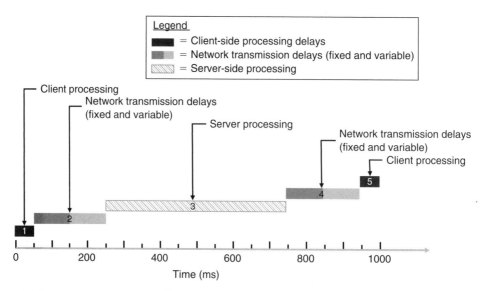

Figure 1.24 Delay components: example interactive data application #1

time target uses a single network transaction (e.g. an HTTP GET) per user transaction, using a minimally sized request (a single packet), with a total of 100 ms of client-side processing (actions 1 + 5) and 500 ms of total server-side processing (action 3). To meet the application response time target requires a network RTT of approximately 400 ms (actions 2 + 4) or less.

If by comparison, as per the example timeline shown in Figure 1.25, an application with the same total client-side, and server-side processing delays, but which instead required two network transactions (a DNS query and an HTTP GET for example) per user transaction, a network RTT of approximately 200 ms or less would be required in order to meet the target.

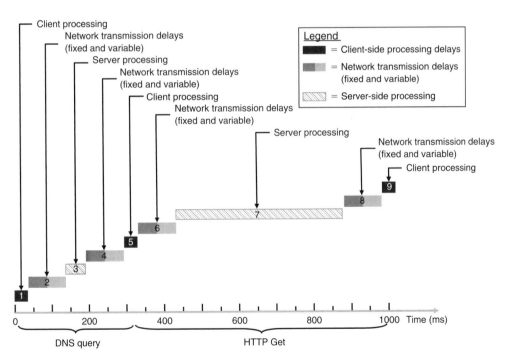

Figure 1.25 Delay components: example interactive data application #2

A badly designed application implementation may impose RTT requirements on the network that are not viable; in this case re-engineering of the application should be considered. Application re-engineering may require re-writing the application to reduce the number of network transactions, or relocating the server to be closer to the client, thereby reducing the network RTT.

Jitter has no explicit impact on interactive data applications; jitter only has an impact on TCP in that it is a component of network delay. Network loss and packet re-ordering can have an impact on interactive data applications in that lost or re-ordered packets may need to be retransmitted which may probabilistically increase the network component of the total transaction delay. The impact of packet loss and resequencing will depend upon the characteristics of the transport layer protocol that is used; the impact of packet loss and resequencing on TCP is discussed in Section 1.3.3.1. For UDP-based interactive data applications, a detailed knowledge of the specific application implementation is required in order to understand the impact of packet loss and resequencing; this would require analysis on an application-by-application basis.

1.3.3.3 On-line Gaming

Multiplayer on-line or networked games are the most popular form of a type of application known as Networked Virtual Environments (NVEs); other uses of NVEs include military simulation. Users in NVEs, who may be in geographically separate locations, interact with each other in a virtual world in real-time. The IEEE Distributed Interactive Simulation (DIS) [IEEE1278] standard covers NVE; however, this is not generally used by the software vendors that produce on-line games who instead use proprietary implementations. The variation in such proprietary implementations means that it is not possible to provide definitive guidance on SLA requirements to support on-line gaming applications, but rather we review the current research on this subject.

Although there are different types of real-time on-line games – the most common game types being: First Person Shooter (FPS), Real-Time Strategy (RTS) and Multiplayer On-line Role-Playing Game

(MORPG) – most use a client-server architecture, where a central server tracks client state and hence is responsible for maintaining the state of the virtual environment. The players' computers are clients, unicasting location and action state information to the server, which then distributes the information to the other clients participating in the game. Most implementations use UDP as a transport protocol.

Most on-line gaming implementations have evolved to work over the public Internet and have bandwidth requirements of less than 64 kbps and in-built mechanisms to deal with packet loss. However, it is noted that these bandwidth requirements may increase over time, with the prevalence of higher bandwidths available to end-users due to broadband access. In addition, some games provide the capability to tweak various network parameters, which can have a significant impact on their bandwidth requirements.

It is commonly cited that low network delay is a requirement of on-line gaming applications; players who experience higher delays to/from the server than others may experience a relative "lag" in play as they receive information from the server later than lower delay users, and similarly the server receives information from them later than from the lower delay user. Consequently, users with lower RTTs may have a game-playing advantage. In terms of setting a bound on the acceptable RTT for on-line gaming, research into FPS games suggests that with delays above 100–250 ms, gamers are deterred from playing and/or their playing performance is inhibited [HENDERSON1, ARMITAGE, PANTEL], although different types of games might have differing requirements. These findings are supported by research in a variety of fields aimed at determining the delay above which performance for interactive applications becomes impaired [G.114, BAILEY, MACKENZIE].

A more recent study by [HENDERSON2] examined the impact that delay has on user behavior, rather than impact on game-play, concluding that high network delay may dissuade a user from joining a particular game server. However, when experiencing high delay after having joined a game server, even when players could notice the delay and their game-play performance was degraded, they were not inconvenienced to the extent that they would leave the server.

This may indicate that players are willing to tolerate higher levels of delay than previous research indicated. In addition, a number of techniques for lag compensation have been shown to be successful [BERNIER].

Research into RTS games [SHELDEN] suggests that RTTs of up to 500 ms have minimal effect on the end-users; even though higher latencies were noticeable to the user they had negligible effect on the outcome of the game; this is attributed to the nature of RTS game play, which is focussed more on strategy, rather than real-time aspects.

1.4 Marketed SLAs versus Engineered SLAs

In practice, there may be a distinction between *marketing SLAs* and *engineering SLAs*. Marketing SLAs apply in SP environments, are contracted between the SP sales channel and their customers, and are aimed to be simple for the customer to understand, competitive for the targeted customer market segment and easy to report against. Marketing SLAs may also define the bounds that represent SLA violation, together with the service-credits/refunds that apply in the presence of such violation. Marketing SLAs do not really have any context in enterprise network environments.

Engineering SLAs apply in both network SP and enterprise environments. In an SP context engineering SLAs are contracted between the SP engineering and support team and their sales channel and are aimed to support the requirements of the applications of the targeted customer market segment; SPs will not normally disclose their engineering SLAs. In an enterprise context, engineering SLAs are contracted by the network engineering and support teams to the enterprise and are aimed to support the requirements of the enterprise's business critical applications. Engineering SLAs define the bounds used in designing and operating the network and are not visible to the end customer. They are necessarily more stringent than their equivalent marketing SLA, to mitigate the risks of paying service-credits/refunds. As the focus of this book is on engineering, the preceding sections and the rest of this book focus on engineering SLAs; how an SP chooses to translate an engineering SLA commitment to a marketing SLA is a choice for the particular service provider.

1.4.1   End-to-End SLAs vs Segmented SLAs

For ease of understanding, marketing SLAs are normally defined end-to-end – that is, from customer premises equipment (CPE) to CPE – in the context of services where the SP manages the CPE. End-to-end SLAs, however, often need to be applicable across an amalgamation of geographic locations and possibly link speeds; therefore, their definition needs to be loose enough to encompass the worst case.

Consequently, to ease the problem of engineering the network, engineering SLAs are most commonly defined in a segmented manner: the access links are designed to meet an edge engineering SLA, while the backbone is designed to meet a core engineering SLA. A small and well-defined set of segmented SLAs could be used to support a larger and more complex set of marketing SLAs. The segmented approach also maps well to use of active SLA monitoring, where segmentation can aid scaling of the deployment of an active SLA probing system (see Chapter 5, Section 5.3).

1.4.2   Inter-provider SLAs

When considering services which span multiple providers' networks, it might be assumed that from a SLA perspective, the end-to-end SLA for a class (assuming there are congruent classes between the two providers) is a simple aggregation of the individual SLAs offered by the providers, e.g. SP A offers a loss rate of 1%, SP B offers a loss rate of 2%, hence the end-to-end loss rate is $1 - (0.98 * 0.97) = \sim 3\%$. However, in practice, the marketing SLA definitions for the two providers are likely to be very different: SP A might define packet-loss by sending end-to-end probes every minute and then averaging daily, while SP B might send probes hourly and average monthly. This illustrates how much scope there is for ambiguity with marketing SLAs.

Marketing SLAs aside, as SPs will actually design their networks to satisfy engineering SLAs with the objective that the target applications for each class of service they offer will actually work across their own network. Hence, although a VoIP service might be able to be supported across SP A and across SP B individually, there is nothing to assure that it will work end-to-end across both SP A and SP B's networks in series. Worse still, the VoIP service might work initially, because both SPs' networks are lightly loaded; however, when their networks become more heavily loaded, the VoIP service may fail, even though neither SP is exceeding their individual SLAs. This applies not just to delay but also to jitter, loss, throughput and availability.

A benefit of using a solution where SPs have cooperated in providing an inter-provider service is that the network has been engineered to support the target applications end-to-end across both providers, and there is some recourse for the end customer if this does not work. There are some current standards efforts, which are looking to formalize the definitions of inter-provider services [IPSPHERE].

1.5 Intserv and Diffserv SLAs

For completeness, Intserv and Diffserv both have their respective SLA terminologies; however, in practice these terminologies are rarely used in explicit SLA definitions:

- *Diffserv*. SLAs in Diffserv [RFC2475 updated by RFC3260] (Diffserv is described in Chapter 2, Section 2.3.4) are defined in terms of the Service Level Specification (SLS) and Traffic Conditioning Specification (TCS):
  - A SLS is a set of parameters and their values which together define the service offered to a traffic stream by a Diffserv domain. The SLS is effectively the engineering SLA that a service has been designed to support.
  - A TCS is a set of parameters and their values, which together specify a set of traffic classifier rules and a traffic profile. A TCS

is an integral element of an SLS. The TCS effectively defines the traffic (both in terms of classification and traffic profile) for which the SLS is committed.

- Diffserv also defines the concept of "Per-Domain Behaviors" (PDBs) which can be considered a definition of the "black box" forwarding behaviors experienced by a class of packets across a differentiated services network, and can be considered to be the Diffserv definition of the end-to-end engineering SLAs described in Section 1.4.

  Only a single PDB has been defined and that is the lower-effort PDB.

- *Intserv.* With Intserv/RSVP [RFC 2210], SLAs are defined in terms of the QOS service level (either Guaranteed Service [RFC 2212] or Controlled-Load Service [RFC 2211]) and the traffic specifier describing the level of traffic for which the service is assured. See Chapter 4, Section 4.4 for more details on Intserv.

References[6]

[802-2001] IEEE standard for local and metropolitan area networks: overview and architecture

[ARMITAGE] G. Armitage, An experimental estimation of latency sensitivity in multiplayer Quake 3, in *Proceedings of the 11th IEEE International Conference on Networks (ICON 2003)*, Sydney, Australia, September 2003

[BAILEY] R. W. Bailey, *Human Performance Engineering – Using Human Factors/Ergonomics to Achieve Computer System Usability*, Prentice Hall, Englewood Cliffs, NJ, USA, second edition, 1989

[BAKER] Mark Baker, Rajkumar Buyya, and Domenico Laforenza, Grids and grid technologies for wide-area distributed computing, *Software – Practice & Experience*, Volume 32, Issue 15, December 2002, pp. 1437–1466

[BERNIER] Y. W. Bernier, Latency compensating methods in client/server in-game protocol design and optimization, in *Proceedings of the 15th Games Developers Conference*, San Jose, CA, USA, Mar. 2001

[BICKFORD] Peter Bickford, Worth the wait? contribution to the Human Interface On-line column of Netscape's View Source, October 1997. Available at: http://developer.netscape.com/viewsource/bickford_wait.htm

[BRATSKMO] L. S. Bratskmo and L. L. Peterson, TCP vegas: End to end congestion avoidance on a global internet, *IEEE Journal on Selected Areas in Communications*, vol. 13, no. 8, pp. 1465–1480, 1995

[BT.500] ITU-R Recommendation BT.500-11, 2002-06, Methodology for the Subjective Assessment of the Quality of Television Pictures

[CHIMENTO] P. Chimento, J. Ishac, Defining Network Capacity, draft-ietf-ippm-bw-capacity-01 (work in progress)

[DICK] M. Dick, O. Wellnitz, L. Wolf, Analysis of factors affecting Players' Performance and Perception in Multiplayer Games, *NetGames'05*, Hawthorne (NY), U.S.A.

[DOHERTY] Walter J. Doherty, Ahrvind J. Thadani, The Economic Value of Rapid Response Time, November, 1982. http://www.vm.ibm.com/devpages/jelliott/evrrt.html

[DUFFIELD] N.G. Duffield, P. Goyal, A.G. Greenberg, P.P. Mishra, K.K. Ramakrishnan, Jacobus E. van der Merwe, Resource management with hoses: point-to-cloud services for virtual private networks, *IEEE/ACM Transactions on Networking*, November 2002

[EBU] http://www.ebu.ch

[ETSI Ts 102 034] Draft Technical Specification ETSI TS 102 034 V<0.0.8> (2004-05-05) Digital Video Broadcasting (DVB) Transport of DVB Services over IP

[CHENG] Cheng Jin et al., FAST TCP: from theory to experiments, *IEEE Network*, 19(1):4–11, January/February 2005

[FRANCOIS] Pierre Francois, Clarence Filsfils, John Evans and Olivier Bonaventure, Achieving subsecond IGP convergence in large IP networks, *ACM SIGCOMM Computer Communication Review*, Vol. 35, Issue 3 (July 2005), pp. 35–44

[G.107] ITU-T Recommendation G.107 (03/2005), The E-model, a computational model for use in transmission planning

[G.114] ITU-T Recommendation G.114, One-way transmission time, International Telecommunication Union, Geneva, Switzerland, Sep. 2003

[G.826] ITU-T Recommendation G.826, End-to-end error performance parameters and objectives for international, constant bit-rate digital paths and connections, International Telecommunication Union, Geneva, Switzerland, Dec. 2002

[H.323] ITU-T Recommendation H.323: Packet-Based Multimedia Communications Systems, International Telecommunication Union, Geneva, Switzerland, Feb. 1998

[HENDERSON1] T. Henderson, Latency and user behaviour on a multiplayer game server, in *Proceedings of the 3rd International Workshop on Networked Group Communication (NGC)*, pp. 1–13, London, UK, Nov. 2001

[HENDERSON2] Tristan Henderson and Saleem Bhatti, Networked games – a QoS-sensitive application for QoS-insensitive users?, *Proceedings of the ACM SIGCOMM workshop on Revisiting IP QoS*, pp. 141–147, Karlsruhe, Germany, August 2003. ACM Press

[IEEE1278] Institute of Electrical and Electronic Engineers, 1278.2-1995, IEEE Standard for Distributed Interactive Simulation – Communication Services and Profiles IEEE, New York, NY, USA, Apr. 1996

[IPFRR] M. Shand, S. Bryant, IP Fast Reroute Framework, Internet Draft, draft-ietf-rtgwg-ipfrr-framework (work in progress).

[IPPM] http://www.ietf.org/html.charters/ippm-charter.html

[IPSPHERE] www.ipsphereforum.org

[J.144] ITU-T Recommendation J.144 (03/2004), Objective perceptual video quality measurement techniques for digital cable television in the presence of a full reference

[JACOBSON] JACOBSON, V, Congestion avoidance and control, In *Proceedings of SIGCOMM '88* (Stanford, CA, Aug. 1988), ACM

[LAOR] Michael Laor, Lior Gendel, The Effect of Packet Re-ordering in a Backbone Link on Application Throughput, *IEEE Network,* Vol. 16, No. 5, pp. 28–36, 2002.

[MACKENZIE] I. S. MacKenzie and C. Ware, Lag as a determinant of human performance in interactive systems, in *Proceedings of the CHI '93 Conference on Human factors in computing systems*, pp. 488–493, Amsterdam, The Netherlands, Apr. 1993

[MATHIS] Matthew Mathis, The Macroscopic Behavior of the TCP Congestion Avoidance Algorithm, *Computer Communication Review,* July 1997

[MCCANN] Ken McCann, DVB + MPEG-4 = New Options for Baseband Systems, *DVB World Conference 2002* – Dublin 6/7 March 2002. Available at: http://www.zetacast.com/Zeta_Publications.htm

[MPEG] ISO/IEC JTC1/SC29 WG11. More information available at: http://www.chiariglione.org/mpeg/

[MPEG-2] ISO/IEC 13818: Generic coding of moving pictures and associated audio information (MPEG-2)

[MPEG-4] ISO/IEC 14496-10:2004, Coding of audio-visual objects – Part 10: Advanced Video Coding

[NIELSEN] Jakob Nielsen, Usability Engineering, Morgan Kaufmann, 1994. Also on-line at: http://www.useit.com/papers/responsetime.html

[P.800] ITU-T Recommendation P.800 (08/96), Methods for subjective determination of transmission quality

[P.862] ITU-T Recommendation P.862 (02/2001) Perceptual evaluation of speech quality (PESQ): An objective method for end-to-end speech quality assessment of narrow-band telephone networks and speech codecs

[PANTEL] L. Pantel and L. C. Wolf, On the impact of delay on real-time multiplayer games, in *Proceedings of the 12th International Workshop on Network and Operating System Support for Digital Audio and Video (NOSSDAV)*, pp. 23–29, Miami Beach, FL, USA, May 2002

[PRO-MPEG] Pro-MPEG Forum Code of Practice #3 – release 2: Transmission of Professional MPEG-2 transport streams over IP networks, Professional-MPEG Forum, www.pro-mpeg.org

[PWE3] http://www.ietf.org/html.charters/pwe3-charter.html

[RFC768] J. Postel, User Datagram Protocol, August 1980

[RFC783] K. Sollins, The TFTP protocol (revision 2), RFC 783, July 1992

[RFC791] J. Postel, Internet Protocol, RFC 791, September 1981

[RFC793] J. Postel, Transmission Control Protocol, RFC 793, September 1981

[RFC2210] J. Wroclawski, The Use of RSVP with IETF Integrated Services, RFC2210, September 1997

[RFC2211] J. Wroclawski, Specification of the Controlled-Load Network Element Service, RFC2211, September 1997

[RFC2212] S. Shenker et al., Specification of Guaranteed Quality of Service, RFC2212, September 1997

[RFC2250] D. Hoffman et al., RTP payload Format for MPEG1/MPEG2 video, RFC 2250, January 1998

[RFC2326] H. Schulzrinne, A. Rao, R. Lanphier, Real-time Streaming Protocol (RTSP), RFC 2326, April 1998

[RFC2330] V. Paxson et al., Framework for IP Performance Metrics, May 1998

[RFC2343] M. Civanlar, G. Cash, B. Haskell, RTP Payload Format for Bundled MPEG, RFC 2343, May 1998

[RFC2475] S. Blake et al., An Architecture for Differentiated Services, RFC2475, December 1998

[RFC2581] W. Stevens, M. Allman, V. Paxson, TCP Congestion Control, RFC 2581, April 1999

[RFC2678] J. Mahdavi, V. Paxson, IPPM Metrics for Measuring Connectivity, RFC 2678, September 1999

[RFC2679] G. Almes, S. Kalidindi, and M. Zekauskas, A One-way Delay Metric for IPPM, RFC 2679, September 1999

[RFC2680] G. Almes, S. Kalidindi, and M. Zekauskas, A One-way Packet Loss Metric for IPPM, RFC 2680, September 1999

[RFC2681] G. Almes, S. Kalidindi, M. Zekauskas, A Round-trip Delay Metric for IPPM, September 1999

[RFC2733] J. Rosenberg et al., An RTP Payload Format for Generic Forward Error Correction, RFC 2733, December 1999

[RFC3148] M. Mathis, M. Allman, A Framework for Defining Empirical Bulk Transfer Capacity Metrics, RFC3148, July 2001

[RFC3260] D. Grossman, New Terminology and Clarifications for Diffserv, RFC3260, April 2002

[RFC3261] J. Rosenberg et al., SIP: Session Initiation Protocol, RFC 3261, June 2002

[RFC3357] R. Koodli, R. Ravikanth, One-way Loss Pattern Sample Metrics, RFC3357, August 2002

[RFC3390] M. Allman, S. Floyd, C. Partridge, Increasing TCP's Initial Window, RFC 3390, October 2002

[RFC3393] C. Demichelis, P. Chimento, IP Packet Delay Variation Metric for IP Performance Metrics (IPPM), RFC3393, November 2002

[RFC3550] H. Schulzrinne, S. Casner, R. Frederick, V. Jacobson, RTP: A Transport Protocol for Real-Time Applications, RFC 3550, July 2003

[RFC3640] J. van der Meer et al., RTP Payload Format for Transport of MPEG-4 Elementary Streams, November 2003

[RFC3649] S. Floyd, HighSpeed TCP for Large Congestion Windows, RFC 3649, December 2003

[RFC3782] S. Floyd, T. Henderson, A. Gurtov, The NewReno Modification to TCP's Fast Recovery Algorithm, RFC3782, April 2004

[RFC3828] L–A. Larzon et al., The Lightweight User Datagram Protocol (UDP-Lite), RFC 3828, July 2004

[RFC4090] P. Pan, Ed., G. Swallow Ed., A. Atlas Ed., Fast Reroute Extensions to RSVP-TE for LSP Tunnels, RFC 4090, May 2005

[RFC4364] E. Rosen, Y. Rekhter, BGP/MPLS IP Virtual Private Networks (VPNs), RFC 4364, February 2006

[RFC4584] J. Ott et al., Extended RTP profile for Real-time Transport Control Protocol (RTCP)-Based Feedback (RTP/AVPF), RFC 4584, July 2006

[RFC4588] J. Rey et al., RTP Retransmission Payload Format, RFC 4588, July 2006

[RFC4737] A. Morton et al., Packet Re-ordering Metric for IPPM. RFC 4737, November 2006

[ROSENBERG] J. Rosenberg. G.729 error recovery for Internet Telephony, Project report, Columbia University, 1997

[SAMVIQ] Franc Kozamernik, Paola Sunna, Emmanuel Wyckens and Dag Inge Pettersen, SAMVIQ – A New EBU Methodology For Video Quality Evaluations In Multimedia, Presented at IBC 2004, Amsterdam, September 2004. Available on-line at: http://www.broadcastpapers.com/ibc2004/ibc04EBUSamviq01.htm

[SHELDEN] Nathan Sheldon, Eric Girard, Seth Borg, Mark Claypool, Emmanuel Agu, The effect of latency on user performance in Warcraft III, *Proceedings of the 2nd workshop on Network and system support for games*, pp. 3–14, May 22–23, 2003, Redwood City, California

[SINGH] A. Singh, A. Konrad, and A. Joseph, Performance evaluation of UDP lite for cellular video, in *Proceedings of NOSSDAV*, June 2001.

[STEINMETZ] R. Steinmetz, Human Perception of Jitter and Media Synchronization, *IEEE Journal Selected Areas in Comm.*, vol. 14, pp. 61–72, January 1996

[STEVENS] W. Stevens, *TCP/IP Illustrated, Volume 1: The Protocols*, Addison-Wesley, 1994

[VC-1] SMPTE 421M-2006, Television – VC-1 Compressed Video Bitstream Format and Decoding Process

Notes

1. Packet header overhead is calculated at 40 bytes comprising: 12 bytes due to RTP header, 8 bytes due to UDP header and 20 bytes due to IP header.

2. The letters in square brackets refer to the components of delay described in Figure 1.5.

3. [ROSENBURG] shows the impact on the Mean Opinion Score (MOS) that loss of consecutive packets has when using a G.729 codec.

4. It is noted that the delay due to the FEC processing operation for a matrix size of m * n reduces in absolute terms as the rate of the encoded MPEG stream increases, because the time to transmit m * n packets reduces accordingly.

5. This paper can be difficult to get hold of, but this advice with respect to response times is also available in [NIELSEN].

6. The nature of the networking industry and community means that some of the sources referred to in this book exist only on the World Wide Web. All Universal Resource Locators (URLs) have been checked and were correct at the time of going to press, but their longevity cannot be guaranteed.

2

Introduction to QOS
Mechanics and Architectures

2.1 What is Quality of Service?

In networking, the term quality of service (QOS) can mean many different things to different people, hence it is key that we start this chapter by defining what "QOS" means in the context of this book.

Firstly, how do we define a "service" in the context of IP networking? We consider that a service is a description of the overall treatment of a customer's traffic across a particular domain. A service is only practically useful if it meets the requirements of the end-user applications it is intended to support. Hence, the aim of the service is to maximize end-user satisfaction with the applications that the service is supporting. Maximizing user satisfaction requires that the end-user applications work effectively.

How then do we define "quality" in the context of a particular IP service? We can define service quality in terms of the underlying requirements for an application which can be defined in terms of the SLA metrics for IP service performance defined in Chapter 1: delay, jitter, packet loss, throughput, service availability, and per flow sequence preservation.

QOS, however, implies more than just ensuring that a network service is able to support the SLA requirements of the applications it is aiming to support. The problem of ensuring that a network can meet these requirements is fundamentally a problem of managing the available network capacity relative to the service load, i.e. a problem of managing congestion. If it is possible to ensure that there is always significantly more capacity available than there is traffic load then delay, jitter and loss will be minimized, throughput will be maximized, and the service requirements will be easy to meet. In practice, however, ensuring that the network is always overprovisioned relative to the actual traffic load is not always cost-effective. Hence, in engineering the QOS of a network service there is implicitly another important constraint, which is to minimize cost. If there is more traffic load than there is capacity to support it, i.e. if congestion occurs, then some traffic will either need to be delayed until there is capacity available or it will need to be dropped. Minimizing cost may demand that multiple services are supported or multiplexed on the same network, by classifying traffic into discrete classes, such that the problem of engineering traffic load relative to capacity can be performed on a per-class basis allowing per-class service differentiation.

In summary, at a high level we can describe QOS in terms of the goals that it is trying to achieve, which effectively define an optimization problem[1] of trying to maximize end-user satisfaction (utility or efficacy) while minimizing cost. Maximizing user satisfaction requires that the end-user applications work effectively, for example, that a voice over IP call quality is acceptable, which requires that the application's SLA requirements are met. Minimizing cost requires that we do not overengineer the network in order to deliver that call quality, which may require the need to differentiate the service levels offered to different applications.

2.1.1   Quality of Service vs Class of Service or Type of Service?

The terms "class of service" (COS) and "type of service" (TOS) are sometimes used interchangeably with quality of service; for the purposes of this book, we explicitly define them here to avoid confusion:

- *Class of service.* As well as being used interchangeably with quality of service, class of service is also sometimes used to refer to the layer 2 QOS capabilities provided by Ethernet or ATM. We prefer to use neither of those definitions but rather use "class of service" or

COS purely in the context of traffic classification. In Section 2.2.1 we define the concept of a traffic class as a set of traffic streams that will have common actions applied to them. Hence, to avoid confusion, we use the term "classes of service" to refer to the classification of an aggregate traffic stream into a number of constituent classes, where different actions will be applied to each individual "class of service."

- *Type of service*. We use the term "type of service" to refer specifically to the use of the Type of Service Octet in the IPv4 packet header as described in Section 2.3.2.

2.1.2 Best-effort Service

Networks engineered to deliver a particular quality of service are often contrasted to "best-effort" networks. "Best-effort" describes a network service which attempts to deliver traffic to its destination, but which does not provide any guarantees of delivery, and hence is without any commitments for delay, jitter, loss, and throughput.

The term best-effort, however, is often misused. Where a network supports multiple service classes simultaneously, best-effort is often used to refer to the service which offers the lowest SLA commitments. By definition, best-effort infers no SLA commitments and hence a service which provides any SLA commitments cannot be defined as best-effort, however lowly those commitments might be. Even if a network supports only a single service class, i.e. where packet forwarding is egalitarian and all packets receive the same quality of service, if that service provides defined SLA commitments, we contend that it cannot be considered a best-effort network service.

Confusion is also sometimes caused because IP can be referred to as a "best-effort" network layer protocol, in that it does not implicitly provide any capabilities to detect or retransmit lost packets. Despite this, however, with appropriate network engineering, it is possible to support IP services which have defined SLA commitments and hence an IP service does not imply a best-effort service. Conversely, TCP is sometimes considered to be a guaranteed transport layer protocol in that it provides the capability to detect and retransmit lost packets. This capability, however, may be of no practical use if the underlying IP service cannot deliver the TCP segments with the SLAs required by applications; the effective SLA of the TCP service is implicitly constrained by the SLA commitments provided by the underlying IP service.

In order to avoid any potential for confusion, we intentionally try not to use the term "best-effort."

2.1.3   The Timeframes that Matter for QOS

We find it useful to consider three timeframes relevant to engineering the quality of service of a network; different QOS techniques are applied in each timeframe:

- *O(milliseconds)*. The first timeframe we consider is in the order of milliseconds. Within this timeframe bursts of individual traffic streams or the aggregation of bursts for different streams at network aggregation points can cause congestion, where the traffic load exceeds the available capacity. QOS mechanisms relevant to this timescale include applying per-hop queuing, scheduling and dropping techniques to provide differentiation and isolation between different types of traffic, to prioritize some types of traffic over others thereby managing delay, and to ensure fair bandwidth allocations. These mechanisms are considered in Section 2.2.

- *O(100 milliseconds)*. The next timeframe we consider is in the order of 100s of milliseconds. This is the timeframe which defines network round trip times (RTT; see Chapter 1, Section 1.2.1). This is the timeframe which is important to applications that used closed-loop feedback between sender and receiver to apply flow control mechanisms, such as TCP-based applications. QOS mechanisms relevant to this timeframe therefore include active queue management (AQM) congestion control techniques such as random early detection (RED) (see Section 2.2.4.2.3).

- *O(10 seconds) or more.* Timeframes of seconds and minutes are relevant to the management of the long-term average network traffic rates and capacity, which is achieved through capacity planning and traffic engineering, which are discussed in Chapter 6.

2.1.4   Why IP QOS?

Layer 2 technologies such as ATM and Ethernet have their own defined QOS capabilities, hence it is a valid question to ask: "why use IP QOS rather than layer 2 QOS mechanisms?" The main reasons for using IP QOS stem from the fact that IP is the end-to-end network layer technology used by the vast majority of applications today. Added to this QOS is an end-to-end discipline where the service that a particular class of traffic receives is limited by the element on the end-to-end path which provides the worst service. Hence, in order to provide a low-delay, low-jitter and low-loss service (thus maximizing user satisfaction) the network must be engineered to remove all points of congestion on the end-to-end path for that service; in order to assure different SLAs for different classes of traffic (hence minimizing cost), we must apply differentiation at all points of congestion. Different underlying layer 2 technologies may be used for different legs of an end-to-end layer 3 path. Therefore, as IP is the lowest common end-to-end layer, it makes fundamental sense to use IP QOS techniques where possible, and to map them to underlying QOS capabilities in lower layer technologies, where required (see Section 2.5), rather than to attempt to map layer 2 QOS capabilities for one leg to the layer 2 QOS capabilities of the next leg. The SLAs provided at the IP layer, however, are implicitly limited by the SLAs of the underlying Layer 2 technology (see Section 2.5).

2.1.5   The QOS Toolset

In practical terms, QOS involves using a range of functions and features (e.g. classification, scheduling, policing, shaping), within the context of overriding architecture (e.g. Integrated Service, Differentiated

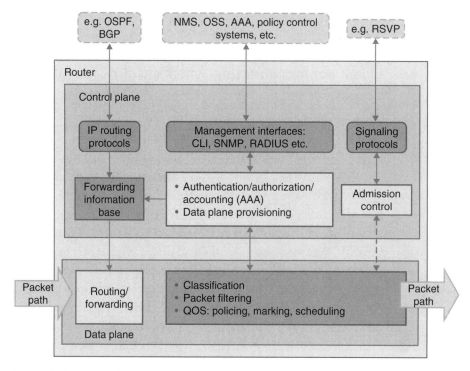

Figure 2.1   Control plane and data plane QOS functions

Services) in order to ensure that a network service delivers the SLA characteristics that the applications targeted by that service need to work effectively. The mechanisms used for engineering the QOS in a network can be broken down into data plane and control plane mechanisms applied on network devices such as routers, as shown in Figure 2.1 and which are introduced here and described in detail in the proceeding sections.

- *Data plane*. Data plane QOS mechanisms are applied at network nodes and can directly impact the forwarding behavior of packets. They are processing intensive functions; in high-performance routers, they are typically implemented in hardware, along with other data plane functions such as packet forwarding lookups and packet filtering. Such data plane QOS mechanisms can be categorized in terms of the primitive behavioral characteristics that they impart to traffic streams to which they are applied:

○ *Classification.* Classification (see Section 2.2.1) is the process of categorizing an aggregate traffic stream into a number of constituent classes, such that any of the following actions can be applied to each individual "class of service."

○ *Marking.* Traffic marking (see Section 2.2.2) is the process of explicitly setting the value of the fields assigned for QOS classification in the IP or MPLS packet headers so that the traffic can subsequently be easily identified.

○ *Maximum rate enforcement.* Policing (see Section 2.2.3) and shaping (see Section 2.2.4.3) can be used to enforce a maximum rate for a traffic class.

○ *Prioritization.* Techniques such as priority scheduling (see Section 2.2.4.1.1) are used to prioritize some types of traffic over others thereby managing delay and jitter.

○ *Minimum rate assurance.* Scheduling techniques such as Weighted Fair Queuing (WFQ) and Deficit Round Robin (DRR) can be used to provide different traffic classes with different minimum bandwidth assurances (see Section 2.2.4.1.2).

• *Control plane.* Control or signaling plane QOS mechanisms typically deal with admission control and resource reservation, and may in some cases be used to set up the data plane QOS functions. Control plane QOS functions are typically implemented as software processes, along with other control plane functions such as routing protocols. In practice, there is only one protocol widely used for control plane QOS signaling; that signaling protocol is RSVP. RSVP is used in several different contexts:

○ *Integrated services architecture.* RSVP is used in the context of the Integrated Services architecture to perform per flow resource reservation and admission control (see Section 2.3.3).

○ *MPLS traffic engineering.* RSVP is used in the context of MPLS traffic engineering, for admission control and to set up MPLS traffic engineering tunnels (see Chapter 6).

These QOS functions and mechanisms are, however, not generally used in isolation, but rather they are used together in concert, within the framework of an overriding QOS architecture, where mechanisms are combined for end-to-end effect. There are two defined IP QOS architectures: the Integrated Services architecture (see Section 2.3.3) and the Differentiated Services architecture (see Section 2.3.4).

2.2 Data Plane QOS Mechanisms

2.2.1 Classification

Classification in the process of identifying flows of packets and grouping individual traffic flows into aggregated streams such that actions can be applied to those streams; the actions that may be applied after classification could be other than QOS actions, for example packet filtering. To complete this definition we define the terms flow, stream and class:

- *Flows*. An IPv4 flow is typically defined by the 5-tuple of source IP address, destination IP address, source TCP/UDP port, destination TCP/UDP port and the transport protocol (e.g. TCP or UDP). Fragmentation, encryption or tunneling can make some flows difficult to classify, as some of these fields may be unavailable. For example, assume that a flow is classified using this 5-tuple, but that the sizes of packets in the flow exceed the size of packets that can be supported (defined by the maximum transmission unit or MTU) on some of the underlying links which the flow transits. Those packets, which exceed the MTU of transit links, will need to be fragmented using IP level fragmentation [RFC 791]. When a packet is fragmented, the TCP/UDP port information is included in the first packet only; hence, it may not be possible to identify uniquely non-first fragments of a packet as belonging to the same flow. IPv6 introduced a Flow Label field which can be used to overcome this problem.

○ More complicated criteria than this 5-tuple may also be used to define a flow, such as using deep packet inspection/stateful inspection techniques (see Section 2.2.1.3).

○ *Stream*. A traffic stream is an aggregation of flows based upon some common classification criteria. For example, all VoIP traffic from a particular VoIP gateway could be identified just by matching the source IP address of that gateway. A traffic stream may consist of a single flow, or a number of flows.

○ *Traffic classes*. A traffic class is an aggregation of individual traffic flows or streams, for the purpose of applying a common action to the constituent flows or streams. For example, a class may represent all VoIP traffic from a particular site, which may consist of streams of traffic from a number of VoIP gateways. A traffic class may consist of a single stream, or a number of streams.

In the following sections we define the concepts "implicit," "complex," "deep packet/stateful" and "simple" when referring to classification techniques.

2.2.1.1   Implicit Classification

From the perspective of IP QOS, we define implicit classification as a broad brush classification approach, which requires no knowledge of the packet header or contents, and may for example use Layer 1/ Layer 2 context such as the received interface, or received virtual circuit (VC) in order to classify traffic.

2.2.1.2   Complex Classification

Complex classification (also known as multi-field classification) allows for more granularity than "implicit" classification and involves identifying traffic based upon values of specific fields or combinations of fields in the IP packet header, which were not explicitly intended for QOS classification. This includes those fields previously defined in the context of the 5-tuple for IP flow classification, i.e. classifying a flow based upon the 5-tuple is an inception of complex classification. Complex classification may also classify traffic using Layer 2 criteria, such as source or destination MAC addresses, e.g. identifying traffic from a specific host by that host's MAC address.

2.2.1.3   Deep Packet Inspection/Stateful Inspection

Some systems have the capability to classify traffic based upon more than the information contained in a single IP packet header. They may be able to look deeper into the packet, at the underlying data; this is referred to as deep packet inspection (DPI). They may also be able to classify flows by keeping state of the information contained in subsequent packets, rather than looking at each packet individually; this is referred to as stateful inspection (SI). When DPI is combined with SI, the combination can be useful to classify applications that cannot be identified using other means, such as some peer-to-peer applications for example.

Due to the traffic demands that can be placed upon the network by peer-to-peer applications, some peer-to-peer application developers intentionally try to make their applications hard to classify, or make them look like other applications, specifically so that they are difficult to classify and hence difficult to control. This situation is comparable to an arms race, where the application developers are constantly trying to stay one step ahead of the DPI/SI capabilities to classify them.

2.2.1.4   Simple Classification

Classification based upon fields in the packet headers which have been explicitly designed for QOS classification. We refer to it as "simple" classification, as it requires no understanding of other fields in the IP packet header or data, and need have no visibility of constituent flows within the traffic stream which may represent an aggregate of flows. The use of simple classification techniques makes QOS designs easier and requires a less complex underlying classification implementation on network equipment. The following schemes are defined for explicit QOS classification in IP and MPLS:

- *Type of service octet.* The original IPv4 specification [RFC 791] defined an 8-bit field to be used for IP QOS classification; this was called the Type of Service octet and is highlighted in Figure 2.2.

Figure 2.2 (IPv4 packet header diagram)

Version	IHL	Type of service/DS field		Total length	
Identification			Flags	Fragment offset	
Time to live		Protocol		Header checksum	
Source address					
Destination address					
Options				Padding	

Figure 2.2   IPv4 packet header

Figure 2.3 (IPv6 packet header diagram)

Version	Traffic class/DS field	Flow label	
Payload length		Next header	Hop limit
Source address			
Destination address			

Figure 2.3   IPv6 packet header

The type of service octet has since been obsoleted by the Differentiated Services field. See Section 2.3.2 for more details on type of service.

• *IPv6 traffic class octet.* [RFC2460] originally defined the 8-bit traffic class field within the IPv6 header for QOS marking as shown in Figure 2.3. The IPv6 traffic class octet has been obsoleted by the Differentiated Services field.

IPv6 packet headers also include a 20-bit flow label field. The flow label helps to unambiguously classify a flow, where some information used to identify the flow may be missing due to fragmentation, encryption or tunneling, for example. The 3-tuple of the flow label and the source and destination IPv6 address fields are used to classify an IPv6 flow [RFC 3697] uniquely.

- *Differentiated Service field*. [RFC2474] obsoleted both the IPv4 type of service octet and the IPv6 traffic class octet, by redefining them as the Differentiated Services (DS) field. Of the 8 bits of the DS field, 6 were defined as the Differentiated Services code point (DSCP), and the 2 low-order bits were initially undefined. See Section 2.3.4.1 for more details on the DS field.

  [RFC3168] later defined the use of the low-order 2 bits for Explicit Congestion Notification (ECN). ECN is described in Section 2.3.4.4.

- *MPLS EXP field*. [RFC3032] defined a 3-bit field in each MPLS header for "experimental use." [RFC3270] went on to redefine the use of this field for QOS marking. See Section 2.3.6.2 for more details on the MPLS EXP field.

- *Layer 2 marking*. In an IP QOS network enabled network, there may also be a need to make use of QOS marking at layer 2. The best example of this is Ethernet, where IEEE 802.1D [802.1D] defines the use of a 3-bit field for QOS marking. See Section 2.5 for more details of QOS at Layer 2 including IEEE 802.1D.

A particular classification policy could contain logical combinations of both complex and simple classification criteria, e.g. matching on all traffic with a particular DS field marking AND which is from a specific source IP address.

Why do we differentiate between complex and simple classification? Primarily because which classification technique you choose to use and how they are applied can have an impact on the complexity and scalability of the resulting QOS design. For example, using a particular server IP address may seem like a sensible way to identify a traffic stream. If this were used as the only classification criteria for that traffic stream, then classifiers would need to be configured throughout the network, which would classify traffic in that stream by matching the source or destination IP address to the address of the server. This would require that every router in the network were configured with this classifier. This may seem viable, but what if there were one hundred servers rather than just one? Further, what if the IP address of one or more of the servers changes? It quickly becomes apparent that manual configuration of complex classifiers throughout a network to classify streams becomes unmanageable. It is also noted that complex classification approaches may have an impact on router platform performance. On software-based platforms, complex classification may be more processor-intensive and have a consequent impact on the packets per second forward performance of the routers; on hardware-based platforms, there may be a limit to the number of complex classifiers that can be supported by the hardware.

Consequently, and as we will discuss later in this book, the QOS architectures used today do not use manually configured complex classification throughout networks. Instead, the Integrated Services architecture (see Section 2.3.4) uses a signaling protocol to set up per flow classifiers, and the Differentiated Services architecture generally uses simple classification, based upon matching aggregates of traffic identified by the marking of the DSCP field, where complex classification is required it is limited to the ingress edges of the network.

2.2.2 Marking

IP packet marking, which is also known as coloring, is the process of setting the value of the fields assigned for QOS classification in the IP or MPLS packet headers so that the traffic can easily be identified later, i.e. using simple classification techniques.

Marking may use any of the schemes described in Section 2.2.1; however, with the obsoletion of the IP precedence and TOS fields, the DSCP and the MPLS EXP field are becoming the main fields used for IP/MPLS packet marking and classification.

Traffic is generally marked at the source end-system or as close to the traffic source as possible in order to simplify the network design:

- *Source marking.* Packet marking may be applied at the source end-system itself; if the end-system is considered to be trusted then this marking may be relied upon throughout the rest of the network, subsequently requiring only simple classification to identify the traffic steam.

• *Ingress marking.* If the end-system is not capable of marking the packets it originates, or cannot be trusted to do so correctly, then on ingress to the network a trusted device close to the source may use implicit or complex classification to identify a traffic stream from the end-system and mark the traffic accordingly, such that it can be subsequently identified using simple classification techniques. If the source is not trusted to mark packets, then any markings that have previously been applied may be overwritten; this is sometimes termed "remarking."

Such traffic marking can be applied unconditionally, e.g. mark the DSCP to 34 for all traffic received on a particular interface. Traffic marking can also be applied as a conditional result of a traffic policer (see Section 2.2.3 for more information on policers), e.g. for traffic received on an interface which conforms to a policer definition mark the DSCP to 34, for traffic which does not conform to (i.e. is in excess of) the policer definition, mark the DSCP to 36. This conditional marking behavior allows the enforcement of a traffic contract with an in- and out-of-contract concept, as described in Section 2.2.3.1.

Even when a source end-system is trusted to mark the traffic it originates, a policer may still be applied to enforce that the traffic stream from the source conforms to the agreed traffic contract. For example, a source may originate all traffic with DSCP 34; simple classification matching DSCP 34 may then be used on ingress to classify the traffic stream, and a policer applied which leaves the DSCP marking at 34 if the traffic conforms to a policer definition (i.e. is "in-contract") and remarks (a.k.a. "demotes") traffic to DSCP 36 if it exceeds the policer definition (i.e. is "out-of-contract").

2.2.3 Policing and Metering

Policing is a mechanism which can be used to ensure that a traffic stream does not exceed a defined maximum rate. A policer is normally visualized as a token bucket mechanism – not to be confused with

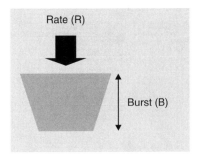

Figure 2.4 Token bucket

a leaky bucket algorithm, which has different properties, and is more commonly used for traffic shaping, as discussed in Section 2.2.4.3.

A simple one-rate token bucket policer has a defined maximum bucket depth (normally in bytes), known as the burst B, and a defined rate R (normally in bps) at which the bucket is filled with byte-sized tokens; see Figure 2.4. Depending upon the particular policer implementation, tokens are added to the bucket at rate R either every time a packet is processed by the policer, or at regular intervals, up to a maximum number of tokens that can be in the bucket, defined by B. The minimum number of tokens in the bucket is zero.

When a token bucket policer mechanism is applied to a traffic stream, and a packet from that stream arrives, the packet size b is compared against the number of tokens currently in the bucket. If there are at least as many byte tokens in the bucket as there are bytes in the packet, then we use the terminology that the packet has "conformed" to the token bucket definition; if there are less tokens in the bucket than bytes in the packet, then the packet has "exceeded" the token bucket definition. If the packet conforms then a number of tokens are decremented from the bucket equal to the packet size b. This simple policer behavior is described in the flowchart in Figure 2.5. Different actions can then be applied depending upon whether the packet conforms or exceeds the token bucket definition. The simplest actions are to transmit the packet if it conforms and to drop the packet if it exceeds; applied in this way the token bucket policer would enforce a maximum rate of R and burst of B on the traffic stream.

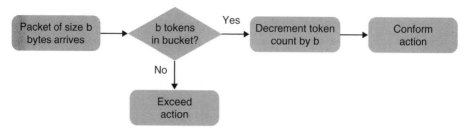

Figure 2.5 Simple one rate policer

The conform and exceed actions of a policer need not only be to transmit the traffic or to drop it; they could also include the marking of traffic or a combination of these actions, hence policers may also be know as markers. Marking is commonly used in conjunction with policing to enforce a defined committed "in-contract" rate on a traffic stream and to allow traffic in excess of this rate to be transmitted but to mark it differently from traffic within the contracted rate (this marking could potentially be to any of the fields described in Section 2.2.2) to indicate that it is "out-of-contract" such that it may potentially be given a less stringent SLA than the in-contract traffic; a more detailed description of applying the concept of in- and out-of-contract marking is given in the following section.

It is important to note that a token bucket policer never delays traffic, whereas a shaper does (see Section 2.2.4.3); there are no packets stored in the bucket; there are only tokens in the bucket! Hence, as a policer does not delay traffic, it cannot re-order or prioritize traffic as a scheduler can (see Section 2.2.4.1).

The simple token bucket policer described in this section is a subset of the functionality of the most commonly used policers, which are described in the following sections.

2.2.3.1 RFC 2697: Single Rate Three Color Marker

A commonly used policer is specified by the "single rate three color marker" (SR-TCM) defined in IETF RFC 2697 [RFC2697]; although this definition refers to a "marker" it can and is used to police traffic as well as to mark traffic. The "three colors" refer to the three possible

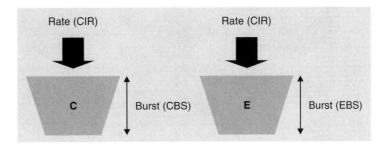

Figure 2.6   RFC 2697: A single rate three color marker

states that are outcomes of the SR-TCM, and which are described using a "traffic light" color scheme.

SR-TCM uses two token buckets, as shown in Figure 2.6, rather than the single token bucket described for the simple policer in the preceding section. The buckets are defined as C and E (for committed and excess, or conform and exceed) with maximum burst sizes CBS and EBS respectively.

Both buckets are filled with tokens at the same rate CIR. When the SR-TCM is applied to a traffic stream and a packet from that stream arrives:

- The packet size b is compared against the number of tokens currently in bucket C. IF there are at least as many tokens in bucket C as bytes in the packet, then the packet has conformed to the SR-TCM definition and the C bucket only is decremented by tokens equal to the number of bytes in the packet. Using the "traffic light" color scheme from RFC 2697 to indicate traffic conformance, in this case the packet is said to be green.

- ELSE IF there are not as many tokens in the C bucket as bytes in the packet, then the packet has exceeded the C bucket of the SR-TCM definition and is now compared against the E bucket. IF there are at least as many byte tokens in the E bucket as there are bytes in the packet, then the E bucket only is decremented by tokens equal to the number of bytes in the packet. Using the traffic light color scheme, in this case the packet is said to be yellow.

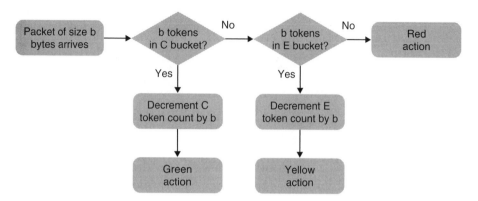

Figure 2.7 RFC 2697: A single rate three color marker (colorblind mode)

- ELSE IF there were neither as many tokens in the C bucket or E buckets as bytes in the packet, then we use the terminology that the packet has "violated" both buckets of the single rate three color token bucket definition. Using the traffic light color scheme, in this case, the packet is said to be red and neither bucket will be decremented. The flowchart in Figure 2.7 shows the operation of the SR-TCM.

CIR and CBS must be set >0, or else all packets will be red. If EBS = 0, then effectively the output of the marker has only two states, and packets will be marked either green or red, and the effective behavior of the SR-TCM is reduced to that of the simple one rate policer described in Section 2.2.3, i.e. "a single rate two color marker."

Different actions, such as transmitting, dropping, or marking the packet can then be applied – possibly in combination – depending upon whether the packet has been designated as green, yellow or red by the SR-TCM:

- Green packets will be transmitted and may be marked also; it makes no sense to apply a drop action to green packets.

- Yellow packets will be transmitted and may also be marked. It makes no sense to apply a drop action to yellow packets if EBS ≠ 0, as the effect would be that all packets which are yellow or red would be dropped, i.e. there would be no differentiation between them.

- Red packets may either be transmitted, or marked and transmitted, or dropped. You might query why there would be a need to transmit red packets without remarking; this may be done if a policer is applied to meter (measure) whether the received traffic exceeds the defined rate (see Section 2.2.3.4).

An application of the SR-TCM could be to set EBS >0 and to apply a green action of {transmit + mark to indicate this traffic is "in-contract"}, a yellow action of {transmit + mark to indicate this traffic is "out-of-contract"} and a red action of drop. Applied in this way the SR-TCM would enforce a maximum rate of CIR and a burst of (CBS + EBS) on the traffic stream, and transmitted traffic would be marked as in- or out-of-contract depending upon whether it conformed or exceeded a burst of CBS. In practice, however, it is difficult to understand what meaningful service benefit is offered by differentiating between in- and out-of-contract traffic depending upon the level of burstiness of the traffic. Alternatively the same marker could be applied with green action of transmit, a yellow action of {transmit + mark to indicate this traffic is out-of-contract} and red action of {transmit + mark to indicate this traffic is "exceedingly-out-of-contract"} respectively; however, in practice it is similarly difficult to understand what meaningful service benefit is offered by differentiating between in-, out-, and exceedingly-out-of-contract traffic depending upon its level of burstiness. Hence, the RFC 2697 "Single Rate Three Color Marker" is not often used practically in this way; more commonly, it is used with EBS = 0; common applications include:

- Enforcing a maximum rate for a voice class of traffic, with EBS = 0 and applying a green action of transmit and red action of drop. Applied in this way the SR-TCM would enforce a maximum rate of CIR and a burst of CBS on the traffic stream, and any traffic in violation of this would be dropped, which is typical of the conditioning behaviors used for the Differentiated Services Expedited

Forwarding Per-Hop Behavior as described in Section 2.3.4.2.1. For a more detailed example like this, see Chapter 3, Section 3.2.2.3.1.

- Marking a certain amount of a traffic class as in-contract, and everything above that as out-of-contract, with EBS = 0 and applying a green action of transmit (if not pre-marked this could be combined with marking in-contract) and red action of {transmit + mark out-of-contract}. Applied in this way the SR-TCM would enforce a maximum rate of CIR and a burst of CBS on the traffic stream; any traffic in violation of this would not be dropped but would be marked out-of-contract, which is typical of the conditioning behaviors used for the Differentiated Services Assured Forwarding Per-Hop Behavior as described in Section 2.3.4.2.2. For a more detailed example like this, see Chapter 3, Section 3.2.2.4.5.2.

2.2.3.2 RFC 2698: Two Rate Three Color Marker

RFC 2698 [RFC2698] defines another commonly used policer/marker: the "two rate three color marker" (TR-TCM). Similarly to the SR-TCM, the TR-TCM uses two token buckets; however, a noticeable difference between the behaviors is that in the case of the two rate marker, the buckets – denoted in this case as C and P, with burst sizes of CBS and PBS respectively – are filled at different rates. C is filled at the committed information rate (CIR), while P is filled at the peak information rate (PIR), where PIR >= CIR and PBS >= CBS as represented in Figure 2.8.

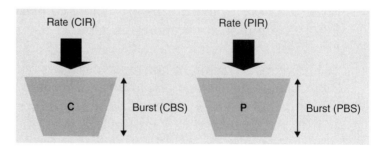

Figure 2.8 RFC 2698: A two rate three color marker

When the TR-TCM is applied to a traffic stream and a packet from that stream arrives:

- The packet size b is compared against the number of tokens currently in bucket P. IF there are fewer tokens in the bucket P than bytes in the packet, then the packet has violated the TR-TCM definition, and neither bucket will be decremented. Using the traffic light scheme, in this case the packet is said to be red.

- ELSE IF there are at least as many tokens in bucket P as bytes in the packet, then the packet is compared against the C bucket. IF there are fewer tokens in the bucket C than bytes in the packet, then the packet has exceeded the C bucket of the TR-TCM definition and the P bucket only is decremented by tokens equal to the number of bytes in the packet. Using the traffic light scheme, in this case the packet is said to be yellow.

- ELSE IF there are at least as many tokens in bucket C as bytes in the packet, then the packet has conformed to the TR-TCM definition and both the C and P buckets are decremented by tokens equal to the number of bytes in the packet. Using the traffic light scheme, in this case the packet is said to be green.

The flowchart in Figure 2.9 shows the operation of the TR-TCM.

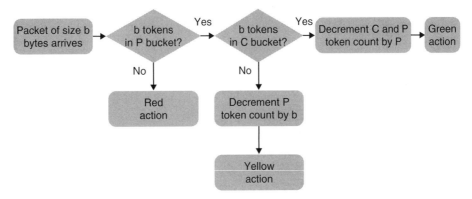

Figure 2.9   RFC 2698: A two rate three color marker (colorblind mode)

As per the SR-TCM, different actions can then be applied, such as transmit, drop, or mark – potentially in combination – depending upon whether the packet has been designated as green, yellow, or red by the TR-TCM.

An example use of the TR-TCM is to mark a certain amount of a traffic class as in-contract, and everything above that as out-of-contract, up to a maximum rate, by applying a green action of transmit (if not pre-marked this could be combined with marking in-contract), yellow action of {transmit + mark out of contract}, and red action of drop. Applied in this way the TR-TCM would enforce a maximum rate of CIR and a burst of CBS on the traffic stream; any traffic in excess would then be marked out-of-contract up to a maximum rate of PIR and a burst of PBS. Although it is possible to have a red action of {transmit + mark}, for the same reasons as discussed for the SR-TCM, in practice it is difficult to understand what meaningful service benefit is offered by differentiating between traffic in terms of in-, out-, and exceedingly-out-of-contract. Hence, in practice the TR-TCM is most commonly used as a "two rate two color marker," i.e. with a red action of drop.

It is noted that if PIR = CIR and PBS = CBS then effectively the output of the marker has only two states, green and red; in this case the effective behavior would be the same as for the simple one rate policer described at the start of Section 2.2.3. Setting PIR < CIR or PBS < CBS may cause unpredictable results, where the same packet may violate the P bucket, i.e. be designated as red, where it would have conformed to the C bucket, i.e. be designated as green.

2.2.3.3 Color-aware Policers

The policing behaviors we have described so far have been color-unaware or "colorblind;" that is, once the packets have been classified into a stream that is being policed, the policer itself applies the policing actions indiscriminately of the packet markings. RFC 2697 and RFC 2698, however, also define "color-aware" modes of operation. When operating in color-aware mode, once the packets have been classified into a stream that is being policed, the policer takes into account any pre-existing markings that may have been set, by a policer at a previous network node for example, when determining the appropriate color-aware policing action for the packet, allowing different actions to be applied depending upon the pre-existing marking.

The RFC 2697 SR-TCM uses exactly the same token bucket definitions in color-aware mode as in colorblind mode. When applied to a traffic stream, the behavior in color-aware mode is as follows:

- IF the packet is pre-colored green and there are at least as many tokens in bucket C as bytes in the packet, then the packet conforms to the C bucket, is designated green and the C bucket only is decremented by tokens equal to the number of bytes in the packet.

- ELSE IF the packet is pre-colored green or yellow and there are at least as many tokens in bucket E as bytes in the packet, then the packet exceeds the C bucket, is designated yellow, and the E bucket only is decremented by tokens equal to the number of bytes in the packet.

- ELSE the packet violates the SR-TCM definition, is designated red and neither bucket will be decremented.

The flowchart in Figure 2.10 shows the operation of the SR-TCM in color-aware mode.

The SR-TCM, when operating in color-aware mode, ensures that packets pre-marked as yellow or red are not accounted against the C bucket and that packets pre-marked red are not accounted against the E bucket.

The RFC 2698 TR-TCM also uses exactly the same token bucket definitions in color-aware mode as in colorblind mode. When applied to a traffic stream, the behavior in color-aware mode is as follows:

- IF the packet is pre-colored red or if there are fewer tokens in the bucket P than bytes in the packet, then the packet violates the TR-TCM definition, is designated red, and neither bucket will be decremented.

- ELSE IF the packet is pre-colored yellow or if there are less tokens in the bucket C than bytes in the packet, then the packet exceeds

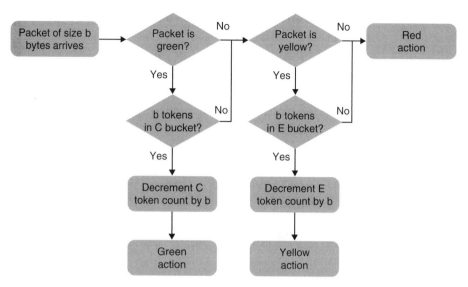

Figure 2.10   RFC 2697: Color-aware single rate three color marker

the C bucket definition, the packet is designated yellow, and the P bucket is decremented by tokens equal to the number of bytes in the packet.

- ELSE the packet conforms to the TR-TCM definition, is designated green, and both the C and P buckets are decremented by tokens equal to the number of bytes in the packet.

The flowchart in Figure 2.11 shows the operation of the TR-TCM in color-aware mode.

Color-aware policers are typically used at trust boundaries, where a downstream node (Node A) is expected to have applied a particular policer definition to condition a traffic stream to adhere to a traffic contract before sending the traffic to an upstream node (Node B). The color-aware policer is applied at Node B to ensure that traffic has been appropriately conditioned by Node A, while also trying to ensure that traffic is no indiscriminately re-marked. If a color-unaware policer was applied both at Node B, then as the policers operate independently, packets determined as green by the policer defined at

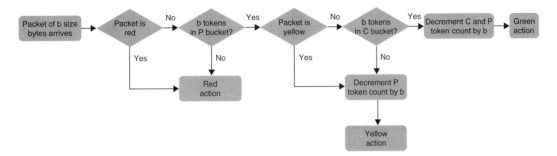

Figure 2.11   RFC 2698: Color-aware two rate three color marker

Node A may be determined to be yellow or red at Node B; similarly packets which A determined as yellow may be determined as green or red at B, and packets which A determined as red may be determined as green or yellow at B. The net effect of this may be that incorrect amounts of traffic are marked as green, yellow, and red, and hence the PIR and CIR commitments may not be met. Using a color-aware policer at Node B in conjunction with a color-unaware policer at Node A will overcome this problem and ensure that at Node B tokens of a particular color are only spent on packets of the same color.

2.2.3.4   Metering

Traffic metering is the process of measuring the rate and burst characteristic of a traffic stream for accounting or measurement purposes. A simple metering function could consist of applying either a single-rate or two-rate policer to a traffic stream, but with green, yellow and red actions all set to transmit; if statistics are maintained for the number of packets and bytes transmitted and dropped then these statistics could be used as a meter of a traffic stream. Alternatively, metering could be performed simply by taking the statistics of packet and bytes transmitted for traffic streams or classes, over a defined time interval; while this approach would provide a means to meter the average rate over the time interval, it would not provide any capability to measure the traffic burst.

2.2.4 Queuing, Scheduling, Shaping, and Dropping

In the most general terms, if the demands placed on any finite resource exceed the resource's ability to service them, contention happens. Scheduling mediates between demands when contention occurs, determining the time or order in which different demands are serviced. www.dictionary.com defines a schedule as *"A list of times of departures and arrivals;"* a scheduler is something that determines a schedule. Scheduling may re-order the demands relative to their arrival times; re-ordering is only possible if unserviced demands are delayed or queued.

In IP QOS terms, when, for example, the arriving traffic demands exceed a link's bandwidth, contention occurs and some of the traffic will need to be delayed or queued before it can be serviced. An IP packet scheduler acts upon the queued packets to determine their departure time (a real-time scheduler) or their departure order (a relative-time scheduler), shuffling packet departures according to rules derived from constraints of rates or priorities. Queues and schedulers are used in conjunction to control queuing delays and give bandwidth assurances to traffic streams.

2.2.4.1 Queuing and Scheduling

Queuing and scheduling in IP QOS has many close analogies in every-day life. Consider a simple example of an airline check-in, where there is single queue and a number of check-in counters, which service the queue in a first-come first-served (FCFS) basis, which is also referred to as first-in first-out (FIFO). The arrival rate at which the passengers turn up, relative to the rate at which the check-in counters are able to service the passengers, determines the length of the queue; arriving passengers start queuing at the "tail" of the queue and are serviced from the "head" of the queue. This is an example of the most basic queuing structure, as shown in Figure 2.12.

Several hours before the plane is due to depart, the rate of arrival of passengers at the check-in is relatively low; most passengers checking in at this time will be serviced straight away. An hour or two before departure, most people are checking in, the arrival rate of

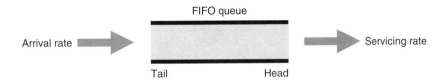

Figure 2.12 FIFO queue

passengers at the check-in is faster than the rate with which they can be serviced and a queue of passengers starts to form. The greater the difference between the arrival rate of the passengers and the servicing rate of the check-in desks, the longer the queue that will form and the greater the potential for delay for passengers in the queue. This case is analogous to a single service class IP network (we refrain from using the term "best-effort" for the reasons described in Section 2.1.2), where packet forwarding is egalitarian; all packets receive the same quality of service, and packets are typically forwarded using a strict FIFO queuing discipline.

If a check-in desk (or desks) is dedicated to business class passengers, which have a dedicated queue, then if the difference between the arrival rate and servicing rate for business class passengers is less than for economy passengers, then the business class queue length should be less than the economy queue and delay at check-in should be less also. Now consider an additional check-in desk and queue dedicated for first class passengers; if the difference between the arrival rate and servicing rate for first class passengers is less than for business passengers, then first class passengers should have even less time to wait. Hence, the queuing delays for the different classes can be managed by controlling the servicing rate (the number of check-in desks) relative to the arrival rate of passengers traveling at that class. The queuing delay for first class passengers could be further minimized by applying a prioritization scheme such that whenever a passenger arrives in the first class queue, they are serviced immediately by whichever check-in counter (economy, business or first class) next finishes servicing a customer. In addition, to make efficient use of resources and ensure that no check-in desks are unnecessarily left empty, if ever a

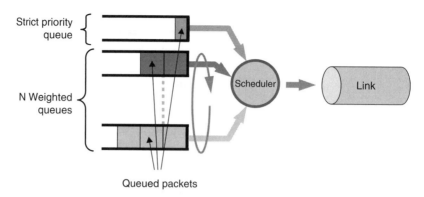

Figure 2.13   Basic IP scheduler

check-in desk (economy, business or first class) has an empty queue, it should next serve a passenger from a non-empty queue.

This airline check-in queuing and servicing scheme is very close to the basic IP scheduler implementations available today. In the same way that an airline check-in desk is a point of aggregation for passengers checking in for a flight, a router may be a point of aggregation for traffic; packets arriving on multiple links may be aggregated onto a single outbound link. Such aggregation can lead to congestion, hence the requirement for queuing and scheduling. Figure 2.13 illustrates the components of a typical basic IP packet scheduler, scheduling packets onto a physical link.

The components of such a scheduler are described in the following sections.

2.2.4.1.1   Priority Scheduling

Typically, most basic IP packet schedulers available today support a queue serviced with a priority scheduler for delay intolerant traffic such as voice and video.

Considered generally, priority scheduling can be either pre-emptive or non-pre-emptive. A pre-emptive priority algorithm would service a priority queue as soon as it becomes active, whereas non-pre-emptive priority algorithm would put the priority queue next on the list of queues to be serviced. In this context, pre-emption could be either at the packet level or at the quantum level. With packet level pre-emption, a non-priority packet currently being scheduled would be pre-empted before it is completely serviced by the scheduler; this approach provides the lowest delay characteristic for the priority queue, but results in bandwidth inefficiencies as the partially sent pre-empted packet needs to be resent in its entirety. With quantum level pre-emption, a non-priority queue currently being scheduled would be pre-empted before its full quanta (which may be a number of packets) has been serviced by the scheduler, but any packet currently being serviced from that queue would be allowed to finish; this approach is bandwidth-efficient, but may result in a higher delay characteristic for the priority queue.

Practical implementations of priority scheduling use quantum level pre-emption, i.e. if the priority queue is active, then the queue will be serviced next after any non-priority packet currently being serviced. This ensures that traffic in the priority queue receives bounded delay and jitter; if a packet arrives in the priority queue and the queue is empty, it should need to wait for at most one packet from another queue, before it is serviced by the scheduler. In practice, the delay impact on the priority queue may be more than just a single packet due to the presence of an interface FIFO queue (as described in Section 2.2.4.1.3).

As the priority queue is serviced with priority above other queues, if the priority queue is constantly active – that is, it always has packets to send – then the other queues may be starved of bandwidth. In order to prevent this from happening, it is common practice to police the traffic entering the priority queue, which enforces a maximum rate for the traffic using that queue. If this maximum rate is less than the available link rate, then there will always be bandwidth available for re-use by the other queues, irrespective of the load in the priority queue. Further, by controlling the offered load for the priority queue, the delay, jitter and loss characteristic for the queue can be bounded.

2.2.4.1.2   Weighted Bandwidth Scheduling

If the priority queue is inactive – that is, there are no packets in the queue – then there are a number of other queues which are each serviced in FIFO order. These queues will generally be serviced in a weighted fashion, where a weighting determines the service offered to one queue relative to another; the weightings effectively determine the share of the link bandwidth to each queue. A scheduling algorithm is used to ensure that the relative servicing between queues is achieved. By controlling the relative differences between the traffic arrival rates and servicing rates (determined by weightings) of different queues, the impact of queuing delays can be controlled and the relative service to those queues can be differentiated.

It is noted that queues can be assigned to discrete traffic flows (as in the case of Integrated Services architecture; see Section 2.3.3) or to traffic classes (as in the case of Differentiated Services architecture; see Section 2.3.4). Due to the scaling challenges of having per flow queues, it is more common to have per-class queues, where a class aggregates a number of flows which have common SLA requirements.

2.2.4.1.2.1 *Weighted Round Robin*   Weighted Round Robin (WRR) is the simplest example of such a weighted bandwidth scheduling algorithm. It is easiest to explain how WRR works by way of an example.

EXAMPLE 1: Weighted Round Robin

Consider a scheduler which has three weighted queues (in addition to any priority queues), denoted as A, B and C with weights of 1, 2 and 4 respectively, as shown in Figure 2.14.

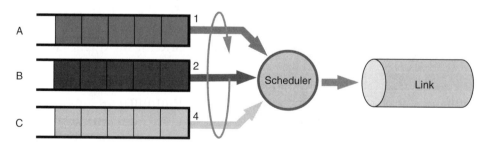

Figure 2.14 WRR scheduling example

In a round of the scheduler, the scheduler visits each queue and services an amount of traffic from that queue determined by the queue's weights. Hence, in this example, in each round, a WRR scheduler would service 1 packet, 2 packets and 4 packets from queues A, B and C respectively. If all queues were permanently full (i.e. their arrival rates constantly exceeded their servicing rates), the scheduling order would be A, B, B, C, C, C, C, A, B, B, C, C, C, C, A . . .

In the above example, the weighting of service between the queues is defined in terms of packets. If all packets in the different queues are the same size, then the allocation of the available link bandwidth is also weighted between the queues in the same proportion. In this case, if the link bandwidth was 512 kbps, queue A would be allocated $1/(1 + 2 + 4) * 512 = {\sim}73$ kbps, queue B would be allocated $2/(1 + 2 + 4) * 512 = {\sim}146$ kbps, and queue C would be allocated $4/(1 + 2 + 4) * 512 = {\sim}293$ kbps. In percentage terms, the link bandwidth has therefore been allocated with approximately 14% to queue A, 29% to queue B and 57% to queue C. Hence, the scheduler is providing these minimum bandwidth assurances for the queues; they are minimum bandwidth assurances as irrespective of the traffic load (but in this particular case not irrespective of packet sizes as we shall see shortly) in the other queues, each queue will be assured its respective bandwidth allocation at a minimum. Depending upon their particular equipment implementation, some vendors require that queues are configured by their relative weights, others allow configuration in terms of absolute (e.g. kbps) or relative percentage minimum bandwidth assurances, which are then converted to weights in order to program the scheduler.

In a WRR scheduler if any queues are inactive, then the scheduler moves on to the next queue and hence the unused bandwidth for the inactive queues is redistributed between the active queues in proportion to their relative weightings, i.e. in proportion to the queues' minimum bandwidth assurances. If queue B in the previous example was inactive, then the 146 kbps minimum bandwidth assurance for queue B would be redistributed between queue A and queue C in proportion to their weightings, i.e. in ratio 1:4. Hence queue A would now be allocated $73 + (146 * 1/5) = {\sim}102$ kbps and queue B would be allocated 292 + (146 * 4/5) = ~410 kbps. Schedulers that exhibit this characteristic – allowing unused bandwidth to be re-used by active queues – are called "work conserving" schedulers – they are only idle when there are no packets to send in any queues; most IP schedulers implemented today are work-conserving schedulers. In the preceding example, unused bandwidth is reallocated in proportion to the minimum bandwidth assurances of the active queues; some more advanced scheduler implementations support additional parameters, which allow the redistribution of unused bandwidth to be configured independently of the minimum bandwidth for the queue [CISCO].

A measure of the effectiveness of an IP scheduler is how closely the scheduler achieves the intended bandwidth allocation; this is referred to as the "fairness" of the scheduler. In the preceding example, WRR is fair as long as the packet sizes in the different queues are the same, and when considered over a complete round of the scheduler. If the average packets sizes in the different queues are the same, then WRR will be fair on average. If the average packet sizes of the different queues are not the same, then the scheduler could potentially normalize the weights of the queues according to the average packet size of each queue.

EXAMPLE 2: Weighted Round Robin

Continuing from the previous example, assume that queues A, B, and C have average packet sizes of 64 bytes, 1500 bytes and 300 bytes respectively and that the link is 512 kbps. With the weightings previously used the queue bandwidth allocations would be:

Queue A: 512 * (1 * 64)/((1 * 64) + (2 * 1500) + (4 * 300)) = ~8 kbps

Queue B: 512 * (2 * 1500)/((1 * 64) + (2 * 1500) + (4 * 300)) = ~360 kbps

Queue C: 512 * (4 * 300)/((1 * 64) + (2 * 1500) + (4 * 30)) = ~144 kbps

If the intended relative bandwidth allocation between the queues is 1:2:4, then this is clearly far from fair!

Normalizing each queue's weight by the average packet size for that queue, and expressing as an integer would give the following queue weightings:

Queue A: weight $= 1/64 = 15 \times 10^{-3} \rightarrow$ weight $= 150$

Queue B: weight $= 2/1500 = 1.3 \times 10^{-3} \rightarrow$ weight $= 13$

Queue A: weight $= 4/300 = 13 \times 10^{-3} \rightarrow$ weight $= 130$

In practice, however, the average packet size in a queue may be difficult to estimate, and may vary over time. In these cases, the limitations of a simple WRR scheduler may be exposed as unfairness where some queues do not get their desired bandwidth allocation.

More advanced schedulers are able to overcome this issue, and some can be fair over time periods of less than a round of the scheduler. Fairness is measured by comparing the scheduler behavior against an idealized Generalized Process Sharing (GPS) scheme [KLEINROCK]. A GPS scheduler services an infinitesimally small amount from each queue on each round of the scheduler; hence, it visits all of the active queues in any finite time interval and therefore is fair in any time interval. Queues can have defined weights, and will receive service proportional to this weight whenever they have data in the queue.

A GPS scheduler is idealized in that it assumes that queues can be serviced in infinitesimally small amounts. This is clearly not possible in practice and for IP schedulers; the smallest unit that can be serviced from a queue is a single packet; in the timescale it takes to service a single packet, the scheduler must be unfair to other queues. Hence, no packet scheduler can be as fair as GPS, and in the following two sections we consider two practical scheduler implementations that are commonly used today and which aim to emulate a GPS scheme.

2.2.4.1.2.2 Weighted Fair Queuing Weighted fair queuing (WFQ) [DEMERS] computes the time that a packet would finish being serviced if it was being serviced using a GPS scheme; it then services packets in the order of their finish time, which in effect becomes a sequence number. WFQ is effectively the packet-based version of GPS.

Consider the following example.

EXAMPLE 3: Weighted Fair Queuing

Consider a scheduler that has three weighted queues (in addition to any priority queues): A, B, and C with desired relative bandwidth allocations of 1:2:4 (or 14%, 29%, and 57%) respectively. Assume that queues A, B, and C are permanently full and have packet sizes of 64 bytes, 1500 bytes, and 300 bytes respectively and that the link is 512 kbps. Consider packets arrive back-to-back in the order A1, A2, B1, C1, C2, C3, . . . faster than the scheduler can service the first packet.

In order to determine the servicing time of packets, a WFQ scheduler keeps track of a variable called the round number. If you considered a GPS scheduler servicing each queue byte-by-byte rather than in infinitesimally small amounts, the round number represents the number of complete rounds of byte-by-byte service that the WFQ scheduler has completed.

When a packet arrives at a previously inactive queue, its servicing time (i.e. sequence number) is calculated by taking the current round time and adding the size of the packet multiplied by the queue's weight; consequently with WFQ the bandwidth share of a queue is inversely proportional to that queue's weight. In this case, to achieve the desired bandwidth share of 1:2:4, weights of 4, 2, and 1 are allocated to queues A, B, and C respectively. With WFQ, whether a queue is active can be determined by whether there are any packets in the queue that have a sequence number greater than the current round number. When a packet arrives at an active queue, its sequence number is calculated by adding the size of the arriving packet multiplied by the queue's weight to the highest sequence number of packets already in the queue.

Consider the current round number is 0:

- Packet A1 arrives; the sequence number for the packet is calculated as $0 + 64 * 4 = 256$

- Packet A2 arrives and, as the queue is active, the sequence number for the packet is calculated as $256 + 64 * 4 = 512$

- Packet B1 arrives and, as the queue is inactive, the sequence number for the packet is calculated as $0 + 1500 * 2 = 3000$

- Packet C1 arrives and because the queue is inactive, the sequence number for the packet is calculated as $0 + 300 * 1 = 300$

- Packet C2 arrives and, as the queue is active, the sequence number for the packet is calculated as $300 + 300 * 1 = 600$

- Packet C3 arrives and, as the queue is active, the sequence number for the packet is calculated as $600 + 300 * 1 = 900$.

The scheduler services the packet with the lowest sequence number first, and updates the round to be the equal to the sequence number of that packet. If we compare the sequence numbers of the received packets in this case, we can see that the packets received in order A1, A2, B1, C1, C2, C3, are sent in order A1, C1, A2, C2, C3, B1.

2.2.4.1.2.3 Deficit Round Robin   Deficit Round Robin (DRR) [SHREE-DHAR] modifies WRR such that it can be fair without knowing the average packet sizes of packets in particular queues. This is achieved by keeping track of a deficit counter for each queue. A DRR scheduler visits each queue in a round and aims to service a weight or quantum's worth from each queue. Unlike WRR, the quantum is defined in bytes rather than in packets. When it is a queue's turn to be serviced, the scheduler will attempt to service a complete quantum from the queue. In practice, it is unlikely that the quantum will exactly equal the size of the next packet, or the next few packets at the front of the queue. In this case as many whole packets will be serviced from the front of the queue as can be accommodated by the quantum; if the first packet is greater than the available quantum, then no packets will be serviced from that queue in that round. If there are more packets in the queue than can be accommodated by the quantum, any unused quantum for the queue on that round of the scheduler will be carried forward to the next round, else the deficit counter is reset. In this way, queues which did not get their fair share in one round receive recompense on the next round. Consider the following example.

EXAMPLE 4: Deficit Round Robin

Consider a scheduler, which has three weighted queues (in addition to any priority queues): A, B, and C, which have desired relative bandwidth allocations of 1:2:4 (or 14%, 29%, and 57%) respectively and have quanta of 100, 200, and 400 accordingly. Assume that queues A, B, and C are permanently full and have packet sizes of 64 bytes, 1500 bytes, and 300 bytes respectively and that the link is 512 kbps.

All of the queue deficit counters are initially set to zero. On the first round of the scheduler, the quantum for queue A is 100, and the packets are 64 bytes, so there is sufficient quantum to service one complete packet. As there are more packets in queue A, the remaining quanta will be carried forward as a deficit to the next round; in this case, the deficit counter for queue A will be 100 − 64 = 36 bytes. This will be added to the queue quantum on the next round of the scheduler.

On the first round, after queue A the DRR scheduler next looks at queue B; the quantum for the queue is 200 and the packets are 1500 bytes, so there is insufficient quantum to service any packets and the remaining quantum will be carried forward as a deficit to the next round; in this case the deficit counter for queue B will be 200 bytes. The deficit counter for queue B will continue to increase until round 8, when the deficit counter + quantum will equal 1600 bytes and hence a single 1500-byte packet will be serviced. As there are more 1500-byte packets in the queue, the deficit counter will be set to 1600 − 1500 = 100 bytes and carried forward to round 9.

On the first round, after queue B the DRR scheduler next looks at queue C; the quantum for the queue is 400, and the packets are 300 bytes, so there is sufficient quantum to service one complete packet. As there are more packets in queue C, the remaining quantum will be carried forward as a deficit to the next round; in this case, the deficit counter for queue C will be 400 − 300 = 100 bytes. This will be added to the queue quantum on the next round of the scheduler.

The table in Figure 2.15 shows the status of the queues, in terms of quantum packets sent and deficit, at each round of the scheduler.

Queue		Round 1	Round 2	Round 3	Round 4	Round 5	Round 6	Round 7	Round 8
A	Quantum	100	136	108	144	116	152	124	100
	Pkts sent	1 * 64B {A1}	2 * 64B {A2, A3}	1 * 64B {A4}	2 * 64B {A5, A6}	1 * 64B {A7}	2 * 64B {A8, A9}	2 * 64B {A10, A11}	1 * 64B {A12}
	Deficit	36	8	44	16	52	24	0	36
B	Quantum	200	400	600	800	1000	1200	1400	1600
	Pkts sent	0	0	0	0	0	0	0	1 * 1500B {B1}
	Deficit	200	400	600	800	1000	1200	1400	100
C	Quantum	400	500	600	400	500	600	400	500
	Pkts sent	1 * 300B {C1}	1 * 300B {C2}	2 * 300B {C3, C4}	1 * 300B {C5}	1 * 300B {C6}	2 * 300B {C7, C8}	1 * 300B {C9}	1 * 300B {C10}
	Deficit	100	200	0	100	200	0	100	200

Figure 2.15 Example: DRR queue status (shaded cell indicates packet dequeued)

Over the 8 rounds of the scheduler, the total number of bytes allocated to each queue is as follows:

$$\text{Queue A: } 12 * 64 = 768$$

$$\text{Queue B: } 1 * 1500 = 1500$$

$$\text{Queue C: } 10 * 300 = 3000$$

If we add on the value of the deficit counter, we can determine the effective relative bandwidth allocation to each queue over the 8 rounds:

$$\text{Queue A: } = (768 + 36)/((768 + 36) + (1500 + 100) + (3000 + 200)) = {\sim}14\%$$

$$\text{Queue B: } = (1500 + 100)/((768 + 36) + (1500 + 100) + (3000 + 200)) = {\sim}29\%$$

$$\text{Queue C: } = (3000 + 200)/((768 + 36) + (1500 + 100) + (3000 + 200)) = {\sim}57\%$$

Hence, we can see that the DRR demonstrates fairness irrespective of the packet sizes, albeit possibly over a number of rounds of the scheduler; the more rounds it is considered over, the more fair it becomes, as the outstanding deficit counter (which represents bytes not yet sent on that queue) has proportionally less impact.

2.2.4.1.2.4 Which Scheduling Algorithm?   There are a number of characteristics which can be used to differentiate between scheduling algorithms, and which impact where they are used:

- *Fairness.* As previously described, the fairness of a scheduler is a measure of how closely the scheduler achieves the intended bandwidth allocation. Clearly, fairness is a desirable characteristic of any scheduler. Hence why DRR and WFQ are preferred IP packet scheduling algorithms to WRR, which will only provide a fair bandwidth allocation between queues if the packet sizes in the different queues are the same, which will generally not be the case.

- *Worst-case delay bounds.* Some scheduler implementations may attempt to support traffic which has low delay requirements from a weighted bandwidth queue, which is serviced using a scheduling algorithm such as WRR or WFQ. Different scheduling algorithms acting on the same set of queues would result in different packet dequeue orders, even when they may be configured to produce the same desired bandwidth allocation. Consequently, the worst-case delay bounds for a particular queue will depend upon the scheduling algorithm used and may also be dependent upon the number of queues used in the particular implementation. Further, for some scheduling algorithms, the weighting applied to the queue may need to be artificially inflated in order to reduce the worst-case delay bound by increasing the effective queue scheduling rate. By inflating the bandwidth of one class, the relative share of bandwidth available to the other classes may decrease, which can result in coarser relative granularity of bandwidth allocation to the other classes. Hence, it may be a desirable scheduler characteristic that the worst-case delay bound for a particular queue is as low as possible.

  In practical deployments, however, traffic which has low delay requirements is most commonly serviced using a strict priority queue rather than a weighted bandwidth queue. Hence, if a particular weighted bandwidth scheduler implementation is augmented with priority queues for low-delay traffic, the worst-case delay bound characteristic for the weighted bandwidth queues may not be critical when choosing the scheduling algorithm used for the weighted bandwidth queues.

- *Simplicity.* From a platform implementation perspective, there are benefits in an algorithm which is simple to implement; the fewer cycles and less state needed to implement a particular algorithm, the less processing power and memory required and hence the easier it is to scale and the lower the cost impact on the platform. DRR is less computationally intensive and simpler to implement than WFQ, and hence is generally preferred where a high degree of platform scalability is required, either for high-speed links or for a large number of lower-speed connections.

Although there are other scheduling algorithms used in IP networks, we have described those which are by far the most widely implemented together with the key characteristics which determine where the different algorithms are used. For a more detailed understanding of scheduling theory, see [KESHAV].

2.2.4.1.3   Interface FIFO

For most practical router implementations, the scheduler will not actually schedule queues directly onto the physical link, but rather will service its queues into the queue of the hardware line driver on the outgoing interface; this queue is designed to provide buffering before the hardware line driver allowing the line driver to maximize interface throughput. This queue is a FIFO queue, which is variously known as the interface FIFO or transmit ring buffer (tx-ring for short) and which is shown in Figure 2.16.

If the scheduler can dequeue packets into the interface FIFO faster than they can be serviced (i.e. faster that the link rate) then the transmit ring buffer may start to fill. It is common to implement a flow control mechanism to ensure that the interface FIFO does not continue to fill uncontrollably, but rather when the number of queued packets in the interface FIFO exceeds a defined threshold the flow control will stop the scheduler dequeuing any more packets (this is known as a

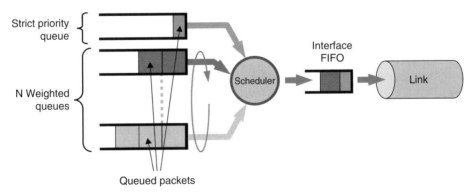

Figure 2.16 Interface FIFO

"flow off"). When the number of packets queued in the interface FIFO buffer falls below a threshold (which must be equal to or lower than the flow-off threshold) the flow control mechanism allows the scheduler to send more packets into the interface FIFO again (this is known as a "flow on"). This type of flow control is sometimes referred to as "back pressure" exerted from the interface FIFO to the scheduler. Therefore packets dequeued by the scheduler may be enqueued behind packets already in the interface FIFO. Even a priority packet can at best be enqueued at the tail of the interface FIFO and consequently the interface FIFO size can impact the queuing delays of all of the scheduler's queues; hence it is important that the size of the interface FIFO is not unnecessarily large.

The impact of even a reasonably sized interface FIFO on the delay of the priority queue can be significant on low-speed access links; optimally it would be tuned to 1-to-2 MTUs, where one packet is being clocked onto the link, while another packet is being enqueued in parallel into the interface FIFO. If the perturbing delay introduced by the interface FIFO exceeds the delay target for traffic in the priority queue, then link level fragmentation and interleaving mechanisms may be required, as described in Section 2.2.5. At higher speeds, i.e. for core network links, the delay impact of a reasonably sized interface FIFO will generally be negligible.

2.2.4.1.4   Advanced Concepts in Scheduling: Multi-level Strict Priority

Whilst the IP scheduler depicted in Figure 2.13 represents the de facto implementation found today, some more advanced implementations are adding support for more than one priority queue. The demand driving this requirement is the concurrent support of voice and video services. As described in Chapter 1, voice services generally have tighter network delay requirements than streaming video services, although the video services still require a delay-bounded service. In addition, video streaming applications often use large sized packets for bandwidth efficiency. Some vendors have implementations that allow multiple subsets of traffic within a class queue to be discretely policed, but to be serviced from the same queue; such implementations may limit the worst-case impact that the streams of traffic have on each other, but there will be an impact nonetheless. Hence, if voice and video are serviced from the same priority queue, large video packets can increase the worst-case delay experienced by the voice traffic; this effect can be significant on low-speed links.

In an alternative deployment approach, using the same scheduler, one of the weighted bandwidth queues could be used to support the video traffic. In this case, as described in Section 2.2.4.1.2.4, the delay bound that the video traffic will experience may vary depending upon the scheduler used, may also be dependent upon the number of other weighted bandwidth queues used in the particular implementation and the traffic in those queues, and at low-link speeds it may not be possible to achieve the required delay targets. Further, for some scheduling algorithms, the weighting applied to the queue may need to be artificially inflated in order to reduce the worst-case delay bound. By inflating the bandwidth of one class, the relative share of bandwidth available to the other classes decreases, which can result in coarser relative granularity of bandwidth allocation to the other classes.

In order to overcome these issues, some more advanced scheduler implementations provide support for more than one priority queue as shown in Figure 2.17.

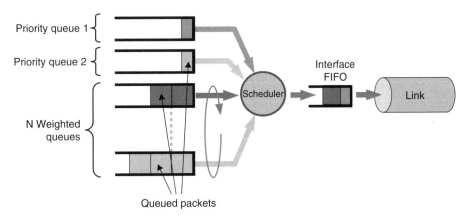

Figure 2.17   Multi-priority queue scheduler

The priority queue with the highest priority is serviced at line rate as soon as it becomes active; once this queue has been serviced, the second priority queue is serviced next. Finally, after the second priority queue, weighted bandwidth queues are serviced. When supporting voice and video, for example, using the highest priority queue for voice traffic, and the next priority queue for video traffic would enable the voice traffic to receive the lowest delay and jitter, while the video traffic would have a bounded delay and jitter, independent of the configuration and load of the weighted bandwidth queues. With multi-priority scheduler implementations such as this, the delay and jitter for the traffic at both levels of priority can be bounded and hence both levels of priority queue are compliant with the Differentiated Services (Diffserv) expedited forwarding (EF) per-hop behavior (PHB) definition, as described in Section 2.3.4.2.1.

While multi-priority queue scheduler implementations are currently the exception, they may become the norm as concurrent support for voice, video, and data services on IP networks becomes more widespread.

2.2.4.2 Dropping

At this point, before considering dropping, it is worth highlighting the difference between buffers and queues. Buffers are the physical memory locations where packets are temporarily stored while they are waiting to be transmitted. Queues on the other hand do not contain packets although it is common parlance to refer to "packets in a queue;" rather, a queue consists of an ordered set of pointers to the locations in buffer memory where packets in that particular queue are actually stored. Fast buffer memory is often an expensive component of a router implementation and hence buffer memory may be shared across all queues for more efficient buffer memory usage, rather than rigidly partitioned between queues. Buffer memory may also be organized in fixed sized chunks (which may be known as particles), which are typically 256–512 bytes, in order to facilitate fast memory lookups while making efficient use of buffer memory. For example, if a system used 256-byte particles, a 576-byte packet would consume three particles of buffer memory.

Considering the scheduler shown in Figure 2.13, if the traffic arrival rate continually exceeds the available link bandwidth, then the number of packets in at least one of the queues must continually increase. As the buffer memory used to queue packets must be finite, at some point, the queue's depth must exceed the available buffer memory, and inevitably packets must be dropped. It is important that routers have sufficient buffer memory to be able to buffer packets being queued in accordance with the configured Diffserv policy; buffer memory starvation can lead to "no buffer" packet drops that occur indiscriminately of class, resulting in violation of the class SLA commitments. Applying limits on the depths of queues has a consequent limiting impact on buffer memory usage.

While limiting buffer memory usage is one reason to drop a packet, in practice today's router platforms generally have sufficient memory that it is not the constraining factor on queues' depths. The main reasons to limit or manage the depth of a queue are either to bound the delay experienced by packets in the queue, or in an attempt to optimize the throughput achieved for traffic in the queue; different dropping techniques are applied depending upon the aim.

2.2.4.2.1   Tail Drop

A "tail drop" mechanism is used to place a hard limit on the number of packets that can be held in a queue. Before a packet is to be enqueued at the tail of a queue, the current depth of packets in the queue is checked and if the depth of the queue exceeds the maximum limit for the queue, which is normally specified in bytes, then the packet will be dropped rather than enqueued. We can consider that the probability of the packet being dropped on enqueue to that queue is zero while the queue depth is less than the tail drop queue limit, q_{limit}, but when the queue limit is reached the probability of being dropped is 100%, as shown in the drop probability graph in Figure 2.18.

Setting the maximum queue limit for a queue can be used to enforce a maximum delay bound on the traffic in the queue. Why might we want to set such a delay bound on a queue? Is it not better to send a packet if we possibly can, rather than to drop it? The answer to these questions depends upon the application. If we return to the

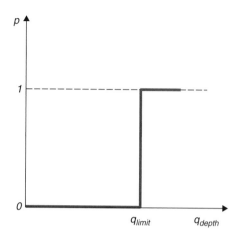

Figure 2.18 Tail drop

airline check-in analogy we introduced in Section 2.2.4.1, if the queue at check-in becomes too long, then the queuing delay may exceed the time to wait before the actual departure of the plane, in this case, there is no point in the passenger queuing as they will miss their plane. Similarly, with some applications such as VoIP, if a packet is delayed too much, it will be of no use and it is better to drop it rather than to consume bandwidth across the network and be dropped at the destination. Section 3.2.2.1.1 in Chapter 3 gives an example delay budget for VoIP, which determines a maximum acceptable delay at each hop in the network. Dropping can be considered the most extreme case of delay; that is, a packet that is infinitely delayed never arrives, and for all intents and purposes can be considered lost or dropped.

If the servicing rate of a queue is known, and the maximum size of the queue is also known, then the worst-case delay bound for a packet in the queue can be determined. If, for example, the servicing rate for a queue is 2 Mbps, and the maximum queue limit for the queue is 4 kilobytes, then the worst-case delay bound for a packet that is enqueued in the queue will be approximately 4096 * 8/2048000 = ~16 ms. Hence, if it is determined that the maximum per-hop delay that an application can sustain is 16 ms, then this may be an appropriate maximum queue depth setting. In practice, however, this is a simpli-fied example, and there may be delays other than just the queuing delay which need to be taken into account and a more thorough analysis of these delays is provided in Chapter 3, Section 3.2.2.4.1.

Head drop (also known as "drop from the front" or DFF) is a possi-ble alternative to tail drop; with head drop packets are dropped from the head of the queue rather than from the tail, when the depth of the queue exceeds the configured maximum limit for the queue. Lakshman et al. [LAKSHMAN] have shown that head drop improves the performance of TCP by allowing the congestion indication signal to reach the sender faster than waiting for the full queue to be trans-mitted first. Head drop, however, has mostly been a subject of aca-demic research and is not generally supported by router vendor's implementations, hence we do not consider it further.

2.2.4.2.2   Weighted Tail Drop

Some queuing implementations support more that one queue limit within a queue; this is sometimes known as "weighted tail drop." The concept behind this is that if there is congestion in the queue – that is, the traffic arrival rate R_a for the queue exceeds the servicing rate R_s – and the queue depth starts to build, then some subset of the traffic in the queue will be preferentially discarded; the arrival rate of the traffic which will be preferentially discarded is R_{a1}, and the remainder is R_{a2}, such that $R_a = R_{a1} + R_{a2}$. The traffic that is to be preferentially discarded may be classified by a different marking from the remainder of the traffic; the traffic may have been differen-tially marked as in- and out-of-contract using a policer as described in Section 2.2.3. The preferential discard is achieved by applying a lower queue limit q_{limit1} to the subset of traffic which is to be dis-carded first than for the remainder, which has a queue limit q_{limit2}. If the arrival rate for the remainder of the traffic R_{a2} is less than the servicing rate of the queue R_s, and the burst of the remainder of the traffic is less than the difference between the two queue limits $(q_{limit2} - q_{limit1})$, then in congestion of the queue, only traffic from the subset to be preferentially discarded will be dropped. This scheme is illustrated by the drop probability graph in Figure 2.19.

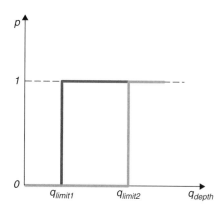

Figure 2.19 Weighted tail-drop

2.2.4.2.3   Random Early Detection

Random early detection (RED) [FLOYD1] is an active queue management (AQM) mechanism. AQM mechanisms detect congestion before queues overflow (i.e. before tail drop is invoked), and provide feedback of this congestion to the end-systems with the aim of avoiding excess packet loss due to congestion and maintaining high network throughput while minimizing queuing delays. Hence, AQM mechanisms are also known as "congestion avoidance" techniques. RED was originally designed as an algorithm aimed at improving throughput for TCP-based sessions, by aiming to prevent the observed behavior of "global synchronization" [DORAN] between TCP sessions. Global synchronization is a behavior which can occur where TCP sessions are aggregated on a single connection (or queue); when congestion occurs, the queue limit is exceeded, causing packet drops across multiple TCP sessions. Due to the adaptive nature of TCP (see Chapter 1, Section 1.3.3.1), on realizing that packets have been dropped the impacted sessions react by each slowing their rate of sending, hence the congestion abates and the effective aggregate throughput drops below line rate. As there is no congestion there are no packets dropped and the sessions then all increase their rate of sending until congestion occurs again and the cycle repeats, potentially creating a sawtooth aggregate throughput characteristic, as illustrated in Figure 2.20.

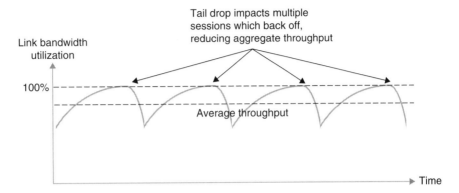

Figure 2.20   TCP "global synchronization"

RED aims to try and break TCP global synchronization by keeping track of the average depth of the queue and using it as an indication of when congestion is approaching; the average queue depth is tracked rather than the actual queue depth, which is used in tail drop, in order to accommodate the bursty nature of TCP. This indication of congestion is fed back to the end-systems by randomly discarding packets from individual sessions as the average queue depth increases, rather than dropping packets across all sessions. The aim of this approach is to cause individual sessions to back off in order to reduce the aggregate throughput in a controlled manner such that a higher aggregate throughput is maintained on average.

RED makes a drop decision prior to enqueuing a packet into a queue based upon the current average queue depth of that queue and a set of four parameters, which are configurable in most implementations:

- The average queue (q_{avg}) depth is calculated using the following formula:

$$q_{avg} = q_{avg\_old} \times \left(1 - \frac{1}{2^w}\right) + \left(q_{current} \times \frac{1}{2^w}\right)$$

where:

q_{avg_old} = the previously calculated average queue depth

$q_{current}$ = the current (not averaged) queue depth

w = the exponential weighting constant

RED uses an exponential weighted moving average; the exponential weighting constant (w, which is normally configurable) determines how closely the average queue depth tracks the actual queue depth; the lower w the more closely the average queue depth tracks the actual queue depth, i.e. the more sensitive the RED drop behavior is to traffic bursts.

- If the current average queue depth (q_{avg}) is below a configurable minimum threshold (q_{minth}), the packet is enqueued.

- If the current average queue depth (q_{avg}) is above a defined maximum threshold (q_{maxth}) then the packet is always dropped; this is referred to as a "forced drop."

- If the current average queue depth (q_{avg}) is above q_{minth} and below q_{maxth}, the packet may be dropped with an increasing, but randomized, probability; this is referred to as a "random drop" and the probability of a random drop (p) is determined by the following formula:

$$p = \left(\frac{q_{avg} - q_{minth}}{q_{maxth} - q_{minth}} \right) \times P_{max} \times RAND(1)$$

where p_{max} is the probability of packet loss at q_{maxth}, which impacts how quickly the probability of the packet being dropped increases between q_{minth} and q_{maxth}.

The RED dropping behavior is illustrated by the drop probability graph in Figure 2.21, where the specific parameters chosen define a particular RED drop profile.

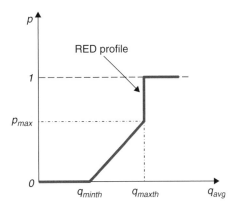

Figure 2.21   Random early detection drop profile

An enhancement to RED was proposed in "Red-Light" [JACOBSON] and is used in some implementations; RED-LIGHT does not have the concept of a configurable exponential weighting constant. Further enhancements to RED have been proposed in [FLOYD2].

The widespread use of RED was advocated in [RFC2309]; however, the benefit of RED is difficult to quantify in practice. AQM has been a favored subject in academic research and some research has recommended against the deployment of RED [MAY]. There have also been a number of new algorithms proposed for AQM; in [BITORIKA] they note that more than 50 new algorithms were proposed between 1999 and 2003 alone. In practice, none of these schemes have been widely implemented today and RED remains the most widely supported AQM algorithm implemented by router vendors, and most widely implemented in networks. In the authors' experience, with appropriate tuning (see Chapter 3, Section 3.4), RED is not generally worse than tail drop; however, the claims of both its benefits and its disadvantages appear to have been overstated.

RED was designed for TCP and as such is used for queues that carry TCP applications. RED is not intended for use with inelastic applications such as VoIP or video, which commonly use UDP as these applications cannot adapt to RED drops. Further, with applications such as voice or video, it is generally preferable to have a bounded worst-case delay for the queue enforced with a firm queue limit. With

RED, however, the maximum queue depth is dependent upon the maximum threshold and current average-queue depth, hence the actual maximum queue depth may be significantly greater than the maximum threshold and the worst-case queuing delay bound may not be easily determined. There are some elastic applications that use UDP rather than TCP, such as the Trivial File Transfer Protocol (TFTP) for example. UDP does not have any implicit reliability or flow control mechanisms built in, hence if they are required they need to be built into the application implementation. For applications such as these detailed knowledge of the specific application implementation is required in order to understand what impact RED would have on them; however, in general the performance with RED should not be significantly worse than with tail drop.

2.2.4.2.4   Weighted Random Early Detection

Weighted RED (WRED) extends the basic concept of RED, by allowing a number of different RED profiles to be used for the same queue, where each profile may be applied to a different subset of the traffic destined for the queue. The concept is very similar to weighted tail drop, in that if there is congestion in the queue, then some subset of the traffic in the queue will be preferentially discarded; this is achieved by having a more aggressive WRED profile (lower q_{minth} and q_{maxth} settings) for the traffic that will be discarded first. The traffic that is to be preferentially discarded may for example be identified using a different marking from the remainder of the traffic; the traffic may have been differentially marked as in- and out-of-contract using a policer as described in Section 2.2.3. The WRED dropping behavior is illustrated by the drop probability graph in Figure 2.22.

2.2.4.2.5   Advanced Concepts in Dropping

A new breed of dropping algorithms has been defined [PAN1, PAN2], which combine FIFO packet scheduling with differential dropping on packet enqueue and are claimed to be capable of approximating a variety of bandwidth allocation and control behaviors including those traditionally supported by scheduling algorithms. Although such mechanisms have yet to be generally implemented or deployed,

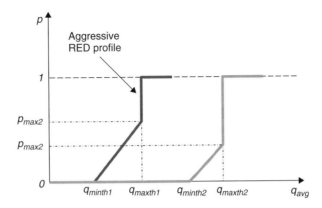

Figure 2.22 Weighted random early detection drop profile

they potentially offer the benefit of scheduling-like bandwidth allocation behaviors with lower complexity implementations.

2.2.4.3 Shaping

Shaping, like policing, is a mechanism which can be used to ensure that a traffic stream does not exceed a defined maximum rate. Also like policing, a shaper can be visualized as a token bucket mechanism like that shown in Figure 2.4, with a defined maximum depth (normally in bytes), known as the burst B, and a defined rate R (normally in bps) at which the bucket is filled with byte-sized tokens. Depending upon the particular shaper implementation, tokens are added to the bucket either every time a packet is processed by the shaper, or at regular intervals, up to a maximum number of tokens that can be in the bucket, defined by B. The minimum number of tokens in the bucket is zero.

The difference between a shaper and a policer becomes apparent when considering what happens when a shaper is applied to a traffic stream. When a packet from that stream arrives, the packet size b is compared against the number of tokens currently in the bucket. If there are at least as many byte tokens in the bucket as there are bytes in the packet, then the packet is transmitted without delay. If there are fewer tokens in the bucket than bytes in the packet, then the packet is delayed (i.e. queued, hence shapers are implicitly used in conjunction with queues) until there are sufficient tokens in the bucket; when there are sufficient tokens in the bucket, the packet is sent and the bucket is decremented by a number of tokens equal to the number of bytes in the packet. In this respect a shaper is significantly different from a policer, which acts to drop or mark non-conformant traffic rather than to delay; a policer can be thought of as a special case of a shaper with a queue with a maximum queue length of zero packets. Hence, while policing acts to cut the peaks off bursty traffic, shaping acts to smooth the traffic profile by delaying the peaks.

It is noted that not all shapers need be implemented with a token bucket mechanism. Another mechanism that is used for shaping is the leaky bucket; leaky buckets and token buckets are often confused but have significant and fundamental differences. With a leaky bucket algorithm, it can be visualized that packets – rather than tokens – are stored in the bucket; arriving packets are placed in a bucket which effectively has a hole in the bottom. The depth of the leaky bucket, B, determines the maximum number of packets that can be queued in the bucket (in effect the same as a queue limit applied to the queue that the bucket represents); if a packet arrives when the bucket is already full, the packet is dropped. Packets drain from the hole in the bucket (i.e. they are transmitted) at a constant rate R, thus smoothing traffic bursts. The best known example of a leaky bucket algorithm is the Generic Cell Rate Algorithm (GCRA) used in traffic shaping of ATM networks [GCRA].

Real-time schedulers, which determine packet dequeue times rather than relative dequeue orders, can also be used to shape traffic streams; such schedulers are non–work-conserving, in that they can be idle (i.e. not sending traffic) even when there is traffic to send, in order to shape the traffic stream. Most practical IP shaping implementations today, however, are based upon token bucket mechanisms. It is noted that while there are standardized definitions of shapers for ATM, and for FR, there are no such standardized definitions for IP.

A shaper can be applied to enforce a maximum rate across all traffic on a physical or logical interface as shown in Figure 2.23.

This could be used to offer a subrate service, for example, where a customer buys a service to provide connectivity to a site from a service provider which defines an aggregate committed rate (i.e. across all classes) for the access connection. The service provider could enforce this service at the edge of their network, either by provisioning the

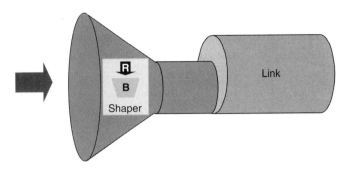

Figure 2.23 Aggregate shaper

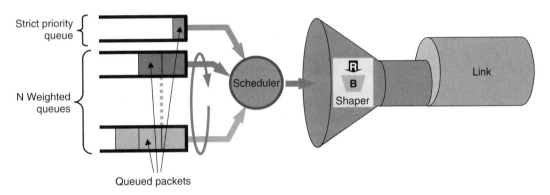

Figure 2.24 Aggregate shaper with class scheduler

access link to the contracted rate, or alternatively by provisioning a higher rate access link and shaping the traffic on the link to the contracted per-customer aggregate rate, which would be sub the line rate; in this way the shaper can acts as an artificial bottleneck, limiting the customer's traffic.

Alternatively, a shaper can be applied to enforce a maximum rate for an individual class of traffic, in which case the delayed traffic will be queuing in the queue for that class. A shaper could also be applied to an aggregate traffic stream which comprises a number of classes; in this case, it is important that a shaper is combined with a scheduler, as shown in Figure 2.24. Such that if the aggregate rate of the traffic exceeds the shaped rate, traffic is delayed in queues per-class, and the scheduler defines the order in which those queues are serviced at the shaped rate, assuring differentiation between different traffic classes.

The example shown in Figure 2.24 is the simplest form of a scheduling/shaping hierarchy; effectively, the shaper and scheduler have a parent/child relationship, where the scheduling policy is a child to the parent shaping policy. Some deployments may require additional levels of shaping and scheduling.

2.2.5   Link Fragmentation and Interleaving

Even with a strict priority scheduler for delay sensitive traffic, such as VoIP, a newly arrived priority packet can at best be enqueued after the last packet to be scheduled. On relatively low-speed links, a single 1500 byte (the maximum transmission unit for Ethernet) non-priority packet scheduled just before a priority packet arrives can have significant impact on the priority packet delay. For a 512 kbps connection this would be ~23 ms which would exceed the 15 ms maximum acceptable access link delay target for a VoIP class derived in the example given in Chapter 3, Section 3.2.2.1.1. In practical implementations, the problem may be worse, with several non-priority packets potentially being queued ahead of a priority packet due to the presence of an interface FIFO (as described in Section 2.2.4.1.3).

Consider, for example, that a particular queuing implementation has been designed such that if a priority queue packet arrives when the priority queue is empty, at most 2 non-priority packets can be serviced before that priority queue packet, i.e. a maximum interface FIFO size of 2 packets, which is representative of practical implementations. If this implementation was used on a 512 kbps link, and assuming non-priority packets of 1500 bytes, then even if a priority packet arrives at the priority queue when it is empty, the packet may be delayed by up to (2 * 1500 * 8/512000) = ~47 ms before the priority packet can even start to be sent out of the interface. This would significantly exceed a typical access link delay budget and consume a significant component of an end-to-end delay budget.

In such cases, link layer fragmentation and interleaving (LFI) mechanisms – such as FRF.12 [FRF12], which is specific to frame-relay or mechanisms which rely on the Multilink Point-to-Point Protocol (MLPPP) [RFC 1990] – are needed to reduce the impact of non-priority packets on priority traffic delay. Link layer fragmentation breaks large non-priority packets into smaller fragments with which priority packets can be interleaved rather than having to wait for whole non-priority packets to be transmitted. Link layer fragmentation therefore reduces the impact of the delay induced by the non-priority packets. The fragments are each transported as unique layer 2 frames, which contain an identifier enabling them to be differentiated from priority packets, and a sequence number enabling the fragments to be reassembled into whole packets at the far end of the link. Typical LFI implementations have a configurable fragment size such that non-priority packets which are greater than the fragment size will be broken up into fragments of at most that size. Consider the previous example: if an LFI technique were used with a fragment size of 300 bytes and a priority queue packet arrives in an empty priority queue it would now be delayed only by 2 * 300 byte fragments in the interface FIFO, i.e. $2 * 300 * 8/512000 = \sim 9$ ms before it could start to be sent out of the interface, and the delay budget would be met. Although IP layer fragmentation could be used to similar effect, it suffers many disadvantages [SHANNON] and is therefore generally not recommended.

Link layer fragmentation and interleaving mechanisms are processor intensive functions and hence they may have a performance impact on software-based router implementations.

2.3 IP QOS Architectures

2.3.1 A Short History of IP Quality of Service

In order to understand the history of IP QOS architectures, we first need to define what an architecture means in this context. QOS architectures define the structures within which we deploy QOS mechanisms to deliver end-to-end QOS assurances or SLAs. To be completely defined, they need to provide the context in which mechanisms such as classification, marking, policing, queuing, and scheduling,

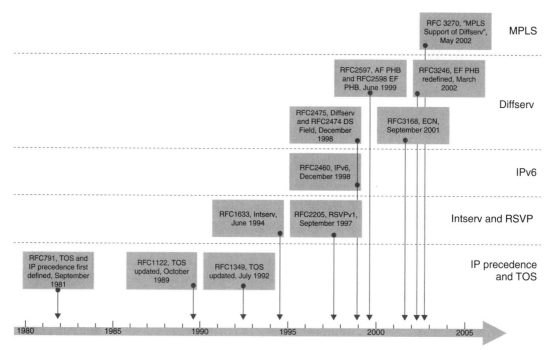

Figure 2.25   IP QOS standards timeline

dropping, and shaping are used together to assure a specified SLA for a service.

The standards which define the different architectures for IP QOS have been defined by the Internet Engineering Task Force (IETF, www. ietf.org). Figure 2.25 shows a timeline for the publication of the major IETF milestones in defining the QOS architectures for IP and MPLS.

The following sections describe the evolution of IP QOS architectures from IP Precedence and Type of Service, through Integrated Services and Differentiated Services, and also describe how IP QOS architectures apply to MPLS.

2.3.2   Type of Service/IP Precedence

In 1981, the original IPv4 specification [RFC 791], defined an 8-bit field to be used for IP QOS classification; this was called the Type of Service

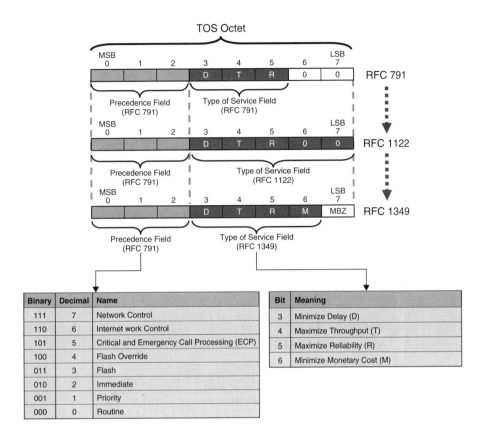

Figure 2.26   Type of service octet evolution

octet. The type of service octet subsequently went through several stages of redefinition in [RFC 1122] and [RFC 1349], as shown in Figure 2.26.

Originally, in RFC 791 the type of service octet was subdivided with 3 bits used for the IP precedence field (bits 0–2), and 3 bits (bits 3–5) used for the type of service (TOS) field; bits 6 and 7 of the type of service octet were listed as "Reserved for Future Use," and are shown set to zero. We note that it is somewhat confusing that the **TOS field** is a subset of the type of service **octet**; we explicitly differentiate between them.

[RFC1122] went on to extend the TOS field to include bits 3–7, although at that time the meaning of the low-order 2 bits (bits 6 and 7) was not defined.

[RFC1349] explicitly defined the meaning of bit 6 of the type of service octet as belonging to the TOS field and being used to indicate a desire to "minimize monetary cost" for packets marked in this way. The use of the low-order bit (bit 7) was redefined as "currently unused" and labeled "MBZ" for "must be zero." RFC 1349 also stated that *"The originator of a datagram sets [the MBZ] field to zero (unless participating in an Internet protocol experiment which makes use of that bit)."*

The specific meanings of the precedence and TOS fields are described in Sections 2.3.2.1 and 2.3.2.2. The definitions of the type of service octet have since been obsoleted by "Definition of the Differentiated Services Field (DS Field) in the IPv4 and IPv6 Headers" [RFC2474], which is described in Section 2.3.4.1.

2.3.2.1 IP Precedence

The use of the IP precedence is only defined in RFC 791, which defines the notion of precedence as *"An independent measure of the importance of this datagram."* Retrospectively, it is apparent that IP precedence defined only a relative priority marking scheme, rather than an overarching QOS architecture.

RFC 791 defined a number of traffic denominations – indicating network control traffic, routing traffic, and various levels of privilege – and an associated marking scheme using the Precedence Field in order to be able to identify to which denomination a particular packet belongs. The bits of the Precedence Field have no individual meaning but rather the field value is taken as a whole to determine the "IP precedence" of a particular packet; hence as there are three precedence bits, there are eight different IP precedence values. The IP precedence values and their corresponding denominations are shown in the table in Figure 2.26; the notation normally used when referring to particular IP precedence values is either to use the decimal values or to use the denomination names shown. Appendix 2.A provides a guide to conversion between precedence, TOS, and DSCP values.

IP precedence provided a capability for marking packets, such that simple classification could be used at later node to determine what scheduling treatment, i.e. by which queue in the scheduler, the packet should be serviced. As such, it allowed packets with different markings to receive different treatments; however, there was no definition either in relative or absolute terms of how traffic with different IP precedence values should be treated with respect to delay, jitter, loss, throughput, or availability. There was no definition, for example, of how a packet marked precedence 3 ("Flash") should be treated compared to a packet marked precedence 2 ("Immediate"). RFC 791 recognizes this: "*Several networks offer service precedence, which somehow treats high precedence traffic as more important than other traffic.*"

Hence, IP precedence did not define the architectural framework of capabilities needed to support services with defined SLA requirements and consequently it did not achieve widespread deployment. Nonetheless, the use of some IP precedence markings have become de facto – e.g. most router vendors today mark routing protocol traffic IP precedence 6 by default. Even though the use of IP precedence has been superseded by the DS field, this de facto marking does not provide any issues with respect to backward compatibility, as Diffserv provides a backward compatibility mode through the use of the class selector code points (see Section 2.3.4.1).

2.3.2.2   Type of Service

The definition of the type of service field evolved through RFC 791, RFC 1122, and RFC 1349. RFC 1349 provides the most recent and comprehensive definition, hence we refer to that definition in this section.

RFC 1349 defined a scheme using the 4-bit TOS field (bits 3–6 of the type of service octet) to indicate in each packet the service that it required from the network. Unlike the precedence field, where individual bits do not have a specific meaning, each bit of the TOS field was set in a packet if that packet required the service represented by that bit as shown in Figure 2.26; all bits set to zero indicates that a packet requires normal service.

As defined in RFC 1349, TOS field marking was not intended to determine which queue a particular packet would be queued in at a network node – that was the function of the IP precedence field – but rather the TOS marking of a packet was to be used to determine which path that packet would take through the network. Specifications for some routing protocols provided support for TOS routing, where a separate (and possibly distinct) set of routes could be calculated for each IP TOS value, such that an IP packet could be routed based upon both the packet's destination IP address and its TOS field value.

While we have already differentiated between the type of service octet and the TOS field, the terms "type of service" or "TOS," when used on their own, are generally referring to the use of the TOS field for TOS routing. The notation generally used when referring to TOS is to take the entire value of the type of service octet (including the precedence field and bit 7 of the type of service octet) expressed in decimal, where bit 0 is taken as the most significant bit; this is generally called the "TOS value." For example, assuming a precedence field value of 101 binary, and a TOS field value of 1000 binary, the TOS value would generally be referred to as "176" decimal (i.e. 10110000 binary). This notation can sometimes cause confusion, because it consumes the IP precedence value; hence even though a packet may have a TOS field value of 0000 binary (i.e. normal service), if the packet has a precedence field value of 101 binary, the TOS value would generally be referred to as "160" decimal (10100000). Appendix 2.A provides a guide to conversion between precedence, TOS, and DSCP values.

With type of service, the markings defined were subjective; it was not defined, for example, how a packet marked with "minimize delay" should be treated relative to one marked without; RFC 1349 goes as far as to say *"setting the TOS field to 1000 (minimize delay) does not guarantee that the path taken by the datagram will have a delay that the user considers 'low'."* Similarly, with IP precedence, type of service did not provide the facilities needed to support services with defined SLA requirements and hence type of service was never widely implemented or deployed. At one time, the Open Shortest Path First (OSPF) [RFC 1583] interior gateway routing protocol specification supported the capability to calculate separate routing topologies for each type of service; however, this was never widely implemented and was subsequently removed from the OSPF specification [RFC 2178].

The limitations in IP precedence and type of service were realized and this led to the definition of the Integrated Services and Differentiated Services QOS architectures, which resulted in the obsoletion of the TOS field by the Differentiated Services field.

2.3.2.3   IPv6 Traffic Class Octet

The IPv6 Traffic Class Octet existed only in theory and for a short period of time, hence it is not worthy of lengthy discussion. The IPv6 Traffic Class was defined in [RFC2460] in December 1998, and then was redefined in the same month by the definition of Differentiated Services (DS) field, which is specified in [RFC2474] (see Section 2.3.4.1).

2.3.3   Integrated Services Architecture

[RFC1633] laid out the philosophy of the Integrated Services or "Intserv" IP QOS architecture. It was designed to address the issues identified with IP precedence and type of service, providing the capabilities needed to support applications with bounded SLA requirements, such as VoIP and video. Intserv tackles the problem of providing services level assurances to applications by explicitly managing bandwidth resources and schedulers on a per flow basis; resources are reserved and admission control is performed for each flow. The resource ReSerVation Protocol (RSVP) is the end-to-end signaling protocol used to setup Intserv reservations. Intserv and RSVP are described in more detail in Chapter 4, Section 4.4.

2.3.4   Differentiated Services Architecture

Scalability concerns with Intserv lead to the definition of the Differentiated Services (DS) or "Diffserv" IP QOS Architecture [RFC 2475]. Diffserv comprises the following key components, which are used together to enable end-to-end differentiated delay, jitter, and loss commitments to be supported on the same Diffserv-enabled IP network – referred to as a *Diffserv domain* – for different types or classes of service. These components are shown in Figure 2.27.

- *Traffic classification and conditioning.* The edge of the Diffserv domain is the provider/customer boundary for the Diffserv-enabled services being offered. This does not, however, infer that Diffserv is only

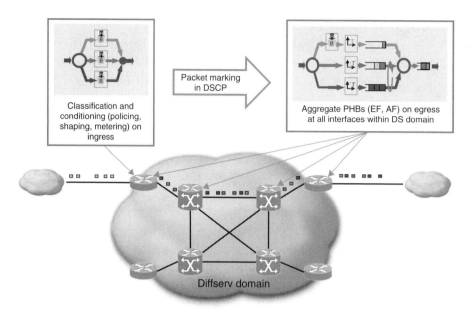

Figure 2.27 Diffserv architecture – RFC 2475

applicable to network service providers; the networking department of an enterprise organization is a service provider to their enterprise. On ingress to the Diffserv domain, the customer's traffic is classified using implicit, simple, or complex classification into a limited number of traffic classes, which are also known as "behavior aggregates" in Diffserv-speak. These aggregates are checked for conformance against agreed profiles – referred to in Diffserv as Traffic Conditioning Agreements (TCAs). QOS mechanisms, such as shaping or policing, are used to "condition" the traffic to ensure that traffic ingressing the Diffserv domain is conformant with the TCA; non-conformant traffic may be delayed, dropped, or re-marked. The TCA is derived from the SLA between the provider and the customer and defines the characteristics of the offered traffic for which the SLA is assured. For example, if a site is provided with a 128 kbps assured VoIP service, the TCA might be to police the received VoIP traffic from that site to 128 kbps (with an appropriate burst), dropping any excess traffic.

- *DSCP marking.* Packets either are pre-marked using the Diffserv Code Point (DSCP) within the DS field in the IP packet header, or are marked on ingress to the Diffserv domain, in order to identify to which particular class or behavior aggregate the packets belong. The marking could be performed by a policer enforcing the TCA, for example. Subsequent Diffserv nodes therefore only need to perform simple classification using the DSCP in order to determine the class of a packet. The DS field and DSCP are described in Section 2.3.4.1.

- *Per-hop behaviors.* The conditioning applied at the edges of the network ensures that all traffic ingressing the Diffserv domain is within the committed TCAs and is appropriately marked. Within the Diffserv domain, the objective is then simply to ensure that the per-class SLAs are met, for the limited number of classes supported. Per-class scheduling and queuing control mechanisms are applied to the traffic classes based upon the DSCP marking in order to ensure per-class SLA differentiation. Diffserv is not prescriptive in defining the scheduling and queuing control algorithms that should be implemented at each hop, but rather, uses a level of abstraction in defining the externally observable forwarding behaviors – termed Per-Hop Behaviors (PHBs) – that can be applied to traffic at each hop. Diffserv PHBs are described in Section 2.3.4.2.

Unlike Intserv, Diffserv configurations are provisioned, either by manual configuration or by an NMS system, rather than being set up by a network signaling protocol.

End-to-end SLAs are assured with Diffserv by ensuring that per-class resources are appropriately provisioned at each hop relative to the traffic load within the class. Per-class traffic loads within the Diffserv domain will change over time and hence performing per-class capacity planning is an essential component of Diffserv to ensure that the per-class resources are appropriately provisioned. Capacity planning is discussed in Chapter 5.

Diffserv achieves scalability by performing complex per-customer QOS functions and maintaining per-customer state (e.g. complex classification criteria), only at the edges of the network. Distributing these functions at the edge of the network facilitates scaling, as the edge of the network naturally expands as the network grows. Unlike Intserv, within the Diffserv domain, there is no per flow or per-customer state, but rather scalability is achieved through using only a limited number of classes, which are simply classified using the DSCP marking within each packet, hence only per-class state is required.

Diffserv can be applied equally to IPv6 as to IPv4. Diffserv can also be applied to MPLS, although the limited size of the field available for QOS marking in MPLS introduces some complexities, which are discussed in Section 3.6.2.

Diffserv is by far the most widely deployed IP QOS architecture; it is widely deployed in enterprise networks and in SP networks providing virtual private network (VPN) services to enterprises. Diffserv is also being deployed to support the move toward so-called "Next Generation Networks" (NGN), which support the migration of PSTN telephony services to IP/MPLS networks. In NGN networks, IP-based PSTN-replacement services coexist on the same network with "best-effort" Internet access services and business oriented VPN services; Diffserv is used to ensure that the SLA requirements for each service are met and that there is isolation between the behaviors of the different services.

SLAs based upon Diffserv are not generally committed for Internet access services, i.e. services to the wider Internet, because services accessing the Internet may transit a number of different service provider networks, and unless they all provide aligned Diffserv capabilities, there would be no benefit in a single provider supporting Diffserv for such services. Further, as Internet access services are at the commodity end of IP service offerings, there is no incentive for service providers to incur the cost and complexity of providing Diffserv-assured Internet access services to their customers.

2.3.4.1 DS Field

The Differentiated Services (DS) field, which is specified in [RFC 2474], redefined the use of the 8-bit field, which had been the type of service octet in IPv4 [RFC1349] and the traffic class octet in IPv6 [RFC 2460]. The DS field definition specified that the first six bits of the

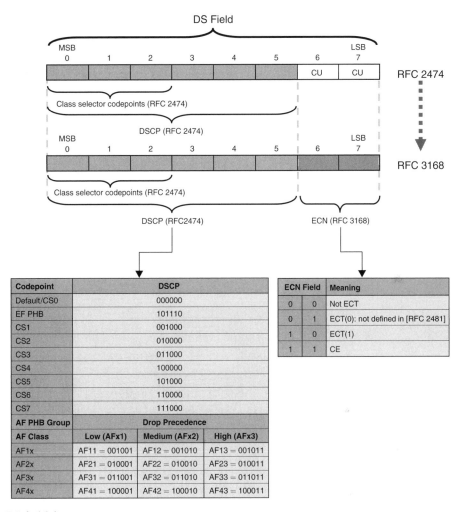

Figure 2.28 DS field format

field (bits 0–5) were designated as the Differentiated Services code point (DSCP). The DSCP field is unstructured and the value of the field is taken as a whole, i.e. there is no distinct meaning for each specific bit. A particular combination of DSCP bits is referred to as a "codepoint," which is set such that it can be used to select the PHB a packet will experience at each node. The DS Field is shown in Figure 2.28.

Codepoints can be expressed in binary or decimal notation. In binary format the notation "xxxxxx" is commonly used, where "x" may be equal to "0" or "1" and the left-most bit signifies bit 0 of the DSCP. In decimal notation all 6 bits of DSCP are expressed in decimal, where bit 0 is taken as the most significant bit; for example, a DSCP of 010000 binary is represented as DSCP 16. Appendix 2.A provides a guide to conversion between precedence, TOS, and DSCP values.

The DSCP is a 6-bit field and therefore it can be used to indicate 64 distinct codepoints. RFC 2474 partitioned this codepoint space into three pools for the purpose of codepoint assignment and management:

- *Pool 1 – standards action.* The first pool consists of the 32 codepoints in the range xxxxx0 were defined to be assigned to standardized PHBs defined in the IETF.

- *Pool 2 – experimental or local use.* The 16 codepoints in the range xxxx11 were reserved for experimental or local use (EXP/LU).

- *Pool 3 – experimental or local use.* The 16 codepoints in the range xxxx01 were also reserved for experimental or local use (EXP/LU). The difference between Pool 3 and Pool 2, however, is that the use of this field may be subsequently redefined for standardized assignments if Pool 1 is ever exhausted.

The DSCP codepoint space assignment is summarized in the table in Figure 2.29.

Some, although not all, of the DSCP values in the Pool 1 codepoint space have been assigned to particular PHBs standardized within the IETF:

- DSCP 0 (000000 binary) has been assigned to the default PHB, which is discussed in Section 2.3.4.2.3.

- The expedited forwarding (EF) PHB, which is discussed in Section 2.3.4.2.1, has been assigned DSCP 46 (101110 binary).

- A set of 12 codepoints, which are shown in Figure 2.28, have been allocated to the AF PHB group, which is discussed in Section 2.3.4.2.2.

Pool	Codepoint Space	Assignment Policy
1	xxxxx0	Standards Action
2	xxxx11	EXP/LU
3	xxxx01	EXP/LU

Figure 2.29   DSCP codepoint space assignment

- A set of codepoints defined as the "Class Selector" (CS) codepoints are any of the eight codepoints in the range "xxx000," where "x" may equal "0" or "1." The notation commonly used for the CS codepoints is "CS" followed by the value of the first three bits of the DSCP expressed in decimal, where bit 0 is taken as the most significant bit, e.g. codepoint 101000 is expressed as CS5.

  The CS codepoints only use the first three bits of the DSCP, which are the bits that were previously defined for the IP precedence field (as described in Section 2.3.2.1), hence use of the CS codepoints provides backward compatibility with IP precedence, i.e. marking or classifying a packet as CS5 is, to all intents and purposes the same as marking or classifying a packet as IP precedence 5 (assuming the TOS field is set to 0). The CS codepoints have an associated PHB definition, which is described in Section 2.3.4.2.4.

As well as being specified in the documents which define a particular PHB, there is a central DS Field Codepoints Registry [DSCR] maintained by the Internet Assigned Numbers Authority (IANA).

Take note that the allocation of Pool 1 codepoints specified above, for standardized PHBs defined in the IETF, are recommended rather than being mandated. This means that while it may make sense to use these values, if there are valid reasons to use DSCP values other than those recommended, then it is up to the network designer's discretion to do so. Hence, contrary to popular opinion, using values other than the recommended values does not mean that a particular IP QOS design is not "Diffserv compliant." Further, while RFC 2474 says, *"Recommended codepoints SHOULD map to specific, standardized PHBs,"* it also says, *"the mapping of codepoints to PHBs MUST be configurable"* in order to allow for alternative configurations, where codepoints other than the recommended codepoints are used.

It is further noted that all packets with the same DSCP should be treated with the same PHB. If packets with the same DSCP were treated with different PHBs, they may for example be placed in different queues, with the result that packets from the same flow may be resequenced. Hence, it is essential to treat all packets with the same DSCP with the same PHB in order to prevent resequencing within a flow due to the adverse impact that packet re-ordering can have on the performance of some applications (this is discussed in more detail in Chapter 1, Section 1.2.5).

Multiple codepoints, however, may be mapped to the same PHB. As a consequence, even though the CS codepoints are defined as those codepoints within the range xxx000, in order to be backward compatible with IP precedence, an alternative approach to be backward compatible is to ignore the markings in bits 3–5 of the DSCP, and classify packets based only on bits 0–2. If this approach were taken, DSCP values of 101000 and 101001 would both be mapped to the same PHB.

RFC 2474 originally defined bits 6 and 7 of the DS field as being reserved and annotated them "Currently Unused" (CU) as shown in Figure 2.28. The use of the field was subsequently redefined in [RFC 3168] for use with Explicit Congestion Notification (ECN), as described in Section 2.3.4.4.

2.3.4.2 Per-Hop Behaviors

Diffserv is not prescriptive in defining the scheduling and queuing control algorithms that should be implemented at each hop, but rather, uses a level of abstraction in defining the externally observable "black box" forwarding behaviors, termed Per-Hop Behaviors (PHBs), that are applied to traffic at each hop.

Four types of PHBs are defined which are described in the following sections. The PHBs are formally defined, such that an implementation which complies with a particular PHB is assured to support the behavioral characteristics intended by that PHB. Each PHB definition consists of two components: a formal definition of the required forwarding behavior and a recommended marking scheme to be used for classifying packets that will be subjected to that PHB.

2.3.4.2.1 The Expedited Forwarding (EF) PHB

The EF PHB [RFC 3246][2] is used to support applications with low-delay, low-jitter, low-loss, assured bandwidth requirements, such as VoIP. The characteristics of an implementation which supports the requirements of the EF PHB are that it is able to service the EF traffic at a specified rate or higher, measurable over a defined time interval and independent of the offered load of any non-EF traffic at the point where the EF PHB is applied. If these characteristics are supported and the EF class traffic rate and burst characteristics are controlled, using a token bucket policer as described in Section 2.2.3 for example, then the delay and jitter for the EF traffic can be bounded. Further, if the available buffer space for the EF class traffic is greater than the burst characteristic, then the loss can also be controlled (i.e. will be zero).

Some scheduler implementations may attempt to support EF traffic using a scheduling algorithm such as WRR or WFQ; however, with such implementations the worst-case delay bounds for the EF traffic will depend upon the particular scheduling algorithm used and may also be dependent upon the number of queues used in the particular scheduler implementation as described in Section 2.2.4.1.2.4. Consequently, the EF PHB is typically implemented using a strict priority queuing mechanism, such as that described in Section 2.2.4.1.1. With implementations that support multiple priority queues, typically they all support the EF PHB as described in Section 2.2.4.1.4.

RFC 3246 also specifies that if the EF PHB is implemented using a scheduler that allows the EF traffic to pre-empt other traffic (e.g. a strict priority queue), then there must also be some mechanism (e.g. a token bucket policer) supported to limit the EF traffic in order to constrain the impact it can have on the other traffic, i.e. to prevent the other traffic from being starved.

Hence, the application of a policer to an EF traffic stream serves two purposes: firstly, to limit the EF traffic load such that when servicing the traffic with an EF PHB, the delay, jitter and loss can be assured; secondly, to limit the impact that the EF traffic can have on non-EF traffic.

The EF PBH is assigned a recommended DSCP of 101110 binary, 46 decimal.

2.3.4.2.2   The Assured Forwarding (AF) PHB

The Assured Forwarding (AF) PHB group [RFC 2597] defines a set of AF classes, which are designed to support data applications with assured bandwidth requirements, such as absolute or relative minimum bandwidth guarantees, with a work-conserving property.

The key concept behind the AF PHB group definition is that a particular class could be used by a DS domain to offer a service, to a particular site for example, with an assurance that IP packets within that class will be forwarded with a high probability as long as the class rate from the site does not exceed a defined contracted rate. If the rate is exceeded, then the excess traffic may be forwarded, but with a probability that may be lower than for traffic which was below the contracted rate.

There are four defined AF classes denoted as AF1x, AF2x, AF3x, and AF4x. Within each class a packet can be assigned to one of three levels of drop precedence, for example AF11, AF12, and AF13 within class AF1x. Within a particular class, the probability of forwarding AFx1 must not be less than for AFx2, which in turn must not be less than for AFx3, i.e. AFx1 has a low drop precedence, AFx2 has a medium drop precedence, and AFx3 has a high drop precedence. Within a class, the drop precedence therefore indicates the relative importance of the packet. A set of twelve recommended DSCP values have been allocated to indicate the four classes and three drop precedence levels within each class, as shown in Figure 2.28. Although only four AF classes are defined, in theory there is nothing, apart from the size of the DSCP field, to limit the number of classes serviced with an AF forwarding behavior. If more than four AF classes are required then as the recommended DSCP markings are only defined for four classes, non-recommended DSCP values need to be used for the additional AF classes.

A particular AF class is realized by combining conditioning behaviors on ingress to the Diffserv domain – where a particular AF class is offered to a customer – which control the amount of traffic accepted at each level of drop precedence within that class and marks the traffic accordingly. At that and subsequent nodes, the AF class bandwidth is allocated to ensure that traffic within the contracted rate is delivered with a high probability. If congestion within the class is experienced, the congested node aims to ensure that packets of a higher drop precedence are dropped with a higher probability than packets with a lower drop precedence. Hence, at a DS node the forwarding assurance of a particular packet depends upon the forwarding resources allocated to the class, the current offered load for that class, and if congestion occurs within the class, the packet's drop precedence within the class.

The edge conditioning behaviors for an AF class will typically be implemented using a one rate or two rate policer as described in Section 2.2.3 respectively. Although both of these policers are capable of marking "3 colors" which can correspond to 3 levels of drop precedence, in practice it is difficult to understand what meaningful service benefit is offered by differentiating between traffic in terms of a 3 color scheme, i.e. "in-contract," "out-of-contract," and "exceedingly-out-of-contract." Hence, it is more common for the policers to be used to mark 2 colors only ("in-contract" and "out-of-contract"), and hence typically use only 2 drop precedence levels, e.g. AFx1 and AFx2.

An AF PHB class is typically allocated to a queue which is serviced from a weighted scheduling mechanism such as WFQ (Section 2.2.4.1.2.2) or DRR (Section 2.2.4.1.2.3), where the weighting for the queue and queue depths are configured to ensure that low drop precedence packets within the class are forwarded with a high probability. If congestion occurs within the class then WRED is commonly used in order to drop, for example, AFx2 traffic with a higher probability than AFx1 traffic; this is done by having a more aggressive RED drop profile for the AFx2 traffic as described in Section 2.2.4.2.4.

As for all of the other defined Diffserv PHBs, it is a requirement that in applying an AF PHB there is no possibility that packets from a single flow will be resequenced, due to the impact that this can have on application performance. Hence packets from the same flow should always be assigned to the same AF PHB, although they may be assigned different drop precedences, such that they will always be serviced from the same queue and hence will always be in sequence, even though they may have different drop probabilities.

2.3.4.2.3   The Default PHB

The default PHB [RFC 2474] is defined as being the PHB used for packets not explicitly mapped to other PHBs. The default PHB is somewhat ambiguously defined as a PHB which has no committed resources and yet cannot be starved by other PHBs, but potentially can re-use unused bandwidth from other classes when available, i.e. has an implied work conserving property. RFC 2474 also says that the default PHB could be supported *"by a mechanism in each node that reserves some minimal resources (e.g., buffers, bandwidth) for default behavior aggregates."* Hence, in practice, the difference between the service provided to an AF PHB, which has a minimal but quantifiable bandwidth assurance and the default PHB is semantic. Hence, to avoid confusion we choose not to use the default PHB; if a class requires only a minimal bandwidth assurance, we consider it as serviced with an AF PHB, which has a minimal but quantifiable bandwidth assurance.

There can be confusion between the default PHB and the concept of a default class for classification purposes. Most router implementations have the concept of a default class to which all packets that are not explicitly classified into other classes are assigned; this default class serves to simplify QOS configuration. The default class will be assigned to a queue and the bandwidth assurances to this queue will generally be configurable; RED will also generally be able to be configured on this queue in order to optimize throughput for TCP. For example, consider a case where traffic consisting of 5 distinct DSCP markings is being classified into 3 separate classes, each being serviced with AF PHBs. If discrete DSCP markings are individually mapped to each of two classes, then the remaining DSCP could be explicitly mapped to the third class, or alternatively if the concept of a default class is supported, they could implicitly be mapped to the default class without requiring explicit configuration.

2.3.4.2.4   Class Selector PHB

[RFC 2474] defines a set of PHB requirements associated with the Class Selector codepoints (Section 2.3.4.1). The intent of the CS PHB requirements is to define a PHB group that could replace (and hence provide backward compatibility with) the behaviors applied to packets based upon their IP precedence marking. In doing so, the CS PHB requirements assume that packets with a numerically higher IP precedence value were treated with a higher probability of forwarding (i.e. lower probability of drop) than packets with numerically lower precedence values. Therefore, RFC 2474 specifies that packets with a higher numerical CS codepoint value must not have a lower probability of timely forwarding than packets with a lower CS codepoint value. The definition for the CS PHB requires a minimum of two classes servicing the eight CS codepoint values; hence, in the minimal case multiple CS codepoint values may need to be mapped to a single CS PHB. Where multiple PHBs are used in this way, they are referred to as a CS compliant PHB group.

In practice, as IP precedence was not really used in a consistent way (as discussed in Section 2.3.2.1), there has been little need to deploy the forwarding behaviors specified by the CS PHB requirements. If this were required, this could effectively be achieved by classifying them into classes based upon their CS codepoint values and configuring the AF classes with the appropriate bandwidth resources relative to class load, to achieve the relative differentiation required of a CS PHB group.

A more common practical reason for using the CS codepoint makings is not to facilitate backward compatibility with IP precedence, but instead to ease the process of mapping IP packet markings to the MPLS experimental field (as described in Section 2.3.6.2.1). In cases such as this, the EF or AF PHBs may be applied to classes where traffic is classified into those classes based upon CS codepoint classification.

2.3.4.3   Per-Domain Behaviors
[RFC 3086] defines Diffserv "Per-Domain Behaviors" (PDBs); PDBs are intended to define particular end-to-end behaviors delivered by a Diffserv domain. PHBs can be considered to be the externally observable "black box" forwarding behaviors experienced at a particular hop in the Diffserv domain, and similarly a PDB can be considered to be a definition of the "black box" forwarding behaviors experienced by a class of packets across the Diffserv domain as a whole. As such,

a PDB can be considered to be the Diffserv definition of the end-to-end engineering SLAs described in Chapter 1, Section 1.4.1.

Only a single PDB has been defined and that is the lower-effort PDB.

2.4.4.3.1   Lower effort PDB

[RFC3662] is an informational RFC which defines "*A Lower Effort (LE) Per-Domain Behavior (PDB).*" The service provided by the LE PDB can be characterized as one where all other traffic takes precedence over LE traffic in consumption of network link bandwidth, but the traffic supported by the LE PHB is able to use unused bandwidth from other classes when available, i.e. it has a work conserving behavior. Hence, if any congestion is experienced in the Diffserv domain, the service provided by the LE PDB may be completely starved; that is, the other classes can consume all of the available bandwidth such that the LE PDB will get nothing. This is different to the end-to-end service that would be provided by using the Default PHB, as the definition of the Default PHB (Section 2.3.4.2.3) explicitly specifies that it should not be starved. The LE PDB and the terms "scavenger class" and "lower than best-effort" are synonymous.

RFC 3662 says of the LE PDB: "*This behavior could be obtained, for example, by using a [class-based queuing] scheduler with a small share and with borrowing permitted.*" Hence, in practice, there is little difference between the LE PDB, and the service provided by the Default PHB. In turn, as discussed in Section 2.3.4.2.3, there is no significant difference between the service provided to an AF PHB, which has a minimal but quantifiable bandwidth assurance, and the default PHB. Hence, as per the default PHB, we choose not to use the LE PDB; rather, if the required bandwidth assurance for a class is negligible, we consider it as serviced with an AF PHB, which has a minimal bandwidth assurance.

2.3.4.4   Explicit Congestion Notification

As described in Chapter 1, Section 1.3.3.1, TCP effectively treats the network as a "black box," in that it does not rely on any explicit network behaviors when performing flow control, in order to determine the status of available network bandwidth and whether congestion has occurred. Instead, TCP relies on TCP timeouts or the reception of duplicate ACKs to determine implicitly when packets are dropped. AQM mechanisms such as RED are used to detect congestion before the queues overflow (i.e. before tail drop), and selectively drop packets to feedback indication of this congestion to the end-systems so that they will reduce their rate of sending with the aim of avoiding excess packet loss due to congestion and maintaining high network throughput while minimizing queuing delays.

Explicit congestion notification (ECN) aims to further improve throughput for TCP (and potentially for other transport protocols) and reduce queuing delays by adding the capability for the network to explicitly indicate to end-systems when congestion has occurred; support for explicit congestion notification (ECN) was added to Diffserv in [RFC 3168]. The main concept underlying ECN is that, rather than using AQM mechanisms like RED to drop packets when congestion is experienced, they are instead used to explicitly mark packets; the end-system TCP stacks would then use the packet marking to determine when congestion has occurred and hence to slow their rate of sending. ECN relies on the proactive indication of congestion before packets are actually dropped, rather than reacting to packet loss as with non-ECN TCP stacks, hence ECN reduces packet loss and improves overall throughput.

This explicit indication is provided by marking the ECN field, which RFC 3168 defined as bits 6 and 7 of the DS field, which were previously undefined. The ECN field is set both by end-systems, to indicate that they are using an ECN capable transport (ECT) layer protocol, and by routers, to indicate explicitly when congestion is experienced (CE). The possible markings (referred to as codepoints) of the ECN field are given in Figure 2.28.

From Figure 2.28 it can be seen that there are two values of the ECN field which indicate ECT; either can be used by end-systems and routers should treat both values as equivalent. Thus although the ECN field has four possible values, effectively it defines only three states. The reason for having two values to indicate ECT is largely a legacy from the first experimental definition of ECN in [RFC 2481]. RFC 2481 defined that the first bit of the ECN field be used for ECT and the second bit for CE, therefore the 01 codepoint was not undefined; this was changed as per Figure 2.28 by RFC 3168, which obsoleted RFC 2481.

ECN requires the following behaviors in ECN capable end-systems and routers:

- Before using ECN, the transport protocol might employ negotiation between the end-systems to determine that they are both ECN capable. In the case of TCP, this is done during session establishment using two new flags in the TCP header, the ECN-Echo (ECE) and Congestion Window Reduced (CWR) flags, which are defined in RFC 3168 and are shown in Figure 2.30.

  Negotiation of the use of ECN between two TCP end-systems, A and B, where A is the initiator, requires that when A sends the TCP SYN to B it sets both the ECE and CWR flags to indicate that it is ECN capable. If B is also ECN capable, it responds with a SYN-ACK with the ECE flag set and the CWR flag unset.

  With ECN negotiation complete, both A and B can originate packets on this TCP session with ECT set, indicating that they both support ECN.

- A router which receives an ECT packet uses a mechanism such as RED (see Section 2.2.4.2.3) to determine whether or not to set CE; the modified RED behavior to support ECN is as follows:
  - When there is no congestion, i.e. if the current average queue depth (q_{avg}) is below the configurable minimum threshold (q_{minth}), the packet is enqueued. ECT packets received with CE already set are left unchanged and the packet is enqueued as normal.

0	1	2	3	4	5	6	7	8	9	10	11	12	13	14	15
Header Length				Reserved				C W R	E C E	U R G	A C K	P S H	R S T	S I N	F I N

Figure 2.30 TCP header updated with flags ECN

- ○ If there is moderate congestion, i.e. the current average queue depth (q_{avg}) is above q_{minth} and below q_{maxth}, the packet will be marked CE (instead of being dropped as would be the case for a non-ECT packet) with an increasing, but randomized, probability, using the formula defined in Section 2.2.4.2.3.
- ○ If there is extreme congestion, i.e. the current average queue (q_{avg}) depth is above the defined maximum threshold (q_{maxth}) then the ECT packet will always be dropped, as for non-ECT packets.

- Upon receiving a packet with CE set the receiver sets the ECN-Echo flag in its next TCP ACK sent to the sender.

- Upon receiving a TCP ACK with the ECE flag set, the sender applies the same congestion control algorithms as would be applied by a non-ECT end-system in the presence of a single dropped packet (see Chapter 1, Section 1.3.3.1). The sender also sets the CWR flag in the TCP header of the next packet sent to the receiver to acknowledge its receipt of and reaction to the ECN-Echo flag.

Even though ECN was designed to be incrementally deployable, it has not been widely deployed. End-users will not get any benefit from ECN until it is supported both in the TCP stacks of their end-systems and by the routers in the networks they use, and one reason often cited for the lack of deployment of ECN is a chicken and egg problem with respect to the availability of ECN capable implementations:

- Support for ECN by router vendors will inevitably require development efforts and they are unlikely to undertake this development unless they have requests for support from their enterprise or SP customers.

- Enterprise or SP customers are unlikely to ask their router vendors to add support for ECN until it is supported in end-systems' TCP stacks.

- There is no incentive for the vendors of TCP stacks to develop support for ECN, if there is no support by router vendors.

Another oft-cited reason for the lack of deployment of ECN has been concerns over the potential for subversion of the use of ECN capabilities, where packets are falsely indicating ECN capability, for example. If the falsely ECT marked packets encounter moderate congestion at an ECN capable router, the router may set the CE codepoint instead of dropping the packet. If the transport protocol in fact is not ECN-capable or is not adhering to the defined ECN behaviors, then the transport protocol may not reduce its rate of sending, as intended by ECN. The consequences of this action are two-fold:

- The end-systems that are falsely claiming to be ECN-capable receive a lower probability of packet loss when moderate congestion is experienced than others which are correctly indicating that they are not ECN-capable.

- If the end-systems that are falsely claiming to be ECN-capable do not reduce their rate of sending when they should due to CE marking, the level of congestion may increase, thereby increasing the rate of packet marking or dropping impacting all flows.

Hence, the benefits of ECN are only really gained when all end-systems cooperate in adhering to the ECN behaviors; if this cannot be assured the benefits of ECN also cannot be assured. Similar reasons are often cited for the lack of deployment of equivalent layer 2 mechanisms used for adaptive shaping such as forward explicit congestion notification (FECN) in Frame Relay and Explicit Forward Congestion Indication (EFCI) in ATM.

In comparing ECN in IP to FECN in frame-relay or EFCI in ATM, other than the obvious difference that ECN is applied at layer 3, the main difference is that frame-relay and ATM implementations generally use a notion of the actual queue depths at a transit node to determine when to set FECN/EFCI, whereas ECN relies on AQM mechanisms such as RED, which set ECN based upon a measure of the average queue depth at a transit node in order to try and achieve a more stable network-wide behavior. Notionally, assuming that frame-relay and ATM networks supported a REDlike capability, a router which received frames or cells with FECN/EFCI set, could also use this as an indication to set CE in the corresponding IP packet. Where ATM and frame-relay networks are used as links in an end-to-end IP network, this would facilitate the mapping between IP QOS and the layer 2 QOS provided by the underlying ATM and frame-relay networks. This is, however, somewhat of a moot discussion because like ECN, neither FECN nor EFCI have been widely deployed in frame-relay or ATM.

There are some proposals to re-use the capability to mark the ECN bits for admission control; this is discussed in more detail in Chapter 4, Section 4.6. [RFC4774] defines considerations on the re-use of the ECN field.

2.3.4.5   Diffserv Tunneling Models

There are a number of ways to "tunnel" IP traffic within IP traffic, where tunneling involves encapsulating a received IP packet within another IP packet header at the tunnel source, such that packets within the tunnel have two headers (actually at least two headers – as it is possible to have tunnels within tunnels). Such tunneling is commonly used to create a virtual or simulated physical connection between two networks across an intermediate network. Packets which are within the tunnel, i.e. between the tunnel source and tunnel destination, are routed using only the outer packet header. At the tunnel destination the outer IP header is stripped off, revealing the underlying IP packet (and possibly layer 2 headers), which is then forwarded as normal. There are a number of IP tunneling techniques used including:

- simple IP-in-IP tunnels such as [RFC 2003] and GRE [RFC 2784]

- multi-protocol tunnels, such as IP in PPP [RFC 1661] in L2TP [RFC 2661]

- secure tunneling techniques such as IPSec [RFC 2401].

Whichever particular tunneling technique is used, when used with Diffserv, if a tunnel is not used end-to-end (i.e. from traffic source to traffic destination) then as the DSCP of the underlying "tunneled"

IP packet is not visible to nodes on the tunnel path, consideration needs to be given to how the DSCP of the tunnel (outer) packet header is set at the tunnel source, relative to the inner (tunneled) packet. In addition, if the DSCP of the tunnel packet is changed (i.e. re-marked) by an intermediate node somewhere between the tunnel source and tunnel destination, consideration needs to be given as to if and how the DSCP of the underlying IP packet is changed relative to the outer (i.e. "tunnel") DSCP at the tunnel destination, where the "tunnel" IP header, which contains the re-marked DSCP value, is stripped off.

[RFC 2983] defines two conceptual models to describe how to deal with the treatment of Diffserv in the context of IP tunnels, which are described in the following sections.

It is noted that individual IP tunnels are unidirectional entities. If bidirectional behavior is required then a tunnel will be required in each direction and the respective tunneling models will need to be applied to each tunnel.

2.3.4.5.1 IP Uniform Model

With the uniform model, any classification, marking, and re-marking are performed using the DSCP field of the outermost IP packet header only. At the tunnel source, the DSCP value of the underlying IP data packet is copied into the DSCP value of the tunnel IP header, and then at the destination of the tunnel the DSCP of the tunnel IP header is copied back into the DSCP value of the underlying data packet IP header. In this way, the DSCP value of the underlying IP packet propagates up through any added layers of tunnel header and should the outermost DSCP be re-marked, this re-marked value is similarly propagated down to the underlying IP packet when the tunnel header is stripped off at the tunnel destination.

Consider the example shown in Figure 2.31 and the following description:

1. Before entering the IP tunnel, in this example, IP data packets are marked with DSCP 34 (i.e. AF41).

2. At the tunnel source (Router B), the IP tunnel header is added and the DSCP value of the data packet IP header (DSCP 34) is copied

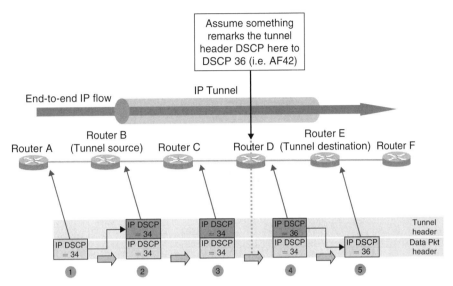

Figure 2.31 IP tunnel: uniform model

into the DSCP of the tunnel header, i.e. the DSCP of both the tunnel and data packet headers are 34.

3. On egress to Router B and intermediate routers between the tunnel source and tunnel destination, e.g. at Router C, when classifying tunnel packets by DSCP, they will look only at the DSCP value of the tunnel header (the outermost tunnel header where multiple layers of tunnel are used), which in this case is DSCP 34 and happens to be the same as the DSCP of the underlying data packet.

4. Assume that some function at Router D re-marks some or all of the tunneled packets to DSCP 36 (i.e. AF42); the re-marking only affects the DSCP of the tunnel header, hence the DSCP of the (outermost) tunnel header is now DSCP 36 (i.e. AF42), while the DSCP of the underlying IP data packet header is still DSCP 34 (i.e. AF41). Router D and any subsequent routers between the tunnel source and tunnel destination, when classifying tunnel packets by DSCP, will look only at the DSCP value of the tunnel header, which is now DSCP 36.

5. At the tunnel destination, the tunnel header is stripped off and DSCP value of the tunnel IP header is copied back into the DSCP value of the underlying data packet IP header, which is now DSCP 36 and which will be used by all subsequent routers when classifying the packets by DSCP.

Effectively, with the uniform model, for each packet, there is one piece of Diffserv information which is carried end-to-end, which may change along the path and which is always represented by the DSCP of the outermost IP header. Hence, when using the uniform model, with an IP tunnel there is really no difference in the resultant Diffserv behavior compared to where no tunnel is present; similarly, there is no difference in the case that multiple layers of IP tunnels are used. Effectively with the uniform model, tunnels are transparent to Diffserv operations.

2.3.4.5.2   IP Pipe Model

Unlike the uniform model, the pipe model treats the DSCP markings on the inner (data) and outer (tunnel) packet headers as independent (although possibly associated) entities. As for the uniform model, outside of the tunnel, as there is no tunnel header the IP data packet DSCP is used; between the tunnel source and tunnel destination, the DSCP marking in the tunnel header is used. The pipe model differs from the uniform model in that DSCP value of the underlying IP packet is not copied into the tunnel header DSCP at the tunnel source (although the tunnel DSCP setting may be derived from the underlying IP packet DSCP value), nor is the tunnel header DSCP copied back into the underlying IP packet DSCP at the tunnel destination. The pipe model behavior is the same where multiple layers of tunnel are used, with each subsequent tunnel layer being treated independently of the last.

Consider the example shown in Figure 2.32 and the following description:

1. Before entering the IP tunnel, in this example, IP data packets are marked with DSCP 34 (i.e. AF41).

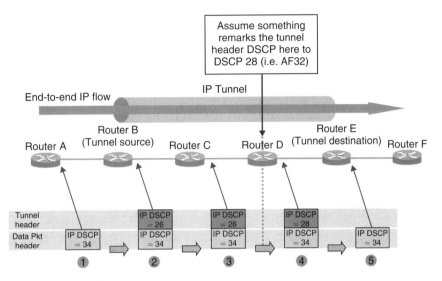

Figure 2.32 IP tunnel: pipe model

2. At the tunnel source (Router B), the tunnel header is added and the DSCP value of the data packet IP header is set. The tunnel DSCP value may be derived from (could be copied from) the DSCP value of the underlying IP packet, or may be set independently of that value. In this example, we assume that the tunnel DSCP is set to DSCP 26 (i.e. AF31) independently of the underlying IP packet DSCP.

3. On egress to Router B and to intermediate routers between the tunnel source and tunnel destination, e.g. at Router C, when classifying tunnel packets by DSCP, they will look only at the DSCP value of the tunnel header (outermost tunnel header where multiple layers of tunnel are used), which in this case is DSCP 26.

4. Assume that some function at Router D re-marks the tunneled packets to DSCP 28 (i.e. AF32); the re-marking only affects the DSCP of the (outermost) tunnel header, hence the DSCP of the underlying IP data packet header is still DSCP 34 (i.e. AF41). On egress to Router D and any subsequent routers between the tunnel source and tunnel destination, when classifying tunnel packets by DSCP,

they will look only at the DSCP value of the tunnel header, which is now DSCP 28.

5. At the tunnel destination, the tunnel header is stripped off. In the case of the pipe model, however, the DSCP value of the tunnel IP header is **not** copied back into the DSCP value of the underlying data packet IP header. Hence, the original DSCP value of the underlying data packet IP header is preserved through the tunnel.

Effectively with the pipe model, there are two separate pieces of Diffserv information which are used; one is used within the bounds of the tunnel and another is used outside of the tunnel. Therefore, the pipe model enables different marking schemes to be used within the tunnel than outside the tunnel. This capability can be useful where the tunnel represents a different Diffserv domain than the networks on either side of the tunnel. This could be in the context of a VPN service provided by an SP, where for example the SP uses a different marking scheme within their portion of the network than their customers do at the edge, while allowing their customers' marking scheme to be preserved end-to-end across the SP VPN service. This capability is sometimes referred to as "QOS transparency."

It is noted that a typical default router implementation would copy the DSCP value of the underlying IP packet into tunnel DSCP value at the tunnel source, but would not copy the DSCP value of the tunnel IP header back into the DSCP value of the underlying data packet IP header at the tunnel destination.

Although [RFC 2983] only considers IP tunneling technologies, the concepts can also be applied to "tunnels" formed by encapsulation in layer 2 (link) or MPLS headers. These approaches are not a form of "IP tunneling" as they do not add an additional IP header, but nonetheless, they can be considered a form of "tunnel." MPLS Diffserv Tunneling modes are described in Section 2.3.6.2.3.

2.3.5   IPv6 QOS Architectures

There is a common misperception that IPv6 provides fundamentally better QOS capabilities than IPv4, which is incorrect. The Intserv

(Section 2.3.3) and Diffserv (Section 2.3.4) IP QOS architectures can be applied equally to IPv6 as to IPv4.

The only practical difference between IPv6 and IPv4 from a QOS perspective is that IPv6 packet headers also include a 20-bit flow label field [RFC 3697]. The flow label helps to classify a flow unambiguously, where some information used to identify the flow may be missing due to packet fragmentation or encryption (Section 2.2.1).

2.3.6   MPLS QOS Architectures

MPLS [RFC 3031] enables new forwarding paradigms from conventional IPv4 or IPv6, allowing forwarding based upon criteria other than the destination IP address. When a traffic stream traverses an MPLS network (also known as an MPLS "domain"), the IP packets (or protocol data units [PDUs] from another protocol, as the "M" in MPLS stands for "Multiprotocol") are "labeled" at the ingress edge router of the MPLS domain (referred to as an Edge Label Switched Router or ELSR). The MPLS "label" is 32 bits long, is of local significance and is most commonly "pushed" on top of (or imposed onto) the original IP header as what is known as a "shim" header; in some cases (where MPLS VPNs or MPLS traffic engineering are used, for example) more than one label (a "label stack") may be imposed. The label that is pushed at the ELSR determines the path that the packet will take across the MPLS domain; this path is termed a label switch path (LSP). Each router within the MPLS domain – termed label switched routers or LSRs – will not look at the IP destination address or within the underlying IP header of labeled packets to determine how to forward the packet but rather the label (or topmost label if there is a label stack) is used to determine which interface and outbound label to use when forwarding the packet onwards to the next hop on the LSP. At the egress of the MPLS domain the labels are popped or stripped off the packet by the egress ELSR and are then forwarded using the normal conventions of IP. Where ATM switches are used as LSRs, they do not add a label "shim" header to the IP packet, but rather encode the label stack into the ATM VPI/VCI field; such ATM LSR deployments are no longer common and hence we do not consider this case in detail.

The new forwarding paradigms made possible with MPLS enable IP networks to support new functionality. Different techniques and signaling protocols are used to determine and establish LSP paths, depending upon the particular paradigm being used. MPLS is most commonly deployed by service providers to provide one or more of the following functions:

- To allow many virtual private networks (VPNs) to be built on top of a single IP/MPLS network. These can be layer 3 VPNs, such as using BGP MPLS VPNs as described in [RFC 4364], or layer 2 VPNs such as those defined in the IETF L2VPN working group [L2VPN].

- To provide traffic engineering (TE) capabilities using MPLS RSVP-TE as defined in [RFC 3209], and as described in Chapter 6, Section 6.2.3.

- To provide fast recovery around network element failures using MPLS TE Fast Reroute (FRR) as defined in [RFC 4090], as discussed in Section 2.6.

With multi-protocol label switching (MPLS), there is a common perception that MPLS provides fundamentally better QOS capabilities than IPv4; as for IPv6, this is not correct. The Intserv (Section 2.3.3) and Diffserv (Section 2.3.4) IP QOS architectures can be applied to MPLS, but with some practical differences from "vanilla" IPv4 and IPv6.

2.3.6.1   MPLS and Intserv/RSVP

Intserv requires admission control and resource reservation on a per flow basis – where a flow is identified by the 5-tuple of source and destination IP addresses, source and destination UDP/TCP port numbers and IP protocol number. These fields are not visible to LSRs within an MPLS domain, which forward labeled packets based upon the outermost label only, hence support for Intserv would require that LSPs are provisioned on a per flow basis, which is not a scalable approach. In practice, Intserv/RSVP is supported in the context of providing reservations to aggregations of flows through the use of MPLS TE tunnels, as discussed in more detail in Chapter 4, Section 4.4.5.

2.3.6.2   MPLS and Diffserv

Diffserv can be applied in an MPLS network essentially in the same way as a plain IP networks, as defined in [RFC3270]. Traffic conditioning is performed at the edge of the Diffserv domain in exactly the same way although it is noted that the router at the edge of the MPLS domain (termed the provider edge or PE router) is not necessarily also the router at the edge of the Diffserv domain, which may be at the customer edge, or CE router. Packets are marked to indicate the particular class of traffic to which they belong and then within the core of the MPLS Diffserv network different PHBs are applied depending upon the marking.

There are, however, some differences between how Diffserv is applied to plain IP packets compared to MPLS labeled packets and these stem from the fact that within an MPLS network, all forwarding is done based upon the outermost label rather that the IP packet header. As the DSCP value is in the IP packet header, which is not used by an LSR, this cannot be used for PHB selection within an MPLS domain. Instead, there is a 3-bit field within the MPLS label shim header as shown in Figure 2.33 – termed the EXP field – which is used for classification when Diffserv is used with MPLS.

[RFC3032] initially defined the EXP field for experimental use; this was subsequently updated by [RFC3270] which redefined it for use with Diffserv, although the field is still commonly referred to as the "EXP" bits. There are two mechanisms by which the EXP field is used for PHB selection within an MPLS Diffserv network; these are described in the following sections.

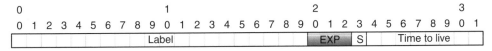

Figure 2.33   MPLS label stack encoding: Label = label value (20 bits), EXP = EXP field (3 bits), S = bottom of stack indicator (1 bit), TTL = time to live field (8 bits)

2.3.6.2.1   EXP Inferred PHB Selection

The most commonly used approach for PHB selection within an MPLS network is to use the EXP field to determine with which PHB a labeled packet should be serviced; this is referred to as EXP Inferred PHB selection.

The EXP field is only three bits long, and therefore it can only represent 8 distinct values, whereas there are 64 possible DSCP values, hence it is not possible to treat the EXP field in labeled packets as directly equivalent to the DS Field in plain IP packets. Therefore, there may need to be a many-to-one mapping of DSCP values to EXP values at the ingress ELSR such that a particular EXP value may need to represent a group of DSCP values, in which case it is referred to as a PHB scheduling class (PSC). LSPs where the EXP field marking is used to determine a PSC are called as EXP-Inferred-PSC LSPs (E-LSPs).

The typical default behavior at an ingress LSR is to copy bits 0 to 2 of the DS field – which are the class selector (CS) codepoints (which are functionally equivalent to the precedence bits) – into the 3 bits of the EXP field in the MPLS label, as shown in Figure 2.34.

The typical default behavior applied at LSRs within the MPLS domain is to copy the EXP field from label-to-label. If additional labels

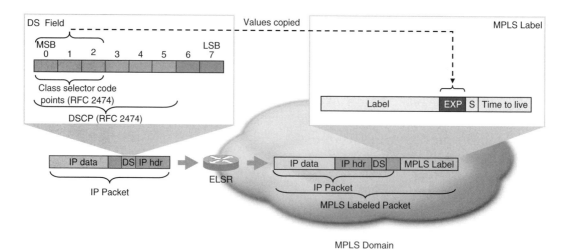

Figure 2.34 Copying CS codepoint to EXP field

are imposed (i.e. a label stack is used), the typical default behavior is to copy the EXP field up the label stack. Hence, where these behaviors are supported, by default the CS codepoint marking of the underlying IP packet is propagated up the label stack. If labels are popped off, the typical default behavior is not to copy the EXP field down the label stack or to the CS codepoints. Therefore if the EXP field marking is changed within the MPLS network this change is not normally propagated down the label stack, but rather the underlying CS codepoint and DSCP values are preserved across the MPLS domain. Behaviors other than this are possible; these are discussed in Section 2.3.6.2.3 on Diffserv MPLS tunnel modes.

2.3.6.2.2   Label Inferred PHB Selection

The use of E-LSPs is the norm in MPLS Diffserv deployments; however, should 8 distinct PSC markings be insufficient to support the number of PHBs required in an MPLS Diffserv network design – or where ATM LSRs are deployed, where a shim header is not used – an alternative approach is defined.

With E-LSPs, a single LSP can be used to carry labeled packets marked with a number of different PSCs; however, [RFC 3270] also defines a scheme where an LSP carries a single PSC only; LSPs that use this scheme are referred to as label-only-inferred-PSC LSPs (L-LSPs). Where a "shim" header is used, the EXP field can then be used to represent the drop precedence to be applied by the LSR to the labeled packet (see the AF PHB, Section 2.3.4.2.2).

ATM LSRs are not widely deployed and in practice there have not been significant requirements for more than 8 distinct PSCs in MPLS Diffserv networks (see the backbone Diffserv deployment case study in Chapter 3, Section 3.3.2). Hence, L-LSPs are not widely used.

2.3.6.2.3   MPLS Diffserv Tunneling Models

[RFC 3270] considers the application of the Diffserv tunneling models (as described in Section 2.3.4.5) and concepts specifically to MPLS. There are a number of conceptual similarities between the Diffserv tunneling models used for IP tunneling and those used for MPLS, where MPLS LSPs are used instead of IP tunnels. As for IP tunnels,

MPLS LSPs are unidirectional. In addition, comparably with IP tunnels, intermediate nodes on the path of an LSP look at the marking of the outermost label only. There are also, however, a number of differences due to the implicit differences between IP and MPLS. [RFC 3270] defines three MPLS Diffserv tunneling models, which are described in the following sections.

2.3.6.2.3.1 MPLS Uniform Model The uniform model for MPLS is conceptually similar to the IP tunneling case. Consider the example shown in Figure 2.35 and the following description. In this example, which describes an IP-to-MPLS forwarding case, only a single level of label is added, which could be assigned by LDP [RFC 3036] for example.

1. Outside of the MPLS domain, e.g. at router 1, assume IP data packets are marked with DSCP 34 (i.e. AF41).

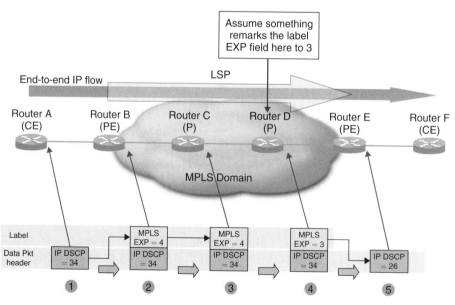

Figure 2.35 MPLS Diffserv tunnel modes: uniform model

2. At the ingress ELSR (Router B), the initial LSP label is imposed and the EXP value for the label is set. The EXP may be derived from the underlying IP packet DSCP value; however, as the EXP field is only 3 bits and the DSCP is 8 bits, it is not possible to copy the whole DSCP value to the EXP field (as would be the case with an IP tunnel). In this example, we assume that bits 0–2 of the DSCP are copied into the label EXP field as described in Section 2.3.6.2.1 with the result that the EXP field would be set to 4. Alternative mappings between the underlying DSCP and the EXP field are possible.

   In an MPLS-to-MPLS forwarding case, where the uniform model is used, the EXP value would be copied up the label stack, as additional layers of label are imposed.

3. Intermediate routers on the LSP, e.g. Router C, will label switch the packet based upon the label value (outermost label value if there is a label stack); as packets are labeled switched, the EXP is by default copied from ingress label to egress label. Hence, in this example, the packet would have an EXP value of 4 on egress to Router C. If there is a label stack, when classifying packets by the EXP field, LSRs will look only at the EXP field of the outermost label.

4. Assuming that some function at Router D re-marks the packets on the LSP from EXP 4 to EXP 3, if there is a label stack, the re-marking only affects the EXP value of the outermost label. Hence, the EXP value of the label is now EXP 3, while the DSCP of the underlying IP data packet header is still DSCP 34 (i.e. AF41). Router D and any subsequent routers on the LSP, when classifying labeled packets by the EXP field, will look only at the EXP field of the outermost label only, which is now EXP 3.

5. In this case, we assume that penultimate hop popping (PHP) is not used, and hence the label is stripped off at the egress ELSR which is the final hop of the LSP, being Router E in this example. The DSCP field value of the underlying IP packet may be re-marked to a value derived from the EXP field value of the deposed label. If the EXP field value were copied back to bits 0–2 of the DSCP field, the resultant DSCP value of the exposed packet on egress to

Router E would be DSCP 26 (i.e. AF31), although alternative mappings between the EXP field and the underlying packet DSCP value are possible. As the label is popped off, on egress to Router E and at subsequent routers the underlying DSCP may be used to classify the packets.

Where PHP is used, the label is popped off at the penultimate hop on the LSP, Router D, in which case as no label is present at Router E, router D would need to perform any required mapping/copying from EXP to DSCP.

The intent with the uniform model is that when used with MPLS, there is really no difference in the resultant Diffserv behavior compared to where MPLS is not used. However, the one factor which prevents total transparency of MPLS to Diffserv operations (unlike the IP tunneling case), is the fact that the MPLS EXP field is only 3 bits long while the DSCP is 8 bits long; this may therefore demand a mapping from DSCP values to EXP values and back to DSCP values, rather than the simple copying which is used in the IP tunneling case.

In practice, it is not normal to apply re-marking within an MPLS domain; rather, such conditioning functions are normally performed at the edge of the Diffserv domain. Hence, the uniform model is rarely used in the context of MPLS and it is defined as optional by [RFC 3270].

2.3.6.2.3.2 *MPLS Pipe Model*

The pipe model for MPLS is conceptually similar to the IP tunneling case, where MPLS LSPs are used instead of IP tunnels, although implicitly there are some differences due to the differences between IP and MPLS. Considering the case of a single level of label (i.e. no label stack), the MPLS pipe model treats the DSCP markings on an underlying IP packet and the MPLS EXP markings on the LSP used by the packet as independent entities. At the start of the LSP, the MPLS EXP field is set; this setting may be derived from the marking in the DCSP of the underlying packet in the case of IP-to-MPLS forwarding, or from the MPLS EXP field of the received label in the case of MPLS-to-MPLS forwarding where a hierarchy of LSPs result in a label stack. Along the path of the LSP, any classification,

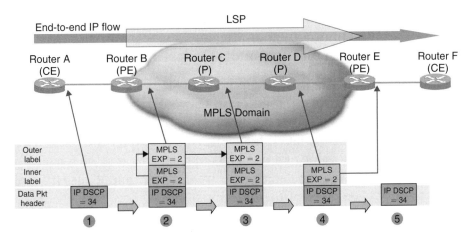

Figure 2.36 MPLS Diffserv tunnel modes: pipe model

marking and re-marking are performed using the EXP field of the outermost label only. Where the outermost label is stripped off, at the end of an LSP (or at the penultimate hop, where PHP is used), the MPLS EXP value of the deposed label is not copied down into the underlying IP packet DSCP or underlying label EXP field.

Consider the example shown in Figure 2.36 and the following description. In this example, which describes an IP-to-MPLS transition, a label stack is used, which could for example represent an MPLS VPN deployment [as per RFC 4364], where the inner label is assigned by Multiprotocol BGP (MBGP) [RFC 2858] and the outer label is assigned by LDP [RFC 3036]. The example also assumes that PHP is used:

1. Outside of the MPLS domain, e.g. at router 1, assume IP data packets are marked with DSCP 34 (i.e. AF41).

2. At the ingress ELSR (Router B), the label stack is imposed and the EXP values for the labels are set. The EXP value for the inner label may be derived from the DSCP value of the underlying IP packet DSCP, or may be set independently of that value. In this example, we assume that the EXP value is set to 2 independently of the underlying IP packet DSCP. As in this example, a label stack is used and

the EXP value of the inner (e.g. MBGP, in the context of MPLS VPN) label is copied up the label stack into the outer (e.g. LDP) label, hence the inner and outer labels both have an EXP value of 2.

3. Intermediate routers on the LSP path, e.g. Router C, will label switch the packet based upon the outermost label value; as packets are labeled switched, the EXP is by default copied from ingress label to egress label, hence in this example, the packet would have an EXP value of 4 on egress to Router C. If there is a label stack, in classifying labeled packets by the EXP field, LSRs will look only at the EXP field of the outermost label.

4. As PHP is used in this example, the outer (e.g. LDP) label is popped off at the penultimate LSR on the LSP, which is Router D in this example. Although the outer label is popped off, the inner (e.g. MBGP) label still remains, hence when classifying labeled packets by the EXP field, on egress Router D will look at the EXP field of this remaining label.

5. Router E, the egress ELSR, will receive the packet with this single (MBGP) label, which it will pop off. Even though it pops off this label, the pipe model defines that Router E retains the value of the EXP field in the received label, such that it can be used to classify the (now unlabeled) packets on egress from Router E to Router F.

   Where a label stack is not used, and penultimate hop popping is used, Router E does not receive a labeled packet, and has no EXP information to retain and use for classification on egress to Router F; therefore, the pipe model cannot be used where penultimate hop popping is used without a label stack.

The pipe model is widely used in MPLS VPN deployments and hence is defined as mandatory by [RFC 3270].

It is noted that the typical default behavior implemented on LSRs is an inception of the pipe model. An ingress LSR will typically copy bits 0 to 2 of the DS field into the 3 bits of the EXP field in the MPLS label by default. The typical default behavior at the egress LSR is not

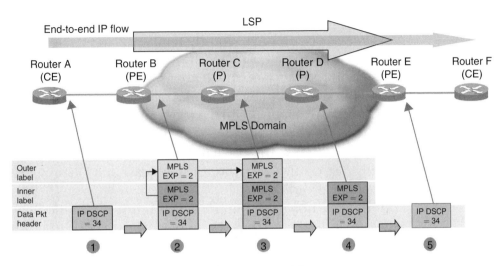

Figure 2.37 MPLS Diffserv tunnel modes: short pipe model

to copy the EXP field down the label stack or to the CS codepoints, as labels are popped.

2.3.6.2.3.3 MPLS Short Pipe Model   The short pipe model is a variation on the pipe model; consider the example in Figure 2.37 and the following description.

Steps 1–4 as per the MPLS pipe model described in Section 2.3.6.2.3.2.

Step 5: The short pipe model differs from the pipe model in terms of the behavior applied at the egress ELSR; rather than retaining the EXP value of the received label, the value of the underlying DSCP is used to classify the (now unlabeled) packets on egress from Router E to Router F.

2.3.7   IP Multicast and QOS

The Intserv (Section 2.3.3) and Diffserv (Section 2.3.4) IP QOS architectures were designed to support both IP unicast and IP multicast [RFC1112] traffic from the outset.

- *IP Multicast and Diffserv*. Support for the basic mechanisms of Diffserv is no different for IP multicast than for IP unicast. Multicast traffic is designated by the destination address of the packets; other than that, the IP headers for multicast traffic are the same as for unicast traffic. Multicast replicated packets have exactly the same DSCP as the original packet, and therefore will be treated with the same PHB as the incoming packets of their respective multicast group. Hence, the DSCP field can be used to mark and classify IP multicast traffic exactly as for IP unicast and Diffserv PHBs can be applied accordingly.

  Implicitly, however, the impact of multicast traffic flows on a network is different from the impact of unicast traffic flows; by definition, multicast flows are point-to-multipoint or multipoint-to-multipoint – a single multicast stream from a source may be replicated to multiple destinations – whereas unicast flows are point-to-point. Hence, the key differences between a unicast and a multicast Diffserv deployment are two-fold:

  ○ *Multicast capacity planning*. Capacity planning in a Diffserv network manages the provisioning of available capacity relative to network load, potentially on a per-class basis. In a multicast deployment, this needs to take into account the traffic matrix (the matrix of ingress to egress flows) resulting from multicast replication. Capacity planning is discussed in detail in Chapter 6.

  ○ *Multicast SLAs*. Whereas a received unicast flow can be limited on ingress to the network and the impact on the network thereby constrained, a received multicast flow may be replicated to many destinations within the network after it is received, and hence the impact on the network may be significantly greater. Any SLA definitions for Diffserv-enabled multicast services must take multicast replication within the network into account.

- *IP Multicast and Intserv/RSVP*. Intserv [RFC1633] and RSVP [RFC2205] were fundamentally designed to cater for multicast as well as unicast reservations. As a consequence, RSVP gives flexible control over the manner in which reservations can be shared along branches of the multicast delivery trees, using "Wildcard Filter" and "Shared-Explicit Filter" reservation styles to allow for reservation state merging. Further, RSVP allows the elementary actions of adding or deleting one sender and/or receiver to or from an existing reservation. Intserv and RSVP are discussed in more detail in Chapter 4, Section 4.4.

2.4 Typical Router QOS Implementations in Practice

Diffserv is the most widely deployed QOS IP QOS architecture and hence most router QOS implementations are optimized for Diffserv deployments. In Section 2.2 we described the main data plane tools that are used in IP QOS: classification, marking, policing, queuing and scheduling, dropping, and shaping. In practice, which of these components are used and how they are combined to create a QOS policy depend upon where they are being applied in the network – at the edge or in the core – and whether they are being applied on egress to an interface or on ingress. Many networks are built with a hierarchy consisting of core routers (CRs), which provide connectivity between distribution routers (DRs), which in turn aggregate connections to routers at remote sites, each of which have local access routers (ARs). If, for example, we consider a Diffserv deployment in this type of network, as shown in Figure 2.38, the access link will normally be the edge of the Diffserv domain, with edge policies being applied outbound on the access router core facing interface and on the access facing interface of the distribution router (which may have

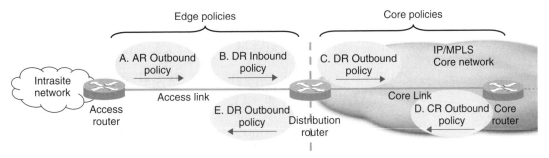

Figure 2.38 Where in the network QOS policies are applied

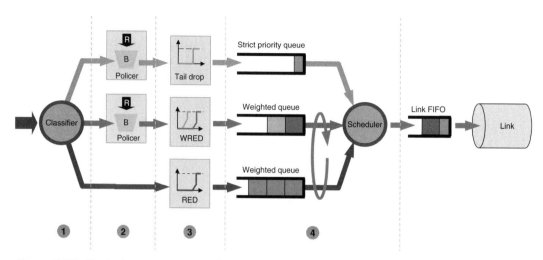

Figure 2.39   Typical access router outbound QOS implementation

inbound policies in some cases also); core policies are then typically applied outbound on the core facing interfaces of the distribution router and outbound on all core router interfaces.

As complex classification and conditioning is performed at the edge of a Diffserv network, router QOS policies applied on routers at the edge of the network (i.e. access routers and distribution routers) are typically more complicated than those used on core routers. Figure 2.39 shows how the different Diffserv QOS components are used together in a typical AR QOS policy applied outbound on the DR facing interface (i.e. policy A in Figure 2.38). Considering Figure 2.39:

- The traffic that is destined for the interface is first classified using simple or complex classification. In this example, we show three classes, although there could be more or less.

- The top traffic class (diagramatically) in Figure 2.39 is serviced from a strict priority queue, for the lowest delay and jitter; this is likely to include applications such as voice and video. An SR-TCM policer with an exceed action of drop is applied to the class before packets are enqueued into the strict priority queue, to enforce a maximum rate for the class and in order to prevent this class from starving the other classes of bandwidth; packets which are dropped by the policer are not enqueued in the class queue. Tail drop is used to impose a maximum queue limit for the queue, hence enforcing a maximum delay bound for traffic in the queue; the tail drop queue limit may be somewhat redundant in the presence of the applied policer as the policer burst will also implicitly limit the maximum queue depth, and hence delay bound.

• The middle traffic class in Figure 2.39 is serviced from a weighted bandwidth queue. An SR-TCM policer may be applied to the class before packets are enqueued in order to enforce a maximum rate for the in-contract traffic within the class. This could for example be achieved with a conform action of transmit (if the traffic is not pre-marked this could be combined with marking in-contract), and violate action of transmit + mark out-of-contract. WRED may be used to maximize throughput for TCP-based applications within the class and to drop in- and out-of-contract traffic differentially, by using a more aggressive WRED profile for the out-of-contract traffic.

• The bottom traffic class in Figure 2.39 is serviced from a weighted bandwidth queue. RED is used to maximize throughput for TCP-based applications within the class.

• The scheduler ensures that the top class is treated with appropriate priority, and that the middle and red classes receive minimum bandwidth assurances due to their respective configured weightings.

• In most practical router implementations a hardware "line driver" will deal with sending the packets onto the actual line and the scheduler will service its queues into the queue of the hardware line driver on the outgoing interface, which is known as the interface FIFO.

From the above description, it can be seen that there is an implied ordering of OQS actions:

1. Classification is performed first to determine which class packets will be assigned to.

2. Then policing and marking functions are applied to the respective classes; packets dropped by the policer will not be enqueued and will not be subject to tail drop or (W)RED drop decisions. Packets should not be re-classified into other classes at this step, or else there would be the possibility of a loop, where a packet is remarked in one class, then reclassified into another class, where it is also remarked, then reclassified into another class and so on.

3. Tail drop or (W)RED decisions are performed before packets are enqueued into their respective queues. If policing/marking policies have been applied to the class in step #2, it is important that an (W)RED profile selection and drop decisions are based upon the resulting markings from that step, such that any in-/out-of-contract marking will be effective for example. Note that, although (W)RED profile selection should be based upon the result of step #2, packets should not be re-classified into other classes at this step, or else there would be the possibility of a classification loop.

4. Then scheduling decisions are performed and the packets are enqueued in the interface FIFO.

The AR outbound QOS implementation described above could further be augmented with the addition of an aggregate shaper, as described in Section 2.2.4.3, where required to offer subline rate services, as shown in Figure 2.40.

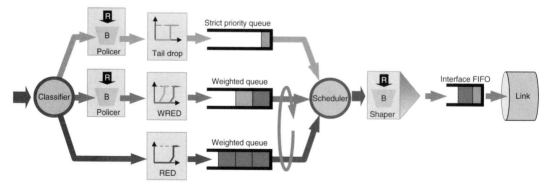

Figure 2.40 Access router outbound QOS implementation with subline rate shaping

Outbound DR QOS policies on AR facing interfaces (i.e. policy E in Figure 2.38) will typically be similar, only with no policers applied to the weighted bandwidth queues, as outbound traffic will have been subjected to traffic conditioning on ingress to the Diffserv domain.

Depending on a particular deployment, QOS policies may be applied inbound on the DR on the AR facing interface (i.e. policy B in Figure 2.38) to perform conditioning on ingress to the Diffserv domain. This is likely to be the case where the access link represents a trust boundary between a network service provider and a customer. While, conceptually, the egress access QOS implementation shown in Figure 2.39 could also be implemented on ingress to a router, this is not commonly done in practice. The ingress to an interface is less commonly an aggregation point for traffic than the egress; if traffic is not aggregated then congestion will not occur, and hence there may be no need to implement scheduling or queuing on ingress to a router. Instead, on ingress to a router interface it is more common to support only per-class policing to perform conditioning, where an SR-TCM or TR-TCM is applied to each class. Figure 2.41 shows a

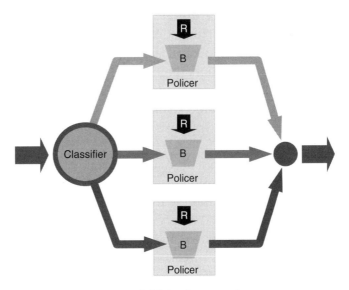

Figure 2.41 Typical distribution router ingress QOS implementation

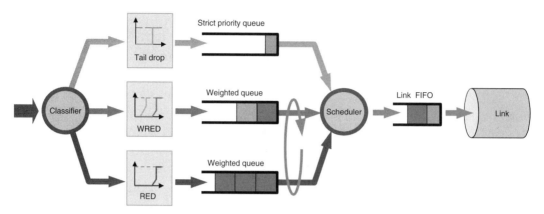

Figure 2.42 Typical core router egress QOS implementation

typical QOS implementation applied to traffic on ingress to a distribution router AR facing interface (i.e. policy B in Figure 2.38).

A typical core router egress QOS implementation (i.e. policy D in Figure 2.38), as shown in Figure 2.42, would generally be a simpler subset of the access router implementation; without policers applied to the weighted bandwidth queues, nor with support for aggregate shapers; the reasons for the differences between core and access router capabilities with respect to QOS are discussed in Section 2.3.4. The same implementation would also typically be used on egress to the DR core facing interfaces (i.e. policy C in Figure 2.38). There are not typically any QOS policies applied on ingress to core interfaces.

When considered as a whole, a typical distribution router QOS implementation supporting a number of access interfaces is shown in Figure 2.43.

Depending upon the architecture of the router, the QOS mechanisms may be implemented centrally in the router, or on distributed platforms, they may be implemented on the interface linecards. On platforms which have a centralized switching fabric, the switching fabric may be a point of aggregation of traffic and hence queuing and scheduling mechanisms may be implemented toward the switching fabric itself. If Diffserv EF/AF forwarding behaviors have an impact on router forwarding performance, the router will support less aggregate

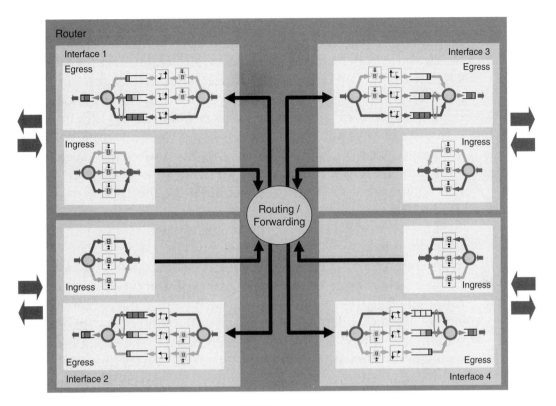

Figure 2.43   Typical distribution router QOS implementation

throughput with Diffserv enabled, and consequently, the per-port cost of the network deployment will be higher. High-performance routers typically implement the EF/AF forwarding behaviors in ASICs, ensuring that there is no forwarding penalty associated with the support of the Diffserv functionality.

The case studies presented in Chapter 3 consider the definition and application of specific QOS policies in more detail.

2.5   Layer 2 QOS

Although the focus of this book is on IP (i.e. layer 3) QOS, IP networks use underlying layer 1 and 2 technologies in order to provide connectivity between layer 3 nodes (i.e. routers). Therefore, in building end-to-end IP services with contracted SLA commitments, it is essential that the underlying layer 1 and layer 2 technologies are able to support the network requirements needed to deliver the contracted SLAs. The SLAs provided at the IP layer are, however, implicitly limited by the SLAs of the underlying layer 2 technology; for example, it would not be possible to deliver an IP service supporting VoIP with a bounded delay, jitter and loss, using an underlying layer 2 network, which did not provide SLAs for delay, jitter and loss at least as good (generally better) as those required for the IP service, e.g. an ATM ABR service.

Some point-to-point layer 2 technologies, such as leased lines delivered on underlying TDM or Synchronous Optical Network (SONET)/Synchronous Digital Hierarchy (SDH) networks, generally have well-defined SLAs at layer 2, which are capable of supporting layer 3 applications with tight SLA requirements. Such connections generally have a defined delay, a defined bit error rate (BER) and committed layer 2 minimum bandwidth, which is normally equal to the maximum bandwidth for the service. In these cases, Intserv or Diffserv queuing policies can be attached directly to the interface that represents the connection; in the case of Diffserv the policy applied would be similar to that illustrated in Figure 2.40.

Other considerations can apply to multiaccess layer 2 technologies, such as ATM, Frame relay and Ethernet, which have some of their own explicit QOS capabilities at layer 2; in such cases end-to-end IP SLAs can be achieved by interworking between layer 3 QOS functions and the underlying layer 2 QOS capabilities as described in the following sections.

2.5.1 ATM

Asynchronous transfer mode (ATM) is a cell relay technology which can be used to provide layer 2 connectivity in IP networks. ATM is a connection-oriented technology in which virtual circuits (VCs) are established between the end points of the connection before data can be exchanged. The ATM Forum Traffic Management Specification Version 4.0 [af-tm-0056] defines the following five service categories that determine the QOS that a particular VC receives:

- *Constant bit rate (CBR)*. The CBR service category was designed to support low delay (cell transfer delay or CTD), low jitter (cell delay variation or CDV), low loss, constant bit rate applications such as circuit emulation. CBR VCs have a specified peak cell rate (PCR); as long as the PCR is not exceeded, the CTD and CDV will be assured.

- *Variable bit rate – real-time (VBR-rt)*. The VBR-rt service category was designed to support low delay, low jitter, low loss, variable bit rate applications such as VoIP and video. VBR VCs (both VBR-rt and VBR-nrt) have a specified sustained cell rate (SCR) but can burst at rates above this up to their defined PCR as defined by the maximum burst size (MBS).

- *Variable bit rate – non-real-time (VBR-nrt)*. The VBR-nrt service category was designed to support bursty, non-real-time applications that require a committed minimum amount of bandwidth but do not have tightly bounded requirements for delay and jitter. With VBR-nrt, the CTD and CDV are not assured and hence VBR-nrt is unsuitable for real-time applications.

- *Available bit rate (ABR)*. Similar to VBR-nrt the ABR service category was designed to support bursty, non-real-time applications that require a committed minimum amount of bandwidth while the VC is active. In addition, however, ABR uses closed-loop feedback conveyed via resource management (RM) cells from the network to the end-systems in order to adapt their rate of sending based upon the congested state of the network. This allows end-systems to increase their transmission rates to take advantage of the available bandwidth when the network is not congested. If the end-systems correctly adapt their rate of sending based upon the network feedback, the network commits to a ratio of dropped cells to transmitted cells defined by the cell loss ratio (CLR).

With ABR, the CTD and CDV can be large and hence ABR is unsuitable for real-time applications. ABR VCs have a specified minimum cell rate (MCR) and PCR; the bandwidth available to a VC at a particular point in time is defined as the available cell rate (ACR), which is between MCR and PCR.

- *Unspecified bit rate (UBR)*. UBR VCs have a specified PCR which defines the maximum rate for the VC; VCs can use up to their configured PCR when bandwidth is available, although no bandwidth reservations are made for the VC within the ATM network. There are no bounds with respect to the CTD or CLR, i.e. cell delivery is not guaranteed; retransmission at higher layers is assumed and hence UBR is unsuitable for real-time applications or applications with committed loss requirements.

  The UBR + variant of UBR allows end-systems to signal a requested MCR to an ATM switch in a connection request, and the ATM network attempts to maintain this as an end-to-end guarantee.

ATM traffic shaping is performed by ATM end-systems at the ingress point to the ATM network (the user-to-network interface or UNI) in order to ensure that the traffic on the VC adheres to the respective VC traffic contract. If the traffic contract is exceeded then policing within the ATM network may drop excess traffic or may set the cell loss priority (CLP) bit within the cell header to 1. If congestion is subsequently experienced within the ATM network cells marked CLP = 1 are discarded in preference to cells marked CLP = 0. VCs may be grouped together in a virtual path (VP), which may also be shaped.

Within the ATM network, schedulers are used to differentiate between traffic from the different service categories. Typical ATM schedulers service the different ATM service categories in strict priority order: CBR is serviced first with highest priority, then VBR-rt, next VBR-nrt, and ABR with UBR last.

The different ATM service classes can be used when supporting Intserv or Diffserv over an ATM connection. This "mapping" of Diffserv to ATM QOS is described in the following section, while Intserv is described in detail in Chapter 4.

2.5.1.1   Mapping Diffserv to ATM QOS

There are two ways that Diffserv can be supported over an intermediate layer 2 ATM connection between two layer 3 nodes:

- *Single VC approach.* With this approach a single VC is used between connected layer 3 nodes and a Diffserv IP QOS policy, i.e. a queuing policy implementing Diffserv PHBs, is applied to that VC. The service category and SLA commitments for the VC need to be sufficient to support the sum of the tightest SLA requirements for constituent Diffserv classes being transported.

  For example, if 256 kbps of VoIP traffic and a minimum of 512 kbps of data traffic needs to be concurrently supported between two sites using ATM, the VC would need to be of a service category that can meet the delay, jitter, and loss requirements of the VoIP service (i.e. typically CBR or VBR-rt), and the VC would need to be provisioned for (512 kbps + 256 kbps) = 768 kbps. The ATM service provider would only assure the delay, jitter, and loss commitments for the VC for up to 768 kbps of traffic, and therefore ATM traffic shaping would be applied to the VC at each of the L3 nodes at either end of the VC. A Diffserv policy would also be applied to each shaped VC, which would use an EF PHB (i.e. priority queue) to prioritize the 256 kbps of VoIP traffic, and an AF PHB (i.e. weighted bandwidth queue) to assure a minimum of 512 kbps of data traffic. The policy applied would be similar to that illustrated in Figure 2.40, where the aggregate shaper was performing ATM traffic shaping. If the VoIP traffic were inactive then the data traffic could potentially re-use the unused bandwidth up to the 768 kbps VC maximum rate.

- *Multi-VC approach.* With this approach, a separate ATM VC is used for each Diffserv PHB type between connected layer 3 nodes. Each VC has a different ATM service category, where the service category and SLA commitments for each VC need to be sufficient to support the SLA requirements of the respective Diffserv classes being transported.

  Considering the previous example, a 256 kbps VC could be used to support the voice (EF) traffic; this VC would need to be of a service category that can meet the delay and jitter requirements of the VoIP service, i.e. typically CBR or VBR-rt. A separate 512 kbps VC would be used to support the data (AF) traffic. The data VC would need to be of a service category that can meet the delay and loss requirements of the data service, i.e. typically VBR-nrt, but potentially ABR or UBR+ depending upon the specific service requirements.

SLAs for ATM services available from ATM network service providers are generally specified on a per-VC basis (unless ATM VPs are used), rather than across a group of VCs. Therefore, this approach can have the disadvantage that the SLAs for the service do not allow for unused capacity on the voice VC to be directly available to be re-used by the data traffic, for example. A potential benefit of this approach, however, is that rental cost of 1×256 kbps CBR VC and 1×512 kbps VBR-nrt VC may be less than for 1×768 kbps CBR VC (VCs with higher priority service categories tend to be more expensive than lower priority categories). This approach may require that the multiple VCs are effectively treated as a single routed connection, with the DSCP of each packet determining which particular VC will be used for that packet.

Section 2.3.4.4 discusses the possible interworking of ATM explicit forward congestion indication (EFCI) with ECN.

2.5.2 Frame-relay

Compared to ATM, the QOS capabilities provided with frame-relay networks are rudimentary. Frame-relay, like ATM, is a connection-oriented technology in which VCs are established between the end points of the connection before data can be exchanged. The service provided by a frame-relay VC is defined in terms of a token bucket traffic shaper, as described in Section 2.2.4.3. The bucket has a specified maximum depth, which is the sum of the committed burst (*Bc*) and the excess burst (*Be*) and is filled at a rate defined by the committed information rate (*CIR*). *CIR* defines the average rate at which the frame-relay network service guarantees to transport data on the VC during a time interval *Tc*. *Bc* defines the maximum amount of data that can be transmitted during the interval *Tc*, i.e. *Bc* = *CIR* * *Tc*. *Be* defines the amount of excess data in addition to *Bc* that can be sent during the first interval after the token bucket is full, i.e. it contains *Bc* + *Be* tokens. Therefore, if the bucket is full *Bc* + *Be* bytes can be sent in the first interval; if these tokens are all used then *Bc* bytes can be sent in the subsequent time interval.

Frame-relay traffic shaping is performed by frame-relay end-systems at the ingress point to the frame-relay network (i.e. at the UNI) in order to ensure that the traffic on the VC adheres to the respective VC traffic contract. If the traffic contract is exceeded then policing within the frame-relay network may drop excess traffic or may set the discard eligibility (DE) bit within the cell header. If congestion is subsequently experienced within the network, the frames with DE set are discarded in preference to frames where DE is not set. Frame-relay provides explicit notification of congestion via forward explicit congestion notification (FECN); if congestion is experienced along the path of a VC, this bit is set in transiting frames; the destination frame-relay end-system will set the backward error congestion notification (BECN) bit in frames sent back to the source end-system. The explicit congestion notification provided by BECN can be used to allow end-systems to increase their transmission rates (through adapting their traffic shaping rates) to take advantage of the available bandwidth when the network is not congested, resorting to sending at CIR if BECN is received.

When Diffserv is applied to frame-relay, a Diffserv IP QOS policy is applied to a shaped frame-relay VC; the policy applied would be similar to that illustrated in Figure 2.40, where the aggregate shaper would be performing frame-relay traffic shaping. Unlike ATM, frame-relay does not have the concept of different service categories and therefore the SLA commitments for the VC assured by the frame-relay service provider would need to be sufficient to support the sum of the tightest SLA requirements for constituent Diffserv classes being transported.

Section 2.3.4.4 discusses the possible interworking of frame-relay forward explicit congestion notification (FECN) with ECN.

2.5.3   Ethernet

The original IEEE 802.3 specifications for Ethernet included no provision for differentiated QOS, i.e. only supported a single service class. The subsequent 802.1Q [802.1Q] project in the IEEE 802 standards process added support for VLAN trunking. The 802.1Q frame format added an extra 4-byte "VLAN tag" to the original Ethernet header, 3-bits of which are defined as the *user_priority* field as shown in Figure 2.44.

The use of the *user_priority* field, to assign a priority indication to each frame, was defined by the 802.1P project (and hence is also commonly referred to as the "802.1P" field), the results of which were merged into 802.1D [802.1D] Annex G. The use of the user_priority field is analogous to the use of the DSCP field in IP and the EXP field in an MPLS network; the field is used to indicate the "priority" of the frame, which is used to determine the forwarding behavior of that frame at each bridging hop. As the field is 3 bits long it can be used to present 8 distinct markings.

Annex G of 802.1D is considered as "informative" only, and provides only a high-level description of behaviors that should be applied based upon *user_priority* markings. 802.1D Annex G acknowledges that not all 8 markings may be used in any particular deployment and specifies strict priority behavior as the minimal implementation where only a few classes are deployed. It acknowledges the need to support schedulers which can provide minimum bandwidth assurances where

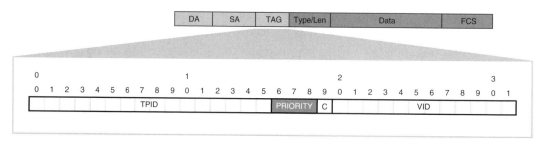

Figure 2.44   802.1Q Frame Format. DA = Destination Address, SA = Source Address, FCS = Frame Check Sequence, TPID = Tag Protocol Identifier (16 bits), PRIORITY = User priority field (3 bits), C = Canonical Format Indicator (1 bit), VID = VLAN Identifier (12 bits)

greater numbers of classes are supported. In practice, in interpreting the specification, most Ethernet switch vendors today support Diffserv like scheduling, with a strict priority queue (i.e. EF-like) and a number of weighted bandwidth queues (i.e. AF-like), to which different *user_priority* values can be assigned.

Hence, in practice, it is often possible to use these capabilities and to treat Ethernet networks, which are components of an end-to-end IP network, almost like any other part of the Diffserv domain, but with EF-like and AF-like behaviors being applied based upon classification of the 802.1Q *user_priority* field. As with MPLS EXP field, it is noted that as the *user_priority* field is 3 bits long and therefore it can only represent 8 distinct values, whereas there are 64 possible DSCP values, hence when used as a component in an end-to-end Diffserv network a particular *user_priority* value may need to represent a group of DSCP values.

2.6 Complementary Technologies

Complementary to IP QOS technologies, there are a set of additional techniques and technologies that have been developed within the IP technical community and which further enable IP networks to be engineered to support tightly bounded SLA commitments. While these technologies are not covered in detail in this book, they are described here in overview.

- *Fast IGP convergence.* Advancements and developments in the implementation and deployment of IGPs have resulted in significant improvements to the IGP convergence times that can be achieved without any compromise in routing protocol stability. This has resulted in convergence times of a few hundred milliseconds being realistically achievable in well-designed IP networks today [FRANCOIS], which significantly reduces the loss of connectivity experienced following network element (e.g. link or node) failures. This reduction in convergence times allows higher availability targets and lower packet loss rates to be offered for SLAs across all service classes. Consequently, fast IGP convergence is also recommended as a foundation for multiservice IP network designs.

- ***Fast reroute technologies***. Developments in local protection schemes for both IP and MPLS – generically termed fast reroute (FRR) technologies – enable further reductions in the loss of connectivity following network element failures.

  ○ *MPLS traffic engineering fast reroute.* The use of MPLS traffic engineering (TE) for admission control is discussed in Chapter 4, and for bandwidth management is discussed in Chapter 6. However, there is another application of MPLS TE which is in the context if MPLS TE Fast Re-route (FRR) [RFC 4090].

  ○ *IP fast re-route.* IP fast re-route [SHAND] is a recent development which provides similar capabilities to MPLS TE FRR, but for IP environments.

  These FRR technologies are local protection schemes, unlike IGP convergence which is a distributed computation process. With FRR, on occurrence of a failure there are no delays associated with the distribution of updated routing information or routing table recalculation prior to IP connectivity being restored. Consequently, the restoration times achieved with FRR are always likely to be faster – typically within fifty milliseconds – and more deterministic than those achieved with IGP fast convergence are. This allows the highest availability of service to be offered in support of VoIP services; for example, ensuring that link failures have minimal impact on IP telephony users. Where such levels of protection are required, a subsecond convergence IGP design should be complemented with the deployment of FRR.

2.7 Where QOS cannot make a difference

In concluding this chapter, we highlight the fact that QOS is not a panacea to all networking ills. There will undoubtedly be cases where, even using QOS mechanisms the SLA requirements cannot be met on a particular network, and hence techniques other than QOS may need to be considered.

- *Network engineering.* In some cases, it may be necessary to re-engineer a network in order to ensure that the SLA requirements of an application can be met. For example, a satellite connection could be replaced by a terrestrial link, in order to reduce the end-to-end delay experienced by an application.

- *Application engineering*. There may be cases where it is more appropriate (cost-effective) to re-engineer an application, or rather re-engineer how an application uses the network such that the applications SLA demands on the network are reduced, than to re-engineer the network to support the original requirements of the application. For example, if the de-jitter buffer on a video end-system is set unnecessarily large it may add unnecessarily to the end-to-end delay, which may increase the channel change time or VoD responsiveness above acceptable thresholds. In this case the right approach to solving the problem is to reduce the de-jitter buffer in the video end-system rather than trying to reduce the network delay. Another example of application engineering is the deployment of distributed application caches throughout the network, which can both reduce the network traffic load due to the application, and also reduce the end-user response times.

References

[802.1D] IEEE Std. 802.1D-2004, Media Access Control (MAC) Bridges

[802.1Q] IEEE Std. 802.1Q-2003, Virtual Bridged Local Area Networks

[af-tm-0056] ATM Forum Traffic Management Specification Version 4.0, April 1996

[BITORIKA] A. Bitorika, M. Robin, and M. Huggard, A survey of active queue management schemes, Trinity College Dublin, Department of Computer Science, Tech. Rep., Sept. 2003

[CISCO]http://www.cisco.com/univercd/cc/td/doc/product/software/ios120/120newft/120limit/120s/120s28/12sl3ncd.htm

[DEMERS] A. Demers, S. Keshav, and S. Shenkar, Analysis and simulation of a fair queueing algorithm, *Journal of Internetworking Research and Experience*, vol. 1, 1990

[DORAN] S. Doran, RED Experience and Differentiated Queueing, *NANOG 13*, June 1998

[DSCR] http://www.iana.org/assignments/dscp-registry

[FLOYD1] S. Floyd, and V. Jacobson, Random Early Detection gateways for Congestion Avoidance, *IEEE/ACM Transactions on Networking*, Volume 1, Number 4, August 1993, pp. 397–413

[FLOYD2] Sally Floyd, Ramakrishna Gummadi, and Scott Shenker, Adaptive RED: An Algorithm for Increasing the Robustness of RED's Active Queue Management, August 1, 2001

[FRANCOIS] Pierre Francois, Clarence Filsfils, John Evans and Olivier Bonaventure, Achieving subsecond IGP convergence in large IP networks, *ACM SIGCOMM Computer Communication Review*, Vol. 35, Issue 3 (July 2005), pp. 35–44

[FRF.12] Frame-Relay Fragmentation Implementation Agreement, FRF.12, Frame-Relay Forum, December 1997

[GCRA] ATM Forum, *ATM User-Network Interface Specification*, Prentice Hall, 1993

[JACOBSON] V. Jacobson, K. Nichols, K. Poduri, RED in a different Light, Technical Report, Cisco Systems, Sept. 1999

[KESHAV] S. Keshav, *An Engineering Approach to Computer Networking*, Addison-Wesley, 1997

[KLEINROCK] L. Kleinrock, *Queueing Systems Vol. 2: Computer Applications*, Wiley, 1976

[L2VPN] IETF L2 VPN working Group: http://www.ietf.org/html.charters/l2vpn-charter.html

[LAKSHMAN] T. V. Lakshman, A. Neidhardt, and T. J. Ott, The Drop from Front Strategy in TCP and in TCP over ATM, *Proc. IEEE INFOCOM*, San Francisco, CA, March 1996

[MAY] M. May, J. Bolot, C. Diot, and B. Lyles, Reasons not to deploy RED, in *Proc. IWQoS'99*, June 1999, pp. 260–262

[PAN1] R. Pan, L. Breslau, B. Prabhakar, S. Shenker, Approximate Fairness through Differential Dropping, *ACM Computer Communication Review*, July 2003

[PAN2] R. Pan, L. Breslau, B. Prabhakar, S. Shenker, A Flow Table-based Design to Approximate Fairness, BEST PAPER AWARD, *Proceedings of Hot Interconnects*, 2002 and by invitation IEEE Micro January/February 2003

[RFC791] Internet Protocol Protocol Specification, RFC 791, September 1981

[RFC1112] S. E. Deering, Host extensions for IP multicasting, *RFC* 1112, 1989

[RFC1122] R. Braden, Editor, Requirements for Internet Hosts – Communication Layers, *RFC* 1122, October 1989

[RFC1349] P. Almquist, Type of Service in the Internet Protocol Suite, *RFC* 1349, July 1992

[RFC1583] J. Moy, OSPF Version 2, *RFC* 1583, March 1994

[RFC1633] R. Braden, D. Clark, S. Shenker, Integrated Services in the Internet Architecture: an Overview, *RFC* 1633, June 1994

[RFC1661] W. Simpson, Editor, The Point-to-Point Protocol (PPP), *RFC* 1661, July 1994

[RFC1990] Skwloer et al., The PPP Multilink Protocol (MP), *RFC* 1990, August 1996

[RFC2003] C. Perkins, IP Encapsulation within IP, *RFC* 2003, October 1996

[RFC2309] D. Clark et al., Recommendations on Queue Management and Congestion Avoidance in the Internet, *RFC* 2309, April 1998

[RFC2328] J. Moy, OSPF Version 2, *RFC* 2328, April 1998

[RFC2401] S. Kent, R. Atkinson, Security Architecture for the Internet Protocol, *RFC* 2401, November 1998

[RFC2460] S. Deering, R. Hinden, Internet Protocol, Version 6 (IPv6) Specification, *RFC* 2460, December 1998

[RFC2474] K. Nichols et al., Definition of the Differentiated Services Field (DS Field) in the IPv4 and IPv6 Headers, *RFC* 2474, December 1998

[RFC2475] S. Blake et al., An Architecture for Differentiated Service, *RFC* 2475, December 1998

[RFC2481] K. Ramakrishnan, S. Floyd, A Proposal to add Explicit Congestion Notification (ECN) to IP, *RFC* 2481, January 1999

[RFC2597] J. Heinanen et al., Assured Forwarding PHB Group, *RFC* 2597, June 1999

[RFC2661] W. Townsley et al., Layer Two Tunneling Protocol 'L2TP', *RFC* 2661, August 1999

[RFC2697] J. Heinanen, R. Guerin, A Single Rate Three Color Marker, *RFC* 2697, September 1999

[RFC2698] J. Heinanen, R. Guerin, A Two Rate Three Color Marker, *RFC* 2698, September 1999

[RFC2784] D. Farinacci et al., Generic Routing Encapsulation (GRE), *RFC* 2784, March 2000

[RFC2858] T. Bates, Y. Rekhter, R. Chandra and D. Katz, Multiprotocol Extensions for BGP-4, *RFC* 2858, June 2000

[RFC2983] D. Black, Differentiated Services and Tunnels, *RFC* 2983, October 2000

[RFC3031] E. Rosen, A. Viswanathan, R. Callon, Multiprotocol Label Switching Architecture, *RFC* 3031, January 2001

[RFC3032] E. Rosen, D. Tappan, G. Fedorkow, Y. Rekhter, D. Farinacci, T. Li, A. Conta, MPLS Label Stack Encoding, *RFC* 3032, January 2001

[RFC3036] L. Andersson et al., LDP Specification, *RFC* 3036, January 2001

[RFC3086] K. Nichols, and B. Carpenter, Definition of Differentiated Services Per Domain Behaviors and Rules for their Specification, *RFC* 3086, April 2001

[RFC3168] K. Ramakrishnan et al., The Addition of Explicit Congestion Notification (ECN) to IP, *RFC* 3168, September 2001

[RFC3209] D. Awduche, L. Berger, D. Gan, T. Li, V. Srinivasan, G. Swallow, RSVP-TE: Extensions to RSVP for LSP Tunnels, *RFC* 3209, December 2001

[RFC3246] B. Davie, ed. et al., An Expedited Forwarding PHB, *RFC* 3246, March 2002

[RFC3270] F. Le Faucheur et al., Multi-Protocol Label Switching (MPLS) Support of Differentiated Services, *RFC* 3270, May 2002

[RFC3270] F. Le Faucheur, L. Wu, B. Davie, S. Davari, P. Vaananen, R. Krishnan, P. Cheval, J. Heinanen, Multi-Protocol Label Switching (MPLS) Support of Differentiated Services, *RFC* 3270, May 2002

[RFC3662] Nichols, K. Wehrle, A Lower Effort Per-Domain Behavior (PDB) for Differentiated Services, R. Bless, K. December 2003

[RFC3697] J. Rajahalme et al., IPv6 Flow Label Specification, *RFC* 3697, March 2004

[RFC4090] P. Pan, Ed., G. Swallow, Ed., A. Atlas, Ed., Fast Reroute Extensions to RSVP-TE for LSP Tunnels, *RFC* 4090, May 2005

[RFC4364] E. Rosen and Y. Rekhter, BGP/MPLS IP Virtual Private Networks (VPNs), *RFC* 4364, February 2006

[REC4774] S. Floyd, Specifying Alternate Semantics for the Explicit Congestion Notification (ECN) Field, November 2006

[SHAND] M. Shand, S. Bryant, IP Fast Reroute Framework, Internet Draft, draft – ietf-rtgwg-ipfrr-Framework (work in progress)

[SHANNON] C. Shannon, D. Moore, and K. Claffy, Beyond Folklore: Observations on Fragmented Traffic, Cooperative Association for Internet Data Analysis (CAIDA), 2002. Available at: www.caida.org/ outreach/papers/2002/Frag/

[SHREEDHAR] M. Shreedhar, George Varghese, Efficient Fair Queuing using Deficit Round Robin, SIGCOMM 1995

Appendix 2.A: Precedence, TOS, and DSCP Conversion

It can be confusing trying to understand how to convert between corresponding IP precedence values, TOS values, and DSCP values, hence this appendix aims to help solve that problem.

2.A.1 Notation

The numeric notations most commonly used for IP precedence, TOS and DSCP values are as follows.

- *IP precedence.* The notation normally used when referring to particular IP precedence values is to take the entire value of the precedence field (bits 0 to 2 of the TOS octet) and express it in decimal, where bit 0 is the most significant bit; e.g. an IP prece- dence value of 010 binary is represented as Precedence 2.
  IP precedence is discussed in detail in Section 2.3.2.1.

- *Type of service.* The notation generally used when referring to the "TOS value" is to take the entire vale of the type of service octet (including the precedence field and bit 7 of the type of service octet) expressed in decimal, where bit 0 is taken as the most significant bit; e.g. assuming a precedence field value of 110 binary, and a

TOS field value of 0100 binary, the TOS value would generally be referred to as 212 decimal (i.e. 11010100 binary).

Type of service is discussed in detail in Section 2.3.2.2.

- *DSCP.* When referring to DSCP values, all 6 bits of the DSCP are expressed in decimal, where bit 0 is taken as the most significant bit; e.g. a DSCP of 010000 binary is represented as DSCP 16.

The DS field is discussed in detail in Section 2.3.4.1.

- *Class selector codepoints.* The numeric notation used for the class selector (CS) codepoints is exactly the same as for IP precedence. When converting to/from the CS codepoints, use the same conversion as for to/from IP precedence.

The use of the class selector codepoints is discussed in Section 2.3.4.1.

2.A.2   Conversion

Use the following formula when converting between the numeric notations most commonly used for IP precedence, TOS and DSCP values:

- *DSCP_value = INT (TOS_value/4)*

- *DSCP_value = PREC * 8*

- *TOS_value = DSCP_value * 4*

- *TOS_value = PREC_value * 32*

- *PREC_value = INT (DSCP_value/8)*

- *PREC_value = INT (TOS_value/32)*

The ready-reckoner in Figure 2.45 provides a quick reference for conversion.

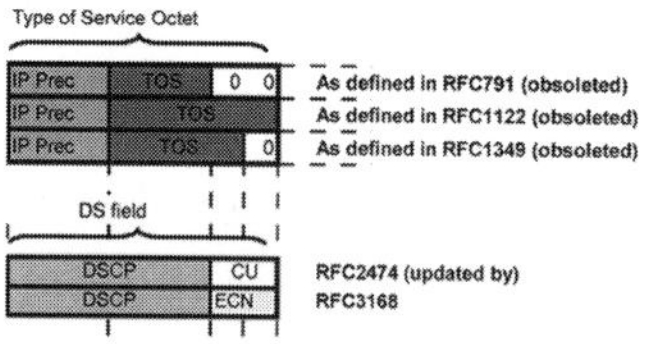

0 (msb)	1	2	3	4	5	6	7 (lsb)	IP Precedence (RFC 791)		TOS Value	Type of Service (RFC 1349) Min. Delay	Max. Thru'put	Max. Reliability	Min. Cost	Diffserv (RFC2474) DSCP	PHB	ECN (RFC3168)
0	0	0	0	0	0	0	0	0	Routine	0					0	Default / CS0	Not-ECT
0	0	0	0	0	0	1	0	0	Routine	2				✓	0	Default / CS0	ECT(0)
0	0	0	0	0	1	0	0	0	Routine	4			✓		1		Not-ECT
0	0	0	0	0	1	1	0	0	Routine	6			✓	✓	1		ECT(0)
0	0	0	0	1	0	0	0	0	Routine	8		✓			2		Not-ECT
0	0	0	0	1	0	1	0	0	Routine	10		✓		✓	2		ECT(0)
0	0	0	0	1	1	0	0	0	Routine	12		✓	✓		3		Not-ECT
0	0	0	0	1	1	1	0	0	Routine	14		✓	✓	✓	3		ECT(0)
0	0	0	1	0	0	0	0	0	Routine	16	✓				4		Not-ECT
0	0	0	1	0	0	1	0	0	Routine	18	✓			✓	4		ECT(0)
0	0	0	1	0	1	0	0	0	Routine	20	✓		✓		5		Not-ECT
0	0	0	1	0	1	1	0	0	Routine	22	✓		✓	✓	5		ECT(0)
0	0	0	1	1	0	0	0	0	Routine	24	Invalid *	Invalid *			6		Not-ECT
0	0	0	1	1	0	1	0	0	Routine	26	Invalid *	Invalid *		✓	6		ECT(0)
0	0	0	1	1	1	0	0	0	Routine	28	Invalid *	Invalid *	✓		7		Not-ECT
0	0	0	1	1	1	1	0	0	Routine	30	Invalid *	Invalid *	✓	✓	7		ECT(0)
0	0	1	0	0	0	0	0	1	Priority	32					8	CS1	Not-ECT
0	0	1	0	0	0	1	0	1	Priority	34				✓	8	CS1	ECT(0)
0	0	1	0	0	1	0	0	1	Priority	36			✓		9		Not-ECT
0	0	1	0	0	1	1	0	1	Priority	38			✓	✓	9		ECT(0)
0	0	1	0	1	0	0	0	1	Priority	40		✓			10	AF11	Not-ECT
0	0	1	0	1	0	1	0	1	Priority	42		✓		✓	10	AF11	ECT(0)
0	0	1	0	1	1	0	0	1	Priority	44		✓	✓		11		Not-ECT
0	0	1	0	1	1	1	0	1	Priority	46		✓	✓	✓	11		ECT(0)
0	0	1	1	0	0	0	0	1	Priority	48	✓				12	AF12	Not-ECT
0	0	1	1	0	0	1	0	1	Priority	50	✓			✓	12	AF12	ECT(0)
0	0	1	1	0	1	0	0	1	Priority	52	✓		✓		13		Not-ECT
0	0	1	1	0	1	1	0	1	Priority	54	✓		✓	✓	13		ECT(0)
0	0	1	1	1	0	0	0	1	Priority	56	Invalid *	Invalid *			14	AF13	Not-ECT
0	0	1	1	1	0	1	0	1	Priority	58	Invalid *	Invalid *		✓	14	AF13	ECT(0)
0	0	1	1	1	1	0	0	1	Priority	60	Invalid *	Invalid *	✓		15		Not-ECT
0	0	1	1	1	1	1	0	1	Priority	62	Invalid *	Invalid *	✓	✓	15		ECT(0)
0	1	0	0	0	0	0	0	2	Immediate	64					16	CS2	Not-ECT
0	1	0	0	0	0	1	0	2	Immediate	66				✓	16	CS2	ECT(0)
0	1	0	0	0	1	0	0	2	Immediate	68			✓		17		Not-ECT
0	1	0	0	0	1	1	0	2	Immediate	70			✓	✓	17		ECT(0)
0	1	0	0	1	0	0	0	2	Immediate	72		✓			18	AF21	Not-ECT
0	1	0	0	1	0	1	0	2	Immediate	74		✓		✓	18	AF21	ECT(0)
0	1	0	0	1	1	0	0	2	Immediate	76		✓	✓		19		Not-ECT
0	1	0	0	1	1	1	0	2	Immediate	78		✓	✓	✓	19		ECT(0)
0	1	0	1	0	0	0	0	2	Immediate	80	✓				20	AF22	Not-ECT
0	1	0	1	0	0	1	0	2	Immediate	82	✓			✓	20	AF22	ECT(0)
0	1	0	1	0	1	0	0	2	Immediate	84	✓		✓		21		Not-ECT
0	1	0	1	0	1	1	0	2	Immediate	86	✓		✓	✓	21		ECT(0)
0	1	0	1	1	0	0	0	2	Immediate	88	Invalid *	Invalid *			22	AF23	Not-ECT
0	1	0	1	1	0	1	0	2	Immediate	90	Invalid *	Invalid *		✓	22	AF23	ECT(0)
0	1	0	1	1	1	0	0	2	Immediate	92	Invalid *	Invalid *	✓		23		Not-ECT
0	1	0	1	1	1	1	0	2	Immediate	94	Invalid *	Invalid *	✓	✓	23		ECT(0)
0	1	1	0	0	0	0	0	3	Flash	96					24	CS3	Not-ECT
0	1	1	0	0	0	1	0	3	Flash	98				✓	24	CS3	ECT(0)
0	1	1	0	0	1	0	0	3	Flash	100			✓		25		Not-ECT
0	1	1	0	0	1	1	0	3	Flash	102			✓	✓	25		ECT(0)
0	1	1	0	1	0	0	0	3	Flash	104		✓			26	AF31	Not-ECT
0	1	1	0	1	0	1	0	3	Flash	106		✓		✓	26	AF31	ECT(0)
0	1	1	0	1	1	0	0	3	Flash	108		✓	✓		27		Not-ECT
0	1	1	0	1	1	1	0	3	Flash	110		✓	✓	✓	27		ECT(0)
0	1	1	1	0	0	0	0	3	Flash	112	✓				28	AF32	Not-ECT
0	1	1	1	0	0	1	0	3	Flash	114	✓			✓	28	AF32	ECT(0)
0	1	1	1	0	1	0	0	3	Flash	116	✓		✓		29		Not-ECT
0	1	1	1	0	1	1	0	3	Flash	118	✓		✓	✓	29		ECT(0)
0	1	1	1	1	0	0	0	3	Flash	120	Invalid *	Invalid *			30	AF33	Not-ECT
0	1	1	1	1	0	1	0	3	Flash	122	Invalid *	Invalid *		✓	30	AF33	ECT(0)
0	1	1	1	1	1	0	0	3	Flash	124	Invalid *	Invalid *	✓		31		Not-ECT
0	1	1	1	1	1	1	0	3	Flash	126	Invalid *	Invalid *	✓	✓	31		ECT(0)

Figure 2.45 Precedence, TOS, DSCP, and ECN ready reckoner

Type of Service Octet

IP Prec	TOS	0 0	As defined in RFC791 (obsoleted)
IP Prec	TOS		As defined in RFC1122 (obsoleted)
IP Prec	TOS	0	As defined in RFC1349 (obsoleted)

DS field

DSCP	CU	RFC2474 (updated by)
DSCP	ECN	RFC3168

m s b   l s b

1	0	0	0	0	0	0	0	4	Flash Overide	128					32	CS4	Not-ECT
1	0	0	0	0	0	1	0	4	Flash Overide	130				✓	32	CS4	ECT(0)
1	0	0	0	0	1	0	0	4	Flash Overide	132			✓		33		Not-ECT
1	0	0	0	0	1	1	0	4	Flash Overide	134			✓	✓	33		ECT(0)
1	0	0	0	1	0	0	0	4	Flash Overide	136		✓			34	AF41	Not-ECT
1	0	0	0	1	0	1	0	4	Flash Overide	138		✓		✓	34	AF41	ECT(0)
1	0	0	0	1	1	0	0	4	Flash Overide	140		✓	✓		35		Not-ECT
1	0	0	0	1	1	1	0	4	Flash Overide	142		✓	✓	✓	35		ECT(0)
1	0	0	1	0	0	0	0	4	Flash Overide	144	✓				36	AF42	Not-ECT
1	0	0	1	0	0	1	0	4	Flash Overide	146	✓			✓	36	AF42	ECT(0)
1	0	0	1	0	1	0	0	4	Flash Overide	148	✓		✓		37		Not-ECT
1	0	0	1	0	1	1	0	4	Flash Overide	150	✓		✓	✓	37		ECT(0)
1	0	0	1	1	0	0	0	4	Flash Overide	152	Invalid *	Invalid *			38	AF43	Not-ECT
1	0	0	1	1	0	1	0	4	Flash Overide	154	Invalid *	Invalid *		✓	38	AF43	ECT(0)
1	0	0	1	1	1	0	0	4	Flash Overide	156	Invalid *	Invalid *	✓		39		Not-ECT
1	0	0	1	1	1	1	0	4	Flash Overide	158	Invalid *	Invalid *	✓	✓	39		ECT(0)
1	0	1	0	0	0	0	0	5	Critical	160					40	CS5	Not-ECT
1	0	1	0	0	0	1	0	5	Critical	162				✓	40	CS5	ECT(0)
1	0	1	0	0	1	0	0	5	Critical	164			✓		41		Not-ECT
1	0	1	0	0	1	1	0	5	Critical	166			✓	✓	41		ECT(0)
1	0	1	0	1	0	0	0	5	Critical	168		✓			42		Not-ECT
1	0	1	0	1	0	1	0	5	Critical	170		✓		✓	42		ECT(0)
1	0	1	0	1	1	0	0	5	Critical	172		✓	✓		43		Not-ECT
1	0	1	0	1	1	1	0	5	Critical	174		✓	✓	✓	43		ECT(0)
1	0	1	1	0	0	0	0	5	Critical	176	✓				44		Not-ECT
1	0	1	1	0	0	1	0	5	Critical	178	✓			✓	44		ECT(0)
1	0	1	1	0	1	0	0	5	Critical	180	✓		✓		45		Not-ECT
1	0	1	1	0	1	1	0	5	Critical	182	✓		✓	✓	45		ECT(0)
1	0	1	1	1	0	0	0	5	Critical	184	Invalid *	Invalid *			46	EF	Not-ECT
1	0	1	1	1	0	1	0	5	Critical	186	Invalid *	Invalid *		✓	46	EF	ECT(0)
1	0	1	1	1	1	0	0	5	Critical	188	Invalid *	Invalid *	✓		47		Not-ECT
1	0	1	1	1	1	1	0	5	Critical	190	Invalid *	Invalid *	✓	✓	47		ECT(0)
1	1	0	0	0	0	0	0	6	Internetwork Control	192					48	CS6	Not-ECT
1	1	0	0	0	0	1	0	6	Internetwork Control	194				✓	48	CS6	ECT(0)
1	1	0	0	0	1	0	0	6	Internetwork Control	196			✓		49		Not-ECT
1	1	0	0	0	1	1	0	6	Internetwork Control	198			✓	✓	49		ECT(0)
1	1	0	0	1	0	0	0	6	Internetwork Control	200		✓			50		Not-ECT
1	1	0	0	1	0	1	0	6	Internetwork Control	202		✓		✓	50		ECT(0)
1	1	0	0	1	1	0	0	6	Internetwork Control	204		✓	✓		51		Not-ECT
1	1	0	0	1	1	1	0	6	Internetwork Control	206		✓	✓	✓	51		ECT(0)
1	1	0	1	0	0	0	0	6	Internetwork Control	208	✓				52		Not-ECT
1	1	0	1	0	0	1	0	6	Internetwork Control	210	✓			✓	52		ECT(0)
1	1	0	1	0	1	0	0	6	Internetwork Control	212	✓		✓		53		Not-ECT
1	1	0	1	0	1	1	0	6	Internetwork Control	214	✓		✓	✓	53		ECT(0)
1	1	0	1	1	0	0	0	6	Internetwork Control	216	Invalid *	Invalid *			54		Not-ECT
1	1	0	1	1	0	1	0	6	Internetwork Control	218	Invalid *	Invalid *		✓	54		ECT(0)
1	1	0	1	1	1	0	0	6	Internetwork Control	220	Invalid *	Invalid *	✓		55		Not-ECT
1	1	0	1	1	1	1	0	6	Internetwork Control	222	Invalid *	Invalid *	✓	✓	55		ECT(0)
1	1	1	0	0	0	0	0	7	Network Control	224					56	CS7	Not-ECT
1	1	1	0	0	0	1	0	7	Network Control	226				✓	56	CS7	ECT(0)
1	1	1	0	0	1	0	0	7	Network Control	228			✓		57		Not-ECT
1	1	1	0	0	1	1	0	7	Network Control	230			✓	✓	57		ECT(0)
1	1	1	0	1	0	0	0	7	Network Control	232		✓			58		Not-ECT
1	1	1	0	1	0	1	0	7	Network Control	234		✓		✓	58		ECT(0)
1	1	1	0	1	1	0	0	7	Network Control	236		✓	✓		59		Not-ECT
1	1	1	0	1	1	1	0	7	Network Control	238		✓	✓	✓	59		ECT(0)
1	1	1	1	0	0	0	0	7	Network Control	240	✓				60		Not-ECT
1	1	1	1	0	0	1	0	7	Network Control	242	✓			✓	60		ECT(0)
1	1	1	1	0	1	0	0	7	Network Control	244	✓		✓		61		Not-ECT
1	1	1	1	0	1	1	0	7	Network Control	246	✓		✓	✓	61		ECT(0)
1	1	1	1	1	0	0	0	7	Network Control	248	Invalid *	Invalid *			62		Not-ECT
1	1	1	1	1	0	1	0	7	Network Control	250	Invalid *	Invalid *		✓	62		ECT(0)
1	1	1	1	1	1	0	0	7	Network Control	252	Invalid *	Invalid *	✓		63		Not-ECT
1	1	1	1	1	1	1	0	7	Network Control	254	Invalid *	Invalid *	✓	✓	63		ECT(0)
x	x	x	x	x	x	0	0										Not-ECT
x	x	x	x	x	x	0	1										ECT(1)
x	x	x	x	x	x	1	0										ECT(0)
x	x	x	x	x	x	1	1										CE

Figure 2.45 (Continued)

Notes

1. Whenever an octet represents a numeric quantity the left most bit in the diagram is the high order or most significant bit. That is, the bit labeled 0 is the most significant bit.

2. The EF PHB was first defined in [RFC2598], however, the formal definition was subsequently determined to be incorrect and hence was superseded by RFC3246.

3

Deploying Diffserv

3.1 Introduction

In Chapter 1, we defined the key service level agreement (SLA) parameters for IP applications and services as being: delay, delay variation or jitter, packet loss rate, throughput, availability, and per flow sequence preservation. In Chapter 2, we described the QOS component mechanisms and architectures that can be used in engineering a network to meet SLA targets. In this chapter, we build on the context and understanding created by Chapters 1 and 2, to show how the Differentiated Services architecture (Diffserv) can be practically deployed at the network edge and in the network core in order to satisfy defined application SLA requirements. Diffserv is by far the most widely deployed IP QOS architecture; it is widely deployed both in private enterprise networks and in service provider (SP) networks providing virtual private network (VPN) services to enterprises.

The edge of the Diffserv domain represents the provider/customer boundary for the Diffserv-enabled services being offered; Diffserv achieves scalability by performing complex per-customer QOS functions and maintaining per-customer state, only at the edges of the network. Hence, the policies applied at the edge of the network are different from, and generally more complex than, those applied within the core. Many networks are built with a hierarchy consisting of core routers (CRs), which provide connectivity between distribution routers (DRs), which in turn aggregate connections to routers at remote sites, each of which have local access routers (ARs). If, for example, we consider a Diffserv deployment in this type of network,

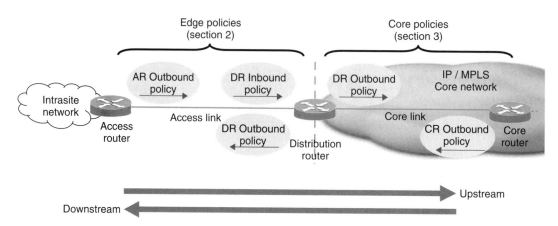

Figure 3.1   Application of Diffserv policies

as shown in Figure 3.1, the access link will normally be the edge of the Diffserv domain, with edge Diffserv policies being applied outbound on the core facing (i.e. upstream) AR interface and outbound on the access facing (i.e. downstream) interface of the DR, which may have inbound policies in some cases also. Core Diffserv policies are then typically applied outbound on the core facing (i.e. upstream) interfaces of the DR and on outbound on all CR interfaces.

In the network core where link bandwidths are high and traffic is highly aggregated, the SLA requirements for a traffic class can be translated into bandwidth requirements, and the problem of SLA assurance can effectively be reduced to that of bandwidth provisioning, which may be on a per-class of service basis. At the network edge, where bandwidth is lower and there is limited aggregation of traffic, different considerations become significant, such as providing isolation between applications. Further, the mechanisms employed on the lower speed access links at the edges of the network to deliver tightly bounded SLA commitments may be different from those used in the core, because factors such as serialization delay become significant at lower speeds.

This chapter focusses on Diffserv designs for the network edge and in the core; in considering Diffserv designs, we apply the following three key design objectives:

- ensuring that the different SLA requirements for each respective class can be met

- optimizing the use of available bandwidth

- keeping the design as simple as possible.

The following sections apply these objectives to Diffserv design case studies supporting applications and services with tightly bounded SLAs for IP service performance. The case studies presented are examples, and as such do not represent the only way of doing things; rather, they aim to describe possible methodologies and the most important aspects to consider with respect to Diffserv designs. In these case studies, where we use the terms service provider and customer, we use them generically. This does not infer, however, that the case studies are only applicable to VPN service providers – the networking department of an enterprise organization is a service provider to their enterprise.

3.2 Deploying Diffserv at the Network Edge

3.2.1 Why is the Edge Key for Tight SLA Services?

In every network, there is a choice about whether or not to deploy QOS mechanisms, such as those defined by Diffserv. Without such QOS mechanisms, however, in order to support services and applications with tightly bound SLA requirements, the available capacity needs to be over-provisioned relative to the peak of the aggregate offered load; this needs to be ensured in the milliseconds timeframe (see Chapter 2, Section 2.1.3). One school of though is that bandwidth will become cheaper and more widely available and hence over-provisioning will be a viable option. At the edge of the network, however, even though access bandwidth speeds have increased and costs have reduced over time, demands for bandwidth from applications combined with end-systems' capabilities to drive such bandwidth has more than kept pace with the availability of bandwidth, and such over-provisioning has not been viable in practice. Access link costs are a significant component of network costs and to minimize operational expenditure, customers will often delay upgrading these links as long as possible; consequently, access links are often under-dimensioned and prone to congestion.

This may change in the future; however, it is very unlikely that this will change in the foreseeable term. Further, unless we provide for the possibility of dealing with congestion (i.e. assuming that over-provisioning is not always going to be possible) then supporting real-time services with requirements for tight bounds on delay, jitter, and loss, will be precluded in cases where congestion occurs. Hence, in the rest of this section, we consider that peak over-provisioning of access links is not a viable option to support services and applications with stringent SLA requirements, as is the case in practice today, and we consider how Diffserv can be deployed to achieve this end.

3.2.2 Edge Diffserv Case Study

In this section, we work through an example edge Diffserv case study, defining the typical class SLA characteristics and describing how Diffserv can be deployed at the network edge to ensure these SLA characteristics are met. In this study, we refer to the access segment SLA, adopting the segmented SLA approach as described in Chapter 1, Section 1.4.1.

We note that Diffserv achieves scalability by performing complex per-customer QOS functions and maintaining per-customer state, only at the edges of the network; hence, implicitly the Diffserv edge design is more complicated than the core design.

3.2.2.1 SLA Specification

We start by considering a simple case, where a leased line of bandwidth Xkbps provides the connectivity between the AR and the DR, and where four service classes are supported, each with a different SLA. We define the SLA characteristics for three "customer-facing" classes and one class that is used by the service provider for essential network service control functions, and which is not available to the end customer:

- *VoIP class (VoIP).* This class targets interactive applications with requirements for defined bandwidth, low loss, and tight bounds on delay, such as VoIP bearer traffic.

- *Premium data throughput-optimized class (Prm-th).* This class targets business applications, that should receive priority access to the available bandwidth over standard applications, but which do not have a defined delay requirement; this might include business critical file transfer applications, for example.

- *Standard class (Std).* The *Std* class is used for all other "customer-facing" traffic, which has not already been classified as *VoIP* or *Prm-th*. This class may be used for email and web applications, for example.

    Note that the term "best-effort" has intentionally not been used for this class, as *best-effort* infers no SLA commitments. Whereas in this case, the *Std* class has defined SLA commitments, they just represent the lowest of the SLA commitments for the classes offered.

- *Control class (Ctrl).* The *Ctrl* class is used by the service provider and is dedicated for network control traffic, ensuring that bandwidth on the access link is guaranteed for essential functions such as for routing protocols and for telnet or SNMP access to the AR. This ensures that congestion of the access link caused by the customer cannot impact the SP's ability to manage the delivery of the service. It also ensures that customer traffic is protected from being impacted by management traffic, such as large file transfers due to router software upgrades, for example.

We start by considering these service classes, as illustrated by Figure 3.2, because they represent the baseline of many Diffserv deployments today. In subsequent sections, we consider additional variations to

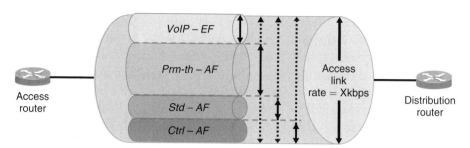

Figure 3.2 Edge case study with four classes

the design, capable of supporting the SLA requirements of the range of applications described in Chapter 1.

The detail of the SLA definitions contracted for each class is defined in the proceeding sections. A summary of the SLA definitions for all of the classes is provided in Section 3.2.2.5.

3.2.2.1.1   VoIP Class (VoIP)

The SLA for the VoIP class is defined in terms of low delay, low jitter, and low loss, and it has a specified bandwidth and availability; attainable throughput is derived from the committed bandwidth and loss rate. The class may support a commitment for per flow sequence preservation.

In agreeing to supply and receive the service, the SP and customer respectively assent to a contract that defines an ingress committed rate (ICR) from the customer site to the SP and an egress committed rate (ECR) from the SP to the customer site (see Chapter 1, Section 1.2.4.2); normally, this relationship is specified symmetrically (i.e. ICR = ECR). The SP enforces the contract by limiting the rate of *VoIP* traffic to/from the customer site using a token bucket policer, with rate R_v and committed burst size B_v; non-conformant traffic will be dropped by the SP. The rate R_v will be selected by the customer and will be offered by the SP up to a defined percentage of the access link speed. The SP will normally limit the maximum percentage of the access link bandwidth that is available for this class in order to ensure that the class latency commitments can be met; for how that maximum percentage is defined, see Section 3.2.2.8. There will also normally be a defined minimum link speed, below which the SP will not offer this class, for example 256 kbps, because increased serialization delay will mean that the delay target for the class is not achievable at lower rates. B_v will be set based on the offered class delay commitment; the maximum burst value effectively limits the maximum latency of traffic in the class.

For conformant traffic, the SP will commit to a maximum one-way edge segment latency, L_v. The edge segment latency is only one component of the ear-to-mouth delay that impacts a VoIP call. Hence, before defining the edge segment latency, the maximum acceptable ear-to-mouth delay for the particular VoIP service must be defined. A network QOS design should then take this budget and apportion it to the various components of network delay (propagation delay through the backbone, scheduling delay due to congestion, and the access link serialization delay) and end-system delay (due to VoIP codec and de-jitter buffer). Consider a typical example VoIP delay budget allocation as follows.

- The end-to-end (ear-to-mouth) delay target is assumed to be 100 ms, adding a significant 50 ms safety margin to the G.114 target of 150 ms to ensure that most users will be very satisfied (see Chapter 1, Section 1.3.1.1). Note that in many situations there may be additional delays incurred due to tandem encoding (repeated encoding and decoding of the signal), which need to be taken into account in the overall delay budget. There may also be cases where a service may span A multiple networks, and a particular network "owns" only a portion of the overall end-to-end delay budget, hence in practice, it is often important to minimize the delay in all portions of the network when supporting VoIP services.

  Next deduct the significant contributors to the fixed components of delay from the end-to-end delay budget, and deduce the remainder to be apportioned to the variable components of delay:
  - 25 ms is deducted for codec delay, assuming G.711–20 ms (see Chapter 1, Section 1.3.1). Other codecs may incur larger delay

and hence consume more of the end-to-end delay budget; lower bandwidth codecs typically incur larger codec delays.

Note that the packetization interval clearly has an impact on the codec delays, hence larger packetization intervals will implicitly result in larger codec delays.

○ Propagation delay is often budgeted for using the widest diameter in the network, which for example, in a national fiber-based network in the US would give a worst-case (coast-to-coast) of approximately 6000 km or ~6000 * 1.25 * 5/1000 = ~40 ms of one-way propagation delay (from Section 1.2.1.1 in Chapter 1).

○ In this example we assume that the minimum per-hop delay (switching delay) is relatively negligible, which may not always be the case; if not then it also needs to be included in the above budget.

Hence, the remainder to be apportioned to the variable components of delay is:

Mouth-to-ear budget	100 ms	
Backbone propagation	−40 ms	(assumes ~6000 km)
Example codec delay	−25 ms	(assumes G.711–20 ms)
Variable delay budget	=35 ms	

- We allocate 5 ms of the variable delay budget to the backbone, where links speeds are higher than the access, and hence a smaller portion of the end-to-end delay budget is consumed.

- This leaves 30 ms of the variable delay budget for the access links; 15 ms is allocated to ingress and 15 ms to egress.

L_v is therefore typically in the range 15 ms–50 ms, depending upon the particular ear-to-mouth delay target, and the delay budgeting for the specific network design. L_v is normally specified for a defined packet size.

End-to-end loss rates of typically less than 0.1% (see Chapter 1, Section 1.3.1.3) are offered for the VoIP class.

The contract will stipulate the classification criteria that the SP will use to identify the *VoIP* class at the network edge. Potentially, the classification criteria for any class may use complex classification (which may match on source or destination IP addresses, for example) or simple classification if the end-system or a downstream element is trusted to pre-mark the traffic. Once classified and policed, conformant traffic will be marked with a defined Diffserv codepoint (DSCP) value D_v, if it is not already pre-marked, such that within the network core, traffic classes can be identified by their DSCP markings rather than requiring complex classification.

3.2.2.1.2 Premium Data Throughput-Optimized Class (*Prm-th*)

The SLA for the *Prm-th* class is defined in terms of a specified bandwidth and availability with a commitment for per flow sequence preservation. Jitter is not important for this class and thus it is not defined.

The SP commits to a minimum class bandwidth, R_t, which is typically set to 80–90% of the remaining access link bandwidth after the *VoIP* class has been serviced. As the *Prm-th* class has a higher bandwidth allocation than the *Std* class, if there were the same offered load in both classes, traffic in the *Prm-th* class should receive better service. This gives the end customer the option of allocating some applications to the *Prm-th* class, such that they receive better service than applications in the *Std* class, dependent on managing the relative loads between the classes. The *Prm-th* class is able to re-use unused bandwidth from any other class up to the available link bandwidth and therefore the maximum rate for the class is not enforced with a policer. Consequently, the class delay and loss are dependent upon the customer's actual offered traffic profile for the class, which is outside of the SP's control. Therefore, although the service for the class may have an implied loss and delay commitment, the SP cannot provide explicit commitments for delay and loss for this class at the network edge, although they may provide such commitments across the backbone. Attainable class throughput for TCP-based applications is dependent upon the actual loss rate and RTT experienced by traffic within the class, capped by the access-link bandwidth.

The contract will also define the classification criteria that the SP will use to identify the class and stipulate that conformant traffic will be marked with a defined DSCP value, D_t.

3.2.2.1.3   Standard Data Class (*Std*)

The *Std class* SLA is defined in terms of a specified bandwidth, availability, and commitment for per flow sequence preservation. Jitter is not important for this class and thus it is not defined.

The SP commits to a minimum class bandwidth, R_s, which is typically set to 10–20% of the remaining access link bandwidth once the *VoIP* class has been serviced. This class can re-use any other class's idle bandwidth up to the available link bandwidth. As for the *Prm-th* class, the SP does not provide delay and loss commitments for the *Std* class at the network edge. Attainable class throughput is again dependent upon the actual loss rate and RTT experienced by the class, capped by the access-link bandwidth. The SP may provide a commitment for loss and delay across the core.

The contract will also stipulate that *Std* class traffic will be marked with a defined DSCP value, D_s.

3.2.2.1.4   Control Class (*Ctrl*)

The *Ctrl* class is assured a minimal share of the access-link bandwidth, e.g. ~1%, although normally with a minimum of ~8–16 kbps. The class also has the ability to re-use bandwidth from the other classes that may be idle, up to the available link bandwidth.

3.2.2.2   Diffserv Meta-Language

In the following sections, we describe the detailed Diffserv design required to support these SLA commitments. To ease the description of the Diffserv design we use meta-language defined in Figure 3.3.

3.2.2.3   High-speed Edge Design

We consider "high-speed" access-links as those where the link rate is high enough that link fragmentation and interleaving mechanisms

Diffserv Meta-Language	
Command	Meaning
`policy <policy_name>`	Defines the start of a Diffserv policy, which may be applied to a particular interface or logical connection.
`class <class_name>`	Defines the start of the definition of the classification criteria and actions applied to a traffic class within a Diffserv policy.
`classify [not] <criteria>`	Defines the classification criteria for the particular class; see Chapter 2 Section 2.2.1. Although a number of complex and simple criteria are possible, we define only the simple criteria "DSCP <D>" and "EXP <E>." Where multiple classification criteria are applied, a logical OR operation is assumed between classification criteria.
`EF`	Indicates that the class will be assigned to a queue serviced with an EF PHB; see Chapter 2 Section 2.3.4.2.1.
`AF (<m>)`	Indicates that the class will be assigned to a queue serviced with an AF PHB with an assured minimum rate *m*; see Chapter 2 Section 2.3.4.2.2.
`mark DSCP (<D>)`	Defines the DSCP marking that will be set for packets in the particular class; see Chapter 2 Section 2.2.2.

`SR-TCM (<cir>, <cbs>, <ebs>)`
    `green-action <action>`
    `yellow-action <action>`
    `red-action <action>`
	Applies an RFC2697 single rate three color marker (SR-TCM) to the class with specified committed information rate (CIR), committed burst size (CBS), and excess burst size (EBS); see Chapter 2 Section 2.2.2. Possible resulting actions are 'drop' or 'transmit' or 'transmit-and-mark DSCP (D)'.

`TR-TCM (<cir>, <cbs>, <pir>, <pbs>)`
    `green-action <action>`
    `yellow-action <action>`
    `red-action <action>`
	Applies an RFC2698 two rate three color marker (TR-TCM) to the class with specified committed information rate (CIR), committed burst size (CBS), peak information rate (PIR) and peak burst size (PBS); see Chapter 2 Section 2.2.3.2. Possible resulting actions are 'drop' or 'transmit' or 'transmit-and-mark DSCP (D)'.

`drop`	This action will drop packets which match the particular condition.
`transmit`	This action will transmit packets which match the particular condition, without changing the DSCP marking of the packets.
`transmit-and-mark DSCP (<D>)`	This action will set the DSCP marking of packets which match the particular condition and transmit them.
`shape (<r>, <b>)`	Applies a token bucket shaper to the class with specified rate *r* and burst *b*; see Chapter 2 Section 2.2.4.3.

Figure 3.3 Diffserv meta-language

Diffserv Meta-Language	
Command	Meaning
`tail-drop-limit (<t>)`	Applies a tail-drop queue-limit to the class queue, dropping packets received for that particular class when the class queue length exceeds *t* bytes; see Chapter 2 Section 2.2.4.2.1.
`RED (DSCP <D>, <minth>, <maxth>, <w>, <pmax>)`	Applies a RED profile to traffic with the specified DSCP within the class queue, with defined minimum threshold (*minth*), maximum threshold (*maxth*), exponential weighting constant (w) and probability of packet loss at *maxth* (p_{max}); see Chapter 2 Section 2.2.4.2.3. Multiple RED profiles can be applied to the same queue to effect WRED.
`RED (EXP <D>, <minth>, <maxth>, <w>, <pmax>)`	Applies a RED profile to traffic with the specified MPLS EXP within the class queue.
<>	Indicates required parameter or parameters.
[]	Indicates optional parameter or parameters.
*	Indicates that the parameter is wild-carded.
{}	Indicates a hierarchy within the Diffserv policy.

Figure 3.3 (*Continued*)

are not required to mitigate the impacts of serialization delay when supporting services with tight SLA bounds for latency; this is typically at link speeds of around 1 Mbps and above; see Section 3.2.2.4.1 for a discussion on low-speed edge designs.

The configuration in Figure 3.4 defines a design to achieve the SLA specification described in Section 3.2.2.1 in terms of the Diffserv meta-language defined in Figure 3.3. This configuration would typically be applied outbound on the core facing (i.e. upstream) AR interface and outbound on the access facing (i.e. downstream) interface of the DR. With this baseline design, there are no inbound policies applied to the AR or DR, although the application of inbound DR policies is required in the design variation discussed in Section 3.2.2.4.3.

Note that within a class the ordering of actions is assumed as described in Chapter 2, Section 2.4.

The following sections describe the design considerations of each class, in order to ensure they support their class SLA commitments.

```
policy outbound-high-speed-edge-policy
  class Voip
    classify DSCP (Dv)
    SR-TCM (Rv, Bv, 0)
      green-action transmit
      red-action drop
    EF
  class Prm-th
    classify <criteria>
    AF (Rt)
    mark DSCP (Dt)
    RED (DSCP(*), <minth>, <maxth>, <w>, <pmax>)
  class Ctrl
    classify DSCP {Dc, 48}
    AF (Rc)
    RED (DSCP(*), <minth>, <maxth>, <w>, <pmax>)
  class Std
    classify *
    AF (Rs)
    mark DSCP (Ds)
    RED (DSCP(*), <minth>, <maxth>, <w>, <pmax>)
```

Figure 3.4 High-speed edge design

3.2.2.3.1 VoIP Class (VoIP)

Considering the *VoIP* class Diffserv configuration in Figure 3.4 it is assumed that VoIP traffic is pre-marked at the source to DSCP D_v, which is used to classify the traffic.

The SLA latency commitment is assured through the following aspects of the design:

- Defining this class as "expedited forwarding" (EF) in order to request the lowest latency service from the scheduler, which would typically be implemented with a strict priority scheduler.

- Ensuring that the arrival rate enforced by the class policer, R_v, is smaller than the servicing rate for the class so that no long-standing buffering can occur. Assuming a strict priority queue EF implementation, the servicing rate for the class would equal the rate of the link where the policy was applied. The class policer, for example, could be the single rate three color marker (SR-TCM) defined in RFC2697, with CIR = R_v, CBS = B_v, with EBS = 0 (i.e. the excess burst is not used in this case) and applying a green action of transmit and a red action of drop. Applied in this way, the SR-TCM would enforce a maximum rate of R_v and a burst of B_v on the traffic stream, and any traffic in excess of this would be dropped.

- Specifying the SLA contract such that the maximum allowed class burst size, B_v, when serviced at the link rate (assuming a strict priority queue EF implementation) ensures that the burst is serviced within the class latency commitment L_v, i.e. $B_v/link\_rate + L_s < L_v$, where L_s represents the worst-case delay impact on EF traffic due to the scheduler and the interface FIFO (see Section 3.2.2.4.1). B_v will in turn determine the maximum percentage of VoIP traffic that can be supported on the access link, as discussed in Section 3.2.2.8.

- With the policer configured, a tail drop queue limit is not required for the *VoIP* class queue. Some vendor implementations, however, may require that one is configured and if so, the queue-limit must be greater than or equal to B_v, to ensure that packets that are within the permitted burst for the class are not dropped. Therefore, the only actual packet loss that conformant traffic within the class should experience is due to layer 1 bit errors or network element failures, which accounts for the committed loss rate for the class offered by the SP.

While this class is targeted at VoIP bearer traffic, there is a design decision to be made as to whether VoIP signaling traffic will share the same class. VoIP signaling traffic generally consists of a small number of small sized packets, hence in some deployments it may be viable to support both VoIP bearer and signaling traffic from the same queue without one having a significant impact on the other.

Some network providers have a policy of ensuring isolation between bearer and signaling, which requires that they are serviced from separate classes, in this case VoIP signaling traffic could be serviced from one of the other AF classes (such as *Prm-th*) or could potentially be assigned its own class.

3.2.2.3.2   Premium Data Throughput-Optimized Class (*Prm-th*)

Considering the *Prm-th* class Diffserv configuration in Figure 3.4, it is assumed that complex classification criteria (which are unspecified in the figure) are used to classify packets into the class. Such criteria could be based upon source or destination addresses, or source or destination UDP/TCP ports, or deep packet inspection/stateful inspection (DPI/SI) for example. The DSCP of all packets classified into the class is set to D_t.

The *Prm-th* class SLA commitment is ensured by treating the class with an AF per-hop behavior (PHB), which provides a minimum bandwidth assurance of R_t. Assuming that a work-conserving scheduler is used, the *Prm-th* class will have access to all unused interface capacity once the *VoIP*, *Std*, and *Ctrl* data classes have been serviced.

The assumption is made that the majority of the *Std* class traffic is TCP/IP [MCCREARY], and hence the random early detection (RED) congestion control mechanism is used within the class queue rather than tail drop to ensure that TCP throughput is maximized when congestion occurs; RED tuning is described in Section 3.4. A tail drop queue limit for the *Prm-th* class queue is not needed when RED is used. Some vendors' implementations, however, require that a queue-limit must also be configured; if one is used, and tail drops were to occur rather than RED drops, then the potential benefit of RED would not be realized. To prevent this, if a queue-limit is used in conjunction to RED, the queue-limit should be set sufficiently greater than the RED maximum threshold so that tail drops do not occur.

3.2.2.3.3   Control Class (*Ctrl*)

Traffic is classified into the *Ctrl* class by matching on the DSCP classification, which is assumed to have been pre-marked at the source: either to DSCP D_c, by network management end-systems for operation, administration and maintenance (OA&M) functions, or to DSCP 48 by routing protocol end-systems. DSCP 48 is used for routing protocol packets, which is equivalent to an IP precedence marking of 6 and which is the de facto marking used by most routers for routing protocol traffic as a result of being the marking originally specified for Internetwork control traffic in RFC 791.

The *Ctrl* class commitments are assured by treating the class with an AF PHB, with a minimal bandwidth assurance of 1% of the link rate, although normally with a minimum of ~8–16 kbps, to ensure that management access to the AR is available even in the presence of congestion of the access-link caused by the customer. A number of applications used for network control and management use TCP (e.g. BGP, SNMP, Telnet), hence RED is used within the *Ctrl* class queue to maximize TCP throughput; RED tuning is described in detail in Section 3.4.

Some designs may choose to engineer the SLA for the control class more precisely. For example, the class bandwidth may be provisioned to ensure that a defined number of routes can be advertised by a particular routing protocol within a specified time period; this effectively provides an SLA for the propagation of routing updates across the access-link.

Care should be taken to ensure that active SLA-monitoring traffic (see Chapter 5, Section 5.3) is not classified into this class because active monitoring traffic should report on the delay, jitter, and loss characteristics of the actual customer-facing class it is monitoring. Consequently, active SLA-monitoring traffic should be classified based on the packets' DSCP marking, which should be the same as for the class it is monitoring.

3.2.2.3.4   Standard Data Class (*Std*)

The configuration in Figure 3.4 assumes that the ordering of the classes within the Diffserv policy implicitly defines an ordering of the classification criteria, i.e. in the case that a packet matches the classification criteria of multiple classes, it will be classified into the first matching class listed in the policy. Therefore, the wildcard classification criteria used for the *Std* class ensures that all traffic that is not classified into the *VoIP*, *Prm-th*, or *Ctrl* classes (which come first in the Diffserv policy) is classified into the *Std* class. The DSCP of all packets classified into the class is set to D_s.

The *Std* class SLA commitment is assured by treating the class with an AF PHB with a minimum bandwidth assurance of R_s. Assuming that a work-conserving scheduler is used, the *Std* class will have access to all unused interface capacity once the *VoIP*, *Prm-th*, and *Ctrl* data classes have been serviced. RED is used within the class queue to ensure TCP throughput within the class is maximized when congestion occurs; RED tuning is described in Section 3.4.

3.2.2.4 Design Variations

In this section, we consider design variations to the baseline edge design described in the preceding sections.

3.2.2.4.1 Low-speed Edge Design

The main difference between the Diffserv edge designs for low-speed links compared to high-speed links relates to the additional use of link layer fragmentation and interleaving mechanisms on low-speed links, to ensure that the delay SLA for classes with tightly bounded delay commitments, such as the *VoIP* class, can be met.

An edge SLA service usually targets a maximum one-way edge latency for VoIP of 15 to 50 ms, as discussed in Section 3.2.2.1.1. Even where a strict priority scheduler is used to implement an EF PHB for delay-sensitive traffic such as VoIP, however, a newly arrived priority packet must wait for any non-priority packet currently being serviced, before it can be serviced by the scheduler (see Chapter 2, Section 2.2.4.1.1). In practical implementations, there may be additional delay, with several non-priority packets potentially being queued ahead of a priority packet due to the presence of an interface FIFO (see Chapter 2, Section 2.2.4.1.3). The impact of the scheduler and interface FIFO on the delay of a priority packet is more significant for lower-speed access connections. Therefore, we define "low-speed" links as those

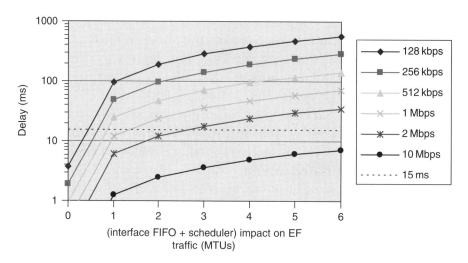

Figure 3.5 Perturbing impact of (Interface FIFO + scheduler) on EF traffic

in which the perturbing impact of non-EF traffic on EF traffic, due to the characteristics of both the scheduler and the interface FIFO, exceeds the latency commitment for the VoIP class, or more generally, the class with the tightest delay commitment. The graph in Figure 3.5 shows the delay of a single 60-byte EF packet (which is the packet size for a G.729A codec with a 20 ms packetization interval) for different rates, with varying impacts due to the interface FIFO and scheduler system, measured in maximum transmission units (MTUs), which are assumed to be 1500 bytes.[1] The actual delay experienced by a VoIP packet may be greater in practice, due to self-induced queuing delay, where there may be multiple VoIP packets in the priority queue, as discussed in Section 3.2.2.8.

As can be seen from Figure 3.5, even where the impact of the interface FIFO and scheduler on EF delay is only 2 * 1500 byte MTUs, which represents a good low-speed implementation in practice, at link speeds of less than 2 Mbps, the perturbing impact on EF delay is sufficient to cause the 15 ms access segment delay budget to be exceeded. In such cases, link layer fragmentation and interleaving mechanisms, such as those provided by Frame-Relay Forum implementation agreement FRF.12 and the multilink point-to-point protocol

(MLPPP) are needed to reduce the impact of non-EF traffic on EF traffic delay. With link-layer fragmentation, large non-EF packets are broken into smaller fragments such that EF packets can be interleaved with the fragments, rather than having to wait for (possibly multiple) whole non-EF packets to be transmitted.

Where link-layer fragment is used, the fragment size F is chosen such that the VoIP latency commitment L_v can be realized. This can be expressed by the following equation:

$$\frac{((T + 1) \times F + n \times V)}{link\_rate} < L_v$$

where T is the number of packet buffers in the interface FIFO; $(T + 1)$ accounts for the worst-case scenario of scheduling an AF packet immediately prior to an EF packet; V is the VoIP packet size; n represents the maximum number of concurrent VoIP packets in the VoIP class queue, which accounts for the self-induced queuing delay due to VoIP traffic contention; see Section 3.2.2.8.

For example, with $T = 2$, $n = 1$, and $V = 60$ bytes, with a link rate of 256 kbps and $F = 1500$ bytes the maximum EF latency could be as high as ~143 ms, which consumes most of an 150 ms ear-to-mouth delay budget. Setting the fragmentation size to ~130 bytes decreases the maximum potential EF latency to ~14 ms. Figure 3.6 shows the EF delay versus fragment size for various link speeds where $T = 2$, $n = 1$, and $V = 60$ bytes; as can be seen, even at 128 kbps it may be possible to achieve an EF delay of ~15 ms, albeit with a fragment size of 100 bytes.

Link layer fragmentation and interleaving mechanisms are processor intensive functions that can have an impact on router forwarding performance, hence, in practice for maximum performance the largest possible fragment sizes should be used that can achieve a particular edge segment latency commitment, which is determined by the following formula:

$$F = \frac{(L_v \times link\_rate) - (n \times v)}{(T + 1)}$$

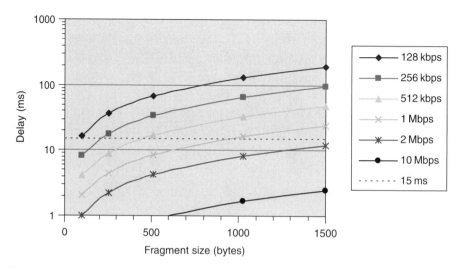

Figure 3.6 EF delay vs fragment size

3.2.2.4.2   Hierarchical Shaping and Scheduling

Distribution routers may potentially aggregate thousands of customer's connections through frame-relay, ATM, TDM (leased line) or metro Ethernet access networks. In the vast majority of deployments, one physical interface will terminate many logical connections using a multiaccess layer 2 technology; each customer site is assigned to one or more virtual links, which would be identified by data link connection identifiers (DLCIs) for frame-relay, virtual circuits (VCs) for ATM, channels for time division multiplexed (TDM) services, or virtual LANs (VLANs) for Ethernet. The distribution and access routers enforce an aggregate rate per-customer site by shaping the virtual link (or links) to a token bucket profile contracted in the SLA to rate R_a and burst B_a. The underlying layer 2 access link virtual connections must guarantee the availability of that traffic profile bidirectionally between the access router and the distribution router with an SLA that is capable of supporting the SLA requirements of the IP services (see Chapter 2, Section 2.5). When the upstream or downstream aggregate offered traffic load is larger than the contracted profile for the access link virtual connections the access router or distribution router shaper delays the packets in the EF/AF scheduler. This creates

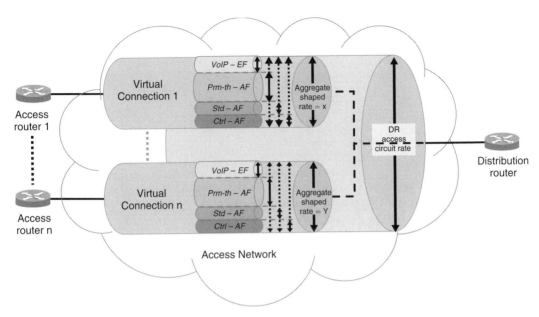

VoIP – EF

Prm-th – AF

Std – AF

Ctrl – AF

Virtual Connection 1

Aggregate shaped rate = x

VoIP – EF

Prm-th – AF

Std – AF

Ctrl – AF

Virtual Connection n

Aggregate shaped rate = Y

DR access circuit rate

Access router 1

Access router n

Access Network

Distribution router

Figure 3.7 Multiaccess DR connectivity: hierarchical shaping and scheduling

a hierarchy where the EF/AF scheduler acts as a child functional block relative to the parent shaper (see Chapter 2, Section 2.4), ensuring that the most important traffic from the customer site gets prioritized access to the committed bandwidth for the logical layer 2 connection. The aggregate rate enforcement serves both to define an aggregate bound on the contract between the SP and the customer, and also to ensure isolation between different customers services which are terminated on the same physical (although different logical) interfaces. This concept is illustrated in the diagram in Figure 3.7.

The configuration in Figure 3.8 augments the design from Section 3.2.2.3 with a parent shaping function, shown in bold text. This configuration would typically be applied outbound on the core facing (i.e. upstream) AR interface and outbound on the access facing (i.e. downstream) interface of the DR. The parent shaping function may need to account for layer 2 overheads, depending upon the layer 2 access technology used, and upon any physical bandwidth constraints (see Chapter 1, Section 1.2.4.1). Where ATM is used as the access

```
policy outbound-shaped-high-speed-edge-policy
  class shaper
    classify *
    shape (Ra, Ba)
      {
        class VoIP
          classify DSCP (Dv)
          SR-TCM (Rv, Bv, 0)
            green-action transmit
            red-action drop
          EF
        class Prm-th
          classify <criteria>
          AF (Rt)
          mark DSCP (Dt)
        RED (DSCP(*), <minth>, <maxth>, <w>, <pmax>)
        class Ctrl
          classify DSCP {Dc, 48}
          AF (Rc)
        RED (DSCP(*), <minth>, <maxth>, <w>, <pmax>)
        class Std
          classify *
          AF (Rs)
          mark DSCP (Ds)
          RED (DSCP(*), <minth>, <maxth>, <w>, <pmax>)
      }
```

Figure 3.8 High-speed edge design with aggregate shaper

network technology, for example, the shaping function will need to take into account the ATM overheads, to ensure that the contracted profile for the ATM VC is not exceeded.

3.2.2.4.3   Unmanaged Access Router Services

The designs discussed so far have been in the context of "managed access router" services – that is, where the network provider (commonly a VPN provider) owns and manages the access router device, in addition to the core and distribution routers, and consequently commits to the SLA end-to-end from access router-to-access router. With *unmanaged access router* service offerings, the network provider owns and manages the core and distribution routers, but does not own and manage the access router. This option is attractive as a wholesale service offering where a network SP supplies a lowest common denominator service to systems integrators who add their own access router to the service, and offer customized access router configurations. Unmanaged access router services are also attractive for end customers who wish to maintain control of the access router.

There are two major differences with respect to the deployment of unmanaged access router services, when compared to managed service offerings. The first is that as the access router is neither owned nor managed by the network SP, they cannot ensure that the correct configuration and management is applied to the access router to be able to commit to an SLA from the access router to the distribution router. Secondly, in order to protect their network from access routers misconfiguration, the network SP may now need to perform inbound on the access facing (i.e. downstream) interface of the DR, the complex per-customer classification and conditioning functions, in terms of rate enforcement, which were distributed to access routers in the managed service context. Conceptually, the hierarchical shaping with queuing functionality, equivalent to that described in Section 3.2.2.4.2, may be applied on ingress to the DR also; however, this functionality is not widely supported on ingress by network equipment vendor's devices today. Alternatively, an example Diffserv conditioning policy, which would be applied inbound on the access facing (i.e. downstream) interface of the DR to the upstream traffic, is shown in Figure 3.9.

In this case, the classification criteria are the same as that used in the managed AR service; however, if it is assumed that the access router is correctly classifying and marking traffic, simple classification based upon the DSCP marking set by the access router may be used instead.

The policy shown in Figure 3.9 uses two instances of the SR-TCM to condition the traffic received by the distribution router: one

```
policy unmanaged-inbound-dr-policy
  class aggregate
    classify *
      SR-TCM (Ra, Ba, 0)
        green-action transmit
        red-action drop
      {
       class VoIP
         classify DSCP (Dv)
         SR-TCM (Rv, Bv, 0)
           green-action transmit
           red-action drop
       class Prm-th
         classify <criteria>
         mark DSCP (Dt)
       class Ctrl
         classify DSCP {Dc, 48}
       class Std
         classify *
         mark DSCP (Da)
      }
```

Figure 3.9 Unmanaged AR service – ingress upstream distribution router policy

enforces an aggregate rate R_a for the received traffic, while the other enforces a rate R_v, for the received *VoIP* class traffic. Note that the use of two policing instances in this way has a fundamentally different effect than the shaping/scheduling hierarchy used in Section 3.2.2.4.2. Assuming that the two SR-TCM instances operate independently, if the rate of one of the policers is exceeded, then the resulting behavior is dependent upon the order in which the policers are applied. If the aggregate policer is applied first then *VoIP* traffic may pass the aggregate policer but may be dropped by the *VoIP* class policer, resulting in underutilization of the aggregate rate. If the VoIP class policer is applied first then *VoIP* traffic may pass the class policer but may be dropped by the *aggregate* policer, resulting in underutilization of the *VoIP* class. Hence, Diffserv policies are generally only applied in this way to protect the SP network from misconfiguration of the AR; if the customer owning the AR has configured the correct policy on the AR (i.e. in this case as described in Section 3.2.2.4.2), this inbound policy on the access facing (i.e. downstream) interface of the DR will have no effect.

3.2.2.4.4   Add Premium Data Delay-optimized Class (*Prm-delay*)

The premium data throughput-optimized class (*Prm-th*) did not support an SLA for delay or loss because the maximum rate for the class was not enforced with a policer and hence the actual class delay and loss are dependent upon the customer's offered traffic profile for that class, which is outside of the SP's control. Therefore, to offer a premium data delay-optimized class (*Prm-delay*) with a defined SLA for loss and latency, the maximum rate and burst for the class must be enforced with a policer. Such a *Prm-delay* class targets business-critical interactive applications with delay requirements such as SNA, SAP R/3, Telnet, and market trading data feed applications.

3.2.2.4.4.1   **Prm-delay SLA**   The *Prm-delay* SLA is defined in terms of a committed delay and loss rate, with a specified bandwidth and availability. Attainable throughput is derived from the loss rate. Jitter is not important for this service class and is not defined. The class may support a commitment for per flow sequence preservation.

As with the *VoIP* class, the SP and the customer agree to a contract with a defined ICR and ECR, which are specified symmetrically in this case study (that is, ICR = ECR), although that need not necessarily be the case. The SP enforces the contract by limiting the rate of *Prm-delay* traffic to/from the customer site using a token bucket policer of rate R_d and burst B_d; non-conformant traffic in excess of the policer will be dropped by the SP. The rate R_d will be selected by the customer and will be offered by the SP up to a defined percentage of the access link speed. As for the VoIP class, SPs will not offer the *Prm-delay* class below a defined minimum link speed, and the value of B_d is set based on the offered class delay commitment.

For conformant traffic, the SP will commit to a maximum one-way edge segment latency, L_d, typically in the range 30–80 ms (for a defined packet size) and an end-to-end loss rate of typically less than 0.1%.

The contract will also define the classification criteria that the SP will use to identify the class and stipulate that conformant traffic will be marked with a defined DSCP value D_d.

3.2.2.4.4.2 **Prm-delay** *Design*   The configuration in Figure 3.10 augments the design from Section 3.2.2.3 with a *Prm-delay* class, which is highlighted in bold text. This configuration would typically be applied outbound on the core facing (i.e. upstream) AR interface and outbound on the access facing (i.e. downstream) interface of the DR.

Considering the *Prm-delay* class Diffserv configuration in Figure 3.10, as per the *Prm-th* class, it is assumed that complex classification criteria (unspecified in the figure) are used to classify packets into the class. The DSCP of all packets classified into the class is set to D_d.

The *Prm-delay* class latency commitment is met by treating the class with an AF per-hop behavior (PHB), which provides a minimum class bandwidth assurance R_d, and by enforcing an average arrival rate of R_d with a policer, such that the arrival rate does not exceed the servicing rate for the class. This could be achieved using the SR-TCM with rate R_d, committed burst size B_d, with EBS = 0 and applying a green action of transmit and mark DSCP and a red action of drop. The SP specifies the SLA contract with the policer's worst-case admitted burst B_d, such that the burst is serviced within the class latency commitment L_d, i.e. $B_d/R_d + L_s < L_d$, where L_s represents the worst-case delay to service the AF traffic (which would be greater than for EF traffic) due to the scheduler and the interface FIFO (see Chapter 2, Section 2.2.4.1.3). A tail drop queue limit is not required for the *Prm-delay* class queue, in addition to the policer.

If a router implementation requires that a queue-limit is configured, the queue-limit must be greater than or equal to B_d, to ensure that packets that are within the permitted burst for the class are not dropped. Therefore, the only actual packet loss that can occur for conformant traffic within the class is due to layer 1 bit errors or network

```
policy high-speed-edge-policy
  class VoIP
    classify DSCP (Dv)
    SR-TCM (Rv, Bv, 0)
      green-action transmit
      red-action drop
    EF
  class Prm-delay
    classify <criteria>
    SR-TCM (Rd, Bd, 0)
      green-action transmit-and-mark DSCP (Dd)
      red-action drop
    AF (Rd)
  class Prm-th
    classify <criteria>
    AF (Rt)
    mark DSCP (Dt)
    RED (*, <minth>, <maxth>, <w>, <pmax>)
  class Ctrl
    classify DSCP {Dc, 48}
    AF (Rc)
    RED (*, <minth>, <maxth>, <w>, <pmax>)
  class Std
    classify *
    AF (Rs)
    mark DSCP (Ds)
    RED (*, <minth>, <maxth>, <w>, <pmax>)
```

Figure 3.10   High-speed edge design with *Prm-delay* class

element failures, which account for the loss rate for the class offered by the SP.

An alternative design is possible using advanced scheduler implementations, which provide support for more than one priority queue as described in Chapter 2, Section 2.2.4.1.4. This would allow the possibility of using the highest priority queue for VoIP class, for example, and the next priority queue for *Prm-delay* traffic, enabling the VoIP class traffic to receive the lowest delay and jitter, while the *Prm-delay* traffic would have a bounded delay and jitter, independent of the scheduler implementation and the configuration and load of the other AF queues.

3.2.2.4.5   Add Premium Data Throughput-optimized Class with Loss Commitment (*Prm-loss*)

The premium data delay-optimized class (*Prm-delay*) added a policer to the premium Data throughput-optimized class (*Prm-th*) configuration to enforce the maximum rate and burst for the class, dropping excess such that an SLA for loss and delay could be supported. A consequence of the way the policer was used with the *Prm-delay* class, however, is that the class was unable to re-use unused bandwidth from other classes within the same policy. Therefore, to offer a premium data throughput-optimized class which has a loss commitment (*Prm-loss*) and which also has the ability to re-use unused bandwidth from other classes within the same policy, a policer is instead applied to mark a certain amount of a traffic class as in-contract, and everything above that as out-of-contract; the SLA for loss is committed for the in-contract traffic only.

3.2.2.4.5.1*   Prm-loss *SLA   The *Prm-loss* SLA is defined in terms of a committed loss rate, with a specified bandwidth and availability. Attainable throughput for TCP-based applications is derived from the loss rate and RTT. Jitter is not important for this service class and is not defined. The class may support a commitment for per flow sequence preservation. Such a class targets the same applications as the *Prm-th* class, but where an explicit loss commitment is required. The practical differences between the *Prm-loss* class and the *Prm-th* class are therefore really in terms of the way that the SLA is exposed to the end-customer; this is most commonly provided in the context of services offered by a network service provider, rather than in the case of an intra-enterprise network.

As with the *VoIP* class, the SP and the customer agree to a contract with a defined ICR and ECR; in this case study ICR = ECR. The SP enforces the contract by limiting the rate of *Prm-loss* traffic to/from the customer site using a token bucket policer of rate R_l and burst B_l; non-conformant traffic will be marked as out-of-contract by the SP. The rate R_l will be selected by the customer and will be offered by the SP possibly up to the access link speed.

For conformant (in-contract) traffic, the SP will commit to an end-to-end loss rate of typically less than 0.1%.

The contract will also define the classification criteria that the SP will use to identify the class and stipulate that conformant traffic within the class be marked with a defined DSCP value D_{lin} and non-conformant traffic will be marked with a defined DSCP value D_{lout}.

In practice, if this class was offered as a service, it would likely be in lieu of the *Prm-th* class, i.e. there is little point in offering both a *Prm-loss* and a *Prm-th* class.

3.2.2.4.5.2 Prm-loss *Design*

The configuration in Figure 3.10 enhances the design from Section 3.2.2.3 with a *Prm-loss* class, which is shown highlighted in bold, instead of the *Prm-th* class. This configuration would typically be applied outbound on the core facing (i.e. upstream) AR interface. A similar policy may be applied outbound on the access facing (i.e. downstream) interface of the DR, only without the class policer, as the in- and out-of-contract conditioning is performed on ingress to the network.

Considering the *Prm-loss class* Diffserv configuration in Figure 3.11, as per the *Prm-th* class it is assumed that complex classification criteria (unspecified in the figure) are used to classify packets into the class.

The *Prm-loss* class loss commitment is met by treating the class with an AF per-hop behavior (PHB), which provides a minimum class bandwidth assurance R_l, and by enforcing an average arrival rate for in-contract traffic of R_l with a policer, such that the in-contract arrival rate does not exceed the servicing rate for the class. This could be achieved using the SR-TCM with rate R_l, committed burst size B_l, with EBS = 0 and applying a green action of transmit-and-mark DSCP D_{lin} and a red action of transmit-and-mark DSCP D_{lout}. Assuming that most of the traffic within the class is TCP-based, B_l, should be set to

```
policy high-speed-edge-policy
  class VoIP
    classify DSCP (Dv)
    SR-TCM (Rv, Bv, 0)
      green-action transmit
      red-action drop
    EF
  class Prm-loss
    classify <criteria>
    SR-TCM (R1, B1, 0)
      green-action transmit-and-mark DSCP (D1in)
      red-action transmit-and-mark DSCP (D1out)
    AF (R1)
    RED (D1in, <minth>, <maxth>, <w>, <pmax>)
    RED (D1out, <minth>, <maxth>, <w>, <pmax>)
  class Ctrl
    classify DSCP {Dc, 48}
    AF (Rc)
    RED (*, <minth>, <maxth>, <w>, <pmax>)
  class Std
    classify *
    AF (Rs)
    mark DSCP (Ds)
    RED (*, <minth>, <maxth>, <w>, <pmax>)
```

Figure 3.11 High-speed edge design with *Prm-loss* class

be sympathetic to the behavior of TCP. If B_l is set too small, due to the bursty nature of TCP, most traffic would be marked as out-of-contract, and the rate commitment for the class may not be achieved in practice. If B_l is set too large, most traffic would be marked as in-contract, and the loss commitment for the class may not be achieved in practice. Most TCP tuning focuses on the concept of the TCP "flight size" [RFC2581] or the "pipesize," which is the amount of unacknowledged data in flight between the TCP sender and the receiver, and is defined by the bottleneck bandwidth * RTT product. For low-speed access with small numbers of TCP flows, setting B_l, equal to R_l * RTT should ensure that the rate and loss commitment for the class can be met for TCP traffic. At higher speeds, as more flows are aggregated, lower values of B_l may be acceptable due to the effect of statistical multiplexing.

Weighted RED (WRED) is then applied to the class queue such that if there is congestion in the queue, then out-of-contract traffic will be preferentially discarded over in-contract traffic. This is achieved by having a more aggressive WRED profile (lower q_{minth} and q_{maxth} settings) for the out-of-contract traffic than for the in-contract traffic (as described in Chapter 2, Section 2.2.4.2.4) and by ensuring that sufficient capacity is provisioned to service the in-contract traffic. The WRED profile for in-contract traffic is set such that the in-contract traffic should not be dropped in normal network operation; it may therefore seem to be redundant; however, it is included in order to maximize throughput for in-contract TCP traffic in the presence of unforeseen in-contract load, due to network element failures, for example. Hence, in normal operation, the only actual in-contract packet loss that should occur is due to layer 1 bit errors or network element failures, which account for the loss rate for the class offered by the SP. WRED tuning is described in Section 3.4.

The TR-TCM may be used as an alternative to the SR-TCM, to mark a certain amount of a traffic class as in-contract, and everything above that as out-of-contract, but up to a maximum rate, with a green action of transmit-and-mark DSCP D_{lin} and a yellow action of transmit-and-mark DSCP D_{lout}, and a red action of drop. Applied in this way the TR-TCM would enforce a maximum rate of CIR and a burst of CBS on the traffic stream; any traffic in excess would then be marked out-of-contract up to a maximum rate of PIR and a burst of PBS.

3.2.2.4.6 Add a Video Class (Video)

As discussed in Chapter 1, Section 1.3.2.1.1, worst-case one-way network delays of 100–200 ms are typically targeted for streaming video applications. If there were a requirement to add support for a video service class there are potentially a number of designs that could be applied to support such a class.

- *Service video from same class as VoIP.* It may be possible to service voice and video from the same class queue, using a design such as that described for the real-time class in Section 3.2.2.3.1. In support of such designs, some vendors have implementations that allow multiple subsets of traffic within a class to be discretely policed to limit the worst-case impact that the subsets of traffic have on each other. Nonetheless, if voice and video are serviced from the same priority queue, large video packets can increase the delay and jitter experienced by the voice traffic; this effect can be significant on low-speed links, but may be acceptable for higher speed access links.

- *Distinct video class using AF queue.* A video service class could be supported using an AF PHB, as per the *Prm–delay* class described in Section 3.2.2.4.4. With this approach, the delay bound that the video traffic can experience may vary depending upon the scheduling algorithm used, may also be dependent upon the number of other AF queues used in the particular implementation and the traffic in those queues, and at low-link speeds it may not be possible to achieve the required delay targets with this approach.

- *Multi-level priority scheduler.* Some advanced scheduler implementations provide support for more than one priority queue as described in Chapter 2, Section 2.2.4.1.4. When supporting voice and video services concurrently, for example, using the highest priority queue for voice traffic, and the next priority queue for video traffic would enable the voice traffic to receive the lowest delay and jitter, while the video traffic would have bounded delay and jitter, independent of the scheduler implementation and the configuration and load of the other AF queues.

Which option is chosen in practice will likely depend upon the nature of the service being offered, and the capabilities of the network equipment used.

Class	Maximum rate (and burst)	Minimum bandwidth assurance	Delay	Loss	DSCP	See Section
VoIP	R_v (B_v)	R_v	L_v	Typically ~0.1%	D_v	3.2.2.3.1
Prm-th	X	R_t	n/a	n/a	D_t	3.2.2.1.2
Std	X	R_s	n/a	n/a	D_s	3.2.2.1.3
Ctrl	X	1%	n/a	n/a	D_c, 48	3.2.2.1.4
Prm-delay	R_d (B_d)	R_d	L_d	Typically ~0.1%	D_d	3.2.2.4.4
Prm-loss: In-contract	R_l (B_l)	R_l	n/a	Typically ~0.1%	D_{lin}	3.2.2.4.5
Out-of-contract	X	n/a	n/a	n/a	D_{lout}	

Figure 3.12 Edge SLA summary

3.2.2.5 Edge SLA Summary

The edge SLA commitments for the different classes described in the preceding sections are summarized in the table in Figure 3.12.

3.2.2.6 How Many Classes are Enough?

At the network's edge, different classes are used for both SLA differentiation and for providing isolation between applications, i.e. ensuring that the behavior of one application cannot impact the SLA committed to another. In the preceding sections, we have described the designs for service classes in support of applications with a number of different SLA requirements. To provide isolation between applications, there may be a requirement to have multiple instances of the same class even though the classes are supporting applications with the same SLA requirements. This leads to the question: how many classes is enough for an edge Diffserv design?

Several efforts in standardization bodies including ITU-T Recommendation G.1010 [G.1010] and [RFC4594] have attempted to categorize applications into QOS services classes based upon their SLA requirements. G.1010 identifies four different categories for user traffic: interactive, responsive, timely, and non-critical; these classes loosely map to the *VoIP*, *Video*, *Prm-delay*, and *Std* classes previously defined. [RFC4594] identifies twelve service class categories, together with recommended traffic forwarding treatments and codepoints for each service class; however, in practice, typical edge Diffserv designs today have less than eight classes [CARTER]. Further, it is not obvious that the requirements for edge classes will naturally increase over time; at some point, adding more classes provides a diminishing return, where the added design and management complexity exceeds the benefit provided. We recommend applying the maxim that the number of classes supported *"should not be multiplied beyond necessity"*[2] [RFC4594] acknowledges: *"[it] is expected that network operators will configure and provide in their networks a subset of the defined service classes."* Hence, the table in Figure 3.13 summarizes the service class categories from [RFC4594] and maps them to the different class designs defined in the previous sections.

There is no general answer to the question of how many classes should be supported in a particular edge Diffserv design; the answer is dependent upon the specific requirements. Some of the main considerations that will drive the number of classes supported are as follows.

- *SLA differentiation.* The need to differentiate SLAs between applications is the primary driver for supporting additional classes. Clearly, there is no need to support a class if there are no applications that will use that class in a particular deployment. Additional classes can be added incrementally as the need arises for them.

- *What level of application isolation is required?* There may be a requirement to deploy different classes for reasons of application isolation rather than SLA differentiation; this may require that multiple classes are deployed supporting the same SLA.

- *Separate classes for different real-time applications?* As discussed in Section 3.2.2.4.6, it may be possible to service different real-time applications, such as voice and video, from the same class, thereby reducing the number of classes needed.

- *Separate classes for routing protocol and management traffic?* Some network designs may choose to use separate classes for routing

Service class name	Example applications	Codepoint	Class design used
Network control	Routing protocols	CS6	*Ctrl* (Section 3.2.2.3.3)
Telephony	IP telephony bearer	EF	*VoIP* (Section 3.2.2.3.1)
Signaling	IP telephony signaling	CS5	*VoIP* (Section 3.2.2.3.1)
Multimedia conferencing	H.323/V2 video conferencing (adaptive)	AF41 AF42 AF43	*Video* (Section 3.2.2.4.6)
Real-time interactive	Video conferencing and Interactive gaming	CS4	*Prm-delay* (Section 3.2.2.4.4)
Multimedia streaming	Streaming video and audio on demand	AF31 AF32 AF33	*Video* (Section 3.2.2.4.6)
Broadcast video	Broadcast TV	CS3	*Video* (Section 3.2.2.4.6)
Low-latency data	Client/server transactions Web-based ordering	AF21 AF22 AF23	*Prm-delay* (Section 3.2.2.4.4)
OAM	Operations, administration & maintenance traffic	CS2	*Ctrl* (Section 3.2.2.3.3)
High throughput data	Store and forward applications	AF11 AF12 AF13	*Prm-th* (Section 3.2.2.1.2) or *Prm-loss* (Section 3.2.2.4.5.1)
Standard	Undifferentiated applications	DF	*Std* (Section 3.2.2.3.4)
Low priority data	Any flow that has no BW assurance	CS1	*Std* (Section 3.2.2.3.4)

Figure 3.13 Traffic service classes summary from [RFC4594]

protocol and management traffic, although in many cases a single edge class is sufficient for this purpose.

- *Separate classes for bearer and signaling?* For applications such as voice and video, there is a choice as to whether application signaling traffic uses the same class as the bearer (media) traffic or is potentially allocated its own class, as discussed in Section 3.2.2.3.1.

3.2.2.7   What Marking Scheme to Use?

Once a decision is made on the number of classes that will be supported, the DSCP marking scheme that will be used to distinctly identify different classes and different drop precedences needs to be decided; a unique codepoint needs to be assigned to each drop precedence within each class.

Although there are recommended codepoints for the EF, AF and default PHBs (see Chapter 2, Section 2.3.4.1), the use of these codepoints is not mandated, which means that while it may make sense to use these values, if there are valid reasons to use DSCP values other than those recommended, then it is up to the network designer's discretion to do so. There is a perception that using recommended marking schemes will facilitate interworking between networks; however, this tends not to be a significant benefit in practice, and the ability to re-mark between different marking schemes at a boundary router is common functionality on routers today. Further, even though two networks may use common DSCP markings, if their SLAs are not aligned for each respective DSCP marking, there may still be a need to re-mark traffic at the network boundary.

There are a number of reasons why markings other than the recommended DSCP markings may be used in practice:

- The use of first three bits of the DS field – which are functionally equivalent to IP precedence bits (see Chapter 2, Section 2.3.2) – can facilitate and simplify mapping of DSCP markings from/to the MPLS Experimental field (see Chapter 2, Section 2.3.6.2), the IEEE 802.1q user_priority field (see Chapter 2, Section 2.5.3), and 802.17 (resilient packet ring), all of which also support 3-bit marking schemes only.

- A particular design may require more than the one EF and four AF classes for which recommended codepoints are specified.

- Some markings, which are not the recommended markings, have become de facto for some applications, and hence using these de facto markings can simplify a design by not requiring that the application's traffic to be re-marked.

When defining a marking scheme for a particular design, there are a few simple rules which can help to avoid pitfalls:

- Only use DSCP 48 for network control traffic such as routing protocols. DSCP 48 is equivalent to an IP precedence value of 6 (i.e. network control), which is the de facto markings used by networking equipment vendors for network control traffic.

- Use DSCP 46 for VoIP traffic, which is the recommended codepoint for EF traffic and is equivalent to an IP precedence value of 5 (i.e. critical), as this is the de facto marking used by VoIP end-system vendors.

- Use DSCP 0 for the "standard class," assuming that this is the majority of traffic, as this avoids unnecessarily re-marking most traffic.

[RFC4594] suggests recommended codepoints for the twelve service classes that it identifies, as shown in Figure 3.13, with the intent of fostering interoperability through consistency between different deployments. It remains to be seen whether the recommendations from [BARBIARZ1] will be widely adopted in networks and by application end-systems; however, if they are, then using this scheme may result in a simplification of designs.

A possible edge-marking scheme, for the different class designs defined in Sections 3.2.2.3 and 3.2.2.4, which aligns with the recommended codepoints in [RFC4594], is given in Figure 3.14.

As the *Prm-loss* and a *Prm-th* classes would not both be supported at the same time, AF11 is used for both classes. Considerations on mapping this edge-marking scheme to a core-marking scheme are provided in Section 3.3.2.5.

3.2.2.8 VoIP – How Much is Enough at the Edge?

In the definition for the *VoIP* class, it was specified that the SP will normally limit the maximum percentage of the access link bandwidth that is available for this class; the reason for applying this limit is to

Edge class		Edge DSCP marking	
VoIP		D_v	= 46 (EF)
Prm-th		D_p	= 10 (AF11)
Std		D_s	= 0
Ctrl:	Routing protocols		= 48 (CS6)
	OA&M	D_c	= 16 (CS2)
Prm-delay		D_d	= 18 (AF21)
Prm-loss:	In-contract	D_{lout}	= 10 (AF11)
	Out-of-contract	D_{lout}	= 12 (AF12)

Figure 3.14   Edge-marking scheme

ensure that the delay commitment for the class can be met. Even though the VoIP class may be serviced with an EF PHB implemented using a strict priority queue, there is a possibility that when a packet within that class arrives, there may already be a packet (or packets) from that class in the VoIP class queue waiting to be serviced. As the VoIP class load increases, the probability that there are other packets in the queue increases, and hence the probability of that packet experiencing higher queuing delays, also increases. At some class load, there will be a significant probability that this delay due to VoIP traffic contention, i.e. the self-induced VoIP queuing delay, will be sufficient that the access segment latency commitment is exceeded. Hence, the percentage of the access link bandwidth that is available for this class is limited to ensure that the delay commitment for the class can be met. There are various commonly cited rules of thumb for what this percentage should be, including 30%, 33%, and 50%; however, these are generalizations, which are generally incorrect and in this section we consider the factors that affect the maximum percentage of VoIP traffic supported on an access link in practice.

For traffic which obeys a random packet arrival distribution (i.e. a Poisson distribution), queuing theory can be used to determine the queuing delay due to VoIP traffic contention, i.e. the delay due to the fact that traffic from different calls can arrive at the same time. In this

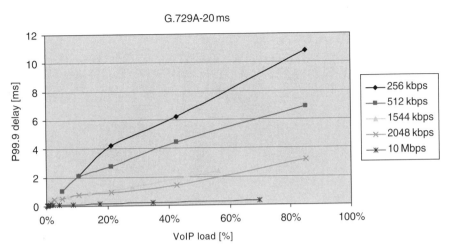

Figure 3.15 Variation of self-induced VoIP queuing delay with rate, assuming a random call arrival distribution

case, the self-induced queuing delay due to VoIP IP traffic contention is a function of two factors:

- the percentage of link utilization due to VoIP traffic

- The VoIP packet size. The serialization delay of a VoIP packet is dependent on the packet size, which in turn is dependent upon the VoIP CODEC used and the packetization interval.

The graph in Figure 3.15 was produced by simulation, where the VoIP self-induced queuing delay was measured when multiple simultaneous calls were established over links of different sizes. The simulation used a random call arrival distribution, with all calls using a G.729A codec (without silence suppression), with a packetization interval of 20 ms (which results in 50 packets per second per call), and a VoIP packet size of 60 bytes. Figure 3.15 shows the variation of the 99.9 percentile VoIP self-induced queuing delay with different levels of VoIP load relative to the access-link rate (i.e. assuming VoIP traffic is serviced from a strict priority queue) for different link rates.

As can be seen from Figure 3.15, for a given codec and packetization interval, the self-induced VoIP queuing delay increases as the

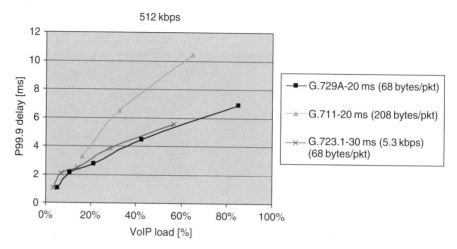

Figure 3.16 Variation of VoIP self-induced queuing delay with codec, assuming a random call arrival distribution

average VoIP traffic increases as a percentage of the link rate. For a given average VoIP traffic load as a percentage of link rate, the self-induced VoIP queuing delay decreases as link rate increases. The graph in Figure 3.16, which is also from simulation, shows the variation of 99.9 percentile VoIP self-induced queuing delay with different codecs (all without silence suppression), for different average VoIP loads, at a link rate of 512 kbps and assuming a random call arrival distribution.

As can be seen from Figure 3.16, for a given percentage of the VoIP traffic average load, the self-induced VoIP queuing delays increase for higher bit rate codecs and for larger packetization intervals.

Therefore, the maximum percentage of VoIP traffic that could be supported on the access link for a particular design is dependent upon the access-link delay budget, from which the worst-case delay through an empty priority queue (i.e. the worst case due to the impact of the interface FIFO and scheduler on EF delay as discussed in Section 3.2.2.4.1, excluding the delay due to VOIP traffic contention itself) should be deducted. The remainder is the delay budget available to VoIP traffic contention, which determines the maximum percentage of VoIP traffic that could be supported on the access link. For example, consider a case where a VoIP class is offered with an access segment delay commitment of 15 ms, for a 2 Mbps link; if the worst-case delay through an empty priority queue is 2 MTUs due to the impact of the scheduler and the interface FIFO, i.e. 12 ms as per Figure 3.5, then this leaves 3 ms of delay budget available to VoIP traffic contention itself. If the VoIP traffic uses a G.729A codec with a 20 ms packetization interval, then from Figure 3.15 the VoIP class load would need to be less than ~85% of the link rate (i.e. supporting a maximum of ~64 simultaneous calls), to ensure that the access segment delay commitment could still be met.

The previous discussion is valid assuming a random (i.e. Poisson) arrival distribution, which may be valid for a VoIP gateway connected directly to an AR, for example, as telephony call arrivals are well modeled with a Poisson process. If the VoIP traffic has been through a number of levels of aggregation, however, the traffic may no longer follow a random arrival distribution and the previous guidance may not apply. In this case, at the edge of the network, the only options to determine the maximum acceptable VoIP load are either to determine the actual traffic distribution, or to assume worst-case analysis, e.g. that packets from all concurrent calls may arrive at the same time.

The question of how much VoIP traffic load can be supported within the core of the network is discussed in Chapter 6, Section 6.1.3.

3.3   Deploying Diffserv in the Network Backbone

Even where Diffserv is deployed at the edge of the network, there is still a choice as to whether Diffserv is deployed in the network core or not.

3.3.1   Is Diffserv Needed in the Backbone?

Unlike at the network edge where bandwidths are lower, in the backbone where there are high bandwidth links and traffic is highly aggregated, SLA requirements for a traffic class can be translated into bandwidth requirements, and the problem of SLA assurance can effectively be reduced to that of bandwidth provisioning. With the aid of a suitable capacity planning process, as discussed in Chapter 6, Section 6.1, designing an IP backbone network to ensure that commitments for low delay, low jitter and low loss can be met can be relatively simple; one simply needs to over-provision the bandwidth compared to the measured average load.

For example, from Chapter 6, Figure 6.5, if we assume that Diffserv is not deployed in the core network and want to achieve a target P99.9 queuing delay of 1 ms to support VoIP traffic on a 155 Mbps link, then the provisioned link bandwidth should be at least 2 times the 5-minute average link utilization. This means that the average link utilization should not be higher than approximately 50% of the link capacity or ~77 Mbps, even if the VoIP traffic contributes a relatively small proportion to the aggregate link load. This approach would actually ensure low-delay, low-jitter, and low loss service for all traffic on the link, because with only a single service class, by definition there is no differentiation between different types of traffic. Without core QOS mechanisms, the network may be simpler to design; however, this benefit comes with the cost of aggregate over-provisioning of the core bandwidth. In addition, if the core capacity planning is not accurate or is not reactive enough to new traffic demands, or in the presence of denial of service attacks or network failure conditions, there may be instances when congestion is unavoidable. In cases such as these, without Diffserv, there would be no differentiation between premium and standard services and in unforeseen congestion all traffic will share the same fate and all services will be impacted.

Diffserv provides a solution to this problem, in that it allows per-class virtual backbones to be built on a single physical backbone. Diffserv simply extends the concept of over-provisioning to multiple classes, giving designers the flexibility to have different over-provisioning factors (the ratio of offered load to available capacity) for each service class, thereby providing SLA differentiation and making more efficient use of network capacity. Using the previous example, this could allow the VoIP class capacity to be over-provisioned by a factor of at least 2 relative to the average class load, hence ensuring that the class receives low-delay, low-jitter and low-loss service, while the aggregate capacity could be over-provisioned by a lower factor, such as 1.2, which is a realistic figure still giving good service. This would result in a bandwidth saving over the non-Diffserv case. In practice as core network links are provisioned in bandwidth increments, this may result in one lower bandwidth increment or one less link being required, which clearly has an associated cost saving. Diffserv also provides isolation between different services classes; in unforeseen congestion; different services no longer need to share the same fate as Diffserv ensures that issues in one service class are isolated from impacting other classes.

Consideration obviously needs to be given to whether the cost of deploying Diffserv outweighs the benefits it provides. There is no generic answer to this question, and the benefits that will be gained will vary deployment by deployment. In the previous example, if the Diffserv deployment cost exceeds the cost of the bandwidth saved (and the router ports, which may be required to terminate that bandwidth) then there may be no sense in deploying Diffserv. For most practical deployments, the maximum potential economic benefit stands to be gained from Diffserv where the traffic requiring the highest SLA targets represents a minor proportion of the overall capacity. As in the previous example, the absence of Diffserv leads the designer to provision capacity equal to the aggregate load across all classes multiplied by the over-provisioning ratio of the class with the tightest SLA; this can be extremely expensive when the tightest-SLA class represents a low proportion of the aggregate traffic. Conversely, when all classes require the same level of service, and hence the same over-provisioning factor, there is no benefit to be gained from deploying Diffserv in the network core. Considering two classes with loads C_1 and C_2, and with over-provisioning factors of OP_1 and OP_2 respectively, the link bandwidth required without Diffserv would be:

$$NoDiffserv\_bandwidth = MAX((OP_1, OP_2) \times (C_1 + C_2))$$

In comparison, with Diffserv, assuming that a work-conserving scheduler is used where class C_1 is serviced with an EF PHB, from a strict priority queue, and class C_2 is serviced with an AF PHB, from a weighted bandwidth queue, the link bandwidth required with Diffserv would be:

$$Diffserv\_bandwidth = MAX((C_1 \times OP_1), (C_1 + (C_2 \times OP_2)))$$

The first term of this formula is to ensure that the over-provisioning factor for C_1 is met; the class is serviced from a strict priority queue, and therefore is serviced at the interface rate, hence the interface bandwidth needs to be at least $C_1 * OP_1$. The second term is to ensure that the over-provisioning factor for C_2 is met; as the scheduler is work conserving, this class is able to re-use all unused bandwidth after class C1 has been serviced, therefore the interface bandwidth needs to be at least $C_1 + (C_2 * OP_2)$.

The benefit of Diffserv can be realized either in terms of less bandwidth being required per link to achieve the same SLAs when compared to the non-Diffserv case, or in more aggregate traffic being supported for the same provisioned bandwidth as the non-Diffserv case. Figure 3.17 illustrates the Diffserv bandwidth gain expressed as the bandwidth required without Diffserv divided by the bandwidth required with Diffserv, to achieve the same SLAs, for different relative

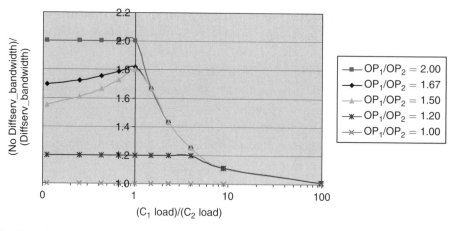

Figure 3.17 Diffserv bandwidth gain

loads of two traffic classes C_1 and C_2, and for different ratios of class over-provisioning factors (i.e. OP_1/OP_2), where $OP_2 = 1$.

As can be seen from Figure 3.17, the most significant relative benefits in terms of bandwidth savings from deploying Diffserv are achieved when the proportion of Class 1 load (the class with the tightest SLA commitment and therefore the highest over-provisioning factor) is low relative to the Class 2 load, and when the ratio of the over-provisioning factor for Class 1 is high relative to the over-provisioning factor for Class 2 (i.e. OP_1/OP_2). Conversely, if all traffic is of the tightest SLA class, intuitively there is no benefit in Diffserv. Chapter 6, Section 6.1.3 discusses the question of what levels of bandwidth over-provisioning are required at different link rates within the core to achieve defined delay and loss commitments.

3.3.2 Core Case Study

We consider a core Diffserv deployment, capable of supporting the SLA requirements of the edge Diffserv classes described in Section 3.2.2.

3.3.2.1 Core Classes of Service and SLA Specification

Clearly, where Diffserv is deployed in the core of the network, the classes supported at the edge need to be able to be mapped to classes in the core, which are capable of meeting the defined classes SLA requirements. At the edge of the network, different classes are used for SLA differentiation and for application isolation, whereas in the core of the network different classes are used for SLA differentiation and for service isolation, where one or more applications may map to a service. Consequently, there may be fewer classes in the backbone than there are at the network edge, with a many-to-one mapping of edge classes to a core class.

Initially we consider support for four core classes, although support for more classes is considered in Section 3.3.2.4, which considers design variations.

- *Real-time (RT)*. This class targets applications such as VoIP and video. The backbone SLA for this class is defined in terms of low delay, low jitter and low loss. A typical SLA for such a class would commit to a one-way delay across the backbone of less than 5 ms (see VoIP delay budget example in Section 3.2.2.1.1) and an average end-to-end loss rate of typically less than 0.1%.

- *Premium data (Prm).* This class targets business-critical applications, which have requirements for bounded delay (albeit less stringent than that of the real-time class) and low loss. An SLA for such a class may commit to a one-way delay or RTT across the backbone and an average loss rate of typically less than 0.1%.

- *Control class (Ctrl).* The *Ctrl* class is dedicated for network control traffic, ensuring that bandwidth on the core links is guaranteed for essential functions typically including routing protocols and for network management traffic, such as telnet or SNMP.

- *Standard class (Std).* The *Std* class is used for all other data traffic, i.e. traffic other than that which is classified as *RT, Prm,* or *Ctrl.* The SLA commitment for such a class may commit to an average RTT across the core and an average loss rate.

These four classes would allow a one-to-one mapping with the four edge classes described in Section 3.2.2.1, as shown in Figure 3.18.

The detailed core network design supporting classes with these SLA requirements is described in the following sections.

3.3.2.2 "Prioritized" Diffserv Core Model
In practice, most backbone Diffserv deployments today have adopted a "Prioritized Diffserv" deployment model. To illustrate the concepts

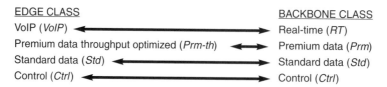

Figure 3.18 Edge to core class mapping

underlying this model, consider a typical design consisting of the four classes defined above, with each class being serviced from its own queue, and serviced with a particular PHB. The *RT* class traffic is serviced with an EF PHB, for example using a strict priority queuing treatment, ensuring that it has the lowest delay and jitter service. The *Ctrl* class is then serviced with an AF PHB, allocated with a minimal bandwidth assurance; let us assume 1% of the interface bandwidth. The *Prm* and *Std* classes are also serviced with AF PHBs, but are configured with a minimum bandwidth allocation such that the remaining bandwidth after the *RT* and *Ctrl* classes have been serviced is allocated with ~90% to the *Prm* class and ~10% to the *Std* class respectively.

Capacity planning is used to ensure that the average measured load for the *RT* and the *Prm* classes is less than their available capacity, i.e. such that their required OP factors are met, hence these classes experience zero packet loss due to congestion, with the only actual packet loss being due to layer 1 bit errors or network element failures. A holistic per-class capacity planning process is essential to ensure this is actually the case; the capacity planning process may take into account network working case conditions (i.e. normal operation) or single or multiple network element failure cases, depending upon the particular goals of the SP; such approaches to capacity planning are discussed in Chapter 6, Section 6.1. Assuming that a work-conserving scheduler is used, even though the standard class is allocated only 10% of the remaining bandwidth, it will have access to all unused interface capacity once the *RT*, *Prm*, and *Ctrl* data classes have been serviced.

A characteristic of this design is that, if interface congestion occurs, assuming the per-class capacity planning process is operating correctly, the loss will be restricted to the *Std* class while the SLAs for the *RT* and *Prm* class will be assured. Further, because the bandwidth available to the *RT* and *Prm* classes is significantly over-provisioned by the scheduler configuration, the scheduler does not need reconfiguring as per-class loads change over time. Rather, when class load thresholds relative to available class bandwidth are such that required over-provisioning factors are not met, the problem is reduced to one of increasing the link bandwidth.

Assuming the per-class capacity planning process is operating correctly, the effect of such a core network Diffserv design is as follows:

- The *RT* class is serviced with priority; capacity planning ensures that the *RT* load is below class thresholds, ensuring that it receives the lowest delay and jitter characteristics and zero packet loss due to congestion.

- The *Prm* class is serviced to its minimum bandwidth assurance; capacity planning ensures that the *Prm* load is below class thresholds, ensuring that it receives zero packet loss due to congestion, and the delay for the class, while not as low as the *RT* class, may be statistically bounded. The class also has the ability to re-use bandwidth from the other classes that may be idle, up to the available link bandwidth, however, if the capacity planning process is operating correctly, it should not need to.

- The *Ctrl* class is serviced to its minimum bandwidth assurance; if the class load is less than the minimum bandwidth assurance for the class it should receive good service with low loss and bounded delay. The class also has the ability to re-use bandwidth from the other classes that may be idle, up to the available link bandwidth, however, it should not need to.

- Due to the work conserving scheduler behavior, the *Std* class is able to re-use unused bandwidth from other classes, up to the available interface rate. The loss and delay characteristics for the class will depend upon the capacity planning load threshold (OP factor) for the class, which need to be managed to achieve the appropriate SLA for the class.

3.3.2.3 Detailed Core Design

The actual core Diffserv policies used to achieve such a design are generally very simple and require relatively minor changes to existing router configurations. Figure 3.19 defines a backbone Diffserv policy designed to achieve the SLA specification described in Section 3.3.2.1 in terms of the Diffserv meta-language defined in Section 3.2.2. This Diffserv policy would be applied outbound to all links in the backbone.

```
policy core-policy
  class RT
    classify DSCP (D_RT)
    classify EXP (E_RT)
    SR-TCM (R_RT, B_RT, 0)
      green-action transmit
      red-action drop
    EF
  class Prm
    classify DSCP (D_p)
    classify EXP (E_p)
    AF (R_p)
    RED (*, <minth>, <maxth>, <w>, <pmax>)
  class Ctrl
    classify DSCP (D_c, 48)
    classify EXP (E_c)
    AF (R_c)
    RED (*, <minth>, <maxth>, <w>, <pmax>)
  class Std
    classify *
    AF (R_s)
    RED (*, <minth>, <maxth>, <w>, <pmax>)
```

Figure 3.19 Backbone Diffserv Policy

As can be seen from the meta-language design described in Figure 3.19, which is representative of real-world router configurations, relatively few lines of configuration are required to implement the Diffserv policy. In backbone Diffserv deployments, these configurations are typically applied once, and then remain static. Furthermore, migrating a backbone to Diffserv can be achieved seamlessly: the backbone configuration can be undertaken independently of the configuration required at the network edge to ensure that traffic is appropriately conditioned and marked on ingress to the network. The benefit of Diffserv for the backbone, however, will not be realized until both edge and backbone components are complete.

The classification criteria used in Figure 3.19 include matching either against DSCP values or against MPLS EXP values. Depending on the particular network deployment and whether MPLS is used in the core network, either or both classification criteria may be required.

3.3.2.3.1   Real-time Class (*RT*)

Considering the *RT* class Diffserv configuration in Figure 3.19, it is assumed that real-time traffic has been marked either at the source or at the edge of the network to one of the DSCP markings within the set D_{RT}, where $D_{RT} = \{D_v, \ldots\}$, or one of the EXP markings within the set E_{RT}.

The per-hop latency commitment is derived from the backbone latency commitment. For example, to achieve an EF backbone delay of less than 5 ms (see VoIP delay budget example in Section 3.2.2.1.1), we assumed 10 router hops through the backbone and apportion a worst-case delay success criterion of 500 µs per hop to ensure that the 5 ms delay target is not exceeded, assuming additive jitter. While jitter might not be additive in practice (see Chapter 6, Figure 6.6, this scenario represents the absolute worst case, and if the deployment can achieve this worst-case per-hop budget, the 5 ms backbone budget will be assured. The per-hop SLA latency commitment is assured by servicing this class with an EF PHB, such that it receives the lowest latency through the scheduler, and by ensuring that the arrival rate enforced by the class policer, R_{RT}, is smaller than the servicing rate for the class.

This could be achieved using the SR-TCM with rate R_{RT}, committed burst size B_{RT}, with EBS = 0 and applying a green action of transmit and a red action of drop. The SP specifies the SLA contract with the policer's worst-case admitted burst B_{RT}, such that the burst is serviced within the class per-hop latency commitment L_{RT}, i.e. $B_{RT}/link\_rate + L_s < L_{RT}$, where L_s represents the worst-case delay impact on EF traffic due to the scheduler and the interface FIFO (see Chapter 2, Section 2.2.4.1.3). Results from [FILSFILS] show that in tests of high-performance routers, L_s was constrained to 125 µs for a 2.5 Gbps interface.

In the backbone, the function of the *RT* class policer is to ensure that the *RT* class cannot starve the other classes of bandwidth, whereas, at the edge of the network policers are also used to ensure that customers do not send more traffic than their SLA commitment allows. In normal operation, and with correct core network capacity planning, the *RT* traffic demands should be known, capacity should be provisioned, and the policer set such that there is sufficient bandwidth and *RT* traffic should not be dropped by the class policer. Therefore, the *RT* policer is typically set higher than the anticipated class load, at a rate whereby it acts as a safety precaution giving protection for the other classes in the case of unplanned for failures, which lead to adversely high *RT* load. Maximum acceptable *RT* rates are discussed in Chapter 6, Section 6.1.3.

If a router implementation requires that a queue-limit is configured, the queue-limit must be greater than or equal to B_{RT}, to ensure that packets that are within the permitted burst for the class are not dropped. Therefore, the only actual packet loss that can occur for the class is due to layer 1 bit errors or network element failures, which account for the loss rate for the class offered by the SP.

3.3.2.3.2 Premium Data Class (*Prm*)

Considering the *Prm* class Diffserv configuration in Figure 3.19, it is assumed that *Prm* traffic has been marked either at the source or at the edge of the network to one of the DSCP markings within the set D_p where $D_p = \{D_t, \ldots\}$, or one of the EXP markings within the set E_p.

The SLA for the *Prm* class is assured by treating the class with an AF PHB, with a minimum bandwidth allocation of ~80–90% of the remaining bandwidth after the *RT* and *Ctrl* classes have been serviced, inline with the prioritized Diffserv model described in Section 3.3.2.2. The RED congestion control mechanism is used within the *Prm* class queue rather than tail drop to maximize TCP throughput. RED tuning is described in detail in Section 3.4.

Capacity planning is used to ensure that the *Prm* load is below class thresholds, such that the required OP factor is achieved, ensuring that it receives zero packet loss due to congestion, with the only actual packet loss experienced by the class being due to layer 1 bit errors or network element failures. This also ensures that the delay for the class, while not as low as for the *RT* class, may be statistically bounded.

3.3.2.3.3   Control Class (*Ctrl*)

Considering the *Ctrl* class Diffserv configuration in Figure 3.19, traffic is classified into the *Ctrl* class by matching on the DSCP which is assumed to have been pre-marked at the source: either to DSCP D_c, by network management end-systems, or to DSCP 48 by routing protocol end-systems or one of the EXP markings within the set E_c.

The *Ctrl* class is assured a minimal share of the access-link bandwidth, e.g. 1% is typically sufficient to support routing protocol and management traffic on high bandwidth core links. The class also has the ability to re-use bandwidth from the other classes that may be idle, up to the available link bandwidth. As a number of applications used for network control and management use TCP (e.g. BGP, SNMP, Telnet) RED is used within the *Ctrl* class queue to ensure TCP throughput within the class is maximized when congestion occurs. RED tuning is described in Section 3.4.

3.3.2.3.4   Standard Data Class (*Std*)

There are two ways that the standard class could be classified:

- either explicitly, based upon DSCP, assuming that *Std* traffic has been marked either at the source or at the edge of the network to one of the DSCPs in the set D_s or one of the EXP markings within the set E_s.

- Or implicitly; as per Figure 3.19, assuming the ordering of classes within the Diffserv policy defines a first match order for classification criteria, the wildcard classification criteria used for the *Std* class ensures that all traffic that has not been classified into the *Real-time*, *Bus*, or *Ctrl* classes is classified into the *Std* class.

The *Standard* class SLA is assured by treating the class with an AF PHB, with a minimum bandwidth allocation of ~10–20% of the remaining bandwidth after the *RT* and *Ctrl* classes have been serviced, in line with the prioritized Diffserv model described in Section 3.3.2.2. RED is used within the *Std* class queue to maximize TCP throughput.

Capacity planning is used to ensure that the required over-provisioning factor for the class is achieved and hence that the loss and delay SLAs for the class are met.

3.3.2.4 Design Variations

In this section, we consider design variations to the basic core design described in the preceding sections, which are needed to support the variations in the edge design described in Section 3.2.2.4. It is noted that the variations to the edge Diffserv design described in Sections 3.2.2.4.1–3.2.2.4.3 (Low-speed Edge Design, Hierarchical Shaping and Scheduling, and Unmanaged Access Router Services) have no impact on the core network design; these variations affect the edge only. Enhancements to the core Diffserv design are required in order to support the edge Diffserv design described in Sections 3.2.2.4.4–3.2.2.4.6:

- *Premium data delay-optimized class (Prm-delay).* There are potentially a number of designs that could be applied to provide support for a *Prm-delay* class across the core:
  - The *Prm-delay* class could potentially be mapped to the real-time class. It is noted that the impact of large data packets on the worst-case delay experienced by other traffic in the same class, is very much less significant on higher speed links, such as those in the backbone. Nonetheless, the delay targets for the *Prm-delay* class are typically less stringent than for VoIP traffic, for example. Hence, for reasons of SLA differentiation and service isolation, it may be required to service the *Prm-delay* service from another class.
  - The *Prm-delay* class could potentially be mapped to the core *Prm* class, defined in Section 3.3.2.3.1, assuming that the class capacity planning thresholds are set to ensure that the *Prm-delay* SLAs for delay can be met.
  - Another core AF class could be added to provide support for the *Prm-delay* class. The approach taken for the class would be similar to that for the *Prm* class; however, this provides the capability to offer service isolation, and SLA differentiation with different

overprovisioning factors and hence capacity planning thresholds for the new class.

○ An alternative design is possible using advanced scheduler implementations, which provide support for more than one priority queue as described in Chapter 2, Section 2.2.4.1.4. This would allow the possibility of using the highest priority queue for RT traffic, and the next priority queue for *Prm-delay* traffic, enabling the RT traffic to receive the lowest delay and jitter, while the *Prm-delay* traffic would have a bounded delay and jitter, independent of the scheduler implementation and the configuration and load of the other AF queues.

• *Business data throughput-optimized class with loss commitment (Prm-loss).* An edge *Prm-loss* class, with in- and out-of-contract capabilities, could be supporting by being mapped to the core *Prm* class, defined in Section 3.3.2.3.1. This would require that WRED be applied to the *Prm* class queue such that if there is congestion in the queue, then out-of-contract traffic will be preferentially discarded over in-contract traffic. This is achieved by having a more aggressive WRED profile (lower minth and maxth settings) for the out-of-contract traffic, as described in Chapter 2, Section 2.2.4.2.4. The WRED profile for in-contract traffic should be set such that the in-contract traffic should not be dropped (see Section 3.4); hence, the only actual packet loss that in-contract traffic within the class can experience is due to layer 1 bit errors or network element failures, which account for the loss rate for the class offered by the SP.

• *Video class.* The possible design options for supporting a video class across the core are ostensibly the same as those for supporting a *Prm-delay* class described above. However, the latency requirements may be tighter for a video class, and the requirements for service isolation may be different, hence the final resulting choice made for supporting a video class may be different from the *Prm-delay* class. A common approach is to service VoIP and video from the same class in the core.

By way of example, we consider how the design would change if support for these three additional classes were provided in the core: we assume that the edge video class is mapped to the core real-time class, and that *Prm-delay* and *Prm-loss* classes are both mapped to the *Prm* class, as shown in Figure 3.20.

The Diffserv policy in Figure 3.21 augments the design from Section 3.2.3 with the modifications required to support these additional edge service classes highlighted in bold.

The changes from the previous design are as follows:

- The classification criteria for the real-time class are changed to classify the DSCP and EXP values corresponding to both VoIP and video classes.

- The classification criteria for the *Prm* class is changed to classify the DSCPs corresponding to the *Prm-loss*, and *Prm-delay* classes.

- WRED, rather than RED, is configured within the *Prm* class queue, to enable different RED profiles for in- and out-of-contract traffic for the *Prm-loss* class.

Further discussion on considerations of mapping and aggregating edge classes to core classes is provided in [BABIARZ].

3.3.2.5   Core-marking Scheme

There is a choice as to what marking scheme is used in the core, and that choice depends upon the type of network technology used in the core, IP or MPLS, and the type of network service that is used, either a private network or a virtual private network (VPN) service built on a public network. We consider the typical combinations:

- *IP core/private network.* If IP is used in the core of a private network, then a consistent marking scheme can be used end-to-end as the full 6-bits of the DS field are available for use both at the edge of the network and within the core. This is typical of private networks, e.g. networks serving the needs of a single enterprise organization.

  Even though a consistent marking scheme is used, there may be fewer classes in the core than at the edge of the network and hence several edge classes may be aggregated into a single core class, with several DSCP values being classified into a single class.

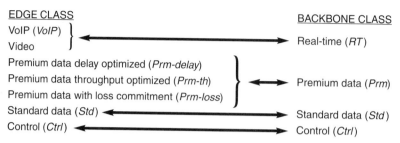

Figure 3.20 Edge to core class mapping: design variations

```
policy core-policy
  class Real-time
    classify DSCP (D_RT)
    classify EXP (E_RT)
    SR-TCM(R_RT, B_RT, 0)
      green-action transmit
      red-action drop
    EF
  class Prm
    classify DSCP (D_d, D_lin, D_lout)
    classify EXP (E_d, E_lin, E_lout)
    AF (R_p)
    RED (D_lin, <minth>, <maxth>, <w>, <pmax>)
    RED (D_lout, <minth>, <maxth>, <w>, <pmax>)
    RED (E_lin, <minth>, <maxth>, <w>, <pmax>)
    RED (E_lout, <minth>, <maxth>, <w>, <pmax>)
  class Ctrl
    classify DSCP (D_c, 48)
    classify EXP (E_c)
    AF (R_c)
    RED (*, <minth>, <maxth>, <w>, <pmax>)
  class Std
    classify *
    AF (R_s)
    RED (*, <minth>, <maxth>, <w>, <pmax>)
```

Figure 3.21 Backbone Diffserv Policy: design variation

- *MPLS core/private network.* If MPLS is used in the core, a mapping will be required from the edge-marking scheme to the core-marking scheme; this mapping requires the edge label switched router (E-LSR) to set the MPLS experimental (EXP) field as a function of the received DSCP for upstream traffic. If more than eight class markings are used at the edge, then as the MPLS EXP field is only 3 bits, and hence can represent only 8 values, there must be a many to one mapping of some of the edge-markings to a single core-marking.

Careful selection of the edge class marking scheme can make the mapping from edge to core classes easier, by making use of the typical default behavior applied at E-LSRs, which is to copy the first three bits of the DSCP (i.e. equivalent to the class selector code-point values), into the MPLS EXP field when a label is imposed (see Chapter 2, Section 2.3.6.2.1). If there were less than eight edge class markings used, then by ensuring that the first 3 bits of the DSCP are unique for each edge class, there would be a unique MPLS EXP field value assigned to each edge class by default. A possible mapping of the edge DSCP markings from Figure 3.14 to a core MPLS marking scheme is given in Figure 3.22.

From Figure 3.22, we note that there are 7 discrete DSCP values used for marking at the edge, which allows a one-to-one mapping

Edge class		Edge DSCP marking		Core class		Core EXP marking		Explicit mapping required?
VoIP		D_v	= 46 (EF)	*Real-time*		E_{rt}	= 5	No
Prm-th		D_p	= 10 (AF11)	*Prm*		E_p	= 1	No
Std		D_s	= 0	*Std*		E_s	= 0	No
Ctrl:	Routing protocols		= 48 (CS6)	*Ctrl:*	Routing protocols		= 6	No
	OA&M	D_c	= 16 (CS2)		OA&M	E_c	= 7	Yes
Prm-delay		D_d	= 18 (AF21)	*Prm*		E_d	= 2	No
Prm-loss:	In-contract	D_{lin}	= 10 (AF11)	*Prm:*	In-contract	E_{lin}	= 1	No
	Out-of-contract	D_{lout}	= 12 (AF12)		Out-of-contract	E_{lout}	= 3	Yes

Figure 3.22 Mapping of edge to core marking schemes

of edge class markings to core class markings. Further, we note with this particular edge scheme the first 3 bits of the DSCP are not unique for each edge class. Therefore, applying the typical default E-LSR behavior, which is to copy the first three bits of the DSCP into the MPLS EXP field, would result in some discrete edge classes incorrectly receiving the same marking within the core. The *Ctrl* class uses CS2 at the edge and the *Prm-delay* class uses AF21; the first three bits of both CS2 and AF21 are 010, hence applying the default E-LSR copying behavior, packets with these markings would both be marked as EXP 2 within the core and would therefore be indistinguishable. Similarly, the *Prm-loss* class uses AF11 and AF12 to represent in- (D_{lin}) and out-of-contract (D_{lout}) traffic at the edge of the network, with DSCP values of AF11 and AF12 respectively. The first three bits of both AF11 and AF12 are 001, hence applying the default E-LSR copying behavior, packets with these markings would both be marked as EXP 1 within the core and would therefore be indistinguishable. There are two possible ways of overcoming this issue:

○ Either explicit mappings can be applied at the ingress E-LSR, rather than the default behavior of copying the first three bits into the EXP field, such that classes can be appropriately distinguished within the core. This is shown in Figure 3.22, where CS2 is explicitly mapped to an EXP marking of 7, so that it is distinguishable from EXP 2, and hence the *Ctrl* class can be distinguished from the *Prm* class within the core. Similarly, AF12 is explicitly mapped to EXP 3, so that in- and out-of-contract traffic within the *Prm* class can be correctly distinguished.

○ Or the edge-marking scheme could be changed such that, when applying the default E-LSR copying behavior, the resulting EXP markings allow the core classes to be appropriately distinguished. In this example, this could be achieved if the edge-markings used for the *Ctrl* class (D_c) and for the out-of-contract traffic within the *Prm-loss* class (D_{lout}) were changed to DSCP 56 (CS7) and DSCP 28 (AF32) respectively.

If there are more than eight edge classes, then ensuring that the first three bits of the DSCP of each edge class represents the core class that it will be mapped to, would allow the default E-LSR copying behavior to be used, rather than requiring any explicit class mappings.

Alternatively, explicit mappings may be used between edge and core classes. This places less constraints on the markings used at the edge, but requires explicit configuration at each E-LSR, to map each edge class to a core class.

- *MPLS core/virtual private network.* When MPLS is used by a network service provider to deliver VPN services, providing network services to a number of enterprises, for example, there are two possible approaches to the core-marking scheme that the network provide can take:
  - *Universal edge-marking scheme.* The network service provider could impose a single edge-marking scheme on all VPN customer networks. This would then allow a single mapping to the core-marking scheme to be used and the options are effectively no different than the "*MPLS core/private network*" model described above, other than the fact that the network service provider defines the marking scheme. This model may represent the simplest solution for the network service provider, but may not be attractive to enterprise organizations, which may have already adopted their own marking scheme, which would have to be changed in migrating to the VPN service.
  - *Per-VPN edge-marking scheme.* Alternatively, the network service provider could support different edge-marking schemes per edge customer. This would require mappings between edge and core-marking schemes on a per VPN customer basis. Use of the Pipe MPLS Diffserv tunneling model described on Chapter 2, Section 2.3.6.2.3.2 would allow the different VPN customer's edge-marking schemes to be preserved transparently across the core. This represents a more complicated model for the network service provider, but can simplify the migration to a VPN for the customer.

- Some deployments may use both IP transport and MPLS transport within the core; in these cases, classification by both DSCP and MPLS EXP classification may be required.

3.4 Tuning (W)RED

The random early detection (RED) congestion avoidance algorithm was originally designed as an algorithm aimed at improving throughput for TCP-based applications, by preventing "global synchronization" between TCP sessions; the operation of RED described in detail in Chapter 2, Section 2.2.4.2.3. Global synchronization is where congestion occurs and queue-limits are exceeded causing drops in multiple sessions, which each back-off, such that the effective aggregate throughput drops below line rate. The sessions then all increase their rate of sending until congestion occurs again and the cycle repeats creating a sawtooth aggregate throughput characteristic. RED aims to prevent this by randomly discarding packets from individual sessions as the average-queue depth increases, such that a higher aggregate throughput is maintained.

RED makes a drop decision prior to enqueuing a packet into a queue, based upon the current average queue depth of that queue and a set of configurable parameters, which hence define the characteristics of RED. A particular set of RED parameters specifies a RED profile, which is defined by a minimum queue threshold (*minth*), maximum queue threshold (*maxth*), and probability of discard at maxth (*maxp*). Weighted RED (WRED) simply extends the basic concept of WRED, by allowing a number of different RED profiles to be used for the same queue, where each profile may be applied to a particular subset of the traffic (normally identified by a specific DSCP or MPLS EXP marking or markings) destined for the queue. This results in different drop characteristics, and consequently probability of drop, per profile. WRED is used for differentiation in the drop probability between in- and out-of-contract traffic in support of classes such as those defined in Section 3.2.2.4.5.2.

The goal of tuning RED is to maximize the link utilization while minimizing the mean queue depth, hence minimizing delay. There are many factors which can impact the tuning of RED, including the number of active TCP sessions, whether those session are long-lived or short-lived, what the RTT is for those sessions, what TCP stacks are used and the particulars of the specific RED implementation itself. These factors vary network-by-network, site-by-site, and probably hour-by-hour, hence optimal RED tuning is probably not achievable in practice. In this section, however, we propose some generic RED tuning guidelines, derived from a number of sources including [FLOYD, CHRISTIANSEN, HOLLOT] which can be fine-tuned as necessary based upon operational experience acquired in the specific deployment environment.

3.4.1 Tuning the Exponential Weighting Constant

The exponential weighting constant (w) determines how closely the average queue depth tracks the actual queue depth. The lower w the more closely the average queue depth tracks the actual queue depth; this has two consequences: the RED drop behavior is more sensitive to traffic bursts, and the closer the maximum instantaneous queue size is to *maxth*, hence the easier it is to limit the maximum latency via RED. For larger w, the converse is true. The following values for w are suggested $w = 1/B$ where B is the output rate expressed in MTU sized packets, i.e.:

$$w = (BW/CMTU * 8)$$

The MTU used in these calculations should be the maximum packet size, which is normally 1500 bytes (the MTU for Ethernet), rather than the MTU of the particular interface, which can often be greater than 1500 bytes. The bandwidth used in the calculations should be the effective servicing rate for the class; for a single class deployment, this would be the link rate.

Note that the enhancement to RED was proposed in "Red-Light" [JACOBSON1], which has been implemented by some vendors, does not have the concept of a configurable exponential weighting constant.

3.4.2 Tuning Minth and Maxth

The minth value should be set high enough to maximize the link utilization; if too low, packets may be dropped unnecessarily, and the link bandwidth will not be fully utilized. The difference between the maxth and the minth should be large enough to avoid global synchronization; if the difference is too small, many packets may be dropped at once, resulting in global synchronization.

Most TCP tuning focuses on the concept of the "pipesize," which is the amount of unacknowledged data in flight between the sender and the receiver, which is the bottleneck bandwidth * RTT product. Where a single RED profile is used in a queue (i.e. no in-/out-of-contract), the following settings (in packets) for minth and maxth are suggested:

For rates < 10 Mbps:

$$minth = MIN [5, 1 * pipesize]$$
$$maxth = 3 * pipesize$$
$$[where\ pipesize = RTT * BW/(MTU * 8)]$$
$$i.e.\ minth = (ROUND(1*RTT*BW/(MTU*8),0))$$
$$maxth = (ROUND(3*RTT*BW/(MTU*8),0))$$

For rates > 10 Mbps:

$$minth = MIN [5, 0.15 * pipesize]$$
$$maxth = 1 * pipesize$$
$$[where\ pipesize = RTT * bw/(MTU * 8)]$$
$$i.e.\ minth = (ROUND(0.15*RTT*BW/(MTU*8),0))$$
$$maxth = (ROUND(1*RTT*BW/(MTU*8),0))$$

The RTT used in these calculations is the round trip time between the TCP hosts. As this varies depending upon queuing delays, access rates, propagation delays, etc., in the absence of other guidance a value of 100–200 ms is suggested. The bandwidth used in the calculations should be the effective servicing rate for the class; for a single class deployment this would be the link rate.

3.4.3   Mark Probability Denominator

It is suggested that a mark probability denominator of 0.1 is used, i.e. the probability of drop at maxth is 0.1.

3.4.4   In- and Out-of-contract

Where WRED is used for differentiation between in- and out-of-contract traffic within the same queue it is suggested that the values for RED recommended in the previous sections are used for the WRED profile applied to the out-of-contract traffic that a "no-drop" RED profile is used for in-contract traffic, i.e. a profile set high enough that in-contract traffic will not be dropped (alternatively, no RED profile or a queue-limit, could be used for out-of-contract traffic). The intended characteristics of this approach are:

- If in-contract traffic is policed such that the arrival rate of the class is not greater than the servicing rate of the queue, then the maximum queue depth should not increase significantly beyond maxth for the out-of-contract profile.

- As there could be both in- and out-of-contract traffic from the same flow, dropping out-of-contract traffic first should reduce the possibility of multiple simultaneous drops from the same flow, and hence be more optimal for aggregate throughput, i.e. across the sum of in- and out-of-contract traffic.

What about using more than two drop WRED drop profiles within a queue, e.g. three drop thresholds as per Diffserv AF11, AF12, AF13? Expressing this in the context of in- and out-of-contract, in practice, it is difficult to understand what meaningful service benefit is offered by differentiating between in-, out-, and exceedingly-out-of-contract traffic. If the intent from such a configuration is to allocate different proportions of bandwidth within a queue to subclasses of that queue, then WRED is not a suitable mechanism to use. To quote [JACOBSON2]: "It is almost always better to run one instance of RED over each of these *x* queues rather than multiple instances of RED over one big queue." Hence, it is not common practice to use more than two WRED drop profiles within a queue, although there may be exceptional cases, where this is warranted.

References

[BABIARZ2] J. Babiarz, K. Chan, F. Baker, Aggregation of DiffServ Service Classes, draft-ietf-tsvg-diffserv-class-aggr, October 2006

[CARTER] S. F. Carter, Quality of service in BT's MPLS-VPN platform, *BT Technology Journal*, Volume 23, Issue 2, pp. 61–72, April 2005

[CHRISTIANSEN] M. Christiansen, K. Jeffay, D. Ott, F. Donelson Smith, Tuning RED for web traffic, in Proceedings of ACM SIGCOMM 2000, pages 139–150, August 2000

[FILSFILS] Clarence Filsfils, John Evans, Engineering a multiservice IP backbone to support tight SLAs, *Computer Networks: The International Journal of Computer and Telecommunications Networking*, v.40 n.1, pp. 131–148, 16 September 2002

[FLOYD] http://www.aciri.org/floyd/REDparameters.txt

[G.1010] ITU-T Recommendation G.1010, End-user multimedia QoS categories, International Telecommunication Union, Geneva, Switzerland, Oct. 2001

[HOLLOT] C. Hollot, V. Misra, D. Towsley, W. Gong

A Control theoretic analysis of RED. In Proceeding of IEEE INFOCOM '01, 2001

[JACOBSON1] V. Jacobson, K. Nichols, K. Poduri, RED in a different light. Technical Report, CISCO Systems, Sept 1999

[JACOBSON2] V. Jacobson. Notes on using RED for Queue Management and Congestion Avoidance, NANOG 13, June 1998

[MCCREARY] S. McCreary, and K. Claffy, Trends in wide area IP traffic patterns – A view from Ames Internet Exchange, *Proceedings of 13th ITC Specialist Seminar on Internet Traffic Measurement and Modeling*, Monterey, CA. 18–20 Sep, 2000

[RFC2581] W. Stevens, M. Allman, V. Paxson, TCP Congestion Control, RFC 2581, April 1999

[RFC4594] J. Babiarz, K. Chan, F. Baker, Configuration Guidelines for Diff Serv Service Classes, RFC 4594, August 2006

Notes

1. 1500 bytes is the MTU size for Ethernet, which is generally the constraining MTU in networks today.

2. This maxim, known as Ockham's razor is a principle attributed to the English logician William of Ockham (circa 1295–1349), which is generally expressed in Latin as *"entia non sunt multiplicanda praeter necessitatem,"* which translates as *"entities should not be multiplied beyond necessity."*

4

Capacity Admission Control

This chapter presents a taxonomy and review of the mechanisms available for capacity admission control in IP networks.

4.1 Introduction

Connection-oriented network technologies such as time division multiplexing (TDM) and asynchronous transfer mode (ATM) have an implicit admission control capability, which is used in establishing the path between sender and receiver, to ensure that there are sufficient resources for the connection. In contrast, IP is connectionless, and has no implicit admission control capability.

In Chapter 3, we described how to deploy the Differentiated Services architecture (Diffserv); Diffserv is by far the most widely deployed IP QOS architecture today, in both enterprise and SP networks. Diffserv effectively provides the capability to manage network capacity on a per-traffic type or class basis. In Chapter 1, we described that the SLAs for IP services are defined in terms of delay, jitter, packet loss rate, throughput, and availability; because the service level experienced by a particular class of traffic is dependent both upon how much capacity has been allocated to that class and upon the current offered load of that class, Diffserv enables differentiated delay, jitter, loss, throughput, and availability commitments to be supported for different classes of traffic.

Diffserv, however, supports no explicit mechanisms for admission control. In order to offer tightly bound service levels for real-time traffic and to assure consistent service within the SLA bounds, admission control mechanisms may be required to ensure that the actual load for a class does not exceed acceptable levels. Without admission control mechanisms, if there is a chance that the available capacity for a real-time traffic class will be exceeded, then for applications using that class which do not degrade gracefully in the presence of congestion, such as VoIP and packet video, the service for all calls or streams in progress may be degraded. Hence, where admission control is not supported for traffic classes used for applications such as VoIP and packet video, the bandwidth for the class must be over-provisioned with respect to the peak load, in order to ensure that congestion does not occur. Such bandwidth over-provision obviously incurs a financial cost. Further, in practice, it may not always be viable to provision every segment of the network to cope for the peak load. In addition, if network capacity planning and provisioning is not accurate or is not reactive enough to new traffic demands, or in failure situations, there may be instances when congestion is unavoidable; in these cases, all calls or streams in progress will be degraded.

Admission control in general is the process of determining whether a new traffic flow, stream or logical connection may be accepted, taking into account resource and policy constraints. Resource admission control is the decision algorithm, which is used to determine whether a new flow can be granted its requested QOS without affecting those flows already granted admission, such that they continue to maintain their committed service. A resource admission control scheme could potentially consider a number of different resource constraints when processing an admission control decision, such as available CPU resources or memory at devices on the path of the requested reservation, or available class bandwidth on the links on the path. In practice, however, from a QOS perspective the main driver for admission control is to ensure that there is sufficient link or class capacity available at the required service level to accept a new request. It is this aspect of admission control which is the focus of this chapter, and we refer to it as "capacity admission control" as opposed to "call admission control" or "connection admission control." Call admission control has voice specific connotations and could relate to policy-based admission control as well as resource-based admission control. Further, "connection admission control" is associated with providing policy or resource-based admission control for traffic "trunks," where a "trunk" is an aggregation of traffic from an ingress point to an egress point. The capability provided by "connection admission control" may not be one of real-time admission control, providing feedback to end-system applications on a per-call or session basis, but rather one of capacity management within the core of an IP or MPLS network, operating in the timescales closer to those of service provisioning, rather than call setup; MPLS traffic engineering is used in this context and is described in Chapter 6. Where the generic terms "admission control" or CAC are used in the remainder of this chapter they refer to capacity admission control.

There are a number of approaches to capacity admission control, none of which is universally deployed today. Different deployments, environments, services, and applications pose different requirements and it is not clear that there is a "one size fits all" solution to the problem of capacity admission control. Further, some technologies for admission control are still evolving. Hence, the rest of the chapter provides a taxonomy and review of the different approaches for capacity admission control, with discussion on the applicability and deployment considerations with each approach.

4.1.1 When is Admission Control Needed?

Considered generally, admission control is only practically useful if the following four conditions are met:

i. Without admission control, the offered load may exceed
   the available capacity

If there is always enough bandwidth for a flow or a class to support the offered load then you simply do not need CAC. Therefore, one approach to providing guaranteed support for services such as voice is to provision sufficient class bandwidth throughout the network to be able to ensure that the peak voice load can be serviced. However, consideration needs to be given to the limitations of guaranteed bandwidth provisioning during different network failure conditions:

- *Network working case conditions*. If there were insufficient bandwidth to support the peak call load in normal working case conditions, then CAC would be required to cover both working and failure cases.

- *Single network element failure conditions*. If sufficient bandwidth provisioning to cope with the peak call load can be assured in network working case conditions only (i.e. in normal operation with no failures) then in all but the most trivial of topologies (i.e. those that are non-resilient) CAC may be required to cover network element (e.g. link or node) failure case conditions. In this case, during network failures, CAC provides the capability to reject new or rerouted service requests so that those already granted admission continue to maintain their committed service. Without CAC, during failure cases or downtime due to planned maintenance, for example, congestion may occur which can degrade all calls.

  Network planning and provisioning methods may be applied which consider single element failures, ensuring that sufficient bandwidth is provisioned when allowing for all single network element failure conditions. In cases such as this, admission control may not be required.

- *Multiple network element failure conditions*. Even where planning and provisioning take single element failures into account, in some topologies there can be unplanned failure cases (e.g. multiple simultaneous network element failures) where there is insufficient bandwidth to support the service load even though IP connectivity exists. In these cases, CAC may be required.

  If sufficient bandwidth can be provisioned to allow for multiple network element failures then admission control is not required; if connectivity verification shows that connectivity exists, then sufficient bandwidth must exist also. However, in meshed topologies, ensuring that sufficient bandwidth exists in multiple network element failure cases may not be a viable approach. Multiple network element failure conditions may seem unlikely, however, in most networks elements will be shut down for planned maintenance; a failure during this time may constitute an instance of multiple network element failures.

Hence, network-by-network consideration is required to determine whether the prevalence, duration and impact of events, such as network element failures, which may lead to congestion resulting in service degradation, is sufficient to justify the cost and complexity of deploying admission control mechanisms.

ii. Service utility will degrade unacceptably as a consequence of
    exceeding available capacity for that flow or class

For some applications, as the bandwidth available to an application flow decreases, the utility of the application also reduces. When browsing the web for example, if the available bandwidth is reduced, the end-user experience may become less satisfactory, but may still be acceptable. Such applications are generally termed elastic applications, examples of which typically include TCP-based applications. An illustrative utility function plot for an elastic application is shown in Figure 4.1.

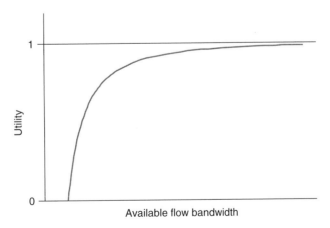

Figure 4.1   Elastic applications' utility function

It is noted that even for elastic applications, there will be some flow bandwidth threshold, below which the utility of the application will be zero, i.e. the application is unusable. Admission control is not generally required for elastic applications. There might be a requirement for admission control for elastic applications if there were the possibility of the application flow bandwidth being reduced to the level of zero utility for a critical elastic application; however, in practice such applications are not prevalent.

There are other applications for which utility is constant above a per flow bandwidth threshold, but when the bandwidth available to the flow falls below an acceptable level, the utility of the application drops to zero. Such applications are generally termed inelastic applications, which typically include VoIP and packet video-based applications. For example, consider a link, which has class capacity to support a maximum of twenty concurrent VoIP calls, within the bounds of the required SLA; if a twenty-first call is allowed to be set up, congestion will occur within that class and the service to all of the calls will be degraded. An illustrative utility function plot for an inelastic application is shown in Figure 4.2.

If there is the possibility of the application flow bandwidth being reduced to the level of zero utility for a critical inelastic application,

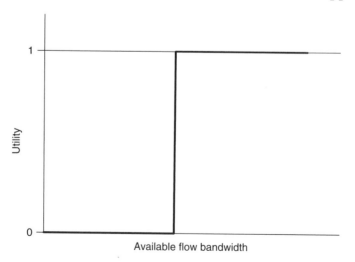

Figure 4.2   Inelastic applications' utility function

then admission control is required to deny a new call or stream if it would reduce the utility of the existing flows, which have already been successfully admitted. If admission control were used in the previous example, it would provide the capability to block the twenty-first call, thereby preventing the existing calls from being degraded and potentially allowing the blocked call to be re-routed where there is sufficient capacity. The mantra for applications which need admission control is that it is much better to refuse a new call than to degrade service for many calls in progress.

In practice, the main drivers for admission control are in support of VoIP and packet video services, both of which are generally inelastic applications. It is noted, however, that there are some VoIP and video which applications may attempt to adjust their rate of sending (and therefore their quality) dynamically based upon the performance they experience from the network (in terms of delay, jitter, and loss), and hence which may be considered in some way elastic. The existence of such applications, however, does not obviate the requirement for admission control. These applications still have minimum bandwidth requirements (i.e. related to minimum quality requirements) and the decision about whether or not admission control is required depends upon whether it is cost effective and practical to ensure that the bandwidth for the flow or class is over-provisioned with respect to the peak load. If it is not, then even for these "elastic" VoIP and video applications, admission control may be required.

iii. The source application knows how to respond to an admission control failure

Admission control is only useful if there is some way of communicating an unsuccessful admission control decision back to the end-system application such that it does not establish the requested flow or stream, and such that it can communicate the failure back to the end-user, e.g. for a VoIP call by returning a busy signal.

iv. It is acceptable from a service perspective to disallow a request

If, from a service perspective, it is not acceptable for admission control to disallow a requested call or session, then rather than CAC, more bandwidth is needed, e.g. for a residential broadcast video service it would generally be unacceptable to have a CAC failure when simply changing channel.

4.1.2 A Taxonomy for Admission Control

As we discussed at the start of the chapter, there are a number of approaches to admission control in IP networks; there are also a number of criteria by which they could be classified. We classify the main approaches into three general classes, as follows:

- *Endpoint measurement-based CAC.* With endpoint measurement-based admission control approaches, admission control decisions are made by the application end points themselves. The end points measure characteristics of traffic to other destination end points to determine if new streams can be accepted to those end points. This approach to admission control is discussed in Section 4.6.

- *On-path network signaled CAC.* With "on-path" or "path-coupled" network signaled approaches to admission control, network nodes on the media (bearer) path between application end points are responsible for making the admission control decisions. This requires a network level signaling protocol to request and reserve resources along the same path that would be used by media traffic for the requested reservation. Such on-path approaches, which ensure that messages used for QOS signaling are routed only through the nodes on the media path, are implicitly topology-aware. Topology-aware approaches have a dynamic understanding of the network topology and are therefore able to adapt to changes in the available network capacity, due to network element (e.g. link and node) failures, for example.

    There are only two protocols, which are defined or being defined, for on-path signaling of such QOS requests in IP networks: RSVP and NSIS.

    ○ *RSVP.* The only practical implementations of topology-aware on-path admission control today use RSVP either as per flow

RSVP (as described in Sections 4.4.1–4.4.4) or as in RSVP-TE (as described in Section 4.4.6).

○ *NSIS.* An effort is currently underway within the IETF to standardize a new suite of extensible IP signaling protocols, which can be used for QOS signaling, and which are referred to generically as "NSIS." These are as described in more detail in Section 4.5.

- *Off-path CAC.* With "off-path" or "path-decoupled" admission control approaches, messages used for QOS signaling are routed through nodes that need not be on the data path for the media traffic. Off-path approaches can be either topology-aware or topology-unaware.

  ○ *Topology-unaware off-path CAC.* Topology-unaware off-path CAC typically consists of applying predefining limits of the available capacity between application endpoint pairs. Being topology-unaware, such approaches have no view of the actual network state, are not able to adapt dynamically to network changes, and hence make inefficient use of the available capacity. This approach to admission control is discussed in Section 4.2.

  ○ *Topology-aware off-path CAC.* There have been a number of recent developments in off-path topology-aware admission control systems, which are also known as "bandwidth managers" or "resource managers." Being topology-aware, this approach can adapt dynamically to the available network capacity and hence does not suffer the bandwidth inefficiency of topology-unaware approaches. This approach to admission control is discussed in Section 4.3.

This admission control taxonomy is illustrated in Figure 4.3.

In addition to the criteria used for the taxonomy, there are a number of other characteristics and capabilities, which can be used to differentiate different admission control approaches:

- *Layer 3 only?* Some admission control approaches only work in IP environments, e.g. they could not be used to make admission control decisions in layer 2 network environments, such as bridged or switched Ethernet networks, for example.

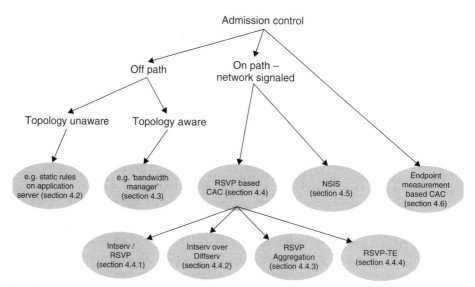

Figure 4.3 IP admission control taxonomy

- *Unicast and multicast?* IP unicast and multicast routing use fundamentally different forwarding paradigms. All admission control approaches described in this chapter support admission control for unicast applications. Although a number of the approaches described could potentially support multicast applications, in practice RSVP is the only approach that currently has this capability.

- *Unidirectional or bidirectional?* Reservations may be unidirectional or bidirectional. Some admission control approaches explicitly support the concept of bidirectional reservations, while other approaches require that bidirectional reservations be modeled as two unidirectional reservations.

- *Control plane or data plane resource reservation?* In Chapter 2, Section 2.1.5, we differentiate between control and data plane QOS functions. Resource admission control is associated with the reservation of resources; if a flow, stream, or connection is successfully admitted, then if that admitted flow's requirements are taken into account before accepting new reservations, by implication resources were reserved for the flow. Depending upon the particular admission control approach that is used, resource reservation can be a control plane only function or both a control plane and data plane function, which for example configures the data plane QOS functions to guarantee resources for successful admissions. Further, depending upon whether the source is considered trusted or untrusted, resource reservation may also be combined with the configuration of data plane conditioning mechanisms to ensure the source is only sending what it is permitted to send.

A summary of the key characteristics and capabilities of the different admission control approaches is provided in Section 4.7.

4.1.3   What Information is Needed for Admission Control?

Whichever admission control approach is used, there is a common set of information needed in order to make an admission control decision:

- *From where to where?* For resources to be reserved, clearly there must be some information to define where the reservation is from and to. For IP-based approaches, this is normally defined by the source and destination IP addresses of the requested reservation.

- *Resources required?* The problem of admission control may often be stated as *"is there enough capacity to support the requested reservation?"* In practice, however, the admission control decision can use parameterized or measurement-based approaches to specify the resources required and determine if sufficient resources are available. The differences between parameterized and measurement-based algorithms are considered in Section 4.1.4.

- *At what service level?* A request for a reservation needs to define the service level at which the prospective reservation is requested. If reservations are being made in a Diffserv network for example, the reservation request could state whether the request is for expedited forwarding (EF) or assured forwarding (AF) resources at each hop. The Integrated Services architecture (Intserv) defines the guaranteed and controlled load service types (see Section 4.4).

- *At what pre-emption priority level?* Some admission control schemes may optionally support the notion of pre-emption, with an associated pre-emption level with each reservation request. If there were insufficient capacity available to accept a new reservation request in addition to all of the existing reservations in progress, this would enable a request with a higher pre-emption priority to be able to pre-empt reservations of a lower priority. This could be used to allow emergency service calls, such as defined in [RFC 4542], to pre-empt standard calls, for example.

4.1.4   Parameterized or Measurements-based Algorithms

With many admission control approaches, there is a choice as to the possible admission control algorithms they can use and whether those algorithms are parameterized or measurement-based; hybrids, which rely on a combination of both approaches, are also possible.

4.1.4.1   Parameterized Algorithms

Parameterized approaches to admission control use resource accounting, in order to make an admission control decision. With such approaches, parameterized traffic descriptors are used to represent resource requirements for requests and a comparable descriptor is used to represent the available resources. The admission control system maintains state information detailing the requests that have been accepted and the remaining resources. When a new request is received, the traffic descriptor for that request is aggregated with those for requests previously admitted (and which are still in progress) and the result is compared against the descriptor of available resources to determine if the new request can be accepted. The performance of such an approach depends upon the accuracy of the parameterized descriptor used to represent traffic requirements and available resources.

The simplest parameterized resource descriptor uses a single variable to describe the traffic profile of the requested reservation, which could represent the peak rate of the reservation, for example. In this case, if the total available capacity (i.e. if no reservation existed) is defined by a (it is presumed that this limit defines the bounds at which the required QOS can be met), the reserved capacity is defined by r, and the capacity requested by a new reservation is n, the new reservation is accepted if the following condition is true:

$$r + n <= a$$

Using a peak rate traffic descriptor, however, makes no allowance for variation in the traffic profile over the duration of the reservation and hence allows no provision for statistical multiplexing gain. For constant bit rate applications this will not be an issue; however, for variable bit rate applications this may result in inefficient use of bandwidth. For variable bit rate applications the variation in traffic profile may be taken into account using a token bucket traffic descriptor, for example, with a specified average rate and a maximum burst characteristic to define the traffic profile of the requested reservation. It can be shown, however, that flows with different traffic profiles could share the same average rate and burst characteristics, and hence functions that aggregate these parameters across a number of flows may not produce a result that accurately reflects the profile of the traffic aggregate. The result of this effect is either that the aggregation functions either need to be conservative (i.e. pessimistic), and hence statistical multiplexing gain is reduced, or inaccuracies may lead to an incorrect decision to accept a new request when insufficient resources are available, and hence SLA guarantees may be violated. This is likely to be more of an issue with a relatively small number of flows; however, where the law of large numbers applies the probability of this issue occurring is low. Further, more complex traffic profile descriptors and aggregation functions are possible [KNIGHTLY], which aim to provide both a reasonable statistical multiplexing gain and statistical QOS guarantees.

4.1.4.2   Measurement-based Algorithms

Measurement-based admission control (MBAC) algorithms rely on using measurements of characteristics, such as the delay, jitter, loss, or utilization from traffic or elements on the path between two end-systems in order to determine whether to accept new reservation requests. MBAC algorithms can use measurements taken either from application end points, or from intermediate nodes on the data path between end-systems. Endpoint-based MBAC approaches can rely either on active monitoring or on passive monitoring of media traffic, and are considered further in Section 4.6.

MBAC approaches that use measurements from intermediate nodes on the data path between end-systems use passive measurement of statistics such as link or class utilizations, in order to estimate whether there is sufficient capacity available to accept a new request. With the simplest measurement-based approach, if the total available capacity (i.e. if no reservation existed) is defined by a (it is presumed that this limit defines the bounds at which the required QOS can be met), the measured load over the past measurement interval is defined by m, and the capacity requested by a new reservation is n, the new reservation is accepted if the following condition is true:

$$m + n <= a$$

More complicated MBAC algorithms are described in [BRESLAU1, JAMIN]. A benefit cited for measurement-based algorithms over parameterized algorithms is that they can achieve higher levels of network utilization (and hence greater statistical multiplexing gain) while meeting user quality of service requirements, as they do not require a traffic descriptor for each reservation and therefore do not suffer the potential issues associated with the aggregation of these traffic descriptors described in the preceding section.

The fundamental assumption, however, that MBAC algorithms are found upon is that measurements taken over the past measurement interval can be used to make accurate admission control decisions in the next measurement interval. This might be the case for high-speed links, such as core links, where a large number of flows are aggregated;

however, in cases where a small number of concurrent flows can cause congestion, this assumption is clearly incorrect. If, for example, multiple flows share a resource, but that resource only has sufficient capacity for a single flow at any point in time, then it is possible for multiple end points to determine that there is capacity available based upon measurements from their past measurement intervals. As a result, they may all start sending within their coincident current measurement intervals, with the result that congestion will occur and their QOS guarantees will be violated. Further, if the state of the network has changed since the last measurement interval, due to a network element failure, for example, then clearly end points may make potentially incorrect decisions to accept new reservations, based upon measurements that are no longer representative of the network's state. Therefore, measurement-based admission control approaches cannot deterministically ensure that congestion does not occur and hence that QOS guarantees will be assured; this is recognized in [BRESLAU1]:

> . . . *traffic measurements are not always good predictors of future behavior, and so the measurement-based approach to admission control can lead to occasional packet losses or delays that exceed desired levels.*

Further, from [JAMIN], which proposed "A measurement-based admission control algorithm for Integrated Service packet networks":

> *Measurement-based approaches to admission control can only be used in the context of service models that do not make guaranteed commitments, such as the [Integrated Services] controlled-load service model.*

Consequently, measurement-based admission control approaches are not generally used for real-time applications such as voice and video (and which would be supported by the Integrated Services guaranteed service model, as described in Section 4.4), which are the main applications demanding admission control today, hence measurement-based admission control is not widely deployed in practice.

4.2 Topology-unaware Off-path CAC

Topology-unaware off-path CAC typically consists of applying pre-defined limits of the available capacity between application end point pairs. Such approaches can be implemented in a distributed manner – on each VoIP gateway as a limit of the number of calls to the other gateways, for example – or in a centralized bandwidth management function, which could be an application server (e.g. video server, call server etc.) or policy server. However this approach is implemented, when a new request is received, it is compared against the currently available capacity between that pair of end points. If sufficient capacity exists, the request is admitted and the available capacity is updated accordingly. If a request would result in the capacity limit between that particular end point pair being exceeded, it would be denied.

Consider the example shown in Figure 4.4. In Figure 4.4, the call server maintains a table of available capacity, in terms of number of calls, from each voice gateway to every other voice gateway. If a user

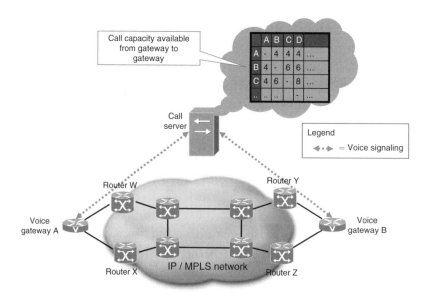

Figure 4.4 Topology-unaware off-path CAC: call server example

connected to voice gateway A attempts to place a call to a user connected to gateway B, in processing the call, the call server performs a lookup in the admission control table. Assuming that there is sufficient capacity available both from A to B, and from B to A as the call is bidirectional, the call will be allowed and the available call capacity in the admission control table would be reduced accordingly. If there were insufficient capacity available for the call to the particular destination, it could be blocked or could potentially be rerouted at the application level to another destination gateway where capacity was available. When the call ends, the admission control table is updated to reflect the consequent increase in available call capacity to the respective destination gateway. This example uses number of calls as the measure of capacity, which may be an acceptable approach where all calls are the same rate; however, where calls can be different rates, a better approach would be to maintain a matrix of the available bandwidth between gateways, and to compare that against the requested bandwidth for new calls.

Topology-unaware off-path CAC represents one of the simplest forms of admission control, but inevitably, it has a number of limitations. This approach may be effective in simple topologies; however, the key issue with all topology-unaware admission control approaches in general is that they do not consider the availability of resources along the specific network path that would be impacted by the request and cannot adapt in real time to changes in network capacity, caused by link or node failures for example. Therefore, in networks with resilient paths, the threshold values used in the tables of available admission control capacity need to defined taking network element failures into account, in order to ensure that such failures will not cause situations where a call is allowed to be placed but there is actually no network capacity available to support the call. In normal network conditions, when there are no failures, these low admission control thresholds do not reflect the state of the network capacity and hence result in inefficient use of available capacity. Consider the access links to gateway A in the example in Figure 4.4: the table shows 4 calls-worth of available capacity between gateway A and gateway B; for this value to be accurate in single element (link or node) failure cases then both of the access links to gateway A would need to be able to support 4 calls independently, i.e. in normal working case conditions site A would be capable of supporting 8 calls in total. If this is the case, but both links are working, then only half of the available capacity can be used. Further inefficiencies may occur where topology-unaware off-path admission control is implemented in a distributed manner, but where the different admission control systems (e.g. different call servers) can share the same network resources and where each system has no visibility of the bandwidth currently reserved by the other systems.

To limit the capacity inefficiencies of topology-unaware off-path admission control approaches, as the network evolves, the tables of available capacity need to be updated accordingly. In large meshed topologies, the ongoing calculation and maintenance of these tables could become a significant operational overhead.

Approaches, which are able to adjust dynamically to changes in the network topology in real-time, overcome these issues. In practice, off-path topology-unaware admission control approaches are only generally used in simple deployments, for example to perform CAC for non-resilient access link connections.

4.3   Topology-aware Off-path CAC: "Bandwidth Manager"

Topology-aware off-path admission control systems, which are also known as "bandwidth managers" or "resource managers," act as an intermediary between the application control plane (e.g. call server, video on demand server etc.) and the network control plane, as shown in Figure 4.5. Such systems track the status of the network and provide the capability to process topology-aware admission control decisions on a per-call or per-stream basis. Being topology-aware, bandwidth manager-based approaches can adapt dynamically to the available network capacity and hence do not suffer the bandwidth inefficiency of topology-unaware approaches. Such off-path topology-aware admission control approaches could potentially provide a solution for most deployment environments: for both the access and for the core, for L2 and L3, for IP and MPLS.

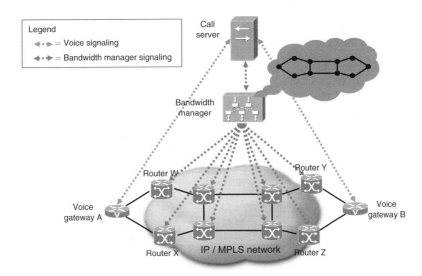

Figure 4.5 Bandwidth manager – topology-aware off-path CAC: call server example

The bandwidth manager maintains a dynamic topology map of the available network bandwidth resources, which in the context of a Diffserv deployment can be maintained on a per-class (service) basis. There are a number of ways that this topology map could be populated, including via an interface to another OSS system in order to extract the required information, or via a discovery process using Telnet/CLI, SNMP or other device protocols, or by participating in routing protocols such as OSPF, ISIS, or BGP. The bandwidth manager also maintains a mapping between these network bandwidth resources and IP addresses of application end points, which may be derived dynamically, from router's routing tables, for example. As requests for resources are received, the bandwidth manager uses the mapping to resolve the addresses of the end points that are passed in the requests to determine which underlying bandwidth resources are impacted by the request. The bandwidth manager verifies that sufficient bandwidth is currently available to satisfy the request; this could be based on bandwidth accounting or potentially use passive measurement statistics retrieved from devices on the data path for the requested reservation. The bandwidth manager then admits or denies the request as appropriate, replies to the application request and updates the bandwidth resource map accordingly.

Effectively the bandwidth manager function is an area of network policy control, making dynamic policy decisions based upon the availability of network bandwidth resources. "Bandwidth managers" can also be considered a practical realization of a subset of the "bandwidth broker" functionality outlined in [RFC 2638]. In addition to performing admission control – which is the key functionality performed by a "bandwidth manager" – the "bandwidth broker" may apply data plane conditioning policies at the ingress points to the network for the requested reservation, and may also perform interdomain communication with bandwidth brokers of adjacent domains.

Off-path resource and bandwidth management functionality has been defined in a number of standards bodies, including the Telecoms & Internet converged Services & Protocols for Advanced Networks (TISPAN) working group within the European Telecommunications Standards Institute (ETSI) [RACS], which currently addresses admission control for the access network and the Multi Service Forum (MSF), which currently addresses admission control for the core network [MSF-TR-ARCH-005-FINAL].

The details of the bandwidth manager operation are most easily illustrated with an example. There are differences in the detail of the different standards in this area and some of the standards are still evolving; hence, the example in the following section is designed to illustrate some of the concepts and considerations of bandwidth manager operation, rather than rigidly representing a particular standard's implementation.

4.3.1 Example Bandwidth Manager Method of Operation: Next Generation Network Voice CAC

With the move to so-called "next generation networks" (NGNs), conventional public switched telephony network (PSTN) voice services are being migrated to IP/MPLS networks. The connection-oriented network technologies traditionally used to support PSTN services implicitly have an admission control capability. One way to provide an equivalent capability with NGNs is by augmenting an IP/MPLS network with a bandwidth manager function, as described in this example.

It is noted that the bandwidth manager could be used in conjunction with a number of different network connectivity models. The choice of network connectivity model has an impact on the characteristics of the resultant admission control system, and affect how the bandwidth manager models and tracks the network topology.

- *IGP-based networks*. In this context, we refer to "IGP-based networks" as networks where forwarding decisions at each hop are determined by an interior gateway routing protocol (IGP), such as OSPF or ISIS, and hence where there is no implicit connection orientation, i.e. no end-to-end signaling function is used to set up the data paths.

  In IGP-based networks, it is possible for the bandwidth manager to participate passively in the IGP routing protocol process in order to model the network topology and to be able to predict the route within the network that a flow would take between two points. If such as system also has a view of the capacity on each of the network's links (either per-class or on aggregate) then it is possible that the system could perform network capacity admission control, receiving and processing requests for network bandwidth reservation and tracking the available capacity. It is noted, however, that the accuracy of such a system is dependent upon how accurately the bandwidth manager predicts the actual behavior of the network; inaccuracies will occur if there are multiple paths with the same IGP metric cost between two end-systems and the bandwidth manager does not model equal cost multipath (ECMP) algorithms (which determine how traffic is load-balanced over the equal cost paths) correctly, for example.

  Further, with conventional IGP routing, in the time interval immediately following network element failures, each router behaves autonomously and hence it is possible that the IGP will reroute traffic affected by the failure, before a new admission control decision can be made by the bandwidth manager, hence transient congestion following network failures is possible with an IGP connection model. This issue is not specific to bandwidth manager deployments, but rather applies to any admission control approaches when they are used with a connectionless IGP-based IP or MPLS network.

- *MPLS traffic engineering-based networks.* MPLS TE (see Section 4.4.6) is implicitly connection-oriented and MPLS TE tunnels provide an explicit routing and signaled network level CAC capability. These capabilities can be used to overcome the issue of transient congestion following network element failures, which can happen with IGP-based network deployments, because re-routing of MPLS TE tunnels cannot happen before a network level admission control decision is made.

  Further, the use of TE tunnels abstracts the bandwidth manager from the task of modeling the detail of the physical network topology. When used in conjunction with a TE deployment the bandwidth manager just needs to track the status of logical TE tunnels and their available bandwidth.

A more detailed discussion on the characteristics of different network level connectivity models when they are used in conjunction with a bandwidth manager is provided in [MSF-TR-ARCH-008-FINAL].

The differences between these approaches highlight the importance of deciding whether CAC is required to cover working case or network failure case scenarios in a particular network deployment; this not only determines whether or not CAC is needed, but also determines which network connectivity models are required in conjunction with the bandwidth manager. If CAC is needed to cover normal working case conditions, and transient congestion following network failures is acceptable, then the combination of a plain IGP deployment in conjunction with a bandwidth manager may be acceptable. If, however, transient congestion following network failures is not acceptable, then MPLS TE is needed in conjunction with the bandwidth manager; MPLS TE also provides capabilities other than CAC, as discussed in Chapter 6, Section 6.2.3.

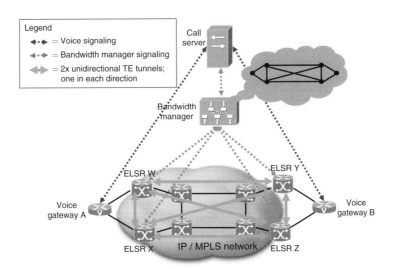

Figure 4.6   Example network topology

For this example, we assume an MPLS TE deployment, as shown in Figure 4.6; Gateway A and gateway B each resiliently connect to respective pairs of MPLS edge label switched routers (ELSRs). A full mesh of TE tunnels is configured to interconnect all of the E-LSRs (for simplicity two unidirectional tunnels are represented with a single bidirectional arrow in Figure 4.6).

The bandwidth manager maintains a map of the key network bandwidth resources needed to make valid admission control decisions, such as contended access connections, core TE tunnels etc. This approach abstracts the bandwidth manager from the detail of modeling the entire network state; TE enables this abstraction for the core. For example, an abstracted bandwidth manager representation of the network from Figure 4.6 is shown in Figure 4.7.

The representation in Figure 4.7 shows symmetrical bidirectional bandwidth resources; however, there is no requirement for bandwidth symmetry and this approach could work with asymmetrical bandwidth resources.

The interaction between the application server, e.g. call manager, and the bandwidth manager will be dependent upon the particular

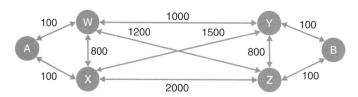

Figure 4.7 Possible bandwidth manager network bandwidth representation

application-signaling model used. In this example, we assume that the session initiation protocol (SIP) [RFC 3261] is used for call signaling, and that Diameter [RFC3588] is used between the call server (in this case SIP proxies) and the bandwidth manager. Diameter is specified as the protocol used for this function by both ETSI/TISPAN [Gq'] and the MSF [MSF2005.187]. Consider the simplified bandwidth manager call flow for a successful two party call setup and tear down shown in Figure 4.8 and the sequence of events that follows.

The call sequence of events is as follows:

- *Steps 1–4.* Conventional call signaling is used to set up a call from SIP End point_A (e.g. Voice Gateway A) to End point_B (e.g. Voice Gateway B).

- *Step 5.* The call server requests admission for a unidirectional call to be set up from Gateway A to Gateway B. The request will contain at least the following information:
  1. IP address of source gateway A
  2. IP address of destination gateway B
  3. Bandwidth requested for the call (or could be the CODEC used)
  4. Call identifier.

  Although this particular application-signaling model uses two separate unidirectional requests to the bandwidth manager per call, some application-signaling models may use a single bidirectional request per call. Unidirectional reservations may also be required for some applications other than voice, such as video-on-demand streams.

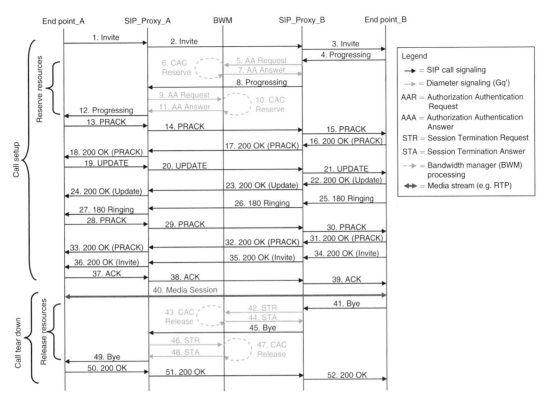

Figure 4.8   Bandwidth manager call flow: basic SIP call

- *Step 6.* Upon receiving the request, the bandwidth manager uses the source and destination gateway addresses to determine which underlying bandwidth resources will be impacted by the request. To do this the bandwidth manager uses an offline path computation function to determine which resources are impacted by the call; this path computation function may rely on IGP or BGP routing information to simulate the routing within the network. In this example, we assume that the path computation function determines that the following resources are impacted by the call:
  - the access link from Gateway A to Router_W
  - the TE tunnel from Router_W to Router_Y
  - the access link from Router_Y to Gateway B.

The bandwidth manager verifies that sufficient bandwidth is available on these resources to support the request. This could potentially use a parameterized or a measurement-based approach, as described in Section 4.1.4. At this stage, the bandwidth manager could also apply policy decisions, for example, that no more than 90% of resources will be used by normal services, allowing headroom for emergency services, e.g. such as defined in [RFC 4542].

- *Step 7*. Assuming that sufficient bandwidth is available to support the call the bandwidth manager replies positively to the call server.

    If there were insufficient bandwidth available on one or more of the resources affected by the call then a number of actions may be performed by the bandwidth manager:

    ○ In the simplest case, the bandwidth manager is aware of the resources in the network, tracks the state of those resources, and manages admission control decisions into available bandwidth accordingly. In this case, if there is insufficient bandwidth to support the request, the bandwidth manager would reply negatively to the call server, and the call would be cleared down as a result. Considering the TE tunnels specifically, either the TE tunnel head-end routers or an offline system, known as a tunnel server or path computation element (PCE) (as being defined by the PCE working group within the IETF [PCE]) would be responsible for tunnel path calculation (see Chapter 6). The head-end routers or PCE perform a constraint-based shortest path first (CSFP) computation to pick the least cost path that satisfies the configured tunnel constraints, including available bandwidth. The bandwidth manager would control admission to the TE tunnel bandwidth and need track only the status of TE tunnels. SNMP, for example, could be used by the bandwidth manager to discover what tunnels are configured on a head-end router and to track the status of tunnels and access network resources.

    ○ A more complicated bandwidth manager implementation could see the bandwidth manager attempt to trigger the resizing of some of the resources dynamically, if possible, such that they could support the requested call. Clearly, an access link may represent a physical bandwidth constraint, which may not be able to be resized dynamically; the bandwidth manager may be able to trigger the resizing of a TE tunnel, however.

For example, when a request is received, the bandwidth manager resolves the request to the underlying resources impacted by the request. If there is sufficient bandwidth available in an impacted tunnel to support the call then the call is admitted; sufficient bandwidth in this context means that the currently allocated tunnel bandwidth is below a defined threshold. If there is not sufficient bandwidth to support the call, then the bandwidth manager may attempt to trigger the resizing (i.e. increasing) of the tunnel bandwidth; the call will be admitted or denied based upon the success or failure of the tunnel resizing. More complicated resizing regimes are possible, e.g. if the currently allocated tunnel bandwidth is greater than 80% utilized, but there is sufficient bandwidth to accept the call, then accept the call AND attempt to increase the tunnel bandwidth by 20%. Similar approaches could be applied to downsize tunnels when calls are cleared.

- *Step 8*. Call signaling continues.

- *Step 9*. The call server requests admission for a unidirectional call to be set up from Gateway B to Gateway A. The request will contain at least the following information:
  1. IP address of source gateway B
  2. IP address of destination gateway A
  3. Bandwidth requested for the call (or could be the CODEC used)
  4. Call identifier

- *Step 10*. Upon receiving the request, the bandwidth manager uses the source and destination gateway addresses to determine which underlying bandwidth resources will be impacted by the request and verifies that sufficient bandwidth is available on these resources to support the request. In this example, we assume that the path computation function determines that the following resources are impacted by the call:

- ○ the access link from Gateway B to Router_Y
- ○ the TE tunnel from Router_Y to Router_W
- ○ the access link from Router_W to Gateway A.

- *Step 11.* Assuming that sufficient bandwidth is available to support the call, the bandwidth manager replies positively to the call server.

- *Steps 12–40.* Call signaling continues. It is noted that the destination phone rings only after the available bandwidth is confirmed in both directions. User B picks up the phone and the media session is successfully established between gateways A and B.

- *Step 41.* User connected to Gateway B hangs-up and call signaling starts to clear the call down.

- *Step 42.* The call server requests that the bandwidth manager clears the reservation from Gateway A to Gateway B for the call.

- *Step 43.* The bandwidth manager clears the reservation from Gateway A to Gateway B.

- *Step 44.* The bandwidth manager confirms that the reservation has been cleared to the call server.

- *Step 45.* Call signaling continues to clear the call down.

- *Step 46.* The call server requests that the bandwidth manager clears the reservation from Gateway B to Gateway A for the call.

- *Step 47.* The bandwidth manager clears the reservation from Gateway B to Gateway A.

- *Step 48.* The bandwidth manager confirms that the reservation has been cleared to the call server.

- *Steps 49–52.* Conventional call signaling continues and the call is cleared down.

4.4 The Integrated Services Architecture/RSVP

[RFC1633] laid out the philosophy of the Integrated Services or "Intserv" IP QOS architecture. Intserv defines an architecture that supports admission control and resource reservation/allocation in IP networks. It was designed to address the issues identified with IP precedence and type of service (see Chapter 2, Section 2.3.2, providing the capabilities needed to support applications with bounded SLA requirements, such as VoIP and video. Intserv tackles the problem of providing services level assurances to applications by explicitly managing bandwidth resources and schedulers on a per flow basis; resources are reserved and admission control is performed for each flow.

Intserv is defined by the following key facets:

- *Classification.* With Intserv, classification is performed on a per flow basis; at each Intserv capable router, complex classification is performed to identify a particular flow using the 5-tuple of source and destination IP addresses, source and destination UDP/TCP port numbers and IP protocol number. This requires per flow data plane state at each Intserv hop.

- *Scheduling.* Intserv requires that scheduling resources are also managed on a per flow basis, in order to ensure that the application requirements for that flow are met. This does not mean that scheduling resources (i.e. queues) have to be provisioned on a per flow basis although they can be. Alternatively, a number of flows may be mapped into a class, which is serviced from a single queue; all packets in the class will then get the same treatment from the scheduler.

- *Admission control.* In order to provide guarantees to each flow, admission control is performed at each hop to ensure that there are sufficient resources available to meet the requirements of the flow. If there are sufficient resources, the flow is admitted, else the flow is rejected. This requires per flow signaling and per flow control plane state at each Intserv hop.

In theory, a number of potential mechanisms could be used to perform admission control and to set up the per flow classifiers and queuing resources associated with an Intserv reservation. This could conceivably be via a centralized management system or via an end-to-end signaling protocol; signaling protocols exchange information between nodes to establish, maintain, and remove control plane state. In practice, however, the only way that Intserv has been implemented is using the resource ReSerVation Protocol (RSVP) as the end-to-end signaling protocol used to set up the Intserv reservation. RSVP was designed to support Intserv, hence Intserv has become synonymous with RSVP.

4.4.1 RSVP

RSVP [RFC2205] is defined by the following key characteristics:

- *IP Protocol*. RSVP does not use a transport layer protocol but rather is identified by IP protocol number 46.

- *Unidirectional reservations*. RSVP provides the capability to establish unidirectional reservations; if bidirectional reservations are required then two RSVP reservations are required, one in each direction.

- *Unicast and multicast*. RSVP supports reservations for both unicast and many-to-many multicast traffic. RSVP has capabilities for state merging and different classification filter styles to support reservations over a multicast distribution tree. Although RSVP supports multiple senders and receivers in support of many-to-many multicast applications, throughout the rest of this section we refer to sender and receiver (singular).

- *Receiver-initiated reservations*. RSVP reservations are initiated by the receiver; to instantiate a reservation, an RSVP receiver sends an RSVP reservation request (Resv) message upstream toward the sender. Each RSVP capable router receiving a Resv message creates reservation state and forwards the message to the next upstream RSVP router, until it reaches the sender. Receiver-initiated reservations are an optimization associated with the merging of reservations on the multicast distribution tree as the reservations get closer to the sender.

Although RSVP reservations are set up by Resv messages which are transmitted from the flow receiver toward the sender, in the case of unicast reservations, a receiver implementation may choose to use the receipt of Path messages sent from the sender as the trigger for generating a Resv message, thereby effecting a source initiated reservation.

- *Routing.* RSVP is not a routing protocol, but rather relies on conventional unicast/multicast IP routing protocols for route determination. RSVP sets up and maintains reservations over an IP path or multicast distribution tree determined by the routing protocol; RSVP consults local routing tables to obtain routes. This approach has three consequences:
  - Routed paths established by interior gateway IP routing protocols (IGPs), such as OSPF and ISIS, may be asymmetrical; that is, the path through the network from a source to a destination may be different to the path from a destination to a source. Clearly then, if the reservation is receiver initiated, some mechanism is needed to ensure that the Resv signaling message from receiver to sender follows the reverse network path to that the media flow would follow from sender to receiver. The mechanism used in RSVP is to transmit an RSVP Path message from the flow sender toward the receiver; routers forward the Path message toward the receiver using conventional routing tables and therefore the Path message follows the same path as the media flow. The Path message sets up forwarding state (called "path state") on RSVP capable routers, which is subsequently used when forwarding the Resv message to ensure that it follows the reverse path to that the media flow will follow from sender to receiver. The sole purpose of path state is to ensure the correct forwarding of Resv messages along the reverse path; reservation state is thereby associated with corresponding path state.
  - If there are insufficient resources on the path chosen by the routing protocol, then a reservation may fail even though there

may be another path through the network with sufficient resources to support the reservation. This issue may be overcome with a constraint-based routing capability, which is provided by MPLS traffic engineering (see Section 4.4.6), which also uses RSVP as its signaling protocol.

○ Following network element failures, the IGP may reroute traffic affected by the failure. If there were flows from existing RSVP reservations, which were rerouted consequently, they may be rerouted before a new admission control decision can be made and before a reservation can be established on the new path. Hence, following network failures there may be a transient period where the service that a flow receives is impacted pending a new RSVP reservation being successfully established.

- *Soft state*. RSVP is a "soft state" protocol; this means that reservations time out if they are not refreshed; Path and Resv messages are sent periodically to refresh the state for each reservation. In the case of multicast flows, reservations can be one-to-many, and the members of the multicast distribution tree can change over the lifetime of the reservation. The soft state model allows RSVP to adapt resource reservations accordingly. The use of soft state also allows RSVP to adapt to changes in network topology, due to network element failures for example. Resending Path and Resv messages periodically also makes RSVP resilient to limited message loss.

- *L3 and L2*. With the "subnet bandwidth manager" extension to RSVP defined in [RFC2814], RSVP can provide admission control over IEEE 802-style LANs.

The use of RSVP within the context of the Integrated Services architecture is defined in [RFC2210]. RFC2210 specifies the structure and contents of the QOS parameters carried by RSVP, when setting up Intserv reservations, which determine how RSVP capable network elements will handle the flow's data. RFC2210 specifies three end-to-end reservation service types:

- *Guaranteed service*. The Intserv guaranteed service (GS) is defined in [RFC2212]; it is intended to support inelastic applications with low-delay, low-jitter, low-loss, assured bandwidth requirements, such as VoIP and video. By comparison, such applications are typically supported with an EF PHB where Diffserv is deployed.

- *Controlled load service.* The Intserv controlled load (CL) service is defined in [RFC2211]; it is intended to support elastic applications with assured bandwidth requirements. By comparison, such applications are typically supported with an AF PHB where Diffserv is deployed. To quote RFC2211, the controlled load service provides: *"A QOS closely approximating the QOS that same flow would receive from an unloaded network element, but uses capacity (admission) control to assure that this service is received even when the network element is overloaded."*

- *Best-effort service.* Best-effort service is defined as the service, which flows receive that have neither had a successful GS or SL reservation established. The Intserv best-effort service is analogous to the service that would be supported with the default PHB where Diffserv is deployed.

The details of RSVP operation are most easily illustrated with an example.

4.4.2   RSVP Example Reservation Setup

The following example considers a unicast reservation, where the receipt of a Path message from the sender is used as the trigger for the receiver to originate a corresponding Resv message. Refer to Figure 4.9:

1. The sender application on the source host passes SENDER_TSPEC and ADSPEC objects to the RSVP stack via the RSVP Application Programmer Interface (API):
   - The SENDER_TSPEC defines the quantity of resources required at a particular service level (GS or GL). This is defined with a traffic specifier, which uses a token bucket definition. The ENDER_TSPEC

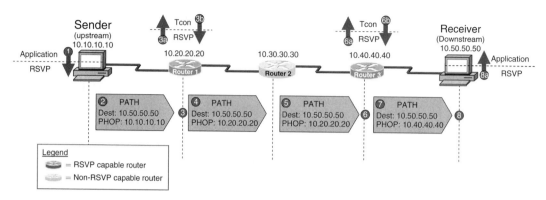

Figure 4.9 RSVP Path message processing example

is generated at the sender and is never modified by intermediate RSVP-capable routers transited en route to the receiver.

- The ADSPEC is generated at the sender and is modified by intermediate RSVP-capable routers transited en route to the receiver to advertise to both the receivers and sender the QOS characteristics of the end-to-end communication path. Receivers use the ADSPEC object to make reservation decisions.

2. The sender generates an RSVP Path message containing the SENDER_TSPEC and ADSPEC objects. In this example, the Path message has an IP source address of 10.10.10.10 and a destination address of 10.50.50.50. The previous hop (PHOP) object in the Path message is set to the sender's address (in this case 10.10.10.10); this is used by the next RSVP hop to set up path state used for Resv message reverse-path forwarding.

   The Path message is forwarded to the next hop on the path toward the IP destination address of the receiver; in this example the next hop is Router 1, which is the sender's default gateway.

3. The Path message is received by Router 1. The Path message has the IP Router Alert Option [RFC2113] set, which alerts the routers to look more closely and examine the contents of the packet, rather than simply forwarding the packet to the destination. As an RSVP capable router, Router 1 determines that the IP protocol

number of the packet is 46, which indicates that it is an RSVP message; the router then passes the Path message to its RSVP function for processing.

In processing the Path message, "path state" is installed which includes the unicast IP address of the previous hop upstream node; this is used for reverse-path forwarding of corresponding Resv messages. Further, the RSVP ADSPEC is passed to the RSVP traffic control function; this is responsible for QOS functions including classification, admission control, and scheduling. The traffic control function may optionally update the ADSPEC with information about the QOS control capabilities available at that point in the path, which might include delay and bandwidth availability information. The updated ADSPEC is then returned to RSVP for delivery to the next hop along the path.

4. Assuming no errors in RSVP processing, Router 1 forwards the Path message, containing the updated ADSPEC object, on toward the destination IP address (10.50.50.50), using its routing table to determine the next hop (hence outbound interface), still with source IP address 10.10.10.10 and destination IP address 10.50.50.50. The previous hop (PHOP) object in the Path message is set to Router 1's address (in this case 10.20.20.20); this is used by the next RSVP hop to set up path state used for Resv message reverse-path forwarding.

If an error were to occur during the RSVP Path message processing – which could be caused if Router 1 has no route to the destination, for example – Router 1 will return a PathErr message to the sender; RSVP error messages are always hop-by-hop routed.

5. Router 2, on determining that the IP protocol number of the packet is 46, as a non-RSVP capable router simply forwards RSVP messages as though they were any other data packet; it uses its routing table to determine the next hop (hence outbound interface) toward the destination IP address (10.50.50.50) and forwards the packet on accordingly without changing it.

6. RSVP Path message processing is repeated at each RSVP capable router as per step 3.

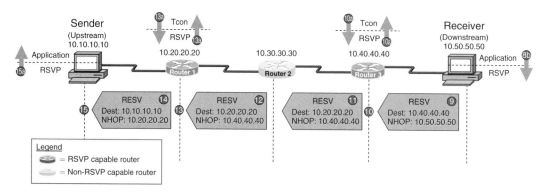

Figure 4.10 RSVP Resv message processing example

7. Assuming no errors in RSVP processing, Router 3 forwards the Path message, containing the updated ADSPEC object, on toward the destination IP address (10.50.50.50), using its routing table to determine the next hop (hence outbound interface), still with source IP address 10.10.10.10 and destination IP address 10.50.50.50. The previous hop (PHOP) object in the Path message is set to Router 3's address (in this case 10.40.40.40); this is used by the next RSVP hop to set up path state used for Resv message reverse-path forwarding.

8. The Path message arrives at the receiver:
   i. The SENDER_TSPEC and ADSPEC are given to the receiving application via the RSVP API.
   ii. Refer to Figure 4.10; the receiver application may use the ADSPEC object to make decisions about the reservation it is about to make. For example, if there were insufficient bandwidth available (as advertised by the ADSPEC) to support a high-definition video stream, the receiving application may decide to request a standard definition stream. The receiver application then supplies RSVP with reservation parameters via the RSVP API, this includes:
   - the requested service level for the reservation, i.e. guaranteed service (GS) or controlled load (CL) service
   - the RECEIVER_TSPEC, which describes the quantity of traffic for which resources should be reserved. This is defined with a traffic specifier, which uses a token bucket definition.

9. The receiver generates an RSVP Resv message which contains a "flow descriptor"; the flow descriptor comprises:
   - The FILTERSPEC, which specifies classification information by which the network can recognize the particular traffic flow that is to receive the QOS defined by the FLOWSPEC. The classifier is defined by the 5-tuple: source IP address, destination IP address, source port, destination port, and IP protocol.
   - The FLOWSPEC, which carries the information generated by the receiving application and which describes the Intserv service characteristics desired for the stream sent by the source in terms of the requested service level (GS or CL), the RECEIVER_TSPEC, and possibly other optional objects.

   The Resv message is forwarded upstream toward the sender. To ensure that the Resv message follows the same path as the Path message in reverse, the Resv message is hop-by-hop routed using Path state information setup during the processing of the Path message. Hence, in this example, the Resv message has an IP source address of 10.50.50.50 and a destination address of 10.40.40.40. In this example, the Resv message is forwarded to Router 3, which is the receiver's default gateway.

10. Router 3 as an RSVP capable router receives the Resv message addressed to it, identifies the RSVP message by IP protocol number 46, and hands the RSVP message over to its RSVP function for processing.
    i. The RSVP traffic control function performs the following functions:
       - Policy control may be performed to provide authorization for the QOS request.
       - Admission control is performed to determine if there are sufficient resources available to satisfy the request at the service level specified in the FLOWSPEC. In this example, the admission control decision would verify that sufficient resources are available on the interface on which the Resv message was received, i.e. the interface to the receiver, in the direction from Router 3 toward the receiver. Available RSVP implementations

generally used a parameterized approach, although a measurement-based approach could potentially be used also, as described in Section 4.1.4.

- Assuming the admission control decision is successful, per flow classifiers are instantiated based upon the FILTERSPEC, and per flow data plane scheduling resources are reserved to assure the quality of service specified for the flow by the FLOWSPEC. The reservation would be on the interface on which the Resv message was received, i.e. the interface to the receiver, in the direction from Router 3 toward the receiver. For a successful GS request, this may consist of assigning the flow to a strict priority queue; for a successful CL request, this may consist of assigning the flow to its own queue within a weighted fair queuinglike system, with a weighting defined to give the flow its requested resources.

ii. State merging, message forwarding, and error handling proceed according to the rules of the RSVP protocol.

11. Assuming no errors in RSVP processing, Router 3 forwards the Resv message upstream to the previous RSVP hop toward the sender. To ensure that the Resv message follows the same path as the Path message in reverse, the Resv message is hop-by-hop routed using path state information set up during the processing of the Path message. Hence, in this example, the Resv message has an IP source address of 10.40.40.40 and a destination address of 10.20.20.20 (i.e. Router 1) and Router 3 uses its routing table to determine how to forward the packet.

If an error were to occur during the RSVP Resv message processing – which could be due to an admission control or policy control failure, for example – Router 3 will return a ResvErr message to the receiver; RSVP error messages are always hop-by-hop routed.

12. Assuming Router 2 – a non-RSVP capable router – receives the Resv message (which may not be guaranteed if there is more than one path between Router 1 and Router 3 as the IGP routing between Router 1 and Router 3 could be asymmetrical), as the router alert option is not set (it is only used in Path messages)

and the message is addressed to Router 1, Router 2 simply forwards the message as any other normal IP datagram. It uses its routing table to determine how to forward the packet on toward the destination IP address (10.20.20.20) and forwards the packet on accordingly without performing any RSVP processing.

Note that if the RSVP reservation for the flow is successfully established, the flow will receive reservationless best-effort service at non-RSVP capable routers.

13. RSVP Resv message processing is repeated at each RSVP capable router as per step 10.

14. Assuming no errors in RSVP processing, Router 1 forwards the Resv message toward the sender. To ensure that the Resv message follows the same path as the Path message in reverse, the Resv message is hop-by-hop routed using path state information set up during the processing of the Path message. Hence, in this example, the Resv message has an IP source address of 10.20.20.20 and a destination address of 10.10.10.10 and Router 1 uses its routing table to determine how to forward the packet.

15. The Resv message reaches the sender and is delivered to the application. The sending application receives the Resv message, knows that the reservation is successful and can start sending traffic belonging to the flow, knowing that the requested QOS is assured.

If the Resv message contains an optional confirmation request object, on receipt of the Resv message the sender will send a ResvConf message back to the receiver. As RSVP is a soft state protocol, path, and reservation state is refreshed by periodic Path and Resv messages. The sender or receiver can terminate the reservation at any time by sending a PathTear or ResvTear message to release path and/or reservation state.

Although it has been standardized and supported by most operating systems for a number of years, RSVP, as we have described it and as it was originally defined, has neither been widely used by applications nor widely deployed. One of the main reasons cited for this is a lack of confidence in the scalability of Intserv, caused by the requirement to perform per flow processing and maintain per flow control plane state (i.e. path and reservation state) and data plane state (i.e. per flow classifiers and queuing resources) at each RSVP capable router. The amount of state that each RSVP capable router has to maintain scales in proportion to the number of concurrent reservations, which can potentially be large on high-speed links. A number of developments have aimed to overcome these control plane and data plane scaling concerns:

- Data plane scaling concerns have been addressed by developments that have defined how to support the Intserv architecture over Diffserv; this is described in Section 4.4.4.

- Control plane scaling concerns have been addressed by several efforts:
  - extensions aimed at reducing processing overhead requirements of refresh messages have been defined in [RFC2961]
  - methods for aggregating individual RSVP flow reservations over aggregate RSVP reservations. This is described in Section 4.4.5.

4.4.3 Application Signaling Interaction

The interaction between the application signaling and RSVP signaling will be dependent upon the particular application-signaling model used. In this example, we assume that SIP [RFC3261] is used for call signaling. Consider the call flow for a successful two party call setup and tear down shown in Figure 4.11 and the sequence of events that follows. The example considers a unicast reservation, where the receipt of a Path message from the sender is used as the trigger for the receiver to originate a corresponding Resv message.

The call sequence of events is as follows:

- *Step 1.* Conventional call signaling is used to set up a call from SIP End point_A (e.g. Voice Gateway A) to End point_B (e.g. Voice Gateway B).

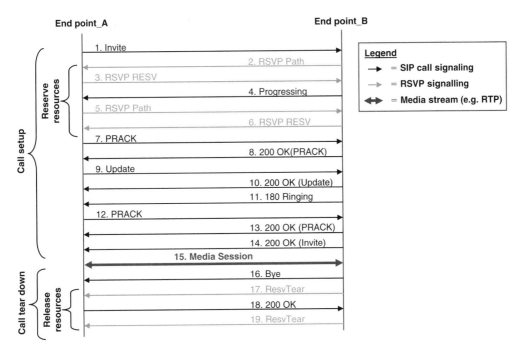

Figure 4.11   Bandwidth manager call flow: basic SIP call

- *Step 2*. SIP End point A originates an RSVP Path message to SIP End point_B.

- *Step 3*. SIP End point B responds with an RSVP Resv message back SIP End point_A to set up the reservation from A to B. Assuming that sufficient bandwidth is available to support the request, the RSVP reservation is successful and the call signaling continues.

- *Step 4*: Call signaling continues.

- *Step 5*. SIP End point B originates an RSVP Path message to SIP End point_A.

- *Step 6*. SIP End point A responds with an RSVP Resv message back SIP End point_B to set up the reservation from B to A. Assuming that sufficient bandwidth is available to support the request, the RSVP reservation is successful and the call signaling continues.

- *Steps 7–15*. It is noted that the destination phone rings only after the available bandwidth is confirmed in both directions. User B picks up the phone and the media session is successfully established between gateways A and B.

- *Step 16*. User connected to Gateway B hangs-up and call signaling starts to clear the call down.

- *Step 17*. SIP End point B originates an RSVP ResvTear message to SIP End point_A, to release the reservation from B to A.

- *Steps 18*. Conventional call signaling continues and the call is cleared down.

- *Step 19*. SIP End point A originates an RSVP ResvTear message to SIP End point_B, to release the reservation from A to B.

4.4.4   Intserv over Diffserv

[RFC 2998] defines "A Framework for Integrated Services Operation over Diffserv Networks" (a.k.a. "Intserv over Diffserv"); in this framework a Diffserv network is viewed as a network element in the end-to-end path of an Intserv reservation.

Consider Figure 4.12, which shows two Intserv regions interconnected with a Diffserv region. Within the Intserv region, RSVP signals per flow resource requirements to the network elements, which apply Intserv admission control to signaled requests. In addition, per flow traffic classifiers and traffic control mechanisms are configured on the network element to ensure that each admitted flow receives the service requested in strict isolation from other traffic. In contrast, within the Diffserv region, traffic is classified into one of a small number of aggregated flows or classes, based on the Diffserv codepoint (DSCP) in the packet's IP header. Intserv over Diffserv describes how end-to-end QOS could be provided in this context by marking the DSCP of RSVP identified flows such that they receive appropriate service within the Diffserv region.

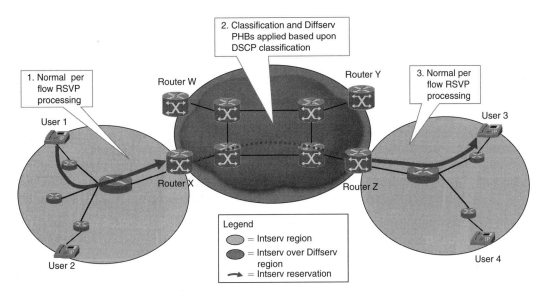

Figure 4.12 Intserv over Diffserv

Consider, for example, what would happen for a successful Intserv request for a flow from User 1 to User 2 in Figure 4.12:

1. Within User 1's local Intserv region, the routers are RSVP capable and normal Intserv/RSVP processing would occur.

2. Within the Diffserv region, the Diffserv-enabled routers would classify traffic based upon the DSCP in the header of each of the packets within the flow. Marking the DSCP of the packets within the flow appropriately would ensure that the packets would be serviced with a per-hop behavior (PHB) that will give them the required service. For example, packets within a flow of an Intserv guaranteed service reservation would be marked such that they were serviced with an EF PHB within the Diffserv domain. This marking could be done either at or close to the sender, or at the routers on the boundary of the Intserv and Diffserv regions, which in this example is at Router X and Router Y.

3. Within User 2's local Intserv region, the routers are RSVP capable and normal Intserv/RSVP processing would occur.

RSVP takes care of admission control in the Intserv regions; however, a number of potential models could be applied for how admission control decisions are made across the Diffserv region:

1. *No admission control over DS region.* In this model, the Diffserv region is statically provisioned and no devices within the Diffserv region are RSVP aware. The routers in the Diffserv region simply ignore RSVP messages. In order for the Intserv reservations to be assured end-to-end the Diffserv region must be capable of supporting the total amount of traffic that is admitted for each PHB.

2. *Admission control at regional boundary only.* In this model, the Diffserv region is statically provisioned and no devices within the Diffserv region are RSVP aware. The boundary routers on the border of the Intserv and Diffserv regions could be considered to have two halves; an Intserv half connecting to the Intserv region and a Diffserv half connecting to the Diffserv region. The border routers maintain a static table of the available resources within the Diffserv domain on a per-PHB basis. As Resv messages are received from the Intserv region destined for the Diffserv region, the border router maps the requested Intserv service level to a Diffserv PHB and performs admission control based upon its table of available resources for that PHB.

   With this approach, the admission control across the Diffserv region is not topology-aware, and therefore it suffers the same issues as all topology-unaware approaches. As described in Section 4.2, they do not consider the availability of resources along the specific path that would be impacted and cannot adapt in real time to changes in network capacity, caused by link or node failures for example, and therefore make inefficient use of the available bandwidth.

3. *Per flow admission control at every hop in DS region.* In this model, all routers within the Diffserv region are "RSVP aware" and are able to participate in some form of RSVP signaling and admission control. However, they classify and schedule traffic on aggregate, based on

DSCP, not based on the per flow classification criteria used by standard RSVP/Intserv routers. RSVP signaling is used for admission control only and per flow classification and scheduling are disabled; effectively the control plane of the routers in the Diffserv region is RSVP while their data plane is Diffserv. As Resv messages are received by a router within the Diffserv region it maps the requested Intserv service level to a Diffserv PHB and performs admission control based upon the currently available resources for that PHB.

This approach provides per flow topology-aware admission control across the Diffserv region. Further, it exploits the signaled admission control (i.e. control plane) benefits of RSVP signaling while maintaining the data plane scalability of Diffserv through aggregate classification, queuing and scheduling. This provides better scaling than "traditional" RSVP because there is no requirement to maintain per flow data plane state, i.e. for classification and scheduling, and hence data plane scaling is independent of number of flows. Hence, Intserv over Diffserv addresses the data plane scalability concerns of RSVP, but it does not address the control plane scalability concerns.

The use of aggregate Diffserv-based classification has its own consequences, however. Following network element failures, the IGP may reroute traffic affected by the failure. If there were flows from existing RSVP reservations that were rerouted as a consequence, they may be rerouted before a new admission control decision can be made and before a new reservation can be established on the new path. With Intserv over Diffserv, there is no isolation between different flows using the same PHB, hence the rerouted traffic may cause congestion within a class; this congestion would impact both rerouted flows and flows that were already successfully admitted onto this path. This service impacting congestion will last until some of the rerouted flows can be torn down. Hence, with Intserv over Diffserv, there may be transient service impacting congestion following network failures; the use of MPLS traffic engineering overcomes this issue (see Section 4.4.6).

It is noted that the example in Figure 4.12 shows distinct Intserv regions interconnected by an Intserv over Diffserv region; however, it is possible that the Intserv over Diffserv region could extend from end-system to end-system with Intserv over Diffserv used end-to-end, which is a more likely deployment model in practice.

4. *Admission control at every hop in DS region via aggregated reservations*. This model aims to address the data plane scalability concerns of RSVP by aggregating individual flow reservations over aggregate RSVP reservations; this is described in more detail in the proceeding section.

4.4.5 RSVP Aggregation

[RFC3175] defines "RSVP aggregation," which allows a number of RSVP reservations to be aggregated into a single larger reservation. RFC3175 defines the concept of an aggregation region, across which a number of end-to-end reservations, which share a common ingress router to the aggregation region (the aggregator) and egress router from the aggregation region (the de-aggregator), can be aggregated into one larger reservation from ingress to egress. This is conceptually similar to the use of virtual paths (VPs) to aggregate virtual circuits (VCs) within ATM.

Consider, for example, what would happen for a successful Intserv request for a flow from User 1 to User 2 across the example network shown in Figure 4.13 and assume that path state has already been set up as required. The following example considers a unicast reservation, where the receipt of a Path message from the sender is used as the trigger for the receiver to originate a corresponding Resv message.

1. As the sender, User 1 originates the Path message toward User 3, the receiver. Within User 1's local Intserv region, the routers are RSVP capable and normal Intserv/RSVP processing occurs.

2. When the aggregation router on the ingress edge of the aggregation region (Router X) receives the Path message on an interface connected to the non-aggregated Intserv region, it performs normal Intserv/RSVP processing and installs path state accordingly.

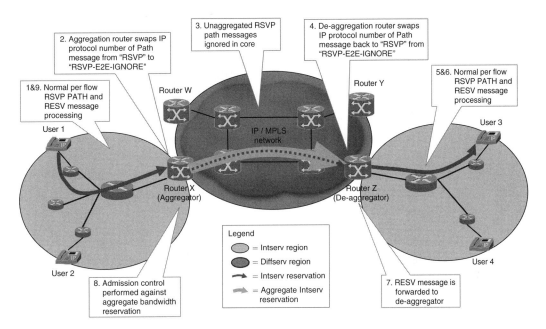

Figure 4.13   RSVP aggregation

Before sending the Path message onwards toward the receiver, however, it changes the IP protocol number of the message from 46 (for RSVP) to 134, which is designated for RSVP-E2E-IGNORE. It then forwards the Path message onwards toward the receiver, which is into the aggregation RSVP region.

3. Within the aggregation region, RSVP capable routers that receive Path messages with IP protocol RSVP-E2E-IGNORE (134), will ignore them rather than performing any RSVP processing. No path state will be installed and the Path messages will be forwarded as any other IP packet.

4. When the de-aggregation router on the egress side of the aggregation region (Router Z) receives the Path messages on an interface connected to the aggregated Intserv region, it installs path state, installing the aggregation router (Router X) as the previous hop upstream node.

Before sending the Path message onwards toward the receiver, however, it changes the IP protocol number of the message back from RSVP-E2E-IGNORE (134) to RSVP (46). It then forwards the Path message onwards toward the receiver, which is into the non-aggregated RSVP region.

In order to determine that a de-aggregator is one part of an aggregator/de-aggregator pair responsible for a particular aggregate reservation, on receipt of a Path message from the aggregation region a de-aggregator also sends a PathErr message back to aggregator, which enables end points for new aggregate reservations to be autodiscovered.

5. Within User 3's local Intserv region, the routers are RSVP capable and normal Intserv/RSVP processing would occur. User 3 receives the Path message and originates a Resv message toward the sender, User 1, in response.

6. When the de-aggregation router (Router Z) receives the Resv message, it performs normal Intserv/RSVP processing for its receiver-facing interface to the Intserv region, performing admission control and instantiating classifiers and scheduling resources accordingly.

   Assuming the Resv message processing is successful, i.e. sufficient resources were available to accept the request, the de-aggregation router then forwards the Resv message upstream to the previous RSVP hop toward the sender, which in this case is Router X.

   As the Resv message is hop-by-hop routed, routers in the aggregated RSVP region will forward the messages as any other IP packet, without performing any RSVP processing. For this reason the IP protocol of the Resv message does not need to be changed to RSVP-E2E-IGNORE.[1]

7. When the aggregation router (Router X) receives the Resv message, assuming that it has a preexisting aggregate RSVP reservation to the de-aggregator, it performs admission control for that request. At the aggregator, however, this admission control decision is not performed against the available resources on its receiverfacing

interface, but rather against the available resources on the aggregate RSVP reservation to the de-aggregator. If the aggregate reservation has not already been established, the receipt of the Resv message could be the trigger to set it up.

If the admission control decision is successful, i.e. if there are sufficient of the aggregate reservation resources available, the aggregation router then forwards the Resv message upstream to the previous RSVP hop toward the sender. If the admission control decision is unsuccessful, this could trigger a resizing on the aggregate reservation.

8. Within User 1's local Intserv region, the routers are RSVP capable and normal Intserv/RSVP processing would occur. Assuming User 1 receives the Resv message, it knows that the requested QOS is assured end-to-end and starts sending traffic associated to the request.

The aggregate RSVP reservation is set up within the aggregation region using an IP protocol of RSVP (46) rather than RSVP-E2E-IGNORE (134) and hence RSVP processing for the aggregate reservation is performed within the RSVP aggregate region. The main difference between the processing of an aggregate reservation and that of a normal reservation is that the data packets associated with the end-to-end reservations do not carry the same IP addresses as the aggregate path and Resv messages and hence cannot be classified using the 5-tuple used with conventional RSVP processing. There are several possible ways that traffic on an RSVP reservation may be classified:

- *Intserv over Diffserv.* If Intserv over Diffserv (see Section 4.4.4) is used in the aggregation region, per flow classification is not required but the DSCP of traffic on aggregate RSVP reservations would be marked such that they receive appropriate service within the Diffserv region.

An issue with this approach is that there is no guarantee that the traffic from the end-to-end reservations using a particular aggregate reservation will follow the same path within the aggregation region as the aggregate reservation itself. From the previous example, this would require that the forwarding path used through the aggregation region for traffic from User 1 to User 3 follows the same path as the Path messages for the aggregate reservation, from the aggregator to the de-aggregator. This may not be the case if there are multiple paths with the same IGP metric cost between Router X and Router W and equal cost multipath (ECMP) algorithms are used, which commonly rely on hashing functions using contexts such as source and destination addresses to determine how traffic is load-balanced over the equal cost paths, for example. Clearly if traffic from the end-to-end reservations follows a path other than that of their aggregate reservation, their QOS on that other path may not be assured. The routing design within a particular deployment may be able to be adjusted to ensure that there are no equal cost paths, and hence that this does not happen. Alternatively, tunneling can be used between the aggregator and de-aggregator.

- *Tunneling.* Traffic using an aggregate reservation may be tunneling from the aggregator to the de-aggregator, using IP-in-IP tunnels, GRE tunnels, or MPLS TE tunnels [draft-ietf-tsvwg-rsvp-dste-02.txt], for example. If tunneling is used, the traffic using an aggregate reservation may be classified by identifying the particular "tunnel" associated with that reservation or Intserv over Diffserv may be used.

  With tunneling approaches, implicitly traffic from the end-to-end reservations using a particular aggregate reservation follows the same path within the aggregation region as the aggregate reservation itself.

  The size of the aggregate reservation needs to be sufficient to support the guarantees of all of the end-to-end reservations that use that particular aggregate reservation. The size of aggregate reservations could be statically configured or dynamically determined using parameterized (i.e. sum the token buckets specified in the SENDER_TSPECs of the end-to-end reservations using that aggregate reservation) or measurement-based approaches, as described in Section 4.1.4. To reduce the frequency of resizing and churn, the aggregate reservation may be resized slowly in bandwidth chunks, with hysteresis being applied to size increases and decreases. For example, if the currently allocated bandwidth from the aggregate reservation is greater than 80% utilized, but there is sufficient bandwidth to accept the call, then accept the call AND attempt to increase the tunnel bandwidth by 20%. Similar approaches could be applied to downsize aggregate reservations when end-to-end reservations are cleared down. Clearly, more complicated sizing schemes and heuristics are possible.

Where RSVP aggregation is used, the control plane (path and reservation) state and data plane (classification and scheduling) state required within the aggregation region is dependent upon the number of aggregate reservations and independent of the number of end-to-end reservations. If this is combined with Intserv over Diffserv, the data plane state it is also independent of the number of aggregate reservations. Further, RSVP aggregation supports the concept of recursive aggregation, allowing aggregate reservations themselves to be further aggregated. This could potentially reduce control plane state even further, at the cost of incurring the complexity of an additional level of aggregation.

4.4.6 RSVP Traffic Engineering

RSVP was originally designed to support an anticipated widespread demand for real-time applications over the Internet, such as teleconferencing. That anticipated demand has not materialized in practice and the widespread deployment of RSVP – at least RSVP as it has been described in the preceding sections, that is – has not resulted. However, the traffic engineering (TE) extension for RSVP [RFC 3209], referred to as RSVP-TE, has been widely deployed by a large number of network service providers.

RSVP-TE is used for traffic engineering within multiprotocol label switching (MPLS) networks. Used in this context, there are some significant differences from RSVP as it has been described in the previous sections. The most significant difference is that rather than using paths already established by the IGP, RSVP-TE is used to set up the data path; RSVP-TE establishes MPLS label switched paths (LSPs), in addition to performing resource reservation and admission control.

In the context of admission control, there are several ways that RSVP-TE could be deployed:

- RSVP-TE could be used in conjunction with MPLS as the tunneling technology underlying RSVP aggregation as described in Section 4.4.5.

- RSVP-TE could be used to provide end-to-end reservations for MPLS attached end-systems, which support MPLS and RSVP-TE. In practice, this type of deployment is most likely in service provider network environments, between large-scale voice-over IP gateways for example.

- RSVP-TE is widely used for traffic engineering within service provider networks; in this context, it provides admission control for traffic "trunks" across the network, where a "trunk" is an aggregation of traffic from an ingress point to an egress point. In this context, the capability provided is not one of real-time admission control, providing feedback to end-system applications, but of capacity management within the core of an IP/MPLS network; traffic engineering in this context is described in Chapter 6, Section 6.2.3.

4.5 NSIS

An effort is currently underway within the Next Steps in Signaling (NSIS) [NSIS] Working Group within the IETF to standardize a new suite of extensible IP signaling protocols, which are referred to generically as "NSIS." QOS signaling is the first explicit use case that the NSIS protocols have addressed; however, they have been designed with the ability to support other use cases such as configuring firewall pinholes and network address translation (NAT) bindings. The NSIS framework is defined in [RFC4080].

NSIS consists of two protocol layers. The lower layer is a generic transport protocol layer referred to as the NSIS Transport Layer Protocol (NTLP); the General Internet Signaling Protocol (GIST) [GIST] is the protocol specified for the NTLP layer. GIST could be used by a number of NSIS Signaling Layer Protocols (NSLPs) at the signaling layer, although currently only two such protocols are defined: an NSLP for QOS Signaling [QNLSP] and a NAT/Firewall NSLP [NNLSP].

Similarly, to RSVP – when augmented with the various enhancements to the original specification, that is – NSIS relies on conventional routing protocols, uses a 5-tuple flow identifier, uses soft state and supports the aggregation of reservations. The NSIS QOS NLSP can also provide signaling capabilities for any QOS model or architecture, including Intserv and Diffserv.

However, NSIS has the following significant differences from RSVP:

- *Bidirectional reservations*. NSIS supports both unidirectional and bidirectional reservations, while RSVP supports unidirectional reservations only.

- *Unicast only*. RSVP supports both unicast and multicast traffic reservations. However, as multicast has not been widely deployed and support for multicast reservations added significantly to the complexity of RSVP, NSIS made the decision to support unicast reservations only.

- *Sender or receiver-initiated reservations*. Unlike RSVP which supports receiver-initiated reservations, NSIS supports both sender and receiver-initiated reservations.

- *L3 only*. NSIS provides no equivalent to the RSVP subnet bandwidth manager functionality, and can be used to make admission control decisions in IP networks only.

NSIS has also been designed to provide mobility and support standard IP security protocols.

NSIS has been designed from the outset with the benefit of knowledge of the issues experienced during the development and deployment of RVSP; however, it is yet to be seen whether the functional capabilities that NSIS provides in addition to those already provided by RSVP will lead to its widespread deployment.

4.6 End-system Measurement-based Admission Control

IP endpoint measurement-based admission control (MBAC), which was first documented in [GIBBONS], relies on application end points to make admission control decisions themselves. End point use measurements of characteristics of traffic to other destination end points, in order to infer the state of the network and hence determine whether new streams can be established to those respective destinations with the required QOS. Endpoint MBAC can rely either on passive or active traffic monitoring (the use of passive and active approaches for network monitoring is discussed in Chapter 5); hybrid approaches are also possible:

- *Active monitoring.* Active network monitoring involves sending synthetic test streams of "probe" packets across the network to characterize the network performance. Endpoint MBAC using active monitoring relies on measuring characteristics of active monitoring probes – such as delay, jitter, loss or number of ECN marked (see Chapter 2, Section 2.3.4.4) probes [KELLY] – sent between end-systems, and using these measurements as basis for making an admission control decision. When an end point needs to set up a new flow, the previously measured characteristics are compared against defined thresholds to determine whether the flow will receive the required QOS and hence can be accepted.

- *Passive monitoring.* Endpoint MBAC using passive monitoring relies on measuring characteristics of pre-existing media streams between end-systems. Where the real-time protocol (RTP) [RFC 3550] is used, for example, the timestamp and sequence number information in the RTP header could be used to determine the delay, jitter, and loss of the received stream at the receiving end-system. As with the active measurement-based approach, these measured characteristics can be used as the basis for making an admission control decision. ECN marking could also be used as an input to the admission control decision with a passive monitoring approach.

A purely passive monitoring approach presumes that there is already an active stream between the two end-systems, i.e. such that there is some current measurement data when a new flow needs to be established, and a new admission control decision is required. If this presumption is not correct then this approach could be augmented with the addition of an active monitoring stream, when there are no bearer streams active.

End-system measurement-based admission control approaches are implicitly topology-aware (assuming that active measurement probes follow the same path as the media traffic; with passive measurement this is implicit), hence can adapt to the available network capacity, and therefore do not suffer the bandwidth inefficiency of topology-unaware approaches. In addition, end-system-based MBAC approaches rely on end-to-end media or probe traffic at layer 4 or above; hence they can provide admission control capabilities transparently of the underlying layers.

Endpoint MBAC suffers the same potential issues as other measurement-based approaches (as discussed in Section 4.1.4.2), that measurements taken over the past measurement interval may not provide a good indication on which to base admission control decisions in the next measurement interval. Hence, despite significant research in endpoint-based admission control schemes [KEY, GANESH, BRESLAU2, BAIN], endpoint MBAC is not yet widely deployed, and it remains to be seen whether endpoint MBAC can provide the deterministic characteristics demanded by real-time applications such as voice and video.

4.7 Summary

At the start of this chapter, we highlighted that there are a number of approaches to capacity admission control, none of which is universally

Approach	Type of approach	Topology aware?	Multicast Support	L3 only?
e.g. Call server or video server based	Off path	No	No	No
Bandwidth manager	Off path	Yes	No	No
RSVP-based	On path network signaling based	Yes	Yes	No
NSIS	On path network signaling based	Yes	No	Yes
End-system MBAC	End-system MBAC	Yes	No	No

Figure 4.14 Summary of admission control approaches

deployed today. Due to the variety of potential deployment scenarios, applications, and services, there is currently no "one size fits all" solution to the problem of capacity admission control, and as a result, some technologies for admission control are still evolving. Hence, we summarize the key characteristics of the different admission control solutions, which are likely to affect their applicability to a particular deployment, in the table in Figure 4.14.

It is noted that admission control need not be implemented end-to-end through the network but rather is only required in those parts of the network where congestion may occur, and then only for those types of traffic that need it. For example, explicit admission control mechanisms may be deployed at the edges of the network, where bandwidth is scarce, and over-provisioning may be relied on in the core of the network. Further, the different approaches to admission control need not be mutually exclusive; it is possible for one approach to be used in the core of the network and another in the access.

References[2]

[BAIN] Alan Bain, Peter Key, Modeling the Performance of In-Call Probing for Multi-Level Adaptive Applications, Microsoft Research Technical Report, MSR-TR-2002-06, Jan 2002. Available online at: http://research.microsoft.com/research/pubs/view.aspx? msr_tr_id= MSR-TR-2002-06

[BRESLAU1] L. Breslau, S. Jamin, and S. Shenker, Comments on the performance of measurement-based admission control algorithms, *Proc. IEEE INFOCOM, 2000*, pp. 1233–1242, March 2000

[BRESLAU2] L. Breslau, E. W. Knightly, S. Shenker, I. Stoica, and H. Zhang, Endpoint admission control: Architectural issues and performance, in *Proc. of ACM SIGCOMM 2000*, pp. 57–69, August 2000

[draft-ietf-tsvwg-rsvp-dste] draft-ietf-tsvwg-rsvp-dste, Francois Le Faucheur et al., Aggregation of RSVP Reservations over MPLS TE/DS-TE Tunnels, IETF draft, September 2006

[draft-ietf-tsvwg-rsvp-ipsec] draft-ietf-tsvwg-rsvp-ipsec, Francois Le Faucheur et al., Generic Aggregate RSVP Reservations, IETF draft, February 2006

[GANESH] A. J. Ganesh, P. B. Key, D. Polis, and R. Srikant, Congestion notification and probing mechanisms for endpoint admission control, *Networking, IEEE/ACM Transactions*, Volume 14, Issue 3, June 2006, pp. 568–578

[GIBBONS] R. J. Gibbens and F. P. Kelly, Measurement-based connection admission control, in *15th International Teletraffic Congress*, volume 2b, pp. 879–888, Elsevier, 1997

[GIST] H. Schuzrinne and R. Hancock, GIST: General Internet Signaling Transport Internet draft, work in progress, July 2005; http://www.ietf.org/internet-drafts/draft-ietf-nsis-ntlp-07.txt

[Gq'] ETSI TS 183 017 Gq' interface based on Diameter protocol

[JAMIN] S. Jamin, P. B. Danzig, S. J. Shenker, and L. Zhang, A measurement-based admission control algorithm for Integrated Service packet networks, *IEEE/ACM Trans. Networking*, Vol. 5, pp. 56–70, February 1997

[KELLY] Frank P. Kelly, Peter B. Key, and Stan Zachary, Distributed Admission Control, *IEEE Journal on Selected Areas in Communications*, Vol. 18, no. 12, pp. 2617–2628, December 2000

[KEY] Peter Key and Laurent Massouli, Probing strategies for distributed admission control in large and small scale systems, *Proceedings of IEEE Infocom*, San Francisco 2003

[KNIGHTLY] E. W. Knightly and N. B. Shroff, Admission control for statistical QOS: Theory and practice, *IEEE Network*, Vol. 13, pp. 20–29, March/April 1999

[MSF2005.187] Olov Schelén, Implementation Agreement for Diameter interface to Bandwidth Manager, MSF Contribution MSF2005.187, May 2006

[MSF-TR-ARCH-005-FINAL] Chris Gallon, Olov Schelén, Bandwidth Management in Next Generation Packet Networks, MSF Technical Report, August 2005. Available at: http://www.msforum.org/ techinfo/reports/MSF-TR-ARCH-005-FINAL.pdf

[MSF-TR-ARCH-008-FINAL] John Evans, Network Engineering to Support the Bandwidth Manager Architecture, MSF White Paper, May 2006. Available at: http://www.msforum.org/techinfo/reports/ MSF-TR-ARCH-008-FINAL.pdf

[NNLSP] M. Stiemerling, H. Tschofenig, and C. Aoun, NAT/ Firewall NSIS Signaling Layer Protocol (NSLP), Internet draft, work in progress, July 2005; http://www.ietf.org/internet-drafts/draftietf-nsis-nslp-natfw-07.txt

[NSIS] http://www.ietf.org/html.charters/nsis-charter.html

[PCE] http://www.ietf.org/html.charters/pce-charter.html

[QNLSP] J. Manner et al., NSLP for Quality-of-Service signaling, Internet draft, work in progress, July 2005; http://www.ietf.org/ internet-drafts/draftietf- nsis-qos-nslp-07.txt

[RFC1633] R. Braden et al., RFC1633, Integrated Services in the Internet Architecture: an Overview, June 1994

[RFC2113] D. Katz, IP Router Alert Option, *RFC 2113*, February 1997

[RFC2205] R. Braden, Ed., Resource ReSerVation Protocol (RSVP) – Version 1 Functional Specification, *RFC 2205*, September 1997

[RFC2210] J. Wroclawski, The Use of RSVP with IETF Integrated Services, *RFC 2210*, September 1997

[RFC2211] J. Wroclawski, Specification of the Controlled-Load Network Element Service, *RFC 2211*, September 1997

[RFC2212] S. Shenker et al., Specification of Guaranteed Quality of Service, *RFC 2212*, September 1997

[RFC2638] K. Nichols and V. Jacobson, A Two-bit Differentiated Services Architecture for the Internet, *RFC 2638*, July 1999

[RFC2814] R. Yavatkar et al., SBM (Subnet Bandwidth Manager): A Protocol for RSVP-based Admission Control over IEEE 802-style networks, *RFC 2814*, May 2000

[RFC2961] L. Berger, RSVP Refresh Overhead Reduction Extensions, *RFC 2961*, April 2001

[RFC2998] Y. Bernet et al., *RFC* 2998, A Framework for Integrated Services Operation over Diffserv Networks, November 2000

[RFC3175] F. Baker et al., Aggregation of RSVP for IPv4 and IPv6 Reservations, *RFC 3175*, September 2001

[RFC3209] D. Awduche et al., RSVP-TE: Extensions to RSVP for LSP tunnels, *RFC 3209*, Dec. 2001; http://www.rfc-editor.org/rfc/rfc 3209.txt

[RFC3261] J. Rosenberg et al., SIP: Session Initiation Protocol, *RFC 3261*, June 2002

[RFC3312] G. Camarillo, Ed. et al., Integration of Resource Management and Session Initiation Protocol (SIP), *RFC 3312*, October 2002

[RFC3550] H. Schulzrinne, RTP: A Transport Protocol for Real-Time Applications, *RFC 3550*, July 2003

[RFC3588] P. Calhoun et al., Diameter Base Protocol, *RFC 3588*, September 2003

[RFC4080] R. Hancock et al., Next Steps in Signaling: Framework, *RFC 4080*, June 2005; http://www.rfc-editor.org/rfc/rfc4080.txt

[RFC4542] F. Baker, J. Polk, Implementing an Emergency Telecommunications Service (ETS) for Real-Time Services in the Internet Protocol Suite, *RFC 4542*, May 2006

Notes

1. Only Path, PathTear and ResvConf messages use an IP protocol of RSVP-E2E-IGNORE (134).

2. The nature of the networking industry and community means that some of the sources referred to in this book exist only on the World Wide Web. All Universal Resource Locators (URLs) have been checked and were correct at the time of going to press, but their longevity cannot be guaranteed.

5

SLA and Network Monitoring

5.1 Introduction

This chapter discusses the technologies and techniques available for
SLA and network monitoring in QOS-enabled IP networks. There are
two main approaches, which are generally used in concert to monitor the performance of a QOS-enabled network service in order to
determine whether SLAs have been or can be met:

- *Passive network monitoring.* With passive network monitoring, network
  devices record statistics on network traffic, which can provide an
  indication of the status at a particular network element. Periodic
  polling is typically used to gather this data for reporting and analysis.
  This is a micromeasure which looks at each device in isolation; by
  looking at multiple network elements an aggregate view of the status of
  a network service may be deduced. Passive network monitoring does
  not require any additional traffic be used for measurement purposes.

- *Active network monitoring.* Unlike passive monitoring, active monitoring involves sending additional traffic into the network. Synthetic
  test streams comprising "probe" packets are sent across the network
  solely for the purpose of characterizing the network performance;
  analysis of the received streams is used for this characterization.
  Active monitoring provides a macromeasure of network SLAs in

---

This chapter has benefitted enormously from the input of Emmanuel Tychon, Technical
Marketing Engineer for Cisco IOS IP Service Level Agreement (IP SLAS), whose contribution formed the basis of the active monitoring section.

that it reports the measured performance across a number of network elements as a system.

Passive and active network monitoring systems may be deployed for a number of reasons:

- For monitoring and reporting that the network service offered is achieving the committed SLA targets, this may include:
  - proactive network and SLA monitoring
  - long-term trending of the relative changes in network SLA performance over time.

    For network service providers (SPs), active and passive network monitoring provide potential value-added service opportunities as end customers look to outsource their end-to-end WAN-related capacity management. Hence, the SP may report enough information to the customer to let them assess their network usage and how well their SLAs were met.

- For monitoring that network performance is sufficient to meet the required application quality of experience (QOE) targets.

- As a feedback loop to network capacity planning processes, results from passive and active monitoring may provide heuristics, allowing capacity planning thresholds to be tuned based upon correlation between network or per-class load and SLA probing reports of delay, jitter, and loss. Capacity planning is discussed in detail in Chapter 6, Section 6.1.

Passive and active network monitoring are discussed in more detail in the following sections.

5.2 Passive Network Monitoring

From a QOS perspective, passive network monitoring involves polling the network devices for statistics which they maintain for QOS functions they perform, such as packet and byte counts, or queue depths, for example. This is typically performed using the Simple Network Management Protocol (SNMP) [RFC1157], to poll for information contained in management information bases or MIBs. The considerations on polling and the types of statistics polled are described in the following sections.

5.2.1 How Often to Poll?

Any polling of network devices for statistics raises the question of how frequently to poll? In practice, this represents a balance between the polling capacity of the network management system (NMS), the number of devices that need to be polled, the load incurred on the polled devices, and the impact of the polling traffic on the network.

Many of the retrieved statistics will be in the form of packet and byte counts; these can be used to determine the average traffic demands over the previous sampling interval. Longer polling intervals implicitly have a larger sample size and may be acceptable for trending purposes; however, the polled data will implicitly be averaged over a longer time and hence issues may be hidden. Therefore, shorter intervals are preferred where measurements that are more granular are required, although this has to be balanced against the increased polling load.

For troubleshooting, proactive measurement and SLA reporting, within the bounds of the NMS and network constraints and capabilities, QOS statistics should be polled as often as possible to prevent visibility of SLA affecting network issues being lost due to the effects of averaging. If the polling is frequent, the data can always be averaged over longer timeframes.

For trending, it may be more appropriate to poll every hour. Longer duration measurements make the comparison between days, months, and years easier and more statistically relevant.

5.2.2 Per-link Statistics

Per-link QOS statistics can be used for different purposes, depending upon from where in the network they are recorded:

- *Access links.* Network access links can be both the boundary of a Diffserv domain and a customer/provider boundary. Hence, access link QOS statistics are used both for faultfinding and for reporting statistics to customers of end-services such that they can provision their edge QOS classes adequately.

- *Core links*. On core links, per-link QOS statistics are used both for faultfinding and as an input to the core network capacity planning processes. Capacity planning is discussed in more detail in Chapter 6, Section 6.1.

Most vendors implement proprietary MIBs, which can be used to retrieve the relevant per-link statistics. They could also be retrieved from the Diffserv MIB [RFC3289], although this is not widely implemented by network equipment vendors. Where it is supported, the Diffserv MIB may be used for both monitoring and configuration of a router or switch that is capable of Differentiated Services functionality. As the Diffserv MIB is designed to be generic across vendors, vendor proprietary MIBs may provide information on QOS statistics that are specific to their implementation, and hence which are not available in RFC3289.

The following sections describe the most important per-link QOS statistics for monitoring Diffserv deployments in terms of the QOS functions and mechanisms that are applied. Consideration is also provided on how these statistics should be interpreted to assure the performance of a QOS-enabled network service. In some cases, it may not be necessary to monitor all of the statistics that are described; some of the statistics are interrelated and hence may be deduced from others without requiring explicit monitoring. This duplication can be useful in providing a means for cross-verifying the retrieved statistics.

5.2.2.1 Monitoring Classification

A router may classify a number of traffic streams into a single traffic class, to which actions may subsequently be applied. The following classification statistics are useful in understanding the offered traffic load in each class, and the constituents of that traffic class:

- *Per-classification rule*. If multiple rules are used to classify traffic streams into a single class, it may be useful to know the total number of packets and their cumulative byte count that have been classified per rule. For example, if traffic marked DSCP 18 (i.e. AF21) and DCSP 20 (i.e. AF22) is to be classified into the same class, which is serviced with an AF PHB, then it may be useful to know how much AF21 traffic (which could, for example represent the "in-contract" traffic) and how much AF22 traffic (which could represent the "out-of-contract" traffic) there is within the class.

Further, by knowing both the number of packets and bytes classified into a class, it is possible to estimate the average packet size for the class. This information can be useful for ensuring that only small VoIP packets are being classified into a voice class, for example. Hence, in general for most QOS statistics polled, the results retrieved include both a packet and a byte count.

- *On aggregate.* Per-traffic class, it is also important to know the total number of packets and bytes that have been classified on aggregate (i.e. across all classification rules) into that particular class.

The main use for classification statistics is to verify that traffic is being correctly classified in the appropriate class. Classification statistics can also be used to verify or deduce other statistics; for example, the total number of packets dropped and transmitted by the other functions applied to a particular class after classification must equal the total number of packets classified into that class.

5.2.2.2 Monitoring Policing

Policers may be applied for a number of reasons as described in Chapter 2, Section 2.2.3. Which statistics are relevant when monitoring policers depends upon the way in which they are used.

- *Enforcing a maximum rate for a voice class.* The single rate three color marker (SR-TCM) defined in [RFC2697] is commonly applied to police the maximum rate of a voice class. This may be used both on core and access links. On core links policers are commonly applied to voice classes to ensure the voice class cannot starve other classes of bandwidth, as per the example in Chapter 3, Section 3.3.2.3.1. On access links policers are used both to prevent starvation of other classes and to enforce a Diffserv edge traffic conditioning agreement (TCA), ensuring that only voice traffic which conforms to the voice class TCA is admitted into the Diffserv network.

In either case when the SR-TCM is used to police a voice class it would typically have a defined CIR and CBS, with EBS = 0, a violate (i.e. red) action of transmit and a conform (i.e. green) action of drop. Applied in this way the SR-TCM would enforce a maximum rate of CIR and a burst of CBS on the voice class and any traffic in violation of this would be dropped.

Wherever a policer is applied to a voice class, the following statistics should be monitored per policer:

○ *Number of packets and bytes conforming (i.e. green)*. This is the number of packets and bytes transmitted by the policer.

○ *Number of packets and bytes violating (i.e. red)*. This is the number of packets and bytes dropped by the policer. Wherever a policer is used to enforce a maximum rate for a voice class, the policer is meant as a protective measure. If the policer actually drops voice packets there is an issue somewhere, which is affecting the service (assuming that the policer has been correctly configured that is) and voice call quality will be affected, hence ideally there should be no packets violating the SR-TCM policer definition. If there are, the resulting actions will depend upon where the policer is being used:

– *Access links*. To resolve drops by a voice class policer on an access link, either the bandwidth provisioned for the voice class (and hence the policer rate) needs to be increased, or controls need to be put in place to limit the offered voice traffic load, e.g. using admission control.

– *Core links*. Drops by a voice class policer are an indication of either a capacity planning failure, or a major network failure or a network attack. In either case, the occurrence of such drops should trigger further investigation to determine the cause of the drops and to prevent a reoccurrence.

• *Marking in- and out-of-contract*. Either the SR-TCM or the two rate three color marker (TR-TCM) defined in [RFC2698] are commonly applied to AF classes to mark certain amounts of traffic in-contract and out-of-contract as described in Chapter 2, Section 2.2.3. When deployed in this way, which statistics are important depends upon whether the SR-TCM or TR-TCM is used:

○ *SR-TCM*. The SR-TCM is commonly used for in-/out-of-contract marking with EBS = 0, a green action of {transmit + mark in-contract} and a red action of {transmit + mark out-of-contract}, as per the example in Chapter 3, Section 3.2.2.4.5. Applied in this way the SR-TCM would enforce a maximum rate of CIR and a burst of CBS on the traffic stream. Conforming traffic would be marked in-contract and any traffic in violation of this would be marked out-of-contract. When deployed in this way the important statistics are:

  – *Number of packets and bytes conforming (i.e. green)*. This is the number of packets marked in-contract by the policer, and their respective byte count.

  – *Number of packets and bytes violating (i.e. red)*. This is the number of packets marked out-of-contract by the policer, and their respective byte count.

The purpose of marking certain amounts of traffic in-/out-of-contract is to be able to offer a committed SLA for a defined "in-contract" rate, and to allow traffic in excess of this rate to be transmitted but to mark it differently to indicate that it is "out-of-contract" such that it may potentially be given a less stringent SLA. Hence, when the SR-TCM is applied in this way, the main use for statistics of packets and bytes conforming and violating is for reporting to customers of end-services such that they can provision their edge QOS classes adequately, rather than for faultfinding.

○ *TR-TCM*. The TR-TCM can be used to mark a certain amount of a traffic class as in-contract, and everything above that as out-of-contract, up to a maximum rate above which all traffic is dropped, by applying a green action of transmit, yellow action of {transmit + mark out-of-contract} and red action of drop. Applied in this way the TR-TCM would enforce a maximum rate of CIR and a burst of CBS on the traffic stream; any traffic in excess would then be marked out-of-contract up to a maximum rate of PIR and a burst of PBS. When deployed in this way the important statistics are:

– *Number of packets and bytes conforming (i.e. green)*. This is the number of packets marked in-contract by the policer, and their respective byte count.
– *Number of packets and bytes exceeding (i.e. yellow)*. This is the number of packets marked out-of-contract by the policer, and their respective byte count.
– *Number of packets and bytes violating (i.e. red)*. This is the number of packets and bytes dropped by the policer.

Similarly to where the SR-TCM is used for in-/out-of-contract marking, where the TR-TCM is used for this purpose, the main use for statistics of packets and bytes conforming and exceeding is for reporting to customers of end-services. However, if there are a significant number of packets which are violating, i.e. dropped, relative to the number of packets transmitted, i.e. conforming + exceeding; this is an indication that the class load is exceeding the available capacity and the performance of all applications within that class may be affected. Hence, consideration should be given to increasing the PIR configured for that class or to reducing the traffic load within the class.

5.2.2.3   Monitoring Queuing and Dropping

For all queuing classes, it is normal to monitor the following statistics:

• *Number of packets and bytes transmitted*. This is the number of packets successfully transmitted from the queue by the scheduler, and their respective byte count.

• *Number of packets and bytes dropped*. This is the number of packets dropped by queue management functions acting on that queue, and their respective byte count. The statistics that matter with respect to dropping mechanisms depend upon the particular dropping mechanisms that are used.

5.2.2.3.1 Monitoring Tail Drop

If simple tail drop is used to enforce a queue limit (see Chapter 2, Section 2.2.4.2.1) then a count of the number of packets and bytes dropped per queue should be monitored.

If a queue limit is applied to a voice or video class queue, it is normal practice for the queue limit to be at least as great as the burst size for the policer configured for the class. In this case, the policer burst should constrain the class burst and there should be no tail drops experienced for that queue; if tail drops are experienced, this would be an indication of an issue. If the queue limit were set less than the policer burst and tail drops were experienced, then the same actions should be taken as if policer drops had occurred as described in Section 5.2.2.2.

If a queue limit is applied to a data class queue and the measured drop rate – that is, the ratio of packets and bytes dropped to packets and bytes transmitted – is high (where high is dependent upon the impact on application performance, as discussed in Chapter 1) then this indicates one of the following:

- either that the queue is operating in significant congestion and hence consideration should be given both to increasing the bandwidth assurance offered to that queue, and to reducing the traffic load within the queue

- or that the queue limit is set too low to accommodate the burst profile of the offered traffic load and hence the queue limit may need retuning.

5.2.2.3.2 Monitoring Weighted Tail Drop

Weighted tail drop is sometimes applied to AF class queues to discard a subset of the traffic within the queue preferentially if congestion is experienced within the queue. This can be used to differentiate between traffic that has been differentially marked as in- and out-of-contract (see Chapter 2, Section 2.2.4.2.2). Traffic that is marked out-of-contract is subjected to a lower queue limit and hence is discarded in preference to traffic that is marked in-contract and which is subject to a higher queue limit.

If weighted tail drop is used, then statistics of the number of packets and bytes dropped and transmitted per weighted tail drop profile should be monitored. If the intent of deploying weighted tail drop in this way is to ensure that in-contract traffic has a low loss rate, then the drop rate for the in-contract (i.e. higher) queue limit should be very low, where low is defined by the in-contract SLA for loss. If this is not the case then the indications and rectifying actions that should be taken with respect to the in-contract traffic are the same as for simple tail drop as described in Section 5.2.2.3.1.

When weighted tail drop is used, it would be expected that the drop rate for out-of-contract traffic would be higher than for in-contract traffic. It should be noted, however, that individual flows might have some packets marked as in-contract and others as out-of-contract. Therefore, if the drop rate for out-of-contract packets is too high, the performance of all applications using that queue may be affected and the indications and rectifying actions that should be taken with respect to the in-contract traffic are the same as for simple tail drop as described in Section 5.2.2.3.1.

5.2.2.3.3   Monitoring RED

Random early detection or RED is an active queue management mechanism, which was designed to improve overall throughput for TCP-based applications; RED is described in Chapter 2, Section 2.2.4.2.3. If RED is applied to a data class queue, then the following statistics should be monitored:

- *The number of packets and bytes enqueued.* This is the number of packets subjected to this RED profile that were successfully enqueued, and their respective byte count. Where only a single RED profile is active on the queue, this should be the same as the number of packets and bytes transmitted from the queue.

- *The number of packets and bytes random dropped.* "Random drops" are RED drops which occur when the measured average queue depth is between the configured minimum threshold and maximum threshold for that particular RED profile. If RED is configured and working correctly then the majority of dropped packets should be random drops. If the drop rate for all RED drops is high relative to the number of packets transmitted then this indicates one of the following:

○ either that the queue is operating in significant congestion and hence consideration should be given to increasing the bandwidth assurance offered to that queue, or to reducing the traffic load within the queue

○ or the configured minimum and maximum thresholds, or exponential weighting constant for that queue are set too aggressively (i.e. too low) to accommodate the burst profile of the offered traffic load and hence may need retuning (see RED tuning in Chapter 3, Section 3.4).

○ or there are applications in that queue, which are not responding to random drops and consideration should be given to whether these applications may be better serviced from a different class queue.

• *The number of packets and bytes force dropped.* Drops that occur when the measured average queue depth is above the configured maximum threshold are referred to as "forced drops." If RED is configured and operating correctly, then random drops should ensure that the average queue limit is below the configured maximum threshold and hence there should be very few forced drops. If there are a significant number of forced drops relative to the total number of RED drops then the possible causes and rectifying actions that should be taken are as described above for high RED drops.

• *Average queue depth.* Polling for the measured RED average queue depth is not essential but provides additional data, which can be used to supplement the RED other statistics. If the measured average queue depth is frequently close to or above the configured RED maximum threshold then this is also an indication that either the queue is operating in significant congestion or the RED configuration is set too aggressively and rectifying actions that should be taken are as for described above for high RED drops.

5.2.2.3.4   Monitoring WRED

Weighted RED (WRED) is commonly applied to AF queues to differentiate between in- and out-of-contract traffic (see Chapter 2, Section 2.2.4.2.4). To achieve this two RED profiles are applied to the same queue and traffic marked out-of-contract is subjected to the more aggressive RED profile (i.e. with lower minimum threshold and maximum threshold) and hence in congestion is discarded in preference to traffic which is marked in-contract and which is subject to a RED profile with higher minimum and maximum thresholds.

Where WRED is used, then the number of packets and bytes dropped and transmitted per RED profile is required. The sum of the packets successfully enqueued across all RED profiles should be the same as the number of packets and bytes transmitted from the queue.

As for weighted tail drop, the intent of deploying WRED in this way is to ensure that in-contract traffic has a low loss rate, then the drop rate for the in-contract RED profile should be very low, where low is determined by the in-contract SLA for loss. If this is not the case then the indications and rectifying actions that should be taken with respect to the in-contract traffic are the same as for RED as described in Section 5.2.2.3.3.

As for weighted tail drop, if the drop rate for out-of-contract packets is too high the performance of all applications using that queue may be affected and the indications and rectifying actions that should be taken with respect to the in-contract traffic are the same as for RED as described in Section 5.2.2.3.3.

5.2.3   System Monitoring

Ideally, all packet drops within a router are handled intelligently by the QOS functions configured on that router, which may be applied outbound on each interface, for example. In practice, however, depending upon how a particular router is architected and implemented, there may be cases where drops can occur on other parts of the system, due to system constraints. If, in the part of the system where these drops occur, there is no understanding of the class of the traffic being dropped, then traffic may be dropped indiscriminately of traffic class.

Clearly, systems should be designed to try to minimize the occurrence of such indiscriminate traffic drops; however, in cases where they can occur it is essential to monitor for them because they can provide an indication of serious system issues that can potentially affect the SLAs across all traffic classes.

The system drops that can occur will depend upon the implementation of a particular device; however, some of the most common types of system drops are as described below:

- *No buffer drops.* In Chapter 2, Section 2.2.4.2 we explained the difference between buffers and queues. Where buffer memory is shared between queues in a system, there may be cases where a packet arrives and there is insufficient packet buffer memory available to store the packet, in which case there is no alternative but to drop the packet. Such "no buffer drops" should be an exception in any well-designed system, rather than the norm; however, the occurrence of "no buffer drops" can be exacerbated in a heavily congested system if RED and queue limit settings are excessively high.

- *Input drops/ignores.* Input drops, which are also known as ignores, occur when there are insufficient packet buffers to store a packet even before a routing or switching decision can be made. Input drops are a symptom of an oversubscribed system, e.g. where the packets per second forwarding performance of the system or component is being exceeded.

System drops such as no buffer drops and input drops will generally need to be monitored using vendor-specific MIBs, as system specific statistics are not available from the Diffserv MIB. Due to the impact they can have on the SLAs of all traffic classes, the occurrence of any such system drops should trigger further investigation to determine the cause of the drops and to prevent a re-occurrence.

5.2.4   Core Traffic Matrix

The core traffic demand matrix is the matrix of ingress to egress traffic demands across the core network. Traffic matrices can be measured or estimated from statistics gathered using passive monitoring techniques. The main benefit of the core traffic matrix is for core network capacity planning, in that it can be used to predict the impact that demand growths can have, and in the simulation of "what-if" scenarios, to predict the impact that the failure of core network elements can have on the utilization of the rest of the network. There are a number of techniques for gathering the core traffic matrix; the application of these techniques and their use in capacity planning is discussed in more detail in Chapter 6.

5.3   Active Network Monitoring

Ideally, it would be possible to measure the delay, jitter, loss, and throughput that actual traffic experiences as it traverses a network. In some cases, it may be possible to retrieve this information from the application end-systems. Where the real-time protocol (RTP) [RFC 3550] is used, for example, the timestamp and sequence number information in the RTP header could be used to determine the delay, jitter, and loss of the received stream at the receiving end-system. This is not generally possible in practice, however, due to the following reasons: many applications do not use RTP; retrieving such statistics from all application end-systems would be unscalable; the end-systems may not be under the same administrative responsibility as the network elements. Further, to provide this information at the network level would require the network elements to identify uniquely a packet at every single hop and to timestamp it very accurately, which is not possible in practice.

Network level active network monitoring is an alternative approach, which is more generally applicable. Active monitoring uses specially tailored synthetic traffic test streams comprising "probe" packets – that aim to emulate actual network traffic – which are sent between active monitoring devices in order to characterize network performance and thereby infer the performance experienced by the emulated traffic. In Diffserv deployments, active monitoring can be used to measure the performance of all classes of traffic.

Active network monitoring requires the deployment of an active SLA probing system, supporting capabilities such as those defined by the IP performance metrics (IPPM) working group [IPPM] within the IETF. In such a system, active monitoring agents are deployed (potentially on existing network elements) and test streams are sent between the agents. The agents measure the received streams and typically keep a statistical analysis of the measured results, which can then be retrieved periodically from the active measuring devices, via SNMP for example. In addition, the active monitoring devices may proactively issue traps, if defined thresholds for the measured performance of the test streams are exceeded.

In deploying an active monitoring system, consideration should be given to the following questions, which are addressed in the proceeding sections:

- What test streams should be used?

- How often should testing be undertaken and for how long?

- What metrics should be measured for the received streams?

- Where should active monitoring devices be deployed and what paths should the active monitoring streams monitor?

To avoid confusion, we differentiate between the active monitoring traffic, i.e. the active measurement probes, and the monitored traffic, the performance of which the active monitoring traffic is trying to estimate.

5.3.1 Test Stream Parameters

The characteristics of the test stream will affect the characteristics of the network that the test stream will measure. These measured test stream results are only useful if they are in some way representative of the performance experienced by the monitored application or traffic class. This gives rise to the question of what test stream parameters are required to ensure that the measured characteristics of the active measurement stream accurately reflects the characteristics (e.g. delay, jitter, loss, packet re-ordering, and availability) of the traffic from the monitored application or traffic class? The answer to this question is still the subject of further study; however, the following sections consider the key parameters to define for an active measurement stream. It is noted that the term "accurately" in this context does not mean that the difference between measured test stream characteristics and the characteristics of the traffic must be small, but is does mean that the two results must be highly correlated, such that it is possible to predict the measured traffic performance from test stream measurements with high fidelity.

5.3.1.1 Packet Size

There are two general approaches to the setting of packet sizes for active monitoring probes:

- *Same size as monitored traffic.* One approach is to use probe packets that are the same size as the packets of the monitored traffic. There are two justifications for this approach:
  - As discussed in Chapter 3, Section 3.2.2.4.1, packet size has a more significant impact on serialization delay with lower-speed links, hence using packets the same size as the packets of the monitored traffic will potentially provide a more accurate measurement of delay. It is noted, however, that if the link speeds on the path are known, adjustments can be made to take differences in serialization delay between monitoring and monitored traffic into account.
  - Packets larger or smaller than the packets of the monitored traffic may experience a different loss than the monitored traffic itself; if congestion occurs in part of the network, as the queue depth increases a smaller packet is more likely to be enqueued than a larger one.

- *Small sized packets.* An alternative approach is to use small sized packets, for two reasons:
  - In environments where there are very low speed links, such as in some mobile environments where the bandwidth is scarce

and expensive, the smallest possible sized packets are used for bandwidth economy.

○ Where a high rate of test packets is needed to achieve measurement accuracy, the use of larger packets may have a significant impact on the traffic being measured. In this case, small sized packets are used to minimize the potential impact.

There is no industry consensus on which approach is best; however, we note the following conclusions from research in this area:

- From simulations studying the effectiveness of active SLA monitoring on a 2 Mbps link, [HILL] concludes that: *"The accuracy of the probes is not really affected by probe size. Both sizes [41-bytes and 850-bytes] show equally good correlation coefficients for delay and loss."* He also concludes that larger sized probes have significantly greater impact on the delay and jitter of the traffic whose performance the test stream is trying to estimate. Therefore, he recommends that probes should be small such that the active monitoring traffic has less impact on the other traffic.

- [SOLANGE] also found no evidence that packet size affected the measurements of packet loss.

In practice, however, most deployments use the same packet size for test streams that are used by the applications they are emulating. It is further noted that on higher speed links, where the impact of serialization delay is less, and the traffic is more highly aggregated, the impact of probe packet sizing is likely to be less significant.

5.3.1.2   Sampling Strategy

The probe sampling strategy determines the distribution of the delay separating consecutive test packets. There are three general probe sampling strategies that may be used:

- *Periodic sampling*. Periodic sampling consists of sending probes at equally spaced intervals, i.e. every *n* seconds. Opponents of this approach argue that one cannot fully characterize the network behavior by "sampling" at regular intervals. There might be some cases where unforeseen synchronization between the sending of probe packets, or possibly other network events, could potentially lead to inaccuracies. This kind of phenomenon, although theoretically possible, is rarely seen in practice. [RFC 3432] describes a methodology for network performance measurement with periodic streams.

- *Random sampling.* Random sampling consists of sending a probe at random intervals, where the interval is regulated by a probability density function. Most commonly, a Poisson process is used to distribute the probe packets, meaning that the interarrivals between probing packets should be independent and exponentially distributed with the same mean. This approach provides an unbiased estimate of the desired time average, which is a property referred to as *"Poisson Arrivals See Time Average"* or PASTA [WOLFF]. This approach is suggested by the IETF, where [RFC 2679] and [RFC 2680] standardize metrics based on Poisson sampling processes. Consequently, the IPPM working group has made the support of Poisson streams mandatory for their one-way active measurement protocol (OWAMP) [RFC4656]. The counterpoint to the use of a variable inter-packet delay is based upon the fact that most of the real world applications, which require tightly bounded delay and jitter and hence which are often a focus of active monitoring, do not have a Poisson distributed interpacket delay. Voice and video applications, for instance, commonly have streams with a constant interpacket delay and so why attempt to measure the performance of these applications on the network with something other than a stream that emulates the application?

  A variation on random sampling is to divide the total sampling period into fixed time intervals and then to send a probe within each interval with a random offset from the start of the interval, where the offset is regulated by a probability density function. The benefit of this approach is that the sample size within a defined number of intervals is known. This approach is referred to as stratified random sampling, where each interval represents a stratum.

- *Batch sampling.* With batch sampling, rather than sending individual probe packets, probes are sent in bursts, where the spacing between bursts may be periodic or random.

These different sampling regimes are illustrated in Figure 5.1.

Several works have attempted to compare both approaches to find if there is a tangible difference between the methods:

- In *"Poisson versus Periodic Path Probing (or, Does PASTA Matter?"* [TARIQ], the authors conclude that: *"The experimental results in this paper indicate that there may not be a significant difference between Poisson and Periodic probing, at least in the context of real Internet measurements."*

- [SOLANGE] conclude that *"... for similar probing rates and coloring, a periodic pattern leads to a slightly better [delay] and [loss] match than Poisson patterns."*

- [HILL] concludes that both random and periodic sampling provide acceptable accuracy for measuring delay and loss for VoIP and TCP, but also concludes that neither approach provides acceptable accuracy for measuring jitter.

- [HILL] suggests that batch sampling be considered to improve jitter measurement (Section 5.3.2.2), while [SOLANGE], who investigated the use of batch sampling, conclude that: *"... when compared [to Poisson] with similar rates, [batch sampling] produced better estimates of delay, jitter and loss."*

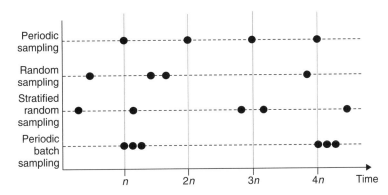

Figure 5.1   Active monitoring sampling strategies

In practice, however, periodic test streams with a constant inter-packet delay are most commonly used because this approach is easier to implement and interpret and because it most closely emulates the applications that the active monitoring is targeting. In recognition of this, [RFC 3432] states: *"Poisson sampling produces an unbiased sample for the various IP performance metrics, yet there are situations where alternative sampling methods are advantageous.... Predictability and some forms of synchronization can be mitigated through the use of random start times and limited stream duration over a test interval."*

5.3.1.3   Test Rate

The test rate determines the amount of packets sent within the test duration, and consequently, it affects the perturbation introduced by the measurement stream on the actual network traffic. For instance, sending a large amount of test traffic over a path with small bandwidth may potentially interfere with the delivery of the actual measured traffic stream that the active monitoring is trying to monitor. Such an effect would clearly invalidate the measured results. Conversely, if the test rate is too low, the measured characteristics of the test stream may not reflect the characteristics of the measured traffic stream itself. Therefore, determining an appropriate test rate is a balance between testing with a high enough rate that the measured result is an accurate reflection of the measured traffic stream, while ensuring that the measuring stream does not interfere with the measured traffic stream significantly, such that it affects the very characteristics it is trying to measure.

There is no general answer to the question of what test rate to use, but rather it depends upon the characteristics of the application or class being monitored.

- Based upon simulations of a 2 Mbps bottleneck link, using both periodic and random sampling, [HILL] concludes that *"both delay and loss can be measured accurately (taking into account the systematic [underestimation]) at around a probe rate of 10 probes per second."* He also notes that *"... higher probe rates report more accurate traffic results*

for [delay and loss]," but suggests using the following rates in order
to measure delay and loss (for jitter, see Section 5.3.2.2):

○ *"For TCP traffic the optimum strategy was to send ... [probes] at a*
  mean rate of ten probes per second," i.e. approximately 0.2% of the
  link rate with probe 41-byte packets.

○ *"For VoIP traffic, the optimum strategy was to send in probes at a*
  rate of 5 probes per second," i.e. approximately 0.1% of the link rate
  with probe 41-byte packets.

• [SOLANGE] conclude that for EF traffic, using Poisson random
  sampling, as low as 2 probes per second (pps) are effective for
  measuring delay and jitter, based upon simulations of a 34 Mbps
  bottleneck link, i.e. approximately 0.01% of the link rate with
  100-byte probe packets.

  However, they report that for AF classes subject to loss and more
  significant jitter, at these probing rates using random sampling there
  is significant overestimation of jitter (see Section 5.3.2.2) and some
  loss events are missed altogether. They also note that while higher
  probing rates improve the measurement accuracy of delay and jitter,
  even at probing rates of 192 pps, some loss events are missed. Hence,
  although higher probing rates provide an improvement, due to the
  overhead incurred and the failure of loss estimation at higher probe
  rates, they suggest that the use of an alternative sampling scheme,
  such as batch sampling, should be considered instead.

5.3.1.4 Test Duration and Frequency

The test duration defines how long an active measurement test case
will run. The test frequency determines how many times the test will
repeat within a specified time window.

Assuming a given test traffic rate, the test duration and frequency
need to be high enough that the measured result is an accurate
reflection of the measured traffic stream. The lower the (*duration x
frequency*) in any given time window, the greater the probability that
significant events will be missed, as illustrated in Figure 5.2.

If the active monitoring devices do not keep the raw data of the
individual probes, but rather keep a statistical representation of the

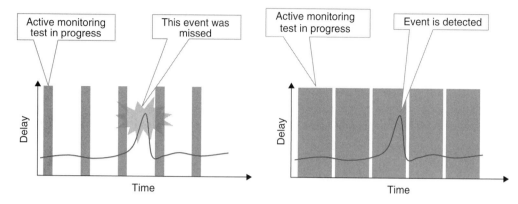

Figure 5.2 Impact of test (*frequency × duration*)

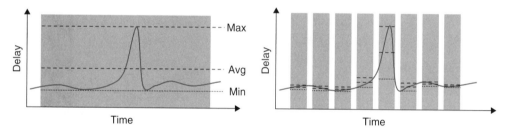

Figure 5.3 Impact of test duration

results over the test duration, as is commonly the case, then assuming a given test traffic rate the test duration will implicitly impact the measured statistics, as shown in Figure 5.3.

Similarly to the discussion on the passive monitoring polling interval in Section 5.2.1, longer active monitoring test durations may be acceptable for trending purposes; however, shorter durations are preferred where more granular measurements are required, although this has to be balanced against the increased polling load. A possible polling scheme could be as follows:

- For troubleshooting, proactive measurement and SLA reporting, a network segment could be measured constantly with a test duration of 2 minutes.

- For trending, it may be more appropriate to measure for one hour every day, during the peak hour previously determined by the more granular measurements. Longer duration measurements make the comparison between days, months and years easier and more statistically relevant.

5.3.1.5 Protocols, Ports, and Applications

In order to ensure that the network characteristics determined by a measuring traffic stream are representative of the traffic stream they are measuring, it is important that the measuring stream is classified the same as the target stream along the end-to-end network path. If Diffserv is deployed the network performance experienced by applications will depend upon how the traffic is classified within the network; if measurement probes are classified differently than the emulated stream in any part of the network, they may experience different delay, jitter, and loss, and hence will not provide representative results.

Where simple classification is used, the probe packets should share the same marking (be it DSCP, IP precedence or even 802.1p based) as the target stream, but need not necessarily share the same IP addressing or protocol as the target stream.

Where complex classification is used (see Chapter 2, Section 2.2.1.2), the criteria used for complex classification should produce the same results for the measuring test stream as for the measured application. If, for example, VoIP traffic is classified by a combination of identifying UDP packets, with even UDP port numbers (e.g. representing RTP data) and from a specific source IP address, then headers of the probe packets should be such that they also match these criteria. If the target traffic stream is TCP-based and complex classification is used, the IP protocol number of the probe packets may also need to be set to 6 to indicate that the packets are TCP.

Where Diffserv is deployed with AF classes supporting the concept of in- and out-of-contract as described in Chapter 2, Section 2.3.4.2.2, the in-contract traffic has a lower probability of packet loss than the traffic. Hence, if monitoring of the in-contract SLA is required, it is important that any policers used to mark traffic as in- or out-of-contract do not re-mark the in-contract probes, else they may be wrongly classified and may not be report the in-contract SLA correctly.

Some probing systems may attempt to characterize application as well as network performance. For example, a probe may record the response time of a DNS query to a particular DNS server or an HTTP GET of a specific web page. In these cases, the results will capture multiple components such as session establishment, end-system processing, sending, and receiving multiple packets between the client and the server, and closing the connection. This kind of application-oriented operation may be useful to measure the user experience, but gives no visibility of the performance of the individual components that make up the measured response.

5.3.2   Active Measurement Metrics

The SLA metrics that are important for defining IP service performance are described in detail in Chapter 1, Section 1.2. Once the appropriate test stream for your particular application has been identified, consideration needs to be given to which metrics to measure, how they are measured and to how the resultant measurements should be interpreted. Multiple metrics can be determined from a single test stream.

5.3.2.1   Delay

Delay can be quantified either as one-way delay, or as round trip delay (round trip time or RTT). Measurement of RTT requires that probes are sent from a sending active monitoring agent to a responder and then back to the sender. In this case the RTT can be determined if the sender timestamps the probes when it sends them (the timestamp is carried in the data of the probe packet) and subtracts this value from the corresponding timestamp when it receives the probe response. Measurement of one-way delay requires that the sender and receiver's local time clocks are synchronized such that the one-way delay can be determined at the receiver, if the receiver also timestamps the probe packets on receipt; the difference between the sending timestamp and receiving timestamp is the one-way delay. Ensuring synchronization between sender and receiver with acceptable accuracy poses challenges; this is discussed in more detail in Section 5.3.3.4. RTT is easier to implement and measure than one-way delay, and may provide sufficiently measurement utility for many applications.

For applications such as VoIP or interactive video conferencing, the important delay metric when considering the engineering of the network is the one-way end-to-end delay in each direction from end-system to end-system. From a monitoring perspective, however, it may be acceptable to monitor the RTT between the end-systems as from a service perspective, it may not matter in which direction excess delay is experienced; if excess is experienced at all, then the service will be impacted. If SLA violations for delay occur, however, RTT hides the detail of in which direction the issue causing the violation occurred. Hence, measurement of one-way delay may be more useful for network troubleshooting.

Delay can provide a number for important indicators of network performance. Most active monitoring end-systems will analyze the received probes and present statistics on the resulting data set, but which statistics are important with respect to delay measurement?

- *Minimum delay.* The minimum network delay is the network delay "baseline," providing an indication of the delay that traffic will experience when the path from source to destination is lightly loaded. This will largely be composed of propagation delay, switching delay, and serialization delay. Delay values above the minimum provide an indication of the congestion experienced along the path. Considering the percentile delay for a low percentile (e.g. 0.1 percentile), will provide an indication of the minimum delay experienced while discounting outliers, e.g. spuriously low results due to measurement system glitches.

- *High percentile delay.* The maximum delay across a network may not be interesting if it is caused by on a very small percentage of outliers; considering the percentile delay for a high percentile (e.g. 99.9 percentile), will provide an indication of the maximum delay experienced while discounting outliers.

- *Threshold exceeded count.* For applications which have a stringent requirement on delay, it may be useful to count the number of probe packets out of the total which experienced a delay in excess of a defined threshold, set to indicate when a packet arrived too late to be useful.

- *Average delay.* The average delay may be interesting for trending purposes, but for purposes of comparison should be recorded together with the standard deviation of the sample; higher than normal standard deviations may be indicative of spurious issues rather than of a trend.

5.3.2.2 Delay-jitter

Delay-jitter (which is also known as jitter), as described in Chapter 1, is generally considered to be the variation of the one-way delay for two consecutive packets. Measurement of one-way delay requires time-stamping at both sending and receiving devices, which requires synchronization between sender and receiver; this is difficult for the reasons discussed in Section 5.3.3.4. Fortunately, to calculate jitter there is no need to know the individual one-way delays: instead, this can be calculated from the difference between timestamps taken on single devices. No operation need be performed between timestamps on two different devices, which makes measurement of one-way delay-jitter simpler than measurement of one-way delay. Consider that $T_s[n]$ is the time when the packet n was sent, and $T_r[n]$ is the time when the packet n was received; the one-way delay of this packet is denoted as $D[n]$. Then, the jitter J between packets n and $n + 1$ can therefore be calculated as:

$$J[n, n + 1] = D[n + 1] - D[n]$$
$$= (T_r[n + 1] - T_s[n + 1]) - (T_r[n] - T_s[n])$$
$$= (T_r[n + 1] - T_r[n]) - (T_s[n + 1] - T_s[n])$$

The most important statistics to report with respect to jitter are high percentile jitter, threshold exceeded count, and average jitter. It is noted that the higher the rate of the traffic stream, the lower will be the measured jitter, as illustrated in Figures 5.4 and 5.5, which show

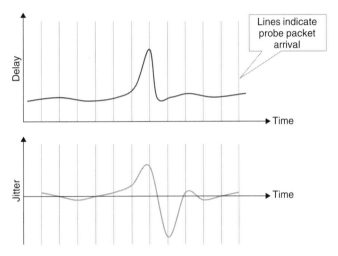

Figure 5.4   Lower rate – higher measured jitter

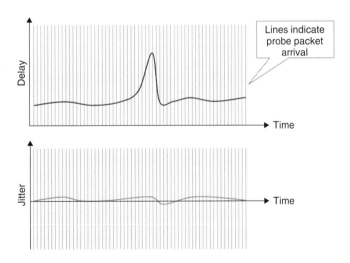

Figure 5.5   Higher rate – lower measured jitter

the variation in queuing delay within a queue, and the resulting jitter measured by probes within that queue, for different probe rates.

Hence, measurements streams at rates below that of the measured traffic will likely report higher jitter than that actually experienced by the traffic itself. This is supported by the findings in [HILL], who suggests a batch sampling strategy to overcome this problem, and [SOLANGE], who concluded that batch sampling produced a better estimate of jitter than random Poisson sampling.

5.3.2.3   Packet Loss

In order to determine packet loss there needs to be a way to distinguish between a lost packet and a packet with a large but finite delay. In practice, depending upon application and end-system implementations, packets delayed beyond a certain threshold will be of no use and hence can be considered lost; acceptable delay thresholds for different applications are discussed in Chapter 1. The loss of an individual packet is a binary measure, however, SLAs for loss are generally defined statistically and hence loss commitments need to be provided over a defined time interval.

The measure of the percentage of packets dropped may be useful for trending purposes; however, it does not say anything about how those packets were dropped. Hence, it is not possible to understand the potential impact on applications from this measure alone. [RFC 3357] introduces some additional metrics, which describe loss patterns and can be used to analyze the possible impact on applications:

- *Loss period*. The loss period defines the frequency and length (loss burst) of loss once it starts

- *Loss distance*. The loss distance defines the spacing between the loss periods.

It is therefore recommended that the loss period and loss distance are measured and compared against application-specific thresholds indicating where the measured loss will unacceptably affect application performance. The impact of packet loss on different applications is discussed in Chapter 1.

5.3.2.4 Bandwidth and Throughput

Application throughput is dependent upon many factors, which can vary widely depending upon end-system implementations and traffic profiles. Hence, active monitoring systems generally do not attempt to characterize application throughput explicitly. Rather, application throughput is generally inferred. Considering TCP for example, TCP performance can be inferred from the measured network RTT and packet loss rate, as discussed in Chapter 1, Sections 1.3.3.1.5–1.3.3.1.7. Active monitoring systems may send packets which appear to be TCP packets (i.e. use IP protocol 6), but they need not – and commonly do not – implement a TCP stack, i.e. the transmission of the packets is not controlled by TCP's flow and congestion control mechanisms.

5.3.2.5 Re-ordering

IP does not guarantee that packets are delivered in the order in which they were sent; as discussed in Chapter 1, packet re-ordering can have an adverse impact on the performance of many applications.

Re-ordering within an active monitoring test stream is determined by adding sequence numbers to the packets transmitted in the stream and then comparing the sequence numbers of the received packets with the order in which they are received. If a packet arrives with a sequence number smaller than its predecessor's then that packet would be defined as out-of-order, or re-ordered.

The simplest metric by which to measure the magnitude of re-ordering is as a re-ordering ratio, which is the ratio of re-ordered packets that arrived, relative to the total number of packets received. A number of other metrics for quantifying the magnitude of re-ordering are defined in [RFC4737].

5.3.2.6 Availability

Availability for IP services is generally defined either as network availability or as service availability, as described in Chapter 1, Section 1.2.6.

- *Network availability*. Bidirectional network availability or connectivity between two active monitoring devices can be determined using probes sent from a sender to a responder and then back to the sender; for each response successfully received the network is considered available and for each not received the network is considered unavailable. As with packet loss, a delay threshold needs to be defined after which a response is considered "lost."

- *Service availability*. Service availability is a compound metric defining when a service is available between a specified ingress point and a specified egress point within the bounds of the committed SLA metrics for the service, e.g. delay, jitter, and loss. This is discussed in more detail in Chapter 1, Section 1.2.6.2.

5.3.2.7   Quality of Experience

Active monitoring end-systems do not normally implement the full end-system behavior for the applications they are trying to measure. Some active monitoring devices, however, will interpret the metrics of a received stream in order to provide an objective measure of the quality of the application performance that will be experienced from the perspective of the end-users, which is also known as the user "quality of experience" or QOE. The most common QOE measure is the "mean opinion score" or MOS, which provides a subjective numeric measure of the QOE of a voice call. ITU standard [G.107] uses a number of measured network parameters to determine a "rating factor," which can be transformed to give estimates of the MOS for calls, which use that network service. QOE is discussed in more detail in Chapter 1, Section 1.2.7.

5.3.3   Deployment Considerations

5.3.3.1   External versus Embedded Agents

An active measurement system uses active monitoring agents to send and receive probe packets. These agents may be implemented in dedicated active monitoring devices or alternatively may be embedded into existing network devices:

- *External agents*. External agents are implemented in dedicated active monitoring devices, which may either use specialized hardware or dedicated but off the shelf computers running active monitoring software. This approach decouples the forwarding path (routers and switches) from the measurement devices; the dedicated active monitoring devices appear as customers connected to the network and hence this approach may provide the closest view to the end-customer experience. The use of dedicated devices, however, requires addition network equipment, which incurs additional cost in terms of capital expenditure, accommodation, power, management, and maintenance. Hence, for end-user or small branch office locations the use of dedicated active monitoring devices is generally not viable.

- *Embedded agents.* Some network hardware vendors implement software active monitoring agents embedded in products, which may be network devices such as routers or switches or could be end-systems such as IP phones. The use of embedded agents in devices which are already on the data switching path allows the installed base of network equipment to be leveraged, enabling the rapid roll-out of an active SLA monitoring system without requiring the deployment of new network equipment.

5.3.3.2 Active Monitoring Topologies

When deploying an active monitoring system, a key question is where to deploy the active monitoring devices, be they external or embedded agents. In general, the measurements from active monitoring should represent the application's experience, and hence the active monitoring devices should be as close to the application end-system as possible. In all deployments, however, there are constraints, which limit the location of such devices; there may be parts of the network that are not under the control of the measuring organization, for example. In large deployments, scalability of the active monitoring system is an additional consideration.

The selection of the active monitoring topology depends upon these constraints. Consider the example physical network topology shown in Figure 5.6. A number of different active SLA monitoring topologies – where the active SLA monitoring topology is defined by

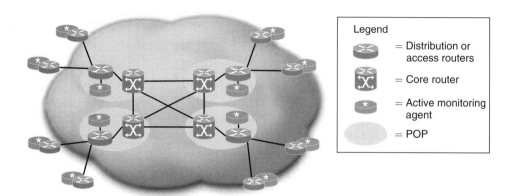

Figure 5.6   Example physical network topology

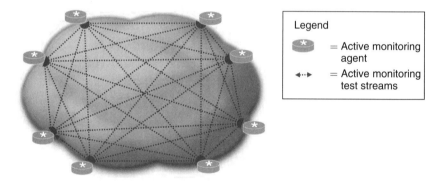

Figure 5.7   Full mesh active monitoring topology

the sources and destinations of the active monitoring test streams –
can be overlaid on this physical topology:

- *Full mesh*. A full mesh requires probes from every active monitoring location to every other active monitoring location, as shown
  in Figure 5.7. This approach is the most accurate because it measures end-to-end paths between all locations and gives full network coverage.
  In practice, however, the full mesh approach does not scale
  well; as the number of active monitoring nodes (*n*) increases, the

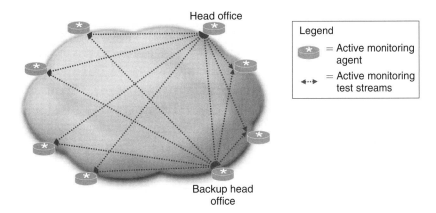

Figure 5.8   Partial mesh active monitoring topology

number of bidirectional active monitoring test streams required to interconnect them is $n * (n − 1)/2$, which increases more than linearly with the number of nodes. Beyond a few nodes, the full mesh approach may result in a configuration burden, the test streams may use a significant amount of bandwidth and the retrieval of the measurement data from all nodes may incur significant management system overhead. For these reasons, a full mesh active monitoring topology is only used where there are a limited number of sites to be monitored.

- *Partial mesh*. A partial mesh involves running a mesh of test streams on a subset of the topology. For example, this could be a hub and spoke active monitoring topology in networks where remote sites (the spokes) only communicate with the head offices (the hubs), as shown in Figure 5.8.

  A partial mesh reduces the number of test streams required and provides end-to-end monitoring between a subset of locations. In a hub and spoke topology, if round-trip active monitoring is used, the hub sites may be configured as the active monitoring probe senders, with the spoke sites acting as responders; in this case, the active monitoring measurement data need only be retrieved from the hub sites.

- *Hierarchical mesh.* In networks with any-to-any communication between sites, a full mesh may be unscalable, while a partial mesh may not provide sufficient network coverage. In these cases, a hierarchical mesh may be used; with a hierarchical mesh, the active monitoring is segmented. In a typical deployment, centralized active measurement devices are located in each point of presence (POP) and test streams are run from each POP to their connected remote sites in a hub and spoke active monitoring topology. Test streams are then run in a full mesh from each POP to every other POP, as shown in Figure 5.9.

  This approach facilitates the scaling of a network-wide active monitoring system and hence it is commonly used in practice; it significantly reduces the number of test streams required compared to a full mesh, while providing full network coverage and being relatively easy to manage. If the POP active monitoring devices are configured as senders for round-trip probes, with their respective remote sites monitoring devices acting as responders, then the active monitoring measurement data need only be retrieved from the central sites and there is no need to access the remote sites.

  This approach gives segmented measurements for the access links and across the core network and maps well to the concept of

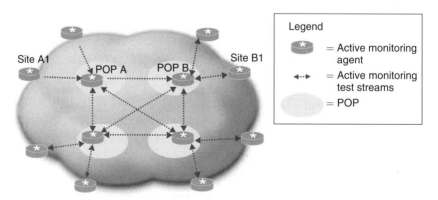

Figure 5.9 Hierarchical mesh active monitoring topology

a segmented SLA discussed in Chapter 1, Section 1.4.1. The disadvantage of this approach is that it does not provide end-to-end monitoring. Hence, if measurements between two sites A1 and B1 were required, they would need to be statistically estimated by combining, where possible, the measured results for each segment in the end-to-end path, i.e. from site A1 to POP A, from POP A to POP B, and from POP B to site B1. For example, it is possible to estimate the average (or a specific percentile) end-to-end delay by summing the average (or specific percentile) measured delay for each segment. To estimate the end-to-end packet loss probability, if the probability of packet loss on segment x is given by P_x, then the end-to-end packet loss probability (P) across n segments is:

$$P = 1 - [(1 - P_1) \times (1 - P_2) \times ... \times (1 - P_n)]$$

It is not, however, possible to estimate end-to-end jitter from the measured jitter of the segments on the end-to-end path because the measured jitter in IP networks is not statistically additive in practice (see Chapter 6, Section 6.1.3). Where a measure of end-to-end jitter is required, end-to-end monitoring should be selectively deployed.

5.3.3.3 Measuring Equal Cost Multiple Paths

Many networks have multiple paths between different parts of the network, for reasons of both resilience and capacity provision. Interior Gateway routing Protocols (IGPs) such as OSPF [RFC 2328] and ISIS [RFC1142] determine which paths will be used between any two points in the network by choosing whichever path has the least total cost, where the path cost is calculated by summing the individual metrics (which express the preference of a link) of the links along the path. If there is more than one least cost path, then the routing protocol will potentially distribute the traffic between the two points across all of those paths. The algorithms that balance the load across the paths are generally referred to as equal cost multi-path (ECMP) algorithms. ECMP algorithms are generally proprietary to each vendor. Different vendors will use different criteria to determine which path will be used for a particular packet, although a common implementation is to perform a hash function using inputs including fields within the packet header, such as source IP address, destination IP address, protocol number, source UDP/TCP port, and destination UDP/TCP port.

ECMP poses a significant issue for active monitoring for which there is no ideal answer; a single measurement can only use one of the many possible paths and not all of them. There are a number of potential resolutions to this issue; however, none of them is a panacea that will provide a solution in all circumstances. It may be possible to vary the source and destination IP addresses and UDP/TCP port numbers of sent probes in order to try to use more than one of the paths. In practice, however, ECMP algorithms can be difficult to predict (some also use a random seed as an input to the hash), hence it may not be possible to guarantee that all paths are being tested. Alternatively, if the test is run from the load-balancing router itself, then it may be possible to force probe packets via each of the load-balancing interfaces in turn; however, this will not guarantee that response probe packets use all return paths also.

5.3.3.4 Clock Synchronization

To achieve highly accurate one-way delay measurements, the clocks on all the network elements participating in the test must be synchronized; any synchronization error will result in an error in the measured one-way delay. Network devices maintain local time using on board clocks, which provide time to the device operating system. There are a number of potential ways that the local clocks on network devices can be synchronized.

The most accurate way to synchronize clocks on network devices is to synchronize each device with an accurate "stratum 1"[1] external clock source such as a GPS clock or radio clock. This is, however, an expensive approach and while it may be viable for devices within the core of the network, it would not be viable for end-user or small branch office locations.

An alternative approach is to distribute stratum 1 time using a protocol, such as the network time protocol (NTP) [RFC 1305]. NTP synchronizes clocks between network devices by exchanging time-stamped messages between a server and its clients. NTP seeks long-term accuracy at the expense of the short-term accuracy; it will, for instance, slow or accelerate the internal clock (or add/subtract time quanta) to adjust the local clock progressively to what it believes is the true time. If measurements are taking place during those adjustments, strange results like negative delay might be observed. NTP can usually maintain time to within 10 ms in wide area networks; this does not generally provide a sufficient level of accuracy for those applications with tight delay bound requirements, which require one-way delay monitoring such as VoIP and video streaming. In local area networks, under good conditions, NTP can usually maintain time to 1 ms or better, which may be sufficient for active monitoring purposes.

Due to the constraints and costs of interdevice clock synchronization, a common deployment model is to distribute time from a stratum 1 clock source to all the devices within a point of presence (POP) using a separate network (commonly the management network), to ensure synchronization via NTP to within 1 ms or better. This enables the measurement of one-way delay between POPs. Synchronization of access routers via NTP is generally not accurate enough and the use of stratum 1 clock sources in these locations is generally not viable, hence SLA reporting of the access links from POP to access router is commonly reported as RTT rather than one-way delay.

References[2]

[G.107] ITU-T Recommendation G.107, The E-model, a computational model for use in transmission planning, International Telecommunication Union, Geneva, Switzerland, Feb. 2003

[HILL] J. Hill, Assessing the Accuracy of Active Probes for Determining Network Delay, Jitter and Loss, MSc Thesis in High Performance Computing, The University of Edinburgh, 2002. Available at: http://www.epcc.ed.ac.uk/msc/dissertations/dissertations-0102/jhill.pdf

[IPPM] http://www.ietf.org/html.charters/ippm-charter.html

[RFC1142] D. Oran, Ed., OSI IS-IS Intra-domain Routing Protocol, *RFC 1142*, February 1999 [republication of ISO DP 10589]

[RFC1157] J. Case et al., A Simple Network Management Protocol (SNMP), *RFC 1157*, May 1990

[RFC1305] D. Mills, Network Time Protocol (Version 3) Specification, Implementation and Analysis, *RFC 1305*, March 1992

[RFC2328] J. Moy, OSPF Version 2, *RFC 2328*, April 1998

[RFC2679] G. Almes, S. Kalidindi, and M. Zekauskas, A One-way Delay Metric for IPPM, *RFC 2679*, September 1999

[RFC2680] G. Almes, S. Kalidindi, and M. Zekauskas, A One-way Packet Loss Metric for IPPM, *RFC 2680*, September 1999

[RFC2697] J. Heinanen, R. Guerin, A Single Rate Three Color Marker, *RFC 2697*, September 1999

[RFC2698] J. Heinanen, R. Guerin, A Two Rate Three Color Marker, *RFC 2698*, September 1999

[RFC3289] Baker, K. Chan, A. Smith, Management Information Base for the Differentiated Services Architecture, *RFC 3289*, May 2002

[RFC3357] R. Koodli, R. Ravikanth, One-way Loss Pattern Sample Metrics, *RFC 3357*, August 2002

[RFC3432] G. Grotefeld, A. Morton, Network performance measurement with periodic streams, *RFC 3432*, November 2002

[RFC3550] H. Schulzrinne, RTP: A Transport Protocol for Real-Time Applications, *RFC 3550*, July 2003

[RFC4656] S. Shalunov et al. A One-way Active Measurement Protocol (OWAMP), *RFC 4656*, September 2006

[RFC4737] A. Morton et al. Packet Re-ordering Metric for IPPM, *RFC4737*, November 2006

[SOLANGE] Solange R. Lima, Paulo M. Carvalho, and Vasco L. Freitas, Measuring QoS in class-based IP networks using multipurpose colored probing patterns, *Proceedings of SPIE*, Volume 5598, September 2004, pp. 171–182

[TARIQ] Muhammad Mukarram Bin Tariq et al., Poisson versus periodic path probing (or, does PASTA matter?), pp. 119–124 of the *Proceedings of the IMC '05*, 2005 Internet Measurement Conference, October 2005

[WOLFF] Ronald W. Wolff, Poisson Arrivals See Time Averages, *Operations Research*, Vol. 30, No. 2, March–April 1982

Notes

1. NTP refers to clock sources by their strata, where stratum 1 sources are considered most accurate; stratum 2 sources derive their time from stratum 1 sources, and so on.

2. The nature of the networking industry and community means that some of the sources referred to in this book exist only on the World Wide Web. All Universal Resource Locators (URLs) have been checked and were correct at the time of going to press, but their longevity cannot be guaranteed.

6

Core Capacity Planning and Traffic Engineering

This chapter addresses core capacity planning and how traffic engineering can be used as a tool to make more efficient use of network capacity.

6.1 Core Network Capacity Planning

Capacity planning of the core network is the process of ensuring that sufficient bandwidth is provisioned such that the committed core network SLA targets of delay, jitter, loss, and availability can be met. In the core network where link bandwidths are high and traffic is highly aggregated, the SLA requirements for a traffic class can be translated into bandwidth requirements, and the problem of SLA assurance can effectively be reduced to that of bandwidth provisioning. Hence, the ability to assure SLAs is dependent upon ensuring that core network bandwidth is adequately provisioned, which is in turn dependent upon core capacity planning.

The simplest core capacity planning processes use passive measurements of core link utilization statistics (i.e. as described in Chapter 5, Section 5.2) and apply rules of thumb, such as upgrading links when they reach 50% average utilization, or some other such general utilization target. The aim of such simple processes is to attempt to ensure that the core links are always significantly over-provisioned

---

This chapter has benefitted enormously from the input of Thomas Telkamp, Director of Network Consulting at Cariden Technologies, Inc. Thomas's work formed the basis of the capacity planning section.

relative to the offered average load, on the assumption that this will ensure that they are also sufficiently over-provisioned relative to the peak load, that congestion will not occur, and hence the SLA requirements will be met. There are, however, two significant consequences of such a simple approach. Firstly, without a network-wide understanding of the traffic demands, even an approach which upgrades links when they reach 50% average utilization may not be able to ensure that the links are still sufficiently provisioned when network element (e.g. link and node) failures occur, in order to ensure that the committed SLA targets continue to be met. Secondly, and conversely, rule of thumb approaches such as this may result in more capacity being provisioned than is actually needed.

Effective core capacity planning can overcome both of these issues. Effective core capacity planning requires a way of measuring the current network load, and a way of determining how much bandwidth should be provisioned relative to the measured load in order to achieve the committed SLAs. Hence, in this section we present a holistic methodology for capacity planning of the core network, which takes the core traffic demand matrix and the network topology into account to determine how much capacity is needed in the network, in order to meet the committed SLA requirements, taking network element failures into account if necessary, while minimizing the capacity and cost associated with over-provisioning.

The methodology presented in this section can be applied whether Diffserv is deployed in the core or not. Where Diffserv is not deployed, capacity planning is performed on aggregate. Where Diffserv is deployed, while the fundamental principles remain the same, capacity planning per traffic class is needed to ensure that class SLA targets are not violated.

6.1.1 Capacity Planning Methodology

We distinguish the following steps in the process of capacity planning:

1. Collect the core traffic demand matrices (either on aggregate or per class) and add traffic growth predictions to create a traffic demand forecast. This step is described in Section 6.1.2.

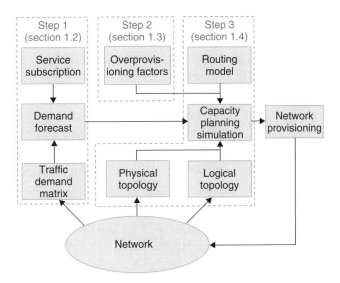

Figure 6.1   Capacity planning methodology

2. Determine the appropriate bandwidth over-provisioning factors (either on aggregate or per class) relative to the measured demand matrices, which are required to ensure that committed SLAs can be met. This step is described in Section 6.1.3.

3. Run simulations to overlay the forecasted demands onto the network topology, taking failure cases into account if necessary, to determine the forecasted link loadings. Analyze the results, comparing the forecasted link loadings against the provisioned bandwidth and taking the calculated over-provisioning factors into account, to determine the future capacity provisioning plan required to achieve the desired SLAs. This step is described in Section 6.1.2.

This capacity planning process is illustrated by Figure 6.1. The steps in the capacity planning process are described in detail in the proceeding sections.

6.1.2   Collecting the Traffic Demand Matrices

The core traffic demand matrix is the matrix of ingress to egress traffic demands across the core network. Traffic matrices can be measured or estimated to different levels of aggregation: by IP prefix, by router, by point of presence (POP), or by autonomous system (AS). The benefit of a core traffic matrix over simple per-link statistics is that the demand matrix can be used in conjunction with an understanding of the network routing model to predict the impact that demand growths can have and to simulate "what-if" scenarios, in order to understand the impact that the failure of core network elements can have on the (aggregate or per-class) utilization of the rest of the links in the network. With simple per-link statistics, when a link or node fails, in all but very simple topologies it may not be possible to know over which links the traffic impacted by the failure will be rerouted. Core network capacity is increasingly being provisioned taking single network element failure cases into account. To understand traffic rerouting in failure cases a traffic matrix is needed which aggregates traffic at the router-to-router level. If Diffserv is deployed, a per-class of service core traffic matrix is highly desirable.

The core traffic demand matrix can be an internal traffic matrix, i.e. router-to-router, or an external traffic matrix, i.e. router to AS, as illustrated in Figure 6.2, which shows the internal traffic demand

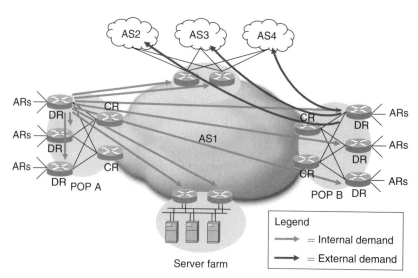

Figure 6.2   Internal and external traffic demands

matrix from one distribution router (DR), and the external traffic demand matrix from another.

The internal traffic matrix is useful for understanding the impact that internal network element failures will have on the traffic loading within the core. An internal matrix could also be edge-to-edge (e.g. DR to DR), or just across the inner core (e.g. CR to CR); a DR to DR matrix is preferred, as this can also be used to determine the impact of failures within a POP. The external traffic matrix provides additional context, which could be useful for managing peering connection capacity provision, and for understanding where internal network failures might impact in the external traffic matrix, due to closest-exit (a.k.a. "hot potato") routing.

There are a number of possible approaches for collecting the core traffic demand matrix statistics. The approaches differ in terms of their ability to provide an internal or external matrix, whether they can be applied to IP or MPLS, and whether they can provide a per-class of service traffic matrix. Further, the capabilities of network devices to provide information required to determine the core traffic matrix can vary depending upon the details of the particular vendor's implementation. Some of the possible approaches for determining the core traffic demand matrix are as follows:

- *IP flow statistics aggregation.* The Internet Protocol Flow Information eXport (IPFIX) protocol [IPFIX] is being defined within the IETF as a standard for the export of IP flow information from routers, probes, and other devices. If edge devices such as distribution routers are capable of accounting at a flow level (i.e. in terms of packet and byte counts), then a number of potential criteria could be used to aggregate this flow information – potentially locally on the device – in order to produce a traffic matrix.

    Where the Border Gateway Protocol (BGP) [RFC4271] is used within an AS, for example, each router at the edge of the AS is referred to as a BGP "peer." For each IP destination address that a peer advertises via BGP it also advertises a BGP next hop IP address, which is used when forwarding packets to that destination. In order to forward a packet to that destination, another BGP router within the AS needs to perform a recursive lookup, firstly looking in its BGP table to retrieve the BGP next hop address associated with that destination address, and then looking in its Interior Gateway Routing Protocol (IGP) routing table to determine how to get to that particular BGP next hop address (for further understanding on the workings of BGP, see [HALABI]). Hence, aggregating IPFIX flow statistics based upon the BGP next hop IP address used to reach a particular destination would produce an edge router to edge router traffic matrix.

- *MPLS LSP accounting.* Where MPLS is used, a label switch path (LSP) implicitly represents an aggregate traffic demand. Where BGP is deployed in conjunction with label distribution by the Label Distribution Protocol (LDP) [RFC3036], in the context of a BGP MPLS VPN service [RFC4364] for example, and each Provider Edge (PE) router[1] is a BGP peer, an LSP from one PE to another implicitly represents the PE-to-PE traffic demand. Hence, if traffic accounting statistics are maintained per LSP, these can be retrieved, using SNMP for example, to produce the PE-to-PE core traffic matrix.

  If MPLS traffic engineering is deployed (see Section 6.2.3) with a full mesh of TE tunnels, then each TE tunnel LSP implicitly represents the aggregate demand of traffic from the head-end router at the source of the tunnel, to the tail-end router at the tunnel destination. Hence, if traffic accounting statistics are maintained per TE tunnel LSP, these can be retrieved, using SNMP for example, to understand the core traffic matrix. If Diffserv-aware TE is deployed (see Section 6.2.3.2) with a full mesh of TE tunnels per class of service, the same technique could be used to retrieve a per-traffic class traffic matrix.

- *Demand estimation.* Demand estimation is the application of mathematical methods to measurements taken from the network, such as core link usage statistics, in order to infer the traffic demand matrix that generated those usage statistics. There are a number of methods that have been proposed for deriving traffic matrices from link measurements and other easily measured data [VARDI, TEBALDI, MEDINA, ZHANG], and there are a number of commercially available tools that use these, or similar, techniques in order to derive the core traffic demand matrix. If link statistics are available on a per-traffic class basis, then these techniques can be applied to estimate the per-class of service traffic matrix.

Further details on the options for deriving a core traffic matrix are provided in [TELKAMP1].

Whichever approach is used for determining the core traffic matrix, the next decision that needs to be made is how often to retrieve the measured statistics from the network. The retrieved statistics will normally be in the form of packet and byte counts, which can be used to determine the average traffic demands over the previous sampling interval. The longer the sampling interval, i.e. the less frequently the statistics are retrieved, the greater the possibility that significant variation in the traffic during the sampling interval may be hidden due to the effects of averaging. Conversely, the more frequently the statistics are retrieved, the greater the load on the system retrieving the data, the greater the load on the device being polled, and the greater the polling traffic on the network. Hence, in practice the frequency with which the statistics are retrieved is a balance, which depends upon the size of the network; in backbone networks it is common to collect these statistics every 5, 10, or 15 minutes.

The measured statistics can then be used to determine the traffic demand matrix during each interval. In order to make the subsequent stages of the process manageable, it may be necessary to select some traffic matrices from the collected data set. A number of possible selection criteria could be applied; one possible approach is to sum the individual (i.e. router to router) traffic demands within each interval, and to take the interval that has the greatest total traffic demand, i.e. the peak. Alternatively, in order to be sensitive to outliers (e.g. due to possible measurement errors), a high percentile interval such as the 95th percentile (P-95) could be taken, that is the interval for which more than 95% of the intervals have a lower value. In order to be representative, the total data set should be taken over at least a week, or preferably over a month, to ensure that trends in the traffic demand matrices are captured. In the case of a small network, it might be feasible to use all measurement intervals (e.g. all 288 daily measurements for 5-minute intervals), rather than to only use the peak (or percentile of peak) interval; this will give the most accurate simulation results for the network.

In geographically diverse networks, regional peaks in the traffic demand matrix may occur, such that most links in a specific region are near their daily maximum, at a time of the day when the total traffic in the network is not at its maximum. In a global network for example, in morning office hours in Europe, the European region may be busy, while the North American region is relatively lightly loaded. It is not very easy to detect regional peaks automatically, and one alternative approach is to define administrative capacity planning network regions (e.g. USA, Europe, Asia), and apply the previously described procedure per region, to give a selected per region traffic matrix.

Once the traffic matrix has been determined, other factors may need to be taken into account, such as anticipated traffic growth. Capacity planning will typically be performed looking sufficiently far in advance that new bandwidth could be provisioned before the network loading exceeds acceptable levels. If it takes 3 months to provision or upgrade a new core link, for example, and capacity planning is performed monthly, then the capacity planning process would need to try and predict at least 4 months in advance. If the expected network traffic growth within the next 4 months was 10%, for example, then the current traffic demand matrix would need to be multiplied with a factor of at least 1.1. Service subscription forecasts may be able to provide more granular predictions of future demand growth, possibly predicting the increase of particular traffic demands.

6.1.3 Determine Appropriate Over-provisioning Factors

The derived traffic matrices described in the previous section are averages taken over the sample interval, hence they lack information on the variation in traffic demands within each interval. There will invariably be bursts within the measurement interval that are above the average rate; if traffic bursts are sufficiently large temporary congestion may occur, causing delay, jitter, and loss, which may result in the violation of SLA commitments even though the link is on average not 100% utilized. To ensure that bursts above the average do not impact the SLAs, the actual bandwidth may need to be over-provisioned relative to the measure average rates. Hence, a key capacity planning consideration is to determine by how much bandwidth needs to be over-provisioned relative to the measured average rate, in order to meet a defined SLA target for delay, jitter, and loss; we define this as the over-provisioning factor (OP).

The over-provisioning factor required to achieve a particular SLA target depends upon the arrival distribution of the traffic on the link, and the link speed. Opinions remain divided on what arrival distribution describes traffic in IP networks. One view is that traffic is self-similar, which means that it is bursty on many or all timescales, i.e. whatever time period the traffic is measured over the variation in the average rate of the traffic stream is the same. An alternative view is that IP traffic arrivals follow a Poisson (or more generally Markovian) arrival process. For Poisson distributed traffic, the longer the time period over which the traffic stream is measured, the less variation there is in the average rate of the traffic stream. Conversely, the shorter the time interval over which the stream is measured, the greater the visibility of burst or the burstiness of the traffic stream. The differences in the resulting measured average utilization between self-similar and Poisson traffic, when measured over different timescales, are shown in Figure 6.3.

For Poisson traffic, queuing theory shows that as link speeds increase and traffic is more highly aggregated, queuing delays reduce for a given level of utilization. For self-similar traffic, however, if the traffic is truly bursty at all timescales, the queuing delay would not decrease with increased traffic aggregation. However, while views on whether IP network traffic tends toward self-similar [PAXON, SAHINOGLU], or Poisson [CAO, ZHANG] are still split, this does not fundamentally impact the capacity planning methodology we are describing. Rather, the impact of these observations is that, for high-speed links, the over-provisioning factor required to achieve a specified SLA target would

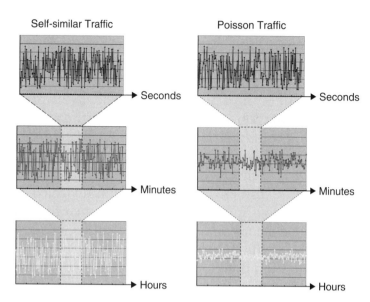

Figure 6.3 Self-similar versus Poisson traffic

need to be significantly greater for self-similar traffic, than for Poisson traffic.

Caveat Lector. A number of studies, both theoretical and empirical, have sought to quantify the bandwidth provisioning required to achieve a particular target for delay, jitter, and loss [FRALEIGH, BONALD, CHARNY, CAO, TELKAMP2], although none of these studies has yet been accepted as definitive. In the rest of this section, by way of example, we use the results attained in the study described in [TELKAMP2], to illustrate the capacity planning methodology. We chose these results because they probably represent the most widely used guidance with respect to core network over-provisioning.

In order to investigate bandwidth provisioning requirements, the authors of [TELKAMP2] captured a number of sets of packet level measurements from an operational IP backbone, carrying Internet and VPN traffic. The traces were used in simulation to determine the bursting and queuing of traffic at small timescales over this interval, to identify the relationship between measures of link utilization that can be easily obtained with capacity planning techniques (e.g. 5-minute average utilizations), and queuing delays experienced in much smaller timeframes,

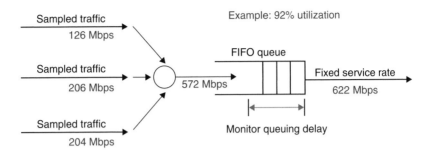

Figure 6.4   Queuing simulation from [TELKAMP2]

in order to determine the over-provisioning factors required to achieve various SLA targets. By using traces of actual traffic they avoided the need to make assumptions about the nature of the traffic distribution.

Each set of packet measurements or "trace" contained timestamps in microseconds of the arrival time for every packet on a link, over an interval of minutes. The traces, each of different average rates, were then used in a simulation where multiple traces were multiplexed together and the resulting trace was run through a simulated fixed speed queue, e.g. at 622 Mbps, as shown in Figure 6.4.

In the example in Figure 6.4, three traces with 5-minute average rates of 126 Mbps, 206 Mbps, and 240 Mbps respectively are multiplexed together resulting in a trace with a 5 minute average rate of 572 Mbps, which is run through a 622 Mbps queue, i.e. at a 5-minute average utilization of 92%. The queue depth was monitored during the simulation to determine how much queuing delay was experienced. This process was then repeated, with different mixes of traffic; as each mix had a different average utilization, multiple data points were produced for a specific interface speed.

After performing this process for multiple interface speeds, results were derived showing the relationship between average link utilization and the probability of queuing delay. The graph in Figure 6.5 uses the results of this study to show the relationship between the measured 5-minute average link utilization and queuing delay for a number of link speeds. The delay value shown is the P99.9 delay, meaning that 999 out of 1000 packets will have a delay caused by queuing which is lower than this value.

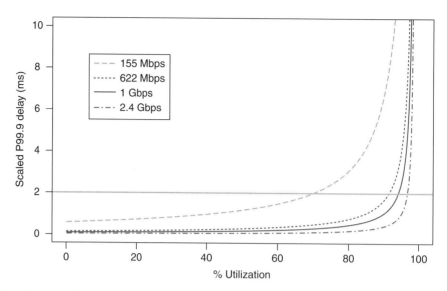

Figure 6.5 Queuing simulation results from [TELKAMP2]

The x-axis in Figure 6.5 represents the 5-minute average link utilization; the y-axis represents the P99.9 delay. The lines show fitted functions to the simulation results for various link speeds, from 155 Mbps to 2.5 Gbps. Note that other relationships would result if the measured utilization was averaged over longer time periods, e.g. 10 minutes or 15 minutes, as in these cases there may be greater variations that are hidden by averaging, and hence lower average utilizations would be needed to achieve the same delay. The results in Figure 6.5 show that for the same relative levels of utilization, lower delays are experiences for 1 Gbps links than for 622 Mbps links, i.e. the level of over-provisioning required to achieve a particular delay target reduces as link bandwidth increases, which is indicative of Poisson traffic.

Taking these results as an example, we can use them to determine the over-provisioning factor that is required to achieve particular SLA objectives. For example, if we assume that Diffserv is not deployed in the core network and want to achieve a target P99.9 queuing delay of 2 ms on a 155 Mbps link, then from Figure 6.5, the 5-minute average link utilization should not be higher than approximately 70% or ~109 Mbps, i.e. an OP of 1/0.7 = 1.42 is required, meaning that the provisioned link bandwidth should be at least 1.42 times the 5-minute average link utilization. To achieve the same objective for a 1 Gbps link the 5-minute average utilization should be no more than ~96% or ~960 Mbps (i.e. OP = 1.04). Although the study from [TELKAMP2] did not focus on voice traffic, in similar studies by the same authors for VoIP-only traffic (with silence suppression) the OP factors required to achieve the same delay targets were similar.

We can apply the same principle on a per-class basis where Diffserv is deployed. To assure a P99.9 queuing delay of 1 ms for a class serviced with an assured forwarding (AF) PHB providing a minimum bandwidth assurance of 622 Mbps (i.e. 25% of a 2.5 Gbps link), the 5-minute average utilization for the class should not be higher than approximately 85% or ~529 Mbps. Considering another example, to assure a P99.9 queuing delay of 500 μs for a class serviced with an expedited forwarding (EF) per-hop behavior (PHB) implemented with a strict priority queue on a 2.5 Gbps link, as the scheduler servicing rate of the strict priority queue is 2.5 Gbps, the 5-minute average utilization for the class should not be higher than approximately 92% or ~2.3 Gbps (i.e. OP = 1.09) of the link rate. Note that these results are for queuing delay only and exclude the possible delay impact on EF traffic due to the scheduler and the interface FIFO as described in Chapter 2, Section 2.2.4.1.3.

The delay that has been discussed so far is *per-link* and not end-to-end across the core. In most cases, traffic will traverse multiple links in the network, and hence will potentially be subject to queuing delays multiple times. Based upon the results from [TELKAMP2], the P99.9 delay was not additive over multiple hops; rather, the table in Figure 6.6 shows the delay "multiplication factor" experienced over a number of hops, relative to the delay over a single hop.

If the delay objective across the core is known, the over-provisioning factor that needs to be maintained per-link can be determined. The core delay objective is divided by the multiplication factor from the table in Figure 6.6 to find the per-hop delay objective. This delay can then be looked up in the graphs in Figure 6.5 to find the maximum utilization for a specific link capacity that will meet this per-hop queuing delay objective. Consider for example, a network comprising

Number of hops	Delay multiplication factor
1	1.0
2	1.7
3	1.9
4	2.2
5	2.5
6	2.8
7	3.0
8	3.3

Figure 6.6 P99.9 delay multiplication factor

155 Mbps links with a P99.9 delay objective across the core network of 10 ms, and a maximum of 8 hops. From Figure 6.5, the 8 hops cause a multiplication of the per-link number by 3.3, so the per-link objective becomes 10 ms/3.3 = 3 ms. From Figure 6.6, the 3 ms line intersects with the 155 Mbps utilization curve at 80%. So the conclusion is that the 5-minute average utilization on the 155 Mbps links in the network should not be more than approximately 80% or ~124 Mbps (i.e. OP = 1.25) to achieve the goal of 10 ms delay across the core.

6.1.4 Simulation and Analysis

After obtaining the demand matrix, allowing for growth, and determining the over-provisioning factors required to achieve specific SLA targets, the final step in the capacity planning process is to overlay the traffic demands onto the network topology. This requires both an understanding of the network routing model – e.g. whether an interior gateway routing protocol (IGP), such as ISIS or OSPF, is used or whether MPLS traffic engineering is used – and an understanding of the logical network topology – i.e. link metrics and routing protocol areas – in order to understand the routing through the network that demands would take and hence to correctly map the demands to the topology. There are a number of commercially available tools, which can perform this function. Some such tools can also run failure case simulations, which consider the loading on the links in network element failures; it is common to model for single element failures, where an element could be a link, a node, or a shared risk link group (SRLG). SRLGs can be used to group together links that might fail simultaneously; to represent the failure of unprotected interfaces sharing a common linecard or circuits sharing a common fiber duct, for example. The concept of SRLGs can also be applied to more than just links, grouping links and nodes which may represent a shared risk, in order to consider what would happen to the network loading in the presence of the failure of a complete POP, for example.

The results of the simulation provide indications of the expected loading of the links in the network; this could be the aggregate loading or the per-class loading if Diffserv is deployed. The forecasted link loadings can then be compared against the provisioned link capacity, taking the calculated overprovisioning factors into account, to determine the future bandwidth provisioning plan required to achieve the desired SLAs. The capacity planner can then use this information to identify links which may be overloaded, such that SLAs will be violated, or areas where more capacity is provisioned than is actually needed.

6.2 IP Traffic Engineering

Capacity planning, as discussed in the proceeding section, is the process of ensuring that sufficient bandwidth is provisioned to assure that the committed core SLA targets can be met. IP traffic engineering is the logical process of manipulating traffic on an IP network to make better use of the network capacity, by making use of capacity that would otherwise be unused, for example. Hence, traffic engineering is a tool that can be used to ensure that the available network capacity is appropriately provisioned.

We contrast traffic engineering to network engineering, which is the physical process of manipulating a network to suit the traffic load, by putting in a new link between two POPs to support a traffic demand between them, for example. Clearly, network engineering and traffic engineering are linked; however, in this section we focus on the options for traffic engineering in an IP network. The outcome of the capacity planning process described in the previous section may drive the need for traffic engineering within a network.

In IP-based networks, traffic engineering is often considered synonymous with MPLS traffic engineering (TE) in particular, which is described in Section 6.2.3; however, there are other approaches in IP networks, including traffic engineering through the manipulation of Interior Gateway Routing Protocol (IGP) metrics – which is described in Section 6.2.2.

6.2.1 The Problem

In conventional IP networks IGPs such as OSPF [RFC2328] and IS-IS [RFC1142] forward IP packets on the shortest cost path toward the destination IP subnet address of each IP packet. The computation of the shortest cost path is based upon a simple additive metric (also known as weight or cost), where each link has an applied metric, and the cost for a path is the sum of the link metrics on the path. Availability of network resources, such as bandwidth, is not taken into account and, consequently, traffic can aggregate on the shortest (i.e. lowest cost) path, potentially causing links on the shortest path to be congested while links on alternative paths are under-utilized. This property of conventional IP routing protocols, of traffic aggregation on the shortest path, can cause suboptimal use of network resources, and can consequently impact the SLAs that can be offered, or require more network capacity than is optimally required.

Consider, for example, the network in Figure 6.7, where each link is 2.5 Gbps and each link has the same metric (assume a metric of 1). If there were a traffic demand of 1 Gbps from R1 to R8, and a traffic demand of 2 Gbps from R2 to R8, then the IGP would pick the same route for both traffic demands, i.e. R1/R2 → R3 → R4 → R7 → R8, because it has a metric of 4 (summing the metric of 1 for each of the links traversed) and hence is the shortest path.

Therefore, in this example, the decision to route both traffic demands by the top path (R3 → R4 → R7) may result in the path being

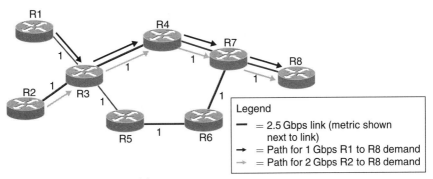

Figure 6.7   Traffic engineering: the problem

congested, with a total offered load of 3 Gbps, while there is capacity available on the bottom path (R3 → R5 → R6 → R7). Traffic engineering aims to provide a solution to this problem.

The problem of traffic engineering can be defined as a mathematical optimization problem; that is, a computational problem in which the objective is to find the best of all possible solutions. Given a fixed network topology and a fixed source-to-destination traffic demand matrix to be carried, the optimization problem could be defined as determining the routing of flows that makes most effective use of (either aggregate or per-class) capacity. In order to solve this problem, however, it is important to define what is meant by the objective "most effective:" this could be to minimize the maximum link/class utilization in normal network working case conditions, i.e. when there are no network element failures. Alternatively the optimization objective could be to minimize the maximum link/class utilization under network element failure case conditions; typically single element (i.e. link, node, or SRLG) failure conditions are considered.

In considering the deployment of traffic engineering mechanisms, it is imperative that the primary optimization objective is defined, in order to understand what benefits the different options for traffic engineering can provide, and where traffic engineering will not help, but rather more bandwidth is required. Other optimization objectives are possible, such as minimizing propagation delay; however, if considered these are normally secondary objectives.

If we apply the primary optimization objective of minimizing the maximum link utilization in network working case (i.e. normal operating) conditions to the network shown in Figure 6.7 then the solution would be to route some subset of the traffic over the top path (R3 → R4 → R7) and the remainder over the bottom path (R3 → R5 → R6 → R7) such that congestion on the top path is prevented. If, however, we apply the primary optimization objective of minimizing the maximum link utilization during single network element failure case conditions, then on the failure of the link between R3 and R4, for example, both traffic demands R1 to R8 and R2 to R8 will be rerouted onto the bottom path (R3 → R5 → R6 → R7), which would be congested, as shown in Figure 6.8.

The example in Figure 6.8 is an illustration that traffic engineering cannot create capacity and that in some topologies, and possibly dependent upon the optimization objective, traffic engineering may not help. In network topologies that have only two paths available in normal network working case conditions, such as ring-based topologies, it is not possible to apply traffic engineering with a primary optimization objective of minimizing the maximum link utilization during network element failure case conditions; there is no scope for sophisticated traffic engineering decisions in network failure case conditions; if a link on one path fails, the other path is taken. In these cases, if congestion occurs during failure conditions then more capacity is simply required. More meshed

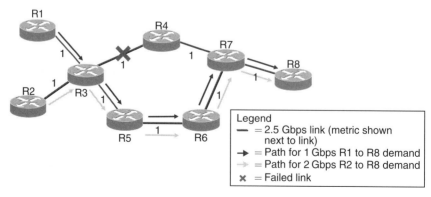

Figure 6.8 Failure case optimization

network topologies may allow scope for traffic engineering in network element failure case conditions.

The chief benefit of traffic engineering is one of cost saving. Traffic engineering gives the network designer flexibility in how to manage their backbone bandwidth in order to achieve their SLAs. The more effective use of bandwidth potentially allows higher SLA targets to be offered with the existing backbone bandwidth. Alternatively, it offers the potential to achieve the existing SLA targets with less backbone bandwidth or to delay the time until bandwidth upgrades are required. The following conditions can all be drivers for the deployment of traffic engineering mechanisms:

- *Network asymmetry.* Asymmetrical network topologies can often lead to traffic being aggregated on the shortest path while other viable paths are under-utilized. Network designers will often try to ensure that networks are symmetrical such that where parallel paths exist, they are of equal cost and hence the load can be balanced across them using conventional IGPs, which support load balancing across multiple equal cost paths. Ensuring network symmetry, however, is not always possible due to economic or topological constraints; traffic engineering offers potential benefits in these cases.

- *Unexpected demands.* In the presence of unexpected traffic demands (e.g. due to some new popular content), there may not be enough capacity on the shortest path (or paths) to satisfy the demand. There may be capacity available on non-shortest paths, however, and hence traffic engineering can provide benefit.

- *Long bandwidth lead-times.* There may be instances when new traffic demands are expected and new capacity is required to satisfy the demand, but is not available in suitable timescales. In these cases, traffic engineering can be used to make use of available bandwidth on non-shortest path links.

The potential benefit of different approaches to traffic engineering can be quantified by using a holistic approach to capacity planning, such as described in Section 6.1, which is able to overlay the network traffic matrix on the network topology, while simulating the relative network loading taking into account different traffic engineering schemes. A network-by-network analysis is required to determine whether the potential TE benefit will justify the additional deployment and operational cost associated with the deployment of these technologies.

Traffic engineering can potentially be performed at layer 2 (i.e. by traffic engineering the underlying transport infrastructure) or at layer 3. In focussing on layer 3, in the following sections we consider possible approaches for IP traffic engineering, and consider traffic engineering at layer 2 to be an inception of network engineering when considered from a layer 3 perspective.

6.2.2 IGP Metric-based Traffic Engineering

The tactical and ad hoc tweaking of IGP metrics to change the routing of traffic and relieve congested hotspots has long been practiced in IP backbone networks. For a long time, however, this approach was not considered viable for systematic network-wide traffic engineering and it was often cited that changing the link metrics just moves the problem of congestion around the network. If we consider the network from Figure 6.7, by changing the metric of the link from R3 to R4 from 1 to 3, as can be seen in Figure 6.9, the traffic demands both from R1 to R and from R2 to R8 are now routed over the bottom path

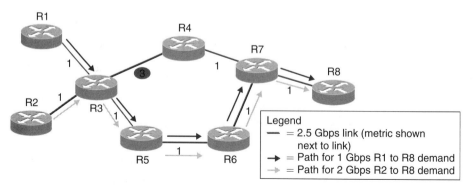

Figure 6.9 Changing link metrics moves congestion

(R3 → R5 → R6 → R7), which is now the least cost path (cost of 5). In this case the congestion has moved to the bottom path.

If instead, the metric of the link from R3 to R4 was changed from 1 to 2 (rather than 1 to 3), however, then the top path (R3 → R4 → R7) and the bottom path (R3 → R5 → R6 → R7) would have equal path costs of 5, as shown in Figure 6.10.

Where equal cost IGP paths exist, equal costs multipath (ECMP) algorithms are used to balance the load across the equal cost paths. There are no standards defining how ECMP algorithms should balance traffic across equal cost paths and different vendors may implement different algorithms. ECMP algorithms typically, however, perform a hash function on fields in the header of the received IP packets to determine which one of the paths should be used for a particular packet. A common approach is to perform the hash function using the 5-tuple of IP protocol, source IP address, destination IP address, source UDP/TCP port, and destination UDP/TCP as inputs. The result of such a hash function is that load balancing across equal cost paths would be achieved for general distributions of IP addresses and ports. Such approaches also ensure that packets within a single flow are consistently hashed to the same path, which is important to prevent resequencing within a flow due to the adverse impact that packet re-ordering can have on the performance of some applications (this is discussed in more detail in Chapter 1, Section 1.2.5).

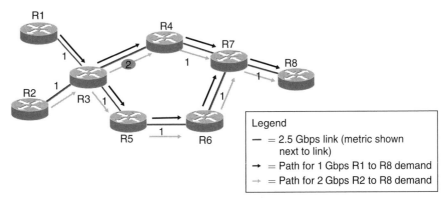

Figure 6.10 Equal IGP path costs

If such an ECMP algorithm were used in the example shown in Figure 6.10, and assuming a general distribution of addresses and ports, the 3 Gbps aggregate demand from R1 and R2 to R8, would be evenly distributed with approximately 1.5 Gbps on the top path and approximately 1.5 Gbps on the bottom path, and therefore the bandwidth would be used effectively and congestion would be avoided. Hence, the mantra that tweaking IGP metrics just moves the problem of congestion around the network is a generalization that is not always true in practice. For some symmetrical network topologies and matrices of traffic, ECMP algorithms may be able to distribute the load effectively without the need for other traffic engineering approaches at all.

In recognition of the possible application of metric-based traffic engineering, there has been a significant recent increase in research in the approach of systematic (i.e. network-wide) traffic engineering by manipulating IGP metrics [FORTZ1, LORENZ, BURIOL, ERICSSON, AMEUR]. Further, IGP metric-based traffic engineering has been realized in the development of automated planning tools, which take inputs of the network logical (i.e. IGP) and physical topology, together with the network traffic demand matrix and derive a more optimal set of link metrics based upon a defined optimization goal. These optimization goals may be to minimize the maximum utilization on aggregate, or per-class.

IGP metric-based traffic engineering provides less granular traffic control capabilities than MPLS traffic engineering (see Section 6.2.3). The effectiveness of IGP metric-based traffic engineering is dependent upon the network topology, the traffic demand matrix, and the optimization goal. [FORTZ2] shows that, for the proposed AT&T WorldNet backbone, they found weight settings that performed within a few percent of the optimal general routing, which is where the flow for each demand is optimally distributed[2] over all paths between source and destination. Studies by [GOUS] conclude that in the six networks they study, metric-based TE can be ~80–90% as efficient as the theoretical optimal general routing. Further, they surmise that the greatest relative difference in performance between IGP metric-based traffic engineering and traffic engineering via explicit routing (such as provided by MPLS traffic engineering) occurs in large networks with heterogeneous link speeds, i.e. where ECMP cannot be readily used to split traffic between parallel circuits with different capacities.

6.2.3   MPLS Traffic Engineering

Unlike conventional IP routing, which uses pure destination-based forwarding, multiprotocol label switching (MPLS), traffic engineering (TE) uses the implicit MPLS characteristic of separation between the data plane (also known as the forwarding plane) and the control plane to allow routing decisions to be made on criteria other than the destination address in the IP packet header, such as available link bandwidth. MPLS TE provides constraint-based path computation and explicit routing capabilities at layer 3, which can be used to divert traffic away from congested parts of the network to links where bandwidth is available and hence make more optimal use of available capacity. Label switched paths (LSPs), which are termed "traffic engineering tunnels" in the context of MPLS TE, are used to steer traffic through the network allowing links to be used which are not on the IGP shortest path to the destination.

It is noted that, as well as being used to solve the traffic engineering problem, MPLS TE has other applications including admission control (as described in Chapter 4, Section 4.4.6), route pinning,[3] and MPLS TE Fast Reroute (see Chapter 2, Section 2.6).

6.2.3.1   MPLS TE Example Tunnel Establishment

Consider the network in Figure 6.11, where every link is 2.5 Gbps and each has the same metric (assume a metric of 1), and where a single MPLS TE tunnel of 1 Gbps is already established from LSR1 to LSR8, using the path LSR1 → LSR3 → LSR4 → LSR7 → LSR8, because it is the shortest path (path cost = 4) with available bandwidth. In this example, it is assumed that the entire network has been enabled for MPLS TE, and that the full bandwidth on each interface is used for MPLS TE.

The following example sequence of events considers the establishment of another TE tunnel, a 2 Gbps tunnel from LSR2 to LSR8.

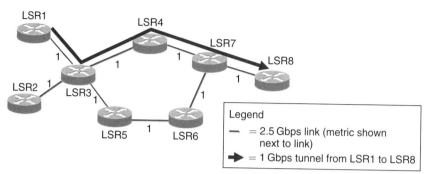

Figure 6.11   MPLS TE example tunnel establishment

1. *Resource/policy information distribution.* Each router within the network floods information on the available bandwidth resources for its connected links, together with administrative policy constraint information, throughout the network by means of extensions to link-state based IGP routing protocols such as IS-IS [RFC3784] and OSPF [RFC3630].

    As TE tunnels are unidirectional, each TE-enabled router maintains a pool of available (i.e. currently unused) TE bandwidth in the egress direction for each interface that it has. Considering LSR3 for example, because the tunnel from LSR1 to LSR8 has already reserved 1 Gbps of bandwidth on the interface to LSR4, LSR3 will only advertise 1.5 Gbps worth of available bandwidth for that interface. For all of its other interfaces, LSR3 will advertise 2.5 Gbps of available bandwidth.

2. *Constraint-based path computation.* All of the routers within the MPLS TE area will receive the information on the available network resources, advertised via IS-IS or OSPF. With MPLS TE, tunnel paths can be specified manually, but more commonly are either dynamically calculated online in a distributed fashion by the TE tunnel sources (known as tunnel "*head-ends*") themselves or determined by an offline centralized function (also know as a tunnel server or path computation element) which then specifies the explicit tunnel path a head-end should use for a particular tunnel. With either approach, constraint-based routing is performed using

a constraint-based shortest path first (CSPF) algorithm to determine the path that a particular tunnel will take based upon a fit between the available network bandwidth resources (and optionally policy constraints) and the required bandwidth (and policies) for that tunnel. This CSPF algorithm is similar to a conventional IGP shortest path first (SPF) algorithm, but also takes into account bandwidth and administrative constraints, pruning links from the topology if they advertised insufficient resources, i.e. not enough bandwidth for the tunnel, or if they violate tunnel policy constraints. The shortest (i.e. lowest cost) path is then selected from the remaining topology. Whether online or offline path calculation is used, the output is an explicit route object (ERO) which defines the hop-by-hop path the tunnel should take and which is handed over to RSVP in order to signal the tunnel label switched path (LSP).

We assume online path calculation by the tunnel head-end, in this case LSR2. There are two possible paths from LSR2 to LSR8, either the top path (LSR2 → LSR3 → LSR4 → LSR7 → LSR8) or the bottom path (LSR2 → LSR3 → LSR5 → LSR6 → LSR7 → LSR8). As the tunnel from LSR2 to LSR8 is for 2 Gbps, there is insufficient bandwidth currently available (1.5 Gbps only) on the links from LSR3 → LSR4 and from LSR4 → LSR7 and hence the top path is discounted by the CSPF algorithm. Therefore, in this example the bottom path is the only possible path for the tunnel from LSR2 to LSR8, and output of the CSPF algorithm is an ERO which specifies the IP addresses of the hops on the path, i.e. LSR2 → LSR3 → LSR5 → LSR6 → LSR7 → LSR8.

3. *RSVP for tunnel signaling.* The Resource ReSerVation Protocol (RSVP) [RFC2205], with enhancements for MPLS TE [RFC3209], is used to signal the TE tunnel. RSVP is used differently in the context of MPLS TE than it is for per flow admission control, as described in Chapter 4, Section 4.4.1.

RSVP uses two signaling messages, a Path message and a Resv message.

   i. The Path message carries the ERO and other information including the requested bandwidth for the tunnel, which is

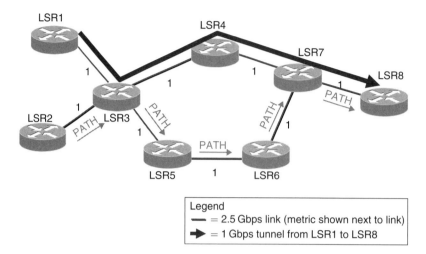

Figure 6.12 MPLS TE example tunnel establishment: Step 3a

used for admission control. An RSVP Path message is sent from the tunnel head-end to the tunnel tail-end, as shown in Figure 6.12, explicitly routed hop-by-hop using the ERO.

At each router that receives the Path message an admission control decision is made to verify that the outbound interface that will be used to forward the Path message to the next hop defined by the ERO, has sufficient resources available to accept the requested bandwidth for the tunnel. This admission control decision may seem redundant as the CSPF algorithm has already picked a path with sufficient bandwidth; however, it is required because it is possible that the head-end router may have performed the CSPF algorithm on information which is now out of date, for example, if another tunnel has been set up in the intervening period since the tunnel path was calculated.

If the admission control decision is successful, the path message is forwarded to the next hop defined by the ERO, until the path message reaches the tail-end router. MPLS TE supports the concept of pre-emption and a lower priority tunnel may be pre-empted to allow a higher priority tunnel to be set up. If the admission control

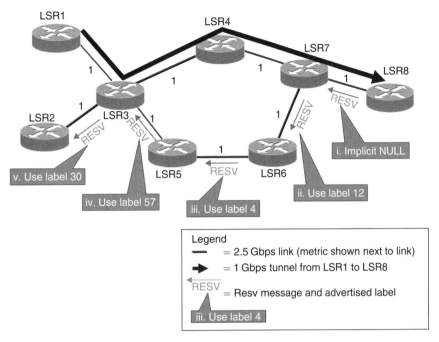

Figure 6.13   MPLS TE example tunnel establishment: Step 3b – label advertisement

decision is unsuccessful at any hop, a PathErr message is returned to the tunnel head-end.

It is noted that where RSVP is used for per flow admission control, rather than for MPLS TE tunnel signaling, the admission control decision is made in response to the receipt of the Resv message.

If the tail-end receives the Path message, then the admission control decisions must have been successful at each hop on the tunnel path. In response, the tail-end router originates a reservation (Resv) message which follows the path defined by the ERO in reverse in order to establish the LSP that defines the tunnel, as shown in Figure 6.13.

At each hop on the tunnel path that receives the Resv message, the tunnel reservation is confirmed. In order to set up the tunnel LSP, the Resv message is then forwarded to the upstream (i.e. closer to head-end) neighbor on the tunnel path, together with MPLS label value that this router expects to be used for traffic on the tunnel received from the upstream neighbor.

In this example, penultimate hop popping (PHP) is assumed and LSR8, as the final hop on the tunnel path, advertises an implicit null label to LSR7 accordingly. LSR7 then advertises label value 12 to LSR6, and so on, until the Resv message reaches the tunnel head-end. This is an example of downstream on demand label binding with upstream label distribution, where upstream/downstream is with reference to the direction of the flow packets on the LSP.

4. *Assigning traffic to tunnels*. When the Resv message reaches the head-end, the tunnel LSP has been successfully established and it can be used for traffic forwarding. There are a number of ways to determine when traffic should use the TE tunnel rather than the conventional IGP path. The simplest is to use static routing with a static route defining that traffic to a particular destination subnet address should use the tunnel rather than the conventional IGP route. Some vendors also support the capability to automatically calculate IP routes to forward traffic over MPLS TE tunnels, by adapting Dijkstra's SPF algorithm as described in [RFC3906].

Having decided to forward some traffic onto the tunnel, the head-end router, in this case LSR2 assigns traffic to that tunnel by forwarding it on the tunnel LSP. It forwards traffic on the TE tunnel by sending it toward LSR3 with label value 30 as shown in Figure 6.14.

LSR3 receives the labeled packet, and label switches it to LSR5 swapping the label from 30 to 57. Note that LSR3 uses only the label to determine how to forward the packet, i.e. it does not look at the underlying IP destination address. The tunneled packet continues on the LSP until it reaches LSR7, which as the penultimate hop, pops off the outer label and forwards it to LSR8, which is the tunnel tail-end. If a label stack is not used, the tail-end router looks at the IP destination address to determine how to forward the received packet; if a label stack is used (e.g. in the context of BGP MPLS VPNs as per RFC4364), the tail-end router uses the

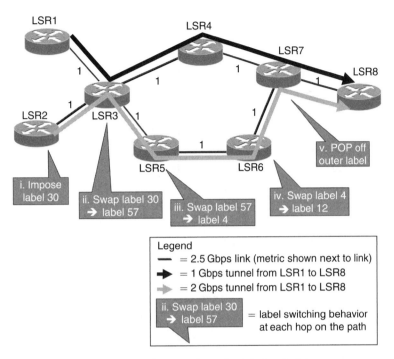

Figure 6.14   MPLS TE example tunnel establishment: Step 4 – label switching

outermost of the remaining labels to determine how to forward the received packet.

5. *TE tunnel control and maintenance.* Periodic RSVP Path/Resv messages maintain the tunnel state. Unlike tunnel setup, Path/Resv messages used for tunnel maintenance are sent independently and asynchronously.

The tunnel head-end can tear down a tunnel by sending a PathTear message. If a network element (link or node) on the tunnel path should fail, the adjacent upstream neighboring router on the tunnel path will send a PathErr message to the head-end, which will then attempt to recalculate a new tunnel path around the failed element. Similarly, if a tunnel is pre-empted, a PathErr message will be sent to the head-end, which will then attempt to recalculate a new tunnel path where bandwidth is available.

6.2.3.2 Diffserv-aware MPLS Traffic Engineering

MPLS TE and Diffserv can be deployed concurrently in an IP backbone, with TE determining the path that traffic takes on aggregate based upon aggregate bandwidth constraints, and Diffserv mechanisms being used on each link for differential scheduling of packets on a per-class of service basis. TE and Diffserv are orthogonal technologies which can be used in concert for combined benefit: TE allows distribution of traffic on non-shortest paths for more efficient use of available bandwidth, while Diffserv allows SLA differentiation on a per-class basis. As it was initially defined and has been described in the previous section, however, MPLS TE computes tunnel paths for aggregates across all traffic classes and hence traffic from different classes may use the same TE tunnels. In this form MPLS TE is aware of only a single aggregate pool of available bandwidth per link and is unaware of what specific link bandwidth resources are allocated to which queues, and hence to which classes.

Diffserv-aware MPLS TE (DS-TE) extends the basic capabilities of TE to allow constraint-based path computation, explicit routing and admission control to be performed separately for different classes of service. DS-TE provides the capability to enforce different bandwidth constraints for different classes of traffic through the addition of more pools of available bandwidth on each link. These bandwidth pools are sub-pools of the aggregate TE bandwidth constraint, i.e. the sub-pools are a portion of the aggregate pool. This allows a bandwidth sub-pool to be used for a particular class of traffic, such that constraint-based routing and admission control can be performed for tunnels carrying traffic of that class, with the aggregate pool used to enforce an aggregate constraint across all classes of traffic. There are two different models that define how the sub-pool bandwidth constraints are applied:

- *Maximum allocation model.* [RFC4127] defines the maximum allocation bandwidth constraints model (MAM) for Diffserv-aware MPLS TE. With the MAM, independent sub-pool constraints can be applied to each class, and an aggregate constraint can be applied across all classes.

- *Russian doll model.* [RFC4125] defines the Russian dolls bandwidth constraints model (RDM) for Diffserv-aware MPLS TE. With the RDM, a hierarchy of constraints is defined, which consists of an aggregate constraint (global pool), and a number of sub-constraints (sub-pools) where constraint 1 is a sub-pool of constraint 0, constraint 2 is a sub-pool of constraint 1, and so on.

The choice of which bandwidth allocation model to use depends upon the way in which bandwidth allocation and pre-emption will be managed between tunnels of different classes. It is noted that if traffic engineering is required for only one of the deployed traffic classes, e.g. for EF traffic only, then DS-TE is not required and standard single bandwidth pool TE is sufficient.

In support of DS-TE, extensions have been added to IS-IS and OSPF [RFC4124] to advertise the available sub-pool bandwidth per link. In addition, the TE constraint-based routing algorithms have been enhanced for DS-TE in order to take into account the constraint of available sub-pool bandwidth in computing the path of sub-pool tunnels. RSVP has also been extended [RFC4124] to indicate the constraint model and the bandwidth pool, for which a tunnel is being signaled.

As described in Section 6.1.3, setting an upper bound on the EF class (e.g. VoIP) utilization per link is necessary to bound the delay for that class and therefore to ensure that the SLA can be met. DS-TE can be used to assure that this upper bound is not exceeded. For example, consider the network in Figure 6.15, where each link is 2.5 Gbps and an IGP and TE metric value of one is applied to each link.

DS-TE could be used to ensure that traffic is routed over the network so that, on every link, there is never more than a defined percentage of the link capacity for EF class traffic, while there can be up to 100% of the link capacity for EF and AF class traffic in total. In this example, for illustration we assume that the defined maximum percentage for EF traffic per link is 50%. LSR1 is sending an aggregate

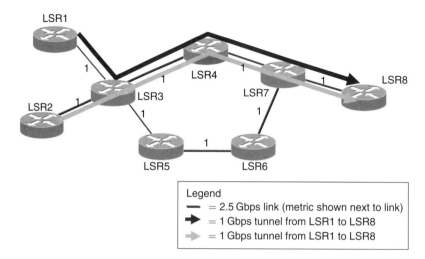

Figure 6.15 DS-TE deployment example 1

of 1 Gbps of traffic to LSR8, and R2 is also sending an aggregate of 1 Gbps of traffic to LSR8. In this case, both the IGP (i.e. if TE were not deployed) and non-Diffserv aware TE would pick the same route. The IGP would pick the top route (R1/R2 → R3 → R4 → R5 → R8) because it is the shortest path (with a metric of 4). Assuming 1 Gbps tunnels were used from both LSR1 and LSR2 to LSR8, TE would also pick the top route, because it is the shortest path that has sufficient bandwidth available (metric of 4, 2.5 Gbps bandwidth available, 2 Gbps required). The decision to route both traffic aggregates via the top path may not seem appropriate if we examine the composition of the aggregate traffic flows.

If each of the aggregate flows were composed of 250 Mbps of VoIP traffic and 750 Mbps of standard data traffic, then in this case the total VoIP traffic load on the top links would be 500 Mbps, which is within our EF class per link bound of 50% = 1 Gbps. If, however, each traffic aggregate is comprised of 750 Mbps of VoIP and 250 Mbps of standard data traffic then such routing would aggregate 1.5 Gbps of VoIP traffic on the R3 → R4 → R5 links, thereby exceeding our EF class bound of 50%. DS-TE can be used to overcome this problem if, for example, each link is configured with an available aggregate bandwidth pool of 2.5 Gbps,

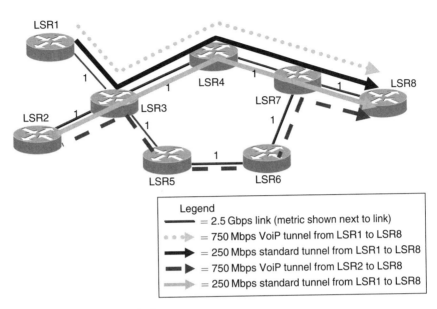

Figure 6.16 DS-TE deployment example 2

and an available VoIP class sub-pool bandwidth of 1.25 Gbps (i.e. 50% of 2.5 Gbps). A VoIP class sub-pool tunnel of 750 Mbps is then configured from R1 to R8, together with a standard class aggregate pool tunnel of 250 Mbps. Similarly, from R2 to R8 a VoIP class sub-pool tunnel of 750 Mbps and a standard class aggregate pool tunnel of 250 Mbps are configured from R2 to R8. The DS-TE constraint-based routing algorithm would then route the VoIP sub-pool tunnels to ensure that the 1.25 Gbps bound is not exceeded on any link, and of the tunnels from R1 and R2 to R8, one VoIP sub-pool tunnel would be routed via the top path (R1/R2 → R3 → R4 → R5 → R8) and the other via the bottom path (R1/R2 → R6 → R7 → R5 → R8).[4] In this particular case, there would be enough available bandwidth for both aggregate pool tunnels to be routed via the top path (R1/R2 → R3 → R4 → R5 → R8), which is the shortest path with available aggregate bandwidth, possibly as shown in Figure 6.16, for example.

Hence, DS-TE allows separate route computation and admission control for different classes of traffic, which enables the distribution of EF and AF class load over all available EF and AF class capacity making optimal use of available capacity. It also provides a tool for constraining the class utilization per link to a specified maximum thus ensuring that the class SLAs can be met. In order to provide these benefits, however, the configured bandwidth for the sub-pools must align to the queuing resources that are available for traffic-engineered traffic.

6.2.3.3 MPLS TE Deployment Models and Considerations

MPLS TE can be deployed either in an ad hoc fashion, with selective tunnels configured tactically to move a subset of traffic away from congested links, or systematically, with all backbone traffic transported in TE tunnels.

6.2.3.3.1 Tactical TE Deployment

MPLS TE can be used tactically in order to offload traffic from congestion hotspots; this is an ad hoc approach, aimed at fixing current problems and as such is generally a short-term reactive operational/ engineering process. When used in this way, rather than all traffic being subjected to traffic engineering, TE tunnels are deployed to reroute a subset of the network traffic from a congested part of the network, to a part where there is more capacity. This can be done by explicitly defining the path that a tunnel should take on a head-end router.

Consider Figure 6.17, for example; in this case there are two links of unequal capacity providing the connectivity between two POPs; one 622 Mbps, the other 2.5 Gbps. Using IGP metrics proportional to link capacity, e.g. a link cost of 1 for the 2.5 Gbps links and a link cost of 4 for 622 Mbps link, in normal working case conditions, the bottom path would be the lowest cost path and the top path would remain unused. Hence, even though there is over 3 Gbps of capacity between the POPs, this capacity could not all be used. If, however, two TE tunnels were configured between LSR 1 and LSR 2, one explicitly defined to use the top path and the other the bottom path, then as MPLS TE supports unequal cost load balancing (which normal IGP routing does not), the traffic demand between Router 1 and Router 2 could be balanced over the tunnels in proportion to the bandwidths of those paths, i.e. 1/5 of the total demand using the top path and 4/5 of the total demand on the bottom path.

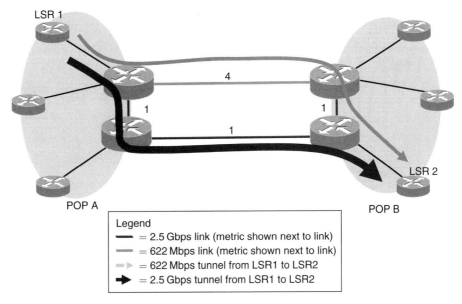

Figure 6.17 Tactical TE deployment – enables unequal cost load balancing

6.2.3.3.2 Systematic TE Deployment

With a systematic TE deployment, all traffic is subjected to traffic engineering within the core; this is a long-term proactive engineering/planning process aimed at cost savings. Such a systematic approach requires that a mesh of TE tunnels be configured, hence one of the key considerations for a systematic MPLS TE deployment is tunnel scaling; a router incurs control plane processing overhead for each tunnel that it has some responsibility for, either as head-end, mid-point, or tail-end of that tunnel. The main metrics that are considered with respect to TE tunnel scalability are the number of tunnels per head-end and the number of tunnels traversing a tunnel mid-point. We consider the key scaling characteristics of a number of different systematic MPLS TE deployment models:

- *Outer core mesh.* In considering a full mesh from edge-to-edge across the core (i.e. from distribution router to distribution router), as MPLS TE tunnels are unidirectional, two tunnels are required between each pair of edge routers hence $n * (n - 1)$ tunnels are

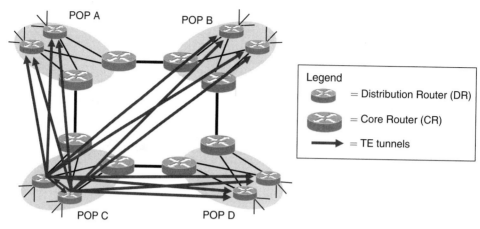

Figure 6.18   Outer core TE mesh

required in total where *n* is the number of edge routers or head-ends. The example in Figure 6.18 shows the tunnels that would be required from the distribution routers within one POP to form a mesh to the distribution routers in other POPs.

If TE is required for *m* classes of traffic each using Diffserv-aware TE then *m * n * (n − 1)* tunnels would be required.

- *Inner core mesh.* Creating a core mesh of tunnels, i.e. from core routers to core routers, can make tunnel scaling independent of the number of distribution routers (there are normally more distribution routers than core routers), as shown in Figure 6.19, which illustrates the tunnels that would be required from the core routers within one POP to form a mesh to the core routers in other POPs.

- *Regional meshes.* Another way of reducing the number of tunnels required and therefore improving the tunnel scalability is to break the topology up into regions of meshed routers; adjacent tunnel meshes would be connected by routers which are part of both meshes, as shown in Figure 6.20, which shows meshes within each of two regions. Although this reduces the number of tunnels required, it may result in less optimal routing and less optimal use of available capacity.

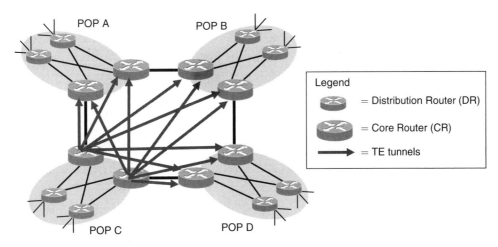

Figure 6.19   Inner core MPLS TE mesh

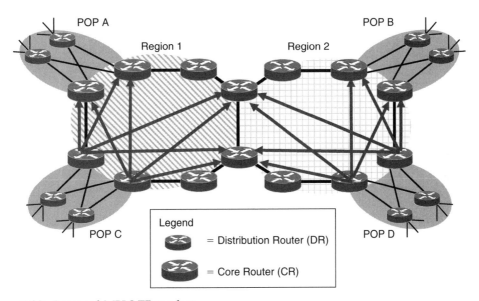

Figure 6.20   Regional MPLS TE meshes

To put these options into context, the largest TE deployments at the time of publication have a full mesh between ~120 head-ends, which results in ~120^2 = ~14 400 tunnels in total with a maximum of ~120 tunnels per head-end and a maximum of ~1500 tunnels traversing a mid-point.

6.2.3.4 Setting Tunnel Bandwidth

Having decided on a particular MPLS TE deployment model, the next most significant decision is how to set the bandwidth requested for TE tunnels. The bandwidth of tunnels is a logical (i.e. control plane) constraint, rather than a physical constraint, hence if the actual tunnel load exceeds the reserved bandwidth, congestion can occur. Conversely, if a tunnel reservation is greater than the actual tunnel load, more bandwidth may be reserved than is required, which may lead to needless rejection of other tunnels and hence underutilization of the network.

The same principles of over-provisioning discussed in Section 6.1.3 could be applied to traffic engineering deployments. The bandwidth pools on each link should be set taking the required over-provisioning ratios into account for that particular link speed. For example, if Diffserv is not deployed in the core network and an OP of 1.42 is determined to be required to achieve a target P99.9 queuing delay of 2 ms on a 155 Mbps link, then the aggregate TE bandwidth pool should be set to 155/1.42 = 109 Mbps. Each tunnel (which represents a traffic demand across the network) should then be sized based upon the measured average tunnel load (or a percentile thereof, as described for the core traffic demand matrices in Section 6.1.2). This will ensure that the measured average aggregate load on each link will be controlled such that the per-link over-provisioning factor is always met, and hence the target SLAs can be achieved, even when there are potentially multiple tunnels that may traverse the link.

Tunnel resizing can be performed online, by the head-end routers themselves, or by an offline system. When online tunnel resizing is used, algorithms run on the head-end routers to automatically and dynamically resize the tunnels which originate from them, based upon some measure of the traffic load on the tunnel over previous measurement periods. Simple algorithms can lead to inefficiencies, however. Consider, for example, an algorithm that sizes the tunnel based upon the peak of the 5-minute average tunnel loads in the previous interval; when traffic is ramping up during the day, the algorithm needs to take into account the traffic growth during the next interval, or else it will under-provision the tunnel. Consequently,

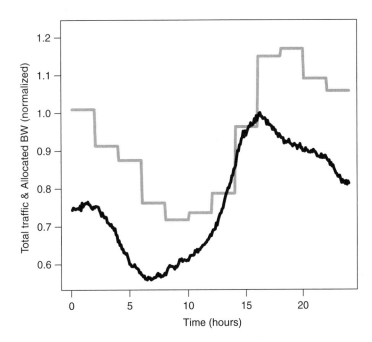

Figure 6.21   Automatic tunnel bandwidth sizing

in the interval following the peak interval of the day, significantly more tunnel bandwidth will be reserved than is necessary, as illustrated by the example in Figure 6.21.

Figure 6.21 plots the total traffic load across all TE tunnels (black line) in a network with a TE tunnel full mesh during a single day. The corresponding sum of the reserved TE tunnel bandwidth is plotted in grey. The tunnel resizing algorithm used in this case resized each tunnel every 2 hours to a multiple of the peak of the 5-minute average load for that tunnel experienced during the preceding 2 hour period. In order to cope with the rapid ramp up in traffic load before the daily peak, a high multiple needed to be used; in this case the multiple was 1.2 times. As a consequence, the reserved tunnel bandwidth is significantly greater than the actual tunnel load during the period after the daily peak load, due to the resizing lag. Hence, tunnel resizing algorithms are most efficient when they rely on a longer history of measurements for tunnel sizing, i.e. day, week, or month.

References[5]

[AMEUR] W. Ben Ameur, N. Michel, E. Gourdin and B. Liau, Routing strategies for IP networks, *Telektronikk*, 2/3, pp. 145–158, 2001

[BONALD] Thomas Bonald, Alexandre Proutiere, James Roberts, Statistical Guarantees for Streaming Flows Using Expedited Forwarding, *INFOCOM 2001*

[BURIOL] L. S. Buriol, M. G. C. Resende, C. C. Ribeiro, and M. Thorup, A memetic algorithm for OSPF routing, in *Proceedings of the 6th INFORMS Telecom*, pp. 187–188, 2002

[CAO] Cao, J., W.S. Cleveland, D. Lin, D.X. Sun, Internet Traffic Tends Toward Poisson and Independent as the Load Increases, in *Nonlinear Estimation and Classification*, New York, Springer-Verlag, 2002

[CHARNY] Anna Charny and Jean-Yves Le Boudec, Delay bounds in a network with aggregate scheduling, in *First International Workshop on Quality of future Internet Services*, Berlin, Germany, 2000

[ERICSSON] M. Ericsson, M. Resende, and P. Pardalos, A genetic algorithm for the weight setting problem in OSPF routing, *J. Combinatorial Optimization*, volume 6, no. 3, pp. 299–333, 2002

[FORTZ1] B. Fortz, J. Rexford, and M. Thorup, Traffic Engineering With Traditional IP Routing Protocols, *IEEE Communications Magazine*, October 2002

[FORTZ2] Bernard Fortz, Mikkel Thorup, Internet traffic engineering by optimizing OSPF weights, *Proc. IEEE INFOCOM, 2000*, pp. 519–528, March 2000

[FRALEIGH] Chuck Fraleigh, Fouad Tobagi, Christophe Diot, Provisioning IP Backbone Networks to Support Latency Sensitive Traffic, *Proc. IEEE INFOCOM 2003*, April 2003

[GOUS] Alan Gous, Arash Afrakhteh, Thomas Telkamp, Traffic Engineering through Automated Optimization of Routing Metrics, presented at Terena 2004 conference, Rhodes, June 2004. Available at:

http://tnc2004.terena.nl/programme/presentations/show.php?pres_
id = 99

[HALABI] Sam Halabi, *Internet Routing Architectures*, Cisco Press, 2000

[IPFIX] B. Claise, Ed., Specification of the IPFIX Protocol for the
Exchange of IP Traffic Flow Information Protocol Specification, IETF
draft draft-ietf-ipfix-protocol, November 2006 [work in progress]

[LORENZ] D. Lorenz, A. Ordi, D. Raz, and Y. Shavitt, How good can
IP routing be?, *DIMACS Technical, Report 2001-17*, May 2001

[MAGHBOULEH] Arman Maghbouleh, Metric-Based Traffic
Engineering: Panacea or Snake Oil? A Real-World Study, *Arman
Maghbouleh, Cariden*, NANOG 27, February 2003

[MEDINA] A. Medina, N. Taft, K. Salamatian, S. Bhattacharyya, and
C. Diot, Traffic matrix estimation: Existing techniques and new directions, in *ACM SIGCOMM* (Pittsburg, USA), August 2002

[PAXON] V. Paxson and S. Floyd, Wide-area traffic: The failure of
Poisson modeling, *IEEE/ACM Transactions on Networking*, vol. 3, no.
3, pp. 226–244, 1994

[RFC1142] D. Oran, Ed., OSI IS-IS Intra-domain Routing Protocol,
RFC 1142, February 1999 [republication of ISO DP 10589]

[RFC2205] R. Braden, Ed., Resource ReSerVation Protocol (RSVP) –
Version 1 Functional Specification, *RFC 2205*, September 1997

[RFC2328] J. Moy, OSPF version 2, *RFC 2328*, April 1998

[RFC3036] L. Andersson et al., LDP Specification, *RFC 3036*, January
2001

[RFC3209] D. Awduche et al., RSVP-TE: Extensions to RSVP for
LSP tunnels, *RFC 3209*, Dec. 2001; http://www.rfc-editor.org/rfc/
rfc3209.txt

[RFC3630] D. Katz, K. Kompella, D. Yeung, Traffic Engineering (TE)
Extensions to OSPF Version 2, *RFC 3630*, September 2003

[RFC3784] H. Smit, T. Li, Intermediate System to Intermediate System (IS-IS) Extensions for Traffic Engineering (TE), *RFC 3784*, June 2004

[RFC3785] Le Faucheur et al., Use of IGP Metric as a second TE Metric, *RFC 3785*, May 2004

[RFC3906] N. Shen, H. Smit, Calculating Interior Gateway Protocol (IGP) Routes Over Traffic Engineering Tunnels, *RFC 3906*, October 2004

[RFC4124] F. Le Faucheur, Ed., Protocol extensions for support of Diff-Serv-aware MPLS Traffic Engineering, *RFC 4124*, June 2005

[RFC4125] F. Le Faucheur, W. Lai, Maximum Allocation Bandwidth Constraints Model for Diffserv-aware MPLS Traffic Engineering, *RFC 4125*, June 2005

[RFC4127] F. Le Faucheur, Ed., Russian Dolls Bandwidth Constraints Model for Diffserv-aware MPLS Traffic Engineering, *RFC 4127*, June 2005

[RFC4271] Y. Rekhter, Ed., T. Li, Ed., S. Hares, Ed., A Border Gateway Protocol 4 (BGP-4), *RFC 4271*, January 2006

[RFC4364] E. Rosen, Y. Rekhter, BGP/MPLS IP Virtual Private Networks (VPNs), *RFC 4364*, February 2006

[SAHINOGLU] Z. Sahinoglu, and S. Tekinay, On Multimedia Networks: Self-Similar Traffic and Network Performance, *IEEE Communications Magazine*, pp. 48–52, January 1999

[TEBALDI] C. Tebaldi and M. West, Bayesian inference on network traffic using link count data, *J. Amer. Statist. Assoc.*, vol. 93, no. 442, pp. 557–576, 1998

[TELKAMP1] Thomas Telkamp, Best Practices for Determining the Traffic Matrix in IP Networks V 2.0, NANOG 35 Los Angeles, October 2005. Available online at: http://www.nanog.org/mtg-0510/telkamp.html

[TELKAMP2] Thomas Telkamp, Traffic Characteristics and Network Planning, NANOG 26, October 2002. Available at: http://www.nanog.org/mtg-0210/telkamp.html

[VARDI] Y. Vardi, Network tomography: estimating source-destination traffic intensities from link data, *J. Am. Statist. Assoc.*, vol. 91, pp. 365–377, 1996

[ZHANG1] Y. Zhang, M. Roughan, N. Duffeld, and A. Greenberg, Fast accurate computation of large-scale IP traffic matrices from link loads, in *ACM SIGMETRICS* (San Diego, California), pp. 206–217, June 2003

[ZHANG2] Z.-L. Zhang, V. Ribeiro, S.Moon, and C. Diot, Small-Time Scaling behaviors of internet backbone traffic: An Empirical Study. In *IEEE Infocom*, San Francisco, Mar. 2003

Notes

1. The distribution routers in the generalized network reference model we use in this book will normally be provider edge (PE) routers in the context of an MPLS VPN deployment.

2. Defined by the solution to the maximum multicommodity flow problem, where the total flow summed over all commodities is to be maximized.

3. Route pinning is the ability to explicitly define the exact path that a particular traffic flow may take through the network.

4. A propagation-delay constraint can also be specified for the sub-pool tunnels to ensure that the chosen path exhibits a propagation delay smaller or equal to the specified value [RFC3785].

5. The nature of the networking industry and community means that some of the sources referred to in this book exist only on the World Wide Web. All universal resource locators (URLs) have been checked and were correct at the time of going to press, but their longevity cannot be guaranteed.

Index